C000081708

Roger Steer is author of twelve books, including *George Müller: Delighted in God*, which has been continuously in print for nearly 30 years. He has been a trustee of Bible Society for many years. He lives in Devon, UK.

Also by Roger Steer:

George Müller: Delighted in God
A Living Reality
Admiring God
George Müller: Heroes of the Cross
Hudson Taylor: A Man in Christ
Love will Find a Way
Dream of Reality: An Evangelical Encounters the Oxford Movement
Hudson Taylor: Lessons in Discipleship
Canvas Conversations
Church on Fire: The Story of Anglican Evangelicals
Letter to an Influential Atheist

GOOD NEWS FOR THE WORLD

200 years of making the Bible heard:

the Story of Bible Society

Roger Steer

MONARCH
BOOKS
Oxford, UK, and Grand Rapids, Michigan

bible society making the bible heard

Copyright © Roger Steer 2004.
The right of Roger Steer to be identified
as author of this work has been asserted by him in
accordance with the Copyright, Designs
and Patents Act 1988.

All rights reserved.
No part of this publication may be reproduced or
transmitted in any form or by any means, electronic
or mechanical, including photocopying, recording, or any
information storage or retrieval system, without
permission in writing from the publisher.

First published in the UK in 2004 by Monarch Books
(a publishing imprint of Lion Hudson plc),
Mayfield House, 256 Banbury Road, Oxford OX2 7DH
Tel: +44 (0) 1865 302750 Fax: +44 (0) 1865 302757
Email: monarch@lionhudson.com
www.lionhudson.com
Co-published with Bible Society

ISBN: 1 85424 663 1 (Monarch, paperback)
ISBN: 0 564 04286 2 (Bible Society, paperback)
ISBN: 0 564 04276 5 (Bible Society, hardback)

Distributed by:
UK: Marston Book Services Ltd, PO Box 269,
Abingdon, Oxon OX14 4YN;
USA: Kregel Publications, PO Box 2607,
Grand Rapids, Michigan 49501.

British Library Cataloguing Data
A catalogue record for this book is available
from the British Library.

Book design and production for the publishers by
Gazelle Creative Productions Ltd,
Concorde House, Grenville Place, Mill Hill, London NW7 3SA.
Printed in Malta.

Contents
A guide to the people you will meet and places you will visit in the drama

Foreword

A cold March day at the London Tavern in Bishopsgate was a strange place for a miracle. But there can be little doubt that the influential group of Christians who met in the tavern's public rooms on 7 March 1804 to form The British and Foreign Bible Society did witness a miracle. Only God could have brought those people together at that time for that purpose!

The 18th century was the age of reason; people were questioning the Bible as never before. God, if he was acknowledged at all, was seen as the great watchmaker. Yes a creator, but not at all engaged with his creation; and weren't the French busy building a new humanist utopia over the channel?

But for many there was another narrative. Throughout the country, ordinary people were experiencing a renewal of lively Christianity under such great leaders as John Wesley and George Whitefield, and the new hymn writers typified by Charles Wesley and John Newton. This was another sort of revolution, but one that barely touched the national power brokers.

Wales, still overwhelmingly speaking its own language, had become a land of revivals. Yet surely rural Wales couldn't impact the whole nation, let alone have a global effect. Or could it? The Welsh Sunday school movement was creating a literate, Christian young population, but Bibles for them to read were in short supply and very expensive.

Enter the young weaver Mary Jones who walked over a mountain for her Bible. It was the man she went to see who provides the key to understanding how all this fits together. Thomas Charles split his time between a far-reaching ministry in the depths of the Welsh hinterland and visits to London where he had the ear of William Wilberforce and other powerful evangelical Christians. It was his urgency that set in motion a series of meetings culminating in the March 1804 gathering in Bishopsgate.

Two centuries later, on another cold March day in 2004, another Welshman was addressing a much larger audience filling the interior of St Paul's Cathedral. Archbishop Rowan Williams spoke powerfully of the importance of the Society in 200 years of translation work and in new programmes to communicate God's Word effectively in today's societies.

"Every language and culture has in it a sort of 'homing instinct' for God...a sleeping beauty to be revived by the word of Christ," he said. "The hidden pull towards Christ" is at work, he added, "even where the style and words of a culture seem least in touch with God."

This is why the work of the Bible societies is as important as it ever was. It is the reason it has grown today into a truly global movement, working together to ensure that the Bible is readily available everywhere and that its voice can be heard by everyone.

This book tells a story of dedicated people often putting their lives on the line. It tells how access to the Bible has led the spread of global Christianity. And it gives astonishing testimony to all that flowed from that strange miracle in a London pub.

Bible Society
March 2004

Acknowledgements

One of the joys of writing this book has been the number of people from all over the world who have so willingly helped by providing me with information, books, documents and suggestions either by email, by phone or in person. I have made many new friends in the process and thank you all. Please forgive me if your favourite gem didn't find a place in the final version. I have put much of the material in the hands of UBS and Bible Society and some of it will be used in other contexts.

My thanks in alphabetical order go to: Anders Alberius, Swedish Bible Society; José Luis Andavert, Bible Society of Spain; Nicky Applegate, BFBS; Ramez Atallah, Bible Society of Egypt; Stephen Batalden, Arizona State University; Hans Bergström, Swedish Bible Society; Valdo Bertalot, Bible Society in Italy; Daphne Bidstrup, Danish Bible Society; Andy Bissex, BFBS; Derek Brown, Heswall Action Group; Gaynor Burrett, BFBS; Lola Calvo, Bible Society of Spain; Douglas Campbell, Scottish Bible Society; Kathleen Cann, Cambridge University Library; James Catford, BFBS; Timóteo Cavaco, Bible Society of Portugal; Joan and Alan Charters, Crediton Action Group; David Cohen, CNEC/Partners International; Tony Collins, Lion Hudson; Alfonso Corzo, Colombian Bible Society; Neil Crosbie, UBS; John Dean, formerly BFBS and UBS; staff at the Devon and Exeter Institution; Clive Dilloway, BFBS; John Doherty, Bible Society in Northern Ireland; Nita Doke, ABS; Hanan Edison, Bible Society of Egypt; Alan Emery, BFBS; Barbara Enholc-Narzyńska, Bible Society in Poland; John Erickson, formerly ABS and UBS; Robert Everitt, Canadian Bible Society; staff at University of Exeter library; Helen Flower, BFBS; Martha Foley, American Bible Society; Richard Gill, BFBS representative in Morecambe; Alan Gordon, Bible Society of West Australia; James Halder, Bangladesh Bible Society; Geoffrey and Jean Hill, formerly

BFBS and UBS; Richard Hitchcock, University of Exeter; Tom Hoglind, Bible Society in Lebanon; Tom Houston, formerly BFBS; Graham and Anne Hutt, UBS; Dafydd Ifans, National Library of Wales; Wyn James, Cardiff University; Urs Joerg, Swiss Bible Society; Tammy Jones, Bank of England; Henry Kathii, Bible Society of Kenya; Alison Knight, BFBS; Margo Koopmans, Netherlands Bible Society; Markku Kotila, Finnish Bible Society; Coral Lazenbury, UBS; Luz Levano, Peruvian Bible Society; Gabriel Linehan, Lambeth Palace Library; Bishop Carlos López Lozano, Anglican Church of Spain; Liana Lupas, American Bible Society; Fergus Macdonald, formerly UBS; Benjamin Martin, Bank of England; Rosemary Mathew, Cambridge University Library; Young-Jin Min, Korean Bible Society; Aloo Mojola, UBS Africa Area, Nairobi; Julie Morris, UBS; Ralf Thomas Müller, German Bible Society; Bruna Ndoci, Interconfessional Bible Society of Albania; Jenni Newman, Exmouth Action Group; Jon Palsson, Icelandic Bible Society; Glen Pitts, Canadian Bible Society; Kate Pool, Society of Authors; Philip Poole, BFBS; B K Pramanik, Bible Society of India; Joan Prebble, UBS; Marc Rakoto, Malagasy Bible Society; Colin Reed, Bible Society in New Zealand; Bill Roop; Shauna Ryan, HM Treasury; Arthur Scotchmer, BFBS; Ashley Scott, UBS; Rodney Shepherd, Lion Hudson; Alan Smallacombe, Hatherleigh Action Group; Julian Smith, BFBS; Ann Soutter, George Borrow Society; Elsie Sparks, Crediton Action Group; Michael Stannard; Hannah Steer; Valdis Teraudkalns, Latvian Bible Society; Neville Turley, Bible Society of South Africa; Tarja Valtonen, Finnish Bible Society; Elliott Wallace, BFBS; Makoto Watabe, Japan Bible Society; Morva White, BFBS; Judy Wilkinson, National Bible Society of Ireland.

Finally, my special thanks to my wife, Sheila, who has put up with the interruption that this, my twelfth book, has brought to our lives. She has supported me 100% every step of the way.

Roger Steer
January 2004

Abbreviations

ABS   American Bible Society
BFBS   British and Foreign Bible Society – from the earliest years and especially in more recent years, known simply as Bible Society
NBS   Netherlands Bible Society
NBSS   National Bible Society of Scotland
RTS   Religious Tract Society
UBS   United Bible Societies

Prologue

The Bible is, and always has been, the best-selling book in the world. Queen Victoria, a member of Bible Society and patron of the Windsor Ladies' Bible Association, maintained that it was the greatest jewel in her imperial crown. The Moderator of the Church of Scotland told our present Queen and current patron of the Society, as he presented her with a Bible at her coronation, that it was "the most valuable thing that this world affords". Napoleon said that the Bible was more powerful that any army, even his, and settled down, during his exile on the island of St Helena, to read and annotate a copy of the French New Testament.

As I write, the leaders of two of the most powerful nations in the world, George W Bush and Tony Blair, are both known to respect the Bible as a book which has profoundly influenced their thinking.

You may think that the Bible has been eclipsed by Harry Potter, *Dr Atkins' New Diet Revolution*, or the IKEA catalogue, but the careful compilers of the latest edition of *Guinness World Records* tell us that "the world's best-selling and most widely distributed book is the Bible, with an estimated 2.5 billion copies sold since 1815".

You can speak to academics, archaeologists, theologians, psychologists, priests, monks, nuns, missionaries, even Islamic scholars or Jewish rabbis, who will tell you that the Bible is the most important collection of documents in the world. You can speak to ordinary Christians who will tell you that it is a book which has changed their lives.

The Bible is unique. It belongs to millions of Christians, Jews and Muslims who look back to Abraham as a man of faith through whom blessing came to the world. People live by the Bible and die for it. It is a brutally honest book which charts failure as well as success, gross moral lapses by its heroes as well as noble deeds performed by scoundrels. It speaks of misfits and dreamers, bad-tempered prophets and talking donkeys.

Those who have scarcely read the Bible speak its language: "the animals go in two by two", he was "as old as Methuselah" and "cast his bread upon the water" just as "the seed fell on good ground". She was "a good Samaritan" and demonstrated "the wisdom of Solomon".

The Bible is a paradoxical book. It can bring out the best and worst in people. It is a book of wisdom, and yet in the wrong hands, it is used to launch a thousand crackpot theories. It is a book which speaks of the Prince of Peace but has been used as an excuse for war. It is an ancient book which is still waiting to be understood. Many busy people promise themselves that one day they will set aside time to grasp what it says.

It is a book which portrays a failed and broken kingdom (Israel) as providing the ideal of true kingship (the Kingdom of God). It speaks of it being better to give than to receive, of losing yourself to find yourself, of dying that you may live, of discovering true freedom in the service of Christ.

It speaks of a man who endured a cruel and brutal death so that he could open a path to a new and dynamic life. And when the risen Lord Jesus joined two sad and weary disciples on the road to Emmaus, they begged him to have a meal with them even though at first they didn't recognise him. When at last they realised who he was they said to one another, "When he talked to us along the road and explained the Scriptures to us, didn't it warm our hearts?"

The book you are about to read is about a succession of sometimes flawed men and women who have had their hearts "warmed by the Scriptures" and for 200 years have had a passion to make the Bible heard.

Curiously enough, although the Bible tells very much a Middle Eastern tale, it is a book which has been gladly received as Good News for the whole world. And nowhere more than in the English-speaking world, as we shall discover in the first act of the drama which is about to unfold.

Act 1

A song for weavers at the shuttle

Little Sodbury, Gloucestershire, 1520s

The Good News has travelled from the Middle East and has been well received in England.

Enter William Tyndale

Working as tutor to the children of Sir John Walsh, sheriff of Gloucestershire, Tyndale is himself an educated man, having studied at Magdalen Hall, Oxford, and then at Cambridge. However, he gets involved in an argument with another scholar.

"If God spare my life," he says, "ere many years I will cause a boy that drives the plough shall know more of the Scripture than you do."

Tyndale has read Erasmus's preface to his Greek New Testament of 1516:

> I totally disagree with those who are unwilling that the Holy Scriptures, translated into the common tongue, should be read by the unlearned. Christ desires his mysteries to be published abroad as widely as possible. I could wish that all women should read the Gospel and St Paul's Epistles, and I would that they were translated into all the languages of all Christian people, that they might be read and known not merely by the Scots and the Irish but even by the Turks and the Saracens. I wish that the farm worker might sing parts of them at the plough, that the weaver might hum them at the shuttle, and that the traveller might beguile the weariness of the way by reciting them.

The knowledge that Luther has given his countrymen the German New Testament in homely and vigorous language encourages Tyndale in his burning desire that an English boy at the plough shall come to know and love the Scriptures. He travels from Gloucestershire to London in the summer of 1523 to find out whether the new Bishop of London, Cuthbert Tunstall, will offer him a residential chaplaincy in his palace that will allow him to translate the Bible into English. After Tunstall declines to offer him a suitable position, Tyndale decides he will leave England to carry out his task.

In the spring of 1524, Tyndale sails for the continent of Europe, never to return to England, and finishes his translation of the New Testament into English in 1525 at Worms. He spends twelve years wandering around from Hamburg to Antwerp, revising his New Testament and translating the Old into a style of English which combines tenderness with majesty and will remain the basis of the Authorised Version of the Bible.

Tyndale's enemies are anxious to arrest him on a charge of heresy. In May 1535 they kidnap him, take him out of Antwerp and imprison him in the fortress of Vilvorde, six miles north of Brussels. From England, Henry VIII's powerful Secretary of State Thomas Cromwell makes an energetic attempt to procure his release and even the King makes some efforts on his behalf. These efforts are unsuccessful and in August 1536 authorities of Charles V, Holy Roman Emperor, find him guilty of heresy. On 6 October he is brought out of Vilvorde's castle and tied to a stake.

"Lord, open the King of England's eyes!" he shouts.

A hangman strangles Tyndale, before attendants light the flames which leap around his dead body. Sadly and ironically, Tyndale almost certainly doesn't know that some months earlier, King Henry has given permission for Coverdale's Bible of 1535, which draws heavily on the martyr's work (unlike Tyndale, Coverdale cannot read Hebrew), to be circulated in England. In the sense which Tyndale intends, the King of England's eyes are opening.

Hampton Court Palace, London, January 1604

Enter King James I

Some months after coming to England (having worn the crown of Scotland for 37 years), James I calls a conference of churchmen and theologians at Hampton Court Palace. The organisers of the conference explain that it is "for the hearing, and for the determining, things pretended to be amiss in the Church". Nothing much comes of the Hampton Court conference except – and it is a notable exception – that Dr John Reynolds of Corpus Christi College, Oxford suggests that a new translation of the Bible be made.

King James seizes eagerly on the proposal. "I profess," he says, "I could never yet see a Bible well translated in English. But I think that, of all, that of Geneva is the worst. I wish that some special pains were taken for an uniform translation, which should be done by the best-learned men in both Universities, then reviewed by the Bishops, presented to the Privy Council, lastly ratified by Royal authority, to be read in the whole Church, and none other."

Richard Bancroft, Bishop of London (soon to be Archbishop of Canterbury), isn't so keen on the idea as the King.

"If every man's humour were followed," Bancroft complains grumpily, "there would be no end of translating. But if there is to be a new translation, let it be without notes."

The King heartily agrees with this.

"I have seen," says the King, "that among the notes annexed to the Geneva Bible some that are very partial, untrue, seditious, and savouring too much of dangerous and traitorous conceits."

And so the resolution at the end of the conference says:

> That a translation be made of the whole Bible, as consonant as can be to the original Hebrew and Greek; and this to be set out and printed, *without any marginal notes*, and only to be used in all Churches of England in time of divine service [my italics].

Though a Protestant, James I favoured lenient treatment of Roman Catholics, made peace with Catholic Spain and persuaded the Assembly of the Church of Scotland to agree to the introduction of Bishops. He probably objected to the fact that the notes in the Geneva Bible (1560) were unashamedly Calvinistic in doctrine.

The decision to make this new translation of the Bible is a landmark in the religious history of English-speaking people. King James is energetic in getting the proposal carried through to its conclusion and deserves credit for the part he plays in the production of the "Authorised Version". Actually, although it will come to be known as the Authorised Version, it acquires this label, not by royal proclamation, or Act of Parliament, but because of the grand words in its preface and, more importantly, the general approval of the people.

At first there are financial difficulties, which the King tries to overcome in various ways which are only partly successful. For almost three years the whole scheme is shelved. Eventually, the King secures an arrangement whereby the translators are supported by various colleges at Oxford and Cambridge and a start on the great task is made.

The members of the translations committee are chosen solely for their fitness for the work. There are 47 of them, including vice-chancellors, five professors, nine clergy in charge of parishes, and one knight who has taught Greek to Queen Elizabeth. They represent every section of the church and they are divided into six groups who have all the books of the Bible, including the Apocrypha, divided up between them. The groups are called "companies" and a set of fifteen rules is drawn up for their guidance.

Each member of a company is to translate a chapter by himself (as far as I know they are all men) and then they meet to decide what parts they are all happy with and to make the needed corrections. As soon as a company finishes a book, they send it to be considered by all the rest, and, if differences arise on any point between two companies, they settle it later at a general meeting of representatives from each company. In any cases of particular difficulty they consult other scholars who are not directly involved in the project. They draw on all the principal translations of the Scriptures that have already appeared. More than any other man, Tyndale leaves his mark on the Authorised Bible.

Beginning in 1606, the companies of translators/revisers complete their task by 1609, and during 1610 the twelve chief translators – two from each company – go over the whole work at Stationers' Hall in London. The Authorised Version is finally printed and published in 1611.

The team of scholars did their work at a time when the English language was at its finest and strongest. It is the language that Shakespeare speaks – and this accounts for the Authorised Version's strength, majesty, simplicity and purity. But there are those who believe that this is not the complete explanation for the excellence of the Authorised Version – they believe that it has the breath of the Spirit of God. Sir Arthur Quiller-Couch says, "Christ did not die for his cadences, still less for the cadences invented by Englishmen almost 1,600 years later; and Englishmen who went to the stake did not die for these cadences... These men were cheerful to die for the *meaning* of the Word and for its authorship – because it was spoken by Christ." His point is that England is the land where men like Latimer, Ridley and Cranmer died for their love of the Bible – lighting a candle for God.

"England became the people of a Book," writes John Richard Green, "and that Book was the Bible. It was, as yet, the one English book which was familiar to every Englishman. It was read in churches, and it was read at home, and everywhere its words, as they fell on ears which custom had not deadened to their force and beauty, kindled a startling enthusiasm... The effect of the Bible in this way was simply amazing. The whole temper of the nation was changed. A new conception of life and man super-seded the old. A new moral and religious impulse spread through every class."

The historian G M Trevelyan says of the Bible: "New worlds of history and poetry were opened in its pages to people who had little else to read – indeed, it created the habit of read-ing and reflection in whole classes of the community and turned a tinker into one of the great masters of the English tongue."

By the end of the 18th century, the Bible has been in print in Britain for over 250 years (Wycliffe's Bible was never printed). Those who do not own their own copy have heard it read many times in church. The people of Britain love their Bible and believe it to be a priceless heritage.

The time is ripe for a new initiative.

Act 2

New life for politicians and the Principality

Llanfihangel-y-Pennant, north Wales, May 1783

Enter Jacob and Mary Jones

In a 12th-century church with an ancient lychgate a young couple exchange their marriage vows. To the north-east looms Cadair Idris mountain, while to the south-west the Dysynni river meanders through a broad valley, joining the sea eight miles away close to the little town of Tywyn. Across St George's Channel, Britain has granted to the Irish Parliament the right to pass its own laws, and on the other side of the Atlantic the Americans have won their independence. Britain now recognises the "United States", as the colonies have called themselves since 1776.

None of this is on the minds of the happy couple or their relatives who have gathered in St Michael's Church to wish them well. Their names are entered in the parish register as "Jacob Jones of this Parish Bachelor and Mary Jones of this Parish Spinster".

Jacob is a weaver and he and his young bride set up their home first at Pen y Bryniau Mawr and then in a tiny cottage at Tyn'y-ddôl about half a mile from the church at Llanfihangel, Merionethshire (since 1974 Gwynedd).

Bala, north Wales, 20 August 1783

Enter Thomas Charles and Sarah Jones

Three months later, another wedding is celebrated 25 miles to the north-east in the town of Bala. Although the bridegroom's parents are not well-to-do, he has received a good education, initially at the grammar school in Carmarthen. At the age of 17, Thomas Charles has gone to Llangeitho, south of Aberystwyth, to hear one of the leaders of the 18th century Welsh revival speak. Llangeitho is being called "Jerusalem" because newly converted or refreshed Christians are making their way there like pilgrims marching to Zion. The preacher, Daniel Rowland, formerly an Anglican curate, is a key figure in early Welsh Methodism. Charles will never forget hearing Rowland preach on 20 January 1773.

"It was a day to remember as long as I live," he says. "Ever since the happy day I have lived in a new heaven and a new earth. The change a blind man who receives his sight experiences does not exceed the change I experienced in my mind. The truths exhibited to my view appeared, for a time, too wonderfully gracious to be believed. I could not believe for very joy. I had before some idea of gospel truths floating in my head – but they never powerfully and with Divine energy penetrated my heart till now."

Eighteen months later, Thomas Charles enters Jesus College, Oxford – the Welshman's college – and gains his BA degree in 1779. He gets to know some of the evangelical leaders of his day, including John Newton, the former slave trader and author of the hymn "Amazing Grace", with whom he spends a summer at Olney. Charles is ordained priest in 1780 but his forthright evangelical views make it difficult for him to hold down curacies in the Church of England.

At the time Thomas and Sarah marry and settle in Bala, Charles is in effect a freelance minister of the Gospel and he soon throws in his lot with the Calvinistic Methodists (now the Presbyterian Church of Wales). He believes this will give him more freedom to proclaim the Good News which so thrills his heart.

Like John Wesley himself – still alive at 80 when the Charleses marry – Thomas never repudiates his Anglican orders. And like most early Methodists, he has few quarrels with the Thirty-Nine Articles of the Anglican Church, but the Welsh revival is bringing with it a new warmth and evangelistic zeal. He will survive financially because his bride, Sarah Jones, is gradually taking over the management and ownership of a large and profitable shop in Bala. The business has been built up by her stepfather who was himself a Methodist preacher. The house where Thomas and Sarah lived in Bala High Street is now a bank.

France and England, autumn 1783

Enter William Pitt and William Wilberforce

In the autumn of the year of these two weddings, two young men of the same age who have become friends at Cambridge enjoy a tour of France. On their return to England, one of them, William Pitt the Younger, becomes, at 24, the youngest Prime Minister in British history. The other, William Wilberforce, who has been a Member of Parliament for four years, is gaining a reputation as an orator — some say, the finest of his generation. His eloquence proves of great assistance to Pitt in his struggles against an unfriendly House of Commons.

Enter Isaac Milner

Next year, Pitt's problems are eased when he wins a large majority in the general election. In the summer, Wilberforce decides on yet another and more extended foreign trip. He travels to Nice, this time with Isaac Milner who has been a master at Hull Grammar School which Wilberforce attended as a boy. The two men read the whole of the New Testament together. The experience makes a new man of Wilberforce. "I renounced the world," he says, "and devoted myself to the fear and service of Almighty God." When he arrives in Nice, he comes across a copy of Doddridge's *Rise and Progress of Religion in the Soul*. He reads it eagerly and it completes his conversion to Christ.

When Wilberforce and Milner return to England, Prime Minister Pitt speaks bluntly to William.

"I cannot understand your uncalled-for enthusiasm for religion," he tells his friend.

Except for one period of tension, though, their friendship will last until Pitt's death in 1806.

Enter Rev. John Newton

Wilberforce visits John Newton, now rector of St Mary Woolnoth in the City of London.

"I think you should advance the cause of Christ in Parliament and public life rather than going into the church," Newton tells him.

Wilberforce has inherited a large fortune and never needs to do a day's work if he doesn't want to. But he will become famous for fighting one of the most successful campaigns in world history – the abolition, in the face of bitter and determined opposition, of first the slave trade and then slavery itself throughout the British Empire.

North Wales, December 1784 A BABY CRIES

Re-enter Jacob and Mary Jones

Jacob and Mary Jones work hard to keep warm during one of the coldest winters of the century. Nine days before Christmas, Mary's first child is born. Three days later, on 19 December 1784, they have the baby christened "Mary" in the little church at Llanfihangel – though everyone calls her "Mari Jacob" after her father and to avoid confusion with her mother.

Unlike Wilberforce, Jacob and Mary Jones never come into money. They supplement their income from weaving through a variety of other activities such as temporary work on local farms and keeping some animals themselves. Life becomes even harder for the mother and daughter when, in March 1789, a few months after Mary turns four, Jacob dies. Poverty increases in rural Wales in the closing years of the 18th century, partly due to the long war with France.

Enter Robert Jones, a fiery Methodist preacher

There is something which brings brightness and a certain excitement into the lives of this mother and daughter. Although Jacob and Mary have had their baby christened in the local Anglican church, they, like the Charleses on the other side of the mountain, have become involved with the Methodists. On a Sunday afternoon, just four years before Mary was born, Robert Jones came to Abergynolwyn, a mile south of Llanfihangel, and preached a powerful sermon – the first to be delivered by a Methodist in the area.

"There was a cruel, angry look on the large crowd that gathered together," Robert Jones reported on that historic open-air meeting, "but I was given comparative peace to hold the meeting and there was a measure of unction on it."

After Robert Jones's visit to Abergynolwyn, travelling Methodist preachers gradually increase the number of meetings they conduct in the area of Wales between Cadair Idris and the sea. About the time of Mary's birth the first *seiat* – the fellowship or society meeting which is such a characteristic of Methodism – is formed in the village where Mary grows up.

Enter William Hugh, a preacher and pastor

When Mary is five or six, William Hugh becomes the first resident preacher in the area. Hugh lives in Llanfihangel parish and sometime in the 1770s he heard Benjamin Evans, then minister of the Independents near Bala, preach. He was surprised by the simplicity of the service and its lack of ceremony compared with services at the parish church. Hugh felt that Evans's sermon gave him "a clear grasp of the truths of the gospel" and he was probably the first person who lived in Mary's part of Wales to become a Methodist.

Over in Bala, in the autumn of 1791, a powerful revival breaks out which Charles describes in letters to his friends. Sometimes, when Mary is seven, William Hugh collects a party of neighbours from Llanfihangel and they walk together to Bala on a Saturday night, listen to rousing sermons on the Sunday and walk home in the evening. Walking to Bala isn't unusual for the sturdy people of Llanfihangel.

Hugh doesn't confine himself to preaching but also visits people in their homes to read the Bible and pray with them; it is almost certainly through his work that Mary Jones hears and comes to love the stories of Jesus.

When she is eight, Mary becomes a member of the Methodist society in Llanfihangel. Children don't normally become members of a *seiat*, but since Mary goes with her mother to the other evening meetings in order to carry the lantern, she is allowed to accompany her mother to the society meeting as well. For many years, the society meets at William Hugh's house, with occasional meetings at Abergynolwyn.

Bala, 1790s SOUNDS OF TEARS AND SHOUTS OF JOY

Re-enter Thomas Charles

Thomas Charles is coming to be in demand as a preacher: his style isn't earthy or rabble-rousing like some of the revivalists, but he is obviously a good and heavenly-minded man. Although he doesn't have the natural gifts of an orator, he touches hearts as well as minds when he preaches.

"The scene," someone who was present to hear Charles preach recalled, "was most affecting. Scores, if not hundreds, melted into tears; some mourning with godly sorrow, others weeping for joy, exulting in their glorious Saviour. Some countenances betrayed the deepest grief, such as became those who were crying out, 'What must we do to be saved?' The countenances of others, though bedewed with tears, were yet glistening with expressions of transport, as if illuminated with the beams of Divine glory."

Thomas Charles is even in demand in London.

Spa Fields, north London, 1791

Enter the Countess of Huntingdon

Thomas Charles accepts a regular annual invitation to preach for some weeks in Spa Fields, north London. A large chapel has been taken over by the strong-minded Lady Huntingdon – previously it was a theatre surrounded by pleasure gardens. To prevent it operating as a place of entertainment, the Earl of Dartmouth, who was one of Lady Huntingdon's more illustrious converts, formed a group which presented it to the Countess so that her chaplains could use it as a place of worship and preaching. In 1768 the indomitable Countess converted the old mansion of Trevecca, near Talgarth in south Wales, into a theological college for her young ministers. Thomas Charles tries for a while to arrange to take over Trevecca College before (following her death in 1791) it is moved to Cheshunt – but the Bala revival and the need to secure as many Bibles as he can for a growing number of converts leads him to change his mind.

North Wales, 1790s THE SOUND OF CHILDREN

The pulpit is not Thomas Charles's overriding passion. He has begun to invite the poor children of Bala into his home for instruction, and so many of them turn up that the Calvinistic Methodists offer him the use of their chapel in the town. And so he begins to establish schools in north Wales on the lines adopted in the south by former vicar Griffith Jones. First, Charles trains a man for the work of teaching, then he sends him to a district for six months, where (for £8 a year) he teaches children, young people and adults reading and the basics of the Christian faith. He adds writing later. Parents and children learn and recite together: it is said that some of the children learn to recite whole Bible books without prompting.

Thomas Charles provides all this education free of charge: the expenses are met by collections made in the Calvinistic Methodist societies, and as the funds increase, Charles multiplies the number of teachers. He writes a Welsh catechism – the basics of the Christian faith summarised in question-and-answer form – for use in his schools and this runs to three editions in just five years.

Charles organises Sunday Schools as well for young people in service who can't attend during the week. William Wilberforce, as well as Charles Grant, John and Henry Thornton are among the philanthropists who contribute to the funds needed for Charles's schools.

The schools founded by Griffiths Jones and Thomas Charles help to make the Welsh one of the first literate peoples of the modern world. Sometimes displays of intense spiritual excitement and zeal break out in the schoolrooms themselves. This makes the people more vocal. And all the time, evangelical Christianity, civilised behaviour and culture are being promoted and encouraged.

Act 3

A long walk for Mary

Abergynolwyn, north Wales, 1795

Enter John Ellis, Mary Jones and Lewis Williams

One of Thomas Charles's earliest teachers is John Ellis of Barmouth, a kind man with an attractive personality who realises that he can get the best out of children through tenderness and love. Somewhere around 1795 he comes to Abergynolwyn to run one of Charles's schools and start a Sunday School. Among the brightest pupils at his day school, as often as she can get there, is Mary Jones. She regularly takes a two-mile walk along a footpath which leaves the present road by the entrance of Castell y Bere and rejoins the road by Nant y Myniawd, a distance of about two miles. She is about ten when Ellis first teaches her, keen to learn and with an exceptional memory. John Ellis is succeeded by Lewis Williams, an energetic and imaginative teacher who lives on to the great age of 88, becoming a useful source of information about Mary for historians.

Thomas Charles's greatest difficulty in carrying on his work is the scarcity of Welsh Bibles. Most of the ordinary people of Wales only speak Welsh. In the late 1780s the wealthy and influential merchant, John Thornton, and the Bible commentator, Thomas Scott, help him secure supplies of Welsh Bibles from the Society for Promoting Christian Knowledge (SPCK). In 1799, when SPCK brings out a new edition, he manages to secure 700 copies of the 10,000 issued. These are released for publication in early 1800 and sell for three shillings and sixpence a copy.

South of Caernarfon, north Wales, 1799

Enter Thomas Charles, on horseback

On a bitterly cold Monday evening on 16 December of the same year that SPCK publishes its Welsh Bible, Thomas Charles is riding south from Caernarfon along the old Roman road at the foot of Snowdon (it is now the A4085). Near the pass of Aberglaslyn a raw, frost-charged wind catches the thumb of his left hand. For eleven months the frostbitten thumb gives Charles "long and grievous pain". There are times that friends worry that he may die, though he continues with his work and engagements and rarely complains.

Llanfihangel parish, 1799–1800

Enter Mary Jones

Now that she has learnt to read at Charles's school at Abergynolwyn, Mary longs to have a Bible of her own. For six years she has saved every halfpenny she earned by doing jobs for neighbours so that she can buy her own copy.

A farmer's wife who lives about two miles from Tyn'y-ddôl, tells her, "You may come to Penybryniau Mawr to read the Bible we keep on the table in the parlour – that's if you'll take your clogs off before you come in!"

From then on, Mary walks there every week in all kinds of weather to learn passages of the Bible by heart.

Enter a man on a white horse

On a stormy Monday morning, while she is walking to the farm-house at Penybryniau Mawr, Mary sees a man wrapped in a cloak, wearing a cloth cap, riding towards her on a white horse. He stops.

"Where are you going through such wind and rain?"

"I am going to a farmhouse where there is a Bible," Mary replies. "There isn't one nearer my home. But the farmer's wife has said I can go and read the Bible she has on the parlour table, providing I take my shoes off and that I save every penny to buy my own. But I don't know where to find one."

"I am Mr Charles," says the horse-rider. "I expect you know that I live in Bala. I am expecting some Bibles from London and may be able to help you."

Bala is 28 miles away, but Mary's mother agrees to her request to be allowed to walk there to buy her Bible.

Fifteen-year-old Mary prepares to set off for Bala early in the hot, dry summer of 1800. She has saved 17 shillings "and a few pennies". Her mother puts the money for the Bible, and some bread and cheese, in one end of her shoulder bag and her one pair of shoes — too precious to be worn on the long walk — in the other. Mary will put them on when she reaches the town.

She sets off from Tyn'y-ddôl along a rough track which takes her along the eastern edge of Cadair Idris above Tal-y-llyn lake, then along the ridge to the top of the pass, turning towards Dinas Mawddwy. At Cae'r Tyddyn Farm she takes the old mountain road across the Wnion valley, coming down beyond Rhydymain. On her way she stops to rest, eat some of her food and wash in a clear stream of water. From Llanuwchllyn, she walks along the north shore of the lake to her destination.

Bala, early summer 1800

Bala is a quiet town at the north end of Bala lake, the largest natural body of water in Wales. The house where Thomas Charles lived in the High Street, now a bank, has a well-preserved plaque on its wall which reads:

> In this house lived the Rev. Thomas Charles B.A., one of the founders of the British and Foreign Bible Society in the year 1804. Psalm CXIX. 162

with another plaque about Mary underneath.

When she arrives in Bala, Mary follows directions she has been given to Thomas Charles's house. She knocks and Charles appears from the study at the back of his house.

"I am afraid the Bibles have not arrived," he tells her.

Mary begins to cry.

"I don't know where I shall stay," she says.

"You shall stay with my maid," Charles tells us, "until the Bibles come from London."

The maid lives in a house at the bottom of Charles's garden. After a day or two, the Bibles arrive and Charles presents Mary, as she will often tell Lizzie Rowlands many years later, with "three for the money, that is, for the price of one".

Mary sets off for home, taking off her shoes lest she should wear them out, and running much of the way home.

Two of the Bibles Thomas Charles handed Mary may still be seen today. One of them – which became Mary's own Bible – is a precious exhibit as part of the Society's collection at Cambridge University Library. It was the last edition of the Welsh Bible prior to the establishment of Bible Society and contains marginal references, the Apocrypha, the Book of Common Prayer, a metrical version of the Psalms and various church tables. Another is in the National Library of Wales at Aberystwyth. Later in our story we will discover how these two Bibles find their way to these august locations. I am not sure what happened to the third. Did Mary's son Ioan take it with him when he emigrated to America? Perhaps an American reader of this book will know the answer.

The loft of Thomas Charles's house in Bala, Sunday 23 November 1800

A group of men and women kneel in prayer

Due to overwork and his severely damaged thumb, the popular minister's health has deteriorated. An old shoemaker named Richard Owen, who is also a deacon in the Bala church, is praying earnestly for Charles, who is now aged 45. Owen remembers how King Hezekiah's life was extended by fifteen years in answer to prayer (2 Kings 20:6).

"Fifteen years, O Lord!" he cries. "Add but fifteen years to the life of your servant! Spare him for fifteen years more to your church and your people!"

He repeats the prayer several times and the earnestness of the prayer thrills the group.

The next day, Thomas Charles endures the agony of a dangerous operation: a surgeon amputates his thumb without anaesthetic. He makes a slow recovery and will live for another fourteen years and 46 weeks.

Act
4

Why not for the world?

Britain 1800–1802

People are increasingly aware of the threat which faces them across the Channel. Napoleon has extended his empire across Europe to the left bank of the Rhine. Even teenagers in Welsh villages such as Llanfihangel begin to hear tales of what "Boney" looks like, what he wears, his private life and his methods of work. A chain of camps extends along the coast of northern Europe from Ostend to Brest and Napoleon is assembling gunboats for an attack. British volunteers are ready to march. The artillery stand harnessed, waiting for the call of the bugle. Over half a million men are armed. Small groups of soldiers keep watch on the cliffs, and night signals from the Thames estuary to Falmouth in Cornwall are ready to flash the news of an imminent invasion. Anyone looking through a telescope can see the movement of troops in France. On 3 August thousands of spectators standing on the heights of Dover watch the ambitious attack on the naval base of Boulogne, planned by the recently promoted Admiral Nelson in order to foil a possible French invasion.

Talks conclude in London in October 1801, putting an end to hostilities for a while, and peace is signed at Amiens on 27 March 1802. The crews of fighting ships are hurriedly paid off and regiments disbanded. The British flock to the continent again and by September there are 12,000 Britons in Paris.

London, November 1802

Enter Thomas Charles

A now-recovered Thomas Charles has come to London to honour his regular preaching engagement at Lady Huntingdon's chapel at Spa Fields, Clerkenwell. He will ask for contributions towards a proposal for contracting with a printer for an edition of the Welsh Bible and hopes to secure some financial help for the distribution of cheap and low-cost Bibles among the Welsh poor.

Although 10,000 copies of the Welsh Bible have sold out within months of publication late in 1799, the Society for the Promotion of Christian Knowledge has turned down requests either to reprint it or bring out a new edition. Bible work only forms one aspect of SPCK's objectives.

One morning, Thomas Charles wakes early. His thoughts turn, as they often do, to the thousands of poor people in Wales who cannot afford to buy a Bible, and thousands more who don't care whether they have a Bible or not: *Why can we not establish a Bible Society in London on a similar basis to the Tract Society?*

He gets up, dresses, and goes out to consult friends on the subject.

Enter Joseph Tarn, member of Spa Fields Chapel

The first person Charles meets is Joseph Tarn, a friend from Spa Hill and Treasurer of the Religious Tract Society. When Tarn was fifteen, his father had taken him to hear Rowland Hill preach at an open-air service. A colourful character from a major landowning family in Shropshire, Rowland Hill (not to be confused with the founder of the penny post) was educated at Shrewsbury, Eton and St John's College, Cambridge. Having come under the influence of Methodism, he delights in delivering open-air sermons despite opposition from the authorities. When he sought ordination, six Bishops rejected him because he wouldn't give up his unlicensed preaching – so he only succeeded in being made a deacon. When he inherited property, he built Surrey Chapel, in Blackfriars Road, London. He conducts popular services there in accordance with the forms of the Church of England, in whose communion he remains. He organises thirteen Sunday Schools which are attached to the chapel, and both there and on his tours of the countryside he attracts immense audiences to hear him preach.

Hill will live to a great age and both he and his brother, Sir Richard Hill, MP for Shropshire, will become active in the affairs of Bible Society.

The Religious Tract Society (RTS), of which Hill was one of the founders, has been recently established to produce plenty of clean and wholesome literature to replace what the members think of as the worldly ballads and stories which hundreds of hawkers are selling door to door. From 1802 Parliament begins to intervene in the development of English education, requiring employers to educate apprentices in basic mathematics, writing, and reading. For the most part this remains only a demand, since most employers are not interested in such education. But self-motivated educators like Andrew Bell and Joseph Lancaster are playing a major role in progress toward an elementary-school system.

RTS's plan is to print short pithy statements of Christian truth for newly literate, working-class people. Evangelicals have joined enthusiastically in the work of the new Society. Zachary Macaulay, former Governor of Sierra Leone, editor of the *Christian Observer* and father of the famous historian and politician, is RTS committee member for Clapham. Charles's friend, Joseph Tarn, is a junior partner in the merchant firm of Hardcastle and Reyner, RTS Treasurer, and an active member of the chapel at Spa Fields. The senior partner, Joseph Hardcastle, is deeply involved with the work of the London Missionary Society (LMS).

But RTS's emphasis is on preparing and distributing religious and character-improving reading for working people rather than concentrating on the Scriptures themselves.

North bank of the Thames between Southwark Bridge and London Bridge, early morning, Tuesday 7 December 1802

Enter Thomas Charles and Joseph Tarn

Two men walk together along Upper Thames Street. They turn into Swan Lane where one of thirteen houses is an 18th-century building comprising offices and a warehouse, close by Old Swan

Stairs, an historic river-landing place. Here, Joseph Hardcastle has recently acquired a counting house with which he is particularly pleased. He believes that one way to put into practice his zeal for the Lord's work is to place the room at the disposal of both RTS and LMS. The building is substantial with thick walls and beams of stout oak.

Charles and Tarn enter through the north door, on the far-thest side from the river, between Corinthian pillars with stone rosettes on the top. They climb a winding staircase and come to a door with an oval window. Inside, the counting house is large, nearly square and rather elegant with an ornamental cornice around the top of the walls. Two windows in the north wall over-look Swan Lane and a third faces west. On the south wall, three windows with a little iron balcony look out on to the river. Already, early though it is, boats and barges are making their way slowly upstream and downstream along the Thames. Candles light the room.

Those present for the RTS committee meeting vote Rev. Matthew Wilks to take the chair. Joseph Hughes, a portly 33-year-old Baptist minister from Battersea and the committee's Secretary, sits at his side. Two other members of the clergy are there, the Revs Steinkopf and Townsend, as well as Messrs Pellatt, Hankey, Mackenzie, Gouldsmith, Shrubsole, Preston, Freshfied, Reyner, Hamilton, Fowler and Shotter. Most of them are London busi-nessmen but Karl Steinkopf is a German who left Basel the previ-ous year to become pastor of the German-speaking Savoy parish in London. He will play a major part in Bible Society history.

After the committee has confirmed the minutes of the pre-vious meeting and dealt with two items of regular business, Joseph Tarn introduces the subject of a regular supply of Bibles for Wales. The Chairman then invites Thomas Charles to enlarge on this by putting his case for establishing a society for the supply of Welsh Bibles. The "country member" of the committee from Bala is rather below ordinary height and has, according to a contempo-rary, "a singularly sweet and winning countenance". As he speaks, the committee members notice that his left thumb is missing.

Charles describes the growth of spiritual life in north Wales.

He tells of his experiences in distributing the 700 copies of the 1799 SPCK edition of the Welsh Bible, and in allotting the grants of Testaments by the Sunday School Society. He speaks of the endless appeals for Bibles which are pouring in from all over Wales and the difficulties which the scarcity of Scriptures is causing him in his work. The copies which are available are too expensive for most ordinary people.

"I beg you to consider establishing a Society similar to the RTS to supply cheap Bibles to Wales," he pleads.

As Thomas Charles finishes speaking, the Chairman temporarily loses control of the meeting and a number of people begin speaking at once. In the confusion, Joseph Hughes is heard to say, "Surely a Society might be formed for such a purpose, and if for Wales, why not also for the Empire and for the world?"

The suggestion contains the germ of Bible Society and will become famous in its history. When the committee rises to adjourn for breakfast, Joseph Hughes writes the following minute in the RTS records.

> Mr Charles of Bala having introduced the subject, which had previously been mentioned by Mr Tarn, of dispersing Bibles in Wales, the Committee resolved that it would be highly desirable to stir up the public mind to the dispersion of Bibles generally, and that a paper in a Magazine to this effect may be singularly useful. The object was deemed sufficiently connected with the object of this Society thus generally to appear in these minutes, and the Secretary who suggested it was accordingly desired to enter it.

Some people think that Charles persuaded his fellow committee members to make a favourable decision by telling them the story of Mary Jones. He may have done so – but we cannot be sure. D E Jenkins, in his three-volume biography of Thomas Charles completed in 1908, examined the evidence and concluded that Charles made no specific mention of Mary, confining himself to speaking in general terms backed by hard facts which demonstrated the high demand and severely inadequate supply of Welsh Bibles. However, we know more of the Mary Jones story now than Jenkins knew in 1908, and there are those in Wales who claim that Charles himself later told both Mary and her (second) teacher, Lewis Williams, that her story had served him very usefully at the meeting in London in 1802.

Some stories suggest that there may well have been a special rapport between Mary and Thomas Charles. Pupils from Charles's Sunday Schools would gather at day festivals to be publicly questioned and catechised. Mary was as faithful as possible at these meetings in her neighbourhood and seems to have excelled at them. They said that her answers "descended in showers as balls of fire". On such occasions, Mary would often meet Thomas Charles, but if she wasn't there Charles would ask, "Where is the weaver today, I wonder?" Mary took up in her teens the trade she was to follow all her life. Erasmus's wish of 1516 that "the weaver might hum the Scriptures at the shuttle" came true in her case.

Old Swan Stairs meetings, 1802–1803

Frivolities like Christmas do not distract the committee from pursuing its new initiative with vigour. When RTS meets a fortnight later, the energetic Joseph Hughes reads a paper which the committee has invited him to draft entitled, "The importance of forming a Society for the distribution of Bibles in various languages". On 28 December they agree that the object of the Society shall be "to promote the circulation of the Holy Scriptures in foreign countries and in those parts of the British Dominions for which adequate provision is not yet made, it being understood that no English translation of the Scriptures will be gratuitously circulated by the Society in Great Britain". Free distribution of Bibles in Britain would unnecessarily upset existing societies like SPCK.

Thomas Charles attends these two meetings and then returns to Wales. But the RTS committee continues to meet weekly throughout the whole of 1803 and the early months of 1804, thrashing out the details of the proposed Society. The committee acts in a thoughtful and thoroughly businesslike way.

Enter William Wilberforce

In February 1803 the RTS members decide to try to involve Wilberforce in their venture. On 5 April Wilberforce records in his diary, "Hughes, Reyner and Grant breakfasted with me on Bible Society formation." Wilberforce attends his first committee meeting on 21 April and records in his private papers that "a few of us met together at Mr Hardcastle's counting house, at a later hour than suited city habits, out of regard to my convenience, and yet on so dark a morning that we discussed by candle-light, while we resolved upon the establishment of the Bible Society".

With Wilberforce on board, the planners of the new Society adopt the same rigorous and painstaking techniques that the campaigners for the abolition of slavery are using to fight the powerful interests who want to retain it.

Before becoming a Baptist minister, Hughes was a Professor at the Baptist College in Bristol. Though a Baptist, he has been accepted into the Anglican evangelical circle at Clapham. Charles Grant has had a successful career in India, served as Chairman of the East India Company and, following his return to England in 1802, has become a Member of Parliament and a near neighbour of Wilberforce at Clapham. The well-known and respected names of Wilberforce and Grant will make it easier for the RTS committee members to gain public acceptance of their idea. A contemporary describes Grant as a "long-faced, blue-eyed Scotchman" with a "fixed, calm look". Hughes, Grant and Wilberforce draw up a questionnaire designed to give them the information they require to evaluate the Bible idea:

1. Can the poor in your neighbourhood read?
2. To what extent are they furnished with the Holy Scriptures?
3. Do they discover a solicitude [anxiety, concern] to read them?
4. What has been done towards supplying this want?
5. Are there persons in your neighbourhood willing further to encourage the distribution of the Holy Scriptures in our own and in foreign lands?

Joseph Hughes circulates the questionnaire throughout the United Kingdom and Ireland while Karl Steinkopf makes similar enquiries on the continent of Europe. Joseph Hardcastle takes the questionnaire to France. As treasurer of LMS, Hardcastle goes with a group of three colleagues to Paris and finds that the ten-day week introduced during the French revolution has been abolished and that Sunday is again respected. However, it takes them four days to find a single copy of the Bible in Paris. On their return, LMS resolves to distribute 2,000 French New Testaments and votes £848 (nearly £34,000 in today's values) to circulate Christian literature in France and Italy.

Battersea, London, early summer 1803

Joseph Hughes sits at his desk, writing

Partly on the basis of the responses to the questionnaire, Joseph Hughes is drafting a paper which he entitles "The Excellency of the Holy Scriptures: an Argument for their more General Dispersion". He sets out the objectives which the new society would be able to achieve. It could

- provide a systematic picture of the whole world's need for the Scriptures
- generate interest both at home and abroad
- collect and administer funds in a businesslike way; and, most strikingly, it could
- encourage Christians from a wide variety of denominations to work together

Hughes writes of the "transcendent excellence of the Holy Scriptures". He lists and describes the various Societies which already are involved in one way or another with circulating religious publications, including Bibles, commends their work and wishes them continued success, but refers to the limitations in their stated objectives which prevent them from concentrating on a work of general distribution.

As he writes, Hughes chooses his words skilfully and his paper is full of good sense: "The projected Society, not refusing to cooperate on the same ground, would traverse scenes which the other Societies are, by their regulations, forbidden to occupy; and, presenting nothing but the inspired volume, would be sure to circulate the truth, and truth alone; hereby avoiding the occasions of controversy, and opening a channel into which Christians of every name might, without scruple, pass their charitable contributions." In this way they could "demolish the invidious wall of partition, cut off the occasion of theological hostilities and invite Christians in general to associate for the more extensive propagation of their common faith...to quit the dark, confined alleys of a party for the open, healthful, and cheerful plains of genuine Catholicism".

If this can be achieved it will be a remarkable achievement in itself. Overall, Hughes writes, "Let us cast a friendly eye over distant countries, and be the parents of the first institution that ever emanated from one of the nations of Europe, for the express purpose of doing good to all the rest."

More cautious men would decide the time is not right for launching a major new initiative. In May 1803 the war bugles begin to blow again and once more Napoleon assembles an army of invasion across the English Channel. Eleven thousand British subjects who are travelling in France are seized as prisoners of war. Napoleon fells the forests of Hanover for his navy, and his Government requisitions all the ship-carpenters and boat-builders in France between the age of fifteen and 60.

Britain responds by preparing 100,000 troops, 80,000 militia and 340,000 volunteers for battle. George III, who has expressed the wish that every child in England might be taught to read the Scriptures, reviews his troops in Hyde Park.

Undisturbed by preparations for war, the RTS committee continues to meet weekly, pursuing its enquiries into the supply of Bibles at home and abroad and securing the cooperation of influential supporters. The members circulate Joseph Hughes's paper widely, including two copies to the Bishop of London's chaplain.

The Bishop's chaplain has been educated at St Paul's School and has had a distinguished career as a Fellow at Corpus Christi College, Cambridge. He has written a number of books. Hughes and Owen have met once or twice and Hughes attaches a note to his paper inviting Owen to accept one copy for his own use, and present the other to the Bishop in the hope that he may come to patronise the proposed Society.

Owen dutifully complies with Hughes's request to the extent of handing one copy of the essay to the Bishop. Beyond that, as he later puts it, he "neither felt himself authorised nor inclined to proceed". The idea of trying to unite people in the established church with other denominations seems to him to be so fraught with difficulties as to be impossible. So he neither attempts to understand the proposal himself nor recommend it to the Bishop. He thinks no more about it for the rest of the year.

London, early 1804

In addition to William Wilberforce and Charles Grant, the committee has secured the support of Granville Sharp, Zachary Macaulay, Lord Teignmouth and Henry Thornton. Samuel Mills drafts a constitution for the proposed Society – and lives to serve on the committee for 43 years.

Thomas Charles is present again at meetings at the turn of 1803/04 and attends a special meeting in January which shortens a more ponderous title to "The British and Foreign Bible Society". In February the RTS committee decides to hold a public meeting at the London Tavern, 123 Bishopsgate Street at noon on Thursday 1 March – this date is later put back by six days.

The planning team produces a "circular address" entitled, "The Importance of a Further Distribution of Bibles", summarising the key points of Joseph Hughes's essay. The address says that the new Society will be called "The British and Foreign Bible Society" and concludes by summarising its objectives as follows:

Its object – to promote the circulation of the Scriptures in some of the principal living languages.

The sphere of its activity – first, the United Kingdom of Great Britain and Ireland, and the European Continent: afterwards, remoter regions, as the state of the finances may admit, and the urgency of particular cases may require.

The object and the sphere of such a Society, considered in their union, distinguish it from all existing Societies.

The Bible Society distributes the Scriptures only, but confines its distributions to the Army and Navy.[1]

The distribution of Bibles in other Societies forms only a part of their plan; and, with a very few exceptions, the exertions of those Societies are limited to Britain.

The projected Society, not refusing to cooperate on the same ground, would traverse scenes which other Societies are, by their regulations, forbidden to occupy; and, presenting nothing but the inspired volume, would be sure to circulate truth, and truth alone; hereby avoiding the occasions of controversy, and opening a channel into which every Christian of every name might, without scruple, pour their charitable contributions.

Several persons have expressed much solicitude on the subject, and, together with those whom it has chiefly interested, look cheerfully forward to the time when a Society, founded on so extensive and liberal principle, shall be able to announce in a very public manner, its ample patronage, and its beneficent exertions.

SIGNED

GRANVILLE SHARP	RICHARD LEA
WILLIAM ALERS	ALEXANDER MAITLAND
JOSEPH BENWELL	SAMUEL MILLS
HENRY BOASE	JOSEPH REYNER
ROBERT COWIE	HERMAN SCHROEDER
SAMUEL FOYSTER	CHRISTOPHER SUNDIUS
JOSEPH SMITH GOSSE	GEORGE WOLFF

---

1. The Naval, Military & Airforce Bible Society existed until recently as part of Scripture Gift Mission. (It is now independent.)

The planners ask Granville Sharp to be prepared to chair the public meeting. Sharp is the grandson of an Archbishop of York. He studied Greek so that he could answer the arguments of a man who denied the deity of Christ, and Hebrew so that he could debate Christianity with a Jew. The direction of Sharp's life suddenly changed as the result of a chance meeting in 1765. Sharp's brother William was a doctor who gave free treatment to the poor of the City of London. While visiting his brother, Sharp noticed a young black man waiting in the queue who had been badly beaten, as it turned out, by his "master", David Lisle. Lisle had beaten the young man, whose name was Jonathan Strong, with the butt of his pistol and had thrown him into the street.

The Sharp brothers took care of Strong and, after two years, he seemed fully recovered. At this point Lisle caught a glimpse of him and realised that the slave he had left for dead could still make him a handsome profit. He arranged for Strong to be kidnapped and sent back to the Caribbean. Strong appealed to his previous benefactors, and Sharp brought his case up before the Lord Mayor of London. The Mayor agreed that Strong had committed no crime and should be set free.

Sharp decided to devote his time to forcing a definitive legal ruling on the question of whether a slave could be compelled to leave the country. As a result of his researches, he published the first major work of anti-slavery by a British author. The book amassed many legal arguments against slavery and brought Sharp into contact with people in America and at home, including John Wesley, who were beginning informally to campaign against slavery.

Sharp became famous with the legal case of James Somerset. Somerset was the property of Charles Stewart, a customs officer from Boston, Massachusetts. Stewart brought Somerset to England but in 1771 he escaped, before being recaptured and imprisoned on a ship bound for Jamaica. Sharp intervened and the captain of the ship was ordered to produce Somerset before the court of King's Bench. After a long trial which heard evidence which Sharp had carefully assembled, the judge made his eagerly-awaited ruling: that "no master was ever allowed here to take a slave by force to be sold abroad because he deserted from his service, or for any other reason whatever" and that "as soon as any slave sets his foot on English ground, he becomes free". Somerset was discharged, and his supporters, who included both black and white Londoners, immediately celebrated a great victory.

However, little provision was made for enforcing the judgement, and slaves were still forcibly taken to the plantations in the years to come. For the next fifteen years, Sharp continued his campaign against slavery as well as involving himself in other charitable and legal campaigns.

In July 1776, since he opposed the war which had just broken out between Great Britain and its American colonies, Sharp resigned his position in the Ordnance Department rather than be part of the Government machine sending war materials to America. After the American revolution many former slaves who had fought on the side of the British were now homeless in the streets of London. Sharp devised a plan to establish a colony of freed slaves on the west coast of Africa. Eventually, he arranged for over a quarter of a million acres of land, including an excellent harbour (St George's Bay), to be purchased from an African chief.

Four hundred former slaves and about 60 Europeans, mostly women, took the maiden voyage to the new colony in April 1787. Out of gratitude for "their original protector and friend", the colonists named their first settlement Granvilletown. The name was later changed to Freetown. In spite of many struggles with slave-traders and disease, the little colony grew and became established.

Sharp continued to play an active role in what was by now the burgeoning abolition movement. In 1787 he was one of the committee of people, mostly Quakers, who set up the Society for Effecting the Abolition of the African Slave Trade – and which is famously associated with the name of Wilberforce. Seen by the committee as "the father of the movement", Sharp was appointed Chairman – although he always hated chairing meetings. However, he continued as an active campaigner, working closely with Thomas Clarkson and William Wilberforce, and personally lobbying both William Pitt, the Prime Minister, and Charles James Fox, the Leader of the Opposition.

On 12 May 1789 Wilberforce delivered his first great abolition speech in Parliament – "one of the ablest and most eloquent ever heard in that or any other place," thought Bishop Porteus. Edmund Burke said of the speech that "the principles were so well laid down, and supported with so much force and order, that it equalled anything he had heard in modern times".

Meanwhile, one copy of the circular address about the proposed new Society arrives at John Owen's home in Fulham. He notices the name of his friend Granville Sharp at the top of the list of signatures, remembers the two copies of the Hughes paper that were sent him the previous summer, and decides to attend the meeting.

On the evening of 6 March, Owen calls to see Sharp at his house on the other side of the Thames in Clapham and they discuss the following day's meeting. The two men agree to go the meeting together.

Act 5

A "new era for Christendom"

Central London, Wednesday 7 March 1804

Enter Granville Sharp and John Owen

Two men walk down Bishopsgate Street (since 1910 known simply as Bishopsgate). One, the 69-year-old, is of medium height, with a pleasant, kindly expression on his face. Before leaving home, he has sung hymns, accompanying himself on his harp. The other, the 38-year-old, walks with the self-assurance of a senior Bishop's chaplain.

They are on their way to a meeting at the London Tavern. The older man is going willingly and with enthusiasm, though the responsibility of chairing the meeting is on his mind. The younger man, though relieved that his friend Granville Sharp's name headed the list of those who signed the circular letter he received inviting him to attend, has accepted with some reluctance.

They arrive at their destination on the west side of the street. A non-religious venue has been chosen so that the Society which is about to be launched will not be identified with any particular church or dissenting body. They enter the great banqueting room of the Tavern "with its fine Turkey carpet and culinary turtles swimming below in cellar vats". (The London Tavern was demolished later in the century and the site occupied for some years by the Royal Bank of Scotland. Today the Fishmarket Restaurant & Champagne Bar, owned by Terence Conran, occupies the site.)

John Owen is ushered into a side room where a busy group is putting the final touches to the resolutions on which the meeting will be invited to vote. He sits down, looks around and notices that among those engaged in animated conversation are "three individuals of respectable appearance" who "from wearing their hats and the peculiarity of their garb" he realises are Quakers. The chaplain to the Bishop of London is astonished. He shares the popular prejudice that Quakers – members of the Society of Friends – rarely either read or recommend the Bible.

The meeting planners, in a shrewd tactical move, hand him a piece of paper on which they have written out the resolutions which will establish the basis of the Society now to be formed.

"If you approve of them," they say, "we should be grateful if you would move their adoption as the basis of the proposed Society."

He agrees but with no great enthusiasm and is led back into the main hall where 300 people from a wide range of denominations have now assembled. At noon, Owen's friend Granville Sharp, a number of whose anti-slave trade friends have turned up, is unanimously invited to chair the meeting. Wilberforce's involvement in the campaign against the slave trade, and the threat of war from France, have prevented him from attending the meeting in person – but he has been intimately involved in the preparations.

Sharp agrees to take the chair, manfully overcoming his hatred of chairing meetings. He much prefers the detailed work of assembling evidence for his campaign to appearing or speaking in public.

Robert Cowie, William Alers, Samuel Mills and Joseph Hughes address the meeting, outlining the need for the Society and the nature and scope of the work they plan it will do. Hughes is eloquent and convincing but a little heavy in his style. While few disagree with what he says, there is no great excitement when he sits down.

And then Karl Steinkopf rises to speak. He is 31 with striking good looks. Educated at Stuttgart, he has taught at the Evangelical Seminary at Tübingen before becoming pastor to the Lutheran church in Savoy. He begins to speak in "broken but good English" and engagingly describes the scarcity of Scriptures on the continent of Europe. He appeals to the compassion of British Christians on behalf of his German brothers and sisters. Owen will never forget his "unaffected simplicity".

When Steinkopf sits down, there is scarcely a dry eye or hard thought in the house. Almost at once, John Owen rises to his feet on an impulse which, as he later records, he has "neither the inclination nor the power to disobey". He makes a powerful speech in support of the proposed Society's objectives.

"The institution which has been described," he concludes, "is manifestly needed."

He moves the adoption of the resolutions which establish the British and Foreign Bible Society and embody its form and constitution. Owen's description of the meeting (referring to himself in the third person) gets to the heart of its significance and successful outcome.

> Surrounded by a multitude of Christians whose doctrinal and ritual differences had for ages kept them asunder, and who had been taught to regard each other with a sort of pious estrangement, or rather of consecrated hostility; and reflecting on the object and the end which had brought them so harmoniously together, he felt an impression which no length of time would entirely remove. The scene was new: nothing analogous to it had perhaps been exhibited before the public since Christians had begun to organise against each other the strife of separation, and to carry into their own camp that war which they ought to have waged in concert against the common enemy. To him it appeared to indicate the dawn of a new era in Christendom; and to portend something like the return of those auspicious days when the multitude of them that believed were of "one heart and one soul"; and when as a consequence of that union, to a certain degree at least, "the Word of God mightily grew and prevailed".

The resolutions are carried unanimously and an executive committee elected. They confirm that Henry Thornton MP, who has earlier been approached, will be Treasurer. Those present subscribe over £700 on the spot – a sum equalling nearly £30,000 today.

A warm speech supporting the key resolutions by the chaplain to the Bishop of London has come as music to the ears of the RTS committee members who have worked so hard for fifteen months to establish the new Society. Many in the Church of

England are suspicious, even contemptuous, of Evangelicals. But now a key figure with a position at the hub of the established church is giving his enthusiastic blessing to an initiative which so far has been pursued by Evangelicals. John Paterson later describes Owen as "the prince of platform speakers". He will become the Church of England Secretary to the Society and its first historian. One of his daughters will marry Wilberforce's eldest son.

Owen thinks it will be important quickly to tell the Bishop of London.

A house in Fulham, 7 March 1804

On his return from the London Tavern, John Owen takes up his pen

The Bishop's chaplain writes a letter to his boss, then living in St James's Square, describing what he has seen. He sets out the evidence which has been produced about the lack of Scriptures both at home and abroad and the broad-minded and open-hearted principles which will govern the Society. He suggests to His Lordship that "the challenge so liberally given on the part of our dissenting brethren ought on our part to be as liberally accepted" and argues that the Church of England should support the new venture.

Will the Bishop of London be more encouraging to the new venture than was his predecessor, Cuthbert Tunstall, to William Tyndale in the early 16th century? The answer is yes: Dr Beilby Porteus takes a keen interest in any initiative he thinks likely to promote "truth, and virtue, and happiness, in any part of the world". Porteus sends Owen an encouraging reply, saying that he very much approves of the idea of Bible Society. He mentions it to friends who also like the scheme.

The Bishop is enthusiastic about the Bible Society because he thinks that distributing Bibles to the world will be hugely expensive and that fundraising and support should not be limited to members of the established church. And he approves of the idea of circulating the Scriptures only, without note or comment.

The Bishop looks forward to great results from a combined

effort by Christians of different views. He hopes that bringing them together to pursue one grand objective will bring an end to the sad divisions which have for so long spoiled the Christian world.

Spa Fields, Clerkenwell, 7 March 1804

On his return from the London Tavern, Joseph Tarn also writes a letter

Joseph Tarn is anxious to share the good news with his friend Thomas Charles. He tells him that the meeting has been attended by "from two to three hundred most respectable men from the several denominations of Christians – and nothing but the utmost harmony was heard". He continues, "We cannot, my dear Brother, but rejoice together when we consider that this work had its beginning in a conversation which took place between us two one weekday morning that is ever to be remembered."

Thomas Charles will reply: "I cannot express the joy I felt on receiving this information of a Society being formed for supplying the various nations of the world with Bibles. I hope it will prove a lasting (supply) of Welsh Bibles, and relieve my anxiety on that head. Those noble institutions, the Missionary, the Sunday-School, together with the Bible Society, added now to the other two, complete the means for the dispersion of divine knowledge far and near." Towards the end of his letter he writes, "Young females, in service, have walked over thirty miles to me with only the bare hope of obtaining a Bible each; and returned with more joy and thanksgiving than if they had obtained great spoils." Even though Mary Jones is not in fact "in service", he almost certainly has her in mind.

Joseph Tarn is early appointed Assistant Secretary and Accountant to the Society, and retains the post for nearly 33 years until the day of his death.

It is remarkable that at a time when tensions and conflicts between the Church of England and Nonconformists are at their most bitter, the Society is formed – by a wholehearted union between them. As those present reflect on the London Tavern meeting, they come to think of it as "fixing an important epoch in the religious history of mankind" and believe they can discern God's hand in the events which have led up to it. Ten days later, the West Indian planters meet in the Tavern to consider a final demand from William Wilberforce that they agree a five-year suspension of the slave trade.

The idea of distributing the Scriptures isn't new. It was one of the objectives of SPCK when it was founded way back in 1698 and of the Society for Promoting the Gospel in Foreign Parts (1701). It is included in the aims of at least three other Societies.

What is new and distinctive about the British and Foreign Bible Society is its interdenominational nature from the start and the enthusiasm and single-mindedness of its founders. They want to print the Scriptures without note or comment and distribute them not only in Britain but throughout the world. Some similar bodies have confined themselves to taking the Bible to particular classes and groups of people. This will be, as Joseph Hughes puts it, an institution which originates in one nation for the good of all.

The boldness and clarity of the Society's objective could well capture the enthusiasm of Christian people for a few years and then be quietly forgotten. But after its first 100 years the Society will be described as "the greatest literary enterprise of the nineteen Christian centuries".

Act 6

Zealous circle in Clapham

As far as we know, Mary Jones never leaves Wales. Later in her life she will get to Methodist Association meetings on the green at Bala, and will enjoy following visiting preachers for a whole day on their visits to her area, but she never ventures anywhere near south-east England. Were she to do so, she would discover that seven of the founders of Bible Society live, like her, in a village. But this particular village is very different from Llanfihangel, and the lifestyle of those who live there is quite unlike anything Mary will ever experience.

Clapham at the turn of the 18th and 19th centuries

Three miles of pleasant meadows lie between London and Clapham, still a village of nightingales, though the number of inhabitants has grown to more than 2,000. Around Clapham Common – a wilderness of gorse bushes, gravel pits and ponds – some merchants, bankers, lawyers and MPs, who want to live in the country and yet be within easy reach of the city, have built a number of substantial homes. Amongst them is an informal group of Anglican Evangelicals whom Sydney Smith in the *Edinburgh Review* nicknames "The Clapham Sect" – the label sticks.

Enter John Venn, rector of Clapham 1792–1813

Son of Henry Venn, vicar of Huddersfield, Venn organises his parish on vigorously evangelical lines, including a Sunday evening service (still a novelty at this time) and a system of district visiting. He seems genuinely to be following his father's example in showing as much concern for his poor parishioners (for the villagers don't all live in big houses) as he is for the well-to-do.

"Mr Venn gave us a most admirable discourse today on

instability in religion, pious and practical," Lord Teignmouth tells a friend in the year the Society is founded. "I hardly ever heard a subject more judiciously treated." Venn preaches every Sunday to what is perhaps the most notable congregation in all England.

As well as being able and successful in the world of business and politics, the members of the Clapham Sect and their wives are devoted to the Church of England, fervent in prayer and diligent in studying their Bibles. Although they dress well and ride well-groomed horses, these men order their lives with strict self-discipline. They are hospitable because they believe this to be a Christian duty. Like all the best Evangelicals of the day, they rise early in the morning and spend time in the presence of God. They map out every hour of the day beforehand, setting aside three hours a day for prayer – from five to six in the morning, from twelve to one at noon, and from five to six in the evening: there are so many hours for study, for business, for rest. They don't regard their wealth as their own but give to the Lord's work generously and methodically.

St James's Square, London, 14 May 1804

Before attending a meeting of the General Committee, John Owen has a long conversation with the Bishop of London about the Society.

"The Committee is concerned about the choice of a President," Owen says.

"Lord Teignmouth," replies the Bishop, "is one of your subscribers, and he would make an excellent President."

Later in the day, Owen tells the Committee of the Bishop's suggestion. The members approve and send an invitation to His Lordship who accepts the position. Before buying his house in Clapham following his return to England, Lord Teignmouth has had a distinguished, if at times controversial, career as Governor General of India. He will hold the post as first President of Bible Society for 30 years, writing the first annual reports himself.

Born John Shore in St James's Street, Piccadilly, the future Lord Teignmouth went at the age of fourteen to Harrow where he was a contemporary of Sheridan. Towards the end of 1768, he sailed for India as a writer for the East India Company. He was rapidly promoted and given official responsibility for a large district and also found the time to study Bengali, Hindustani, Arabic and Persian.

Shore soon gained the confidence of Warren Hastings, the first and most famous of the British Governors General of India, who gave him wide responsibility for revenue collection and adjudication of exchequer cases. In January 1785 he returned to England with Warren Hastings. During the voyage home, Hastings composed a paraphrase of one of Horace's lyric poems which he dedicated to Shore.

Shore visited his brother Thomas who lived at Duryard on the outskirts of Exeter, Devon. Here he met an attractive young woman, Charlotte Cornish, the daughter of a Teignmouth doctor, who was stranded in Exeter during a snowstorm. John and Charlotte fell in love and were married in February 1786. Their marriage lasted until Charlotte's death 48 years later and, from all accounts, was blissfully happy.

Shore and his young wife returned to India in 1787 where he took his seat as a member of the Government of Bengal; he introduced a number of reforms before returning to England in 1790. At this time he refused the offer of a Baronetcy, believing that titles were inappropriate in a world of poverty.

In 1792 it became known that Shore would be invited to become Governor General of India in succession to Lord Cornwallis. Edmund Burke, who had introduced impeachment proceedings against Warren Hastings in the Commons, alleging corruption during his period as Governor General, opposed Shore's name. Although Hastings was acquitted in 1795, Burke sought to link Shore's name and reputation with that of Hastings. Prime Minister William Pitt, however, was unmoved by Burke's manoeuvrings.

"The decision to appoint Shore has been unanimous," Pitt

told Burke firmly. "He has proved one of the ablest and most upright servants of the Company in India."

Shore was duly appointed Governor General of India and took up his duties there in October 1793.

"Grant that I may on all occasions regulate my conduct by the rules and precepts of your Word," he prayed, "and that in all doubts, dangers, and embarrassments, I may always have grace to apply to you for support and assistance. Grant that under my Government, religion and morality may be advanced."

During his period of office as Governor General, the officers of the Indian army mutinied, a turn of events he responded to by granting them concessions which raised some eyebrows. As a reward for his services he did accept the title of Baron Teignmouth in 1798, the year in which he returned to England. The Directors of the East India Company paid tribute to his "long, able, and faithful service in India; and particularly for his distinguished merit and attention, in the administration of every branch of the company's affairs, during the period in which he held the office of Governor General".

Lord Teignmouth became a close friend of the 73-year-old John Newton, the former slave trader and now evangelical rector of St Mary Woolnoth (and opponent of slavery), the two men frequently visiting each other's homes.

John and Charlotte, with their six children (he often referred to them as "the brats" but adored their company), moved to Clapham in August 1802, four months before the momentous RTS meeting at Old Swan Stairs. He bought his house, together with 22 acres of land, from Samuel Thornton. Although living in Clapham allowed him to spend more time with his closest friends and neighbours, especially Wilberforce, Charles Grant, Granville Sharp and Henry Thornton, Lord Teignmouth had no experience either of agriculture or horticulture.

"My farmyard, garden, and hot-houses," he said, "give me more annoyance than I ever experienced governing India."

However, he persevered and never failed to rise early and ride several miles before breakfast. He began to write regular articles for the *Christian Observer*, edited by another member of the

Clapham Sect, Zachary Macaulay (who also became a member of the first General Committee of the Society).

WHAT LORD TEIGNMOUTH BELIEVED

In an article in the *Christian Observer*, Lord Teignmouth set out his Christian beliefs with clarity.

> There is an inherent depravity in man, which can only be subdued by the operation of divine grace; that on this account he is estranged from God, until he is renewed by the sanctifying influence of the Holy Spirit; that Christ our Saviour died for the sins of the world; and that we are redeemed and saved by his death, solely through faith in him, to the exclusion of all merit from our own works or righteousness; that, nevertheless, the only proof which we can give of our faith, is our obedience to the commandments of God, and Christ, which are all comprehended in the injunction of love to God and man; that consequently, no faith can be sound or perfect which does not produce the fruit of a holy life. With this conviction, I endeavour, humbly depending on the divine assistance, to act in all things to the glory of God, and to live in charity with my neighbour; making the Gospel the rule of my conduct; and the conformity of my conduct to its rules, the test of my faith.

With his insistence that "no faith can be sound or perfect which does not produce the fruit of a holy life" Lord Teignmouth acquits himself of the charge of antinomianism – the erroneous belief that Christians are set free by grace from the obligation to observe moral law – which has sometimes been levelled at Evangelicals. Towards the end of his life he described to his son-in-law, Robert Anderson, "his ardent longings after higher degrees of that holiness which is only another name for true happiness".

"I loathe and detest every species and every degree of sin," he told Anderson, "as the transgression of the Divine Law, and as an offence committed against the Majesty and holiness of God. I trust that I do indeed repent of all my transgressions. But I do not trust *in* my repentance. No! I look only to the blood of Jesus for pardon and for peace."

In September 1803, Lord Teignmouth was appointed Vice-Lieutenant of Surrey – a position which involved him in planning for a possible French invasion.

"What do you think of Monsieur Bonaparte?" he asked his father-in-law. "My opinion is that he will risk some thousands of his satellites in an attempt upon us. If he *could* have landed 40,000 two months ago in Kent or Essex they might have come nearer to London than double that number will be now able to do. The metropolis and its environs, if my calculation be correct, would I think furnish 50,000 or 60,000 stout-hearted volunteers. And there is a very stout force in Essex: I was told, from good authority, 30,000, exclusive of cavalry and artillery – all ready to take the field, at an hour's notice."

Besides the regular duties of a county Vice-Lieutenant and presiding regularly at meetings of the magistrates, he found that he also had to take responsibility for the arming and disciplining of 8,000 volunteers who would defend Surrey in case of invasion. He attended the volunteers' drills, reviewed them in various parts of the county, and entertained officers in his home.

Lord Teignmouth was 53 when he accepted the invitation to become President of Bible Society. He thought of the post as more important and honourable than any other office which he held, including being Governor General of India and a Privy Councillor, which he became in 1807. Yet he had no idea when he took on the job how huge a task it would become. Besides drafting the first annual reports himself, he attended regularly the meetings of the General Committee and other committees as they were established. He conducted a huge correspondence with friends, politicians, missionaries, Bible translators, the Society's Secretaries, its supporters and critics.

A few months after the inaugural meeting, in June 1804, he writes to Hubert Cornish, his brother-in-law, about the Society he now presides over.

I have assumed my functions as President of the British and Foreign Bible Society; and was pleased and surprised to find Quakers as well as Dissenters attending our Committee. I doubt if human ingenuity could devise another principle for uniting Christians of various denominations; and it shall be my endeavour to promote a spirit of charity amongst them – they do not want [lack] it at present.

The Bishops of London and Durham have honoured me and the Society by consenting to be Vice-Presidents of it. I tremble sometimes at the responsibility of the situations in which I have been placed, and sincerely pray to God that I may not disgrace my profession.

Introducing the Society's first Treasurer

Henry Thornton was easily recognisable by his powdered hair and blue coat with metal buttons. Bible Society could hardly have had a first Treasurer who was better qualified through ability, experience, connections and integrity. Henry was the third son of John Thornton, said to be the second wealthiest merchant in Europe. John had given generously to Thomas Charles helping him buy Bibles for his schools in north Wales.

In 1790 Henry had bought a house on Battersea Rise with land which stretched up to Clapham Common. He built two houses on this land, lived in one himself and sold the other, named Broomfield, to Wilberforce. The shrubberies of the two houses ran into each other. There, at Wilberforce's suggestion, Thornton built a library, a charming oval building, the walls of which were lined with books and where members of the Clapham Sect and their friends would meet as a break from the hard work of Parliament or business.

Making his own money as a banker and financier, Henry worked closely with his neighbour Wilberforce in the campaign against slavery, having been elected to Parliament for Southwark in 1782 despite refusing to buy votes. Noted for his integrity as well as his anti-slavery views, he held Southwark for 32 years until the end of his life. In Parliament, his contemporaries regarded him as an authority on all matters of finance.

His private life was as exemplary as his public one. We know from a letter his granddaughter wrote to *The Guardian* in 1907 that he always gave away far more than he spent. For example, in 1793 he laid out £1,988 (£106,000 at today's values) on all his extensive household expenses and gave away £6,680 (£356,177 at today's values).

Henry Thornton was an expert monetary theorist and wrote learned papers on the supply of money. But the book through which many 19th century Christian families knew him was his *Family Prayers*.

Members of the General Committee during the Society's first eleven years grew familiar with Thornton's "strong Saxon face, with serene and capacious brows, blue eyes full and scrutinising, lips slightly parted, 'as of one who listens and prepares to speak' and a resolute chin".

England in the early 19th century

Re-enter Wilberforce, leading his campaign

Much of the hard and relentless work underpinning the campaign to abolish both the slave trade and slavery itself is done in Clapham. William Wilberforce and his friends Thomas Clarkson, Granville Sharp, Henry Thornton, Charles Grant, Edward James Eliot, Zachary Macaulay, and James Stephen work tirelessly in the face of formidable opposition. An immense amount of English capital is invested in the trade. The ship-owners, the merchants, the planters and the financiers are united in their determination to keep both the trade and practice of slavery going.

King George III is quite sure the pious men of Clapham are dangerous revolutionaries. Admiral Nelson has no time for Wilberforce. "I was bred in the good old school," he writes from the *Victory*, "and taught to appreciate the value of our West Indian possessions, and neither in the field nor the Senate shall their rights be infringed, while I have any arm to fight in their defence, or a tongue to launch my voice against the damnable doctrine of Wilberforce and his hypocritical allies."

Wilberforce introduces his Bill to abolish the slave trade eleven times, only for it to be debated and defeated. He has to collect witnesses from all over the world. He has to examine the witnesses for the other side and expose their false or misleading assertions. He has to educate public opinion by an endless succession of meetings. He writes hundreds of pamphlets, attends almost daily committees of one kind or another, and organises petitions and deputations. He interviews and briefs Cabinet ministers.

At one stage of the fight, Wilberforce's friends in Clapham agree to sacrifice one night's sleep a week in order to help him sift through the mass of evidence that is pouring in. At last they win the victory, when in 1807 the Bill is carried by 283 votes to 16. After 1807 Wilberforce supports the movement for the complete abolition of slavery (as distinct from the trade in slaves) and this will be achieved by the Emancipation Act of 1833.

From the day in April 1803 when the committee of RTS managed to secure his support for the new Bible Society, Wilberforce is active on its behalf. He speaks at the Society's first General Meeting on 2 May 1804, is a Vice-President of the Society, an eloquent and persuasive speaker promoting its work, and a member of several of its committees.

Act 7

Time for action

Until 1816, when the Society will acquire its own premises in Earl Street, most Committee meetings are held in Joseph Hardcastle's counting house at Old Swan Stairs. Public meetings are held at the London Tavern, Bishopsgate until 1810, when the venue is switched to the Freemasons' Hall in Great Smith Street. From 1831 Exeter Hall will be used for public meetings.

Within a week of the London Tavern meeting, the Society's Committee gets down to work. They have to make arrangements which will meet the approval of all denominations. They decide to appoint three Secretaries: Josiah Pratt, Secretary of the Church Missionary Society, to represent the established church; Joseph Hughes to represent the nonconformist churches; and Karl Steinkopf to represent the foreign Protestant churches. After just a few weeks, they elect John Owen to replace Josiah Pratt at the recommendation and request of Pratt himself, who has more than enough work to do administering the affairs of CMS.

It is agreed that the General Committee shall consist entirely of laymen and that of the 36 members, fifteen will be members of the Church of England, fifteen will be members of other communions, and six will be foreigners resident near London. (Two hundred years later, the Society's constitution still lays down that membership of the General Committee – now known as the Board of Trustees – shall not exceed 36 members with not less than 40% being members of the Church of England and not less than 40% being members of other denominations of Christians.)

As one of the founders will put it later, BFBS "is a society for furnishing the means of religion, but not a religious society". The members meet as lay persons and agree to disagree about points of doctrine. After an early meeting of subscribers to the Society, someone comments that "from the part taken and the sentiments uttered by the persons who take the lead in the conduct of the Society's affairs, he would not be able to ascertain who are the Churchmen and who are the Dissenters".

Administratively, the founders of the Society decide to put the overall direction in the hands of three Secretaries who are all clergy: their skill and experience will enable the new enterprise to sail calmly (most of the time) through the rough seas of denominational differences and the sometimes noisy polemics of the time. But those with the responsibility for the overall strategic decision-making are, and remain, lay people.

"WITHOUT NOTE OR COMMENT"

The first paragraph of the Society's laws and regulations state that the sole object of the Society is "to encourage a wider circulation of the Holy Scriptures without note or comment". The phrase reflects the non-sectarian, non-denominational approach of the Society. Since they want to serve the Bible cause generally, and enlist the help of Christians from across the church spectrum, the founders of Bible Society are wise to adopt the policy of excluding note and comment. Each of the founders certainly has cherished theological positions and interpretations of the Bible – on baptism, what happens to the bread and wine at communion, the second coming, church order, the primacy of the Pope, even (as we shall see) the deity of Christ. But by restraining themselves and the translators they use from adopting and advertising argumentative positions on any issues, and by being ready to work cooperatively in a spirit of tolerance – agreeing to differ – they guarantee the maximum support for their new Society and ensure its rapid growth.

The Society's original laws and regulations also lay it down that

- the subscription one guinea (one pound and one shilling) annually makes you a member of the Society
- the subscription of ten guineas once makes you a life member
- the subscription of five guineas annually makes you a Governor

- the subscription of £50 makes you a Governor for life
- an executor paying a bequest of £50 will be a member for life, and one paying £100 or more will be a Governor for life
- Governors are entitled to attend and vote at all meetings of the Committee
- each member will be entitled to buy Bibles and Testaments, intended for free distribution, at the Society's prices, which will be as low as possible – although the *Society itself* will not give away any Scriptures in Great Britain
- the General Committee will meet on the first Monday of every month "or oftener if necessary"
- at an annual meeting in May, the Treasurer and Committee will be chosen, the accounts audited, and the activities of the previous year reported

Some of these provisions may give today's fundraisers pause for wistful thought! From the outset the Committee meets more than once a month. In the early days of the Society's life, the Bishops of London and Durham send in their names as annual subscribers of five guineas. A few weeks later, both these men plus the Bishops of Exeter and St David's accept the positions of Vice-Presidents, a list which is completed by the addition of the names of Sir William Pepperell, Vice-Admiral (later Lord) Gambier, Charles Grant, William Wilberforce and Henry Thornton (the last three all MPs).

From the start, various sub-committees handle the work of the Society, reporting to the General Committee. Great demands are made on the time of the Committee members and staff. Yet it isn't until 1823, at the death of John Owen, over 18 years after the formation of the Society, that it is agreed that a salary should be attached to the office of Secretary. By this time, the annual revenue of the Society exceeds £90,000 (nearly £4.5 million at today's values).

A prospectus issued in the early weeks of the Society's life sets out its objectives with clarity.

The *reasons* which call for such an institution chiefly refer to the prevalence of ignorance, superstition, and idolatry over so large a portion of the world: the limited nature of the respectable societies [previously referred to], and their acknowledged insufficiency to supply the demand for Bibles in the United Kingdom and foreign countries; and the recent attempts which have been made on the part of infidelity to discredit the evidence, vilify the character, and destroy the influence of Christianity.

The exclusive *object* of this Society is to diffuse the knowledge of the Holy Scriptures by circulating them in the different languages spoken throughout Great Britain and Ireland; and also, according to the extent of its funds, by promoting the printing of them in foreign languages and the distribution of them in foreign countries.

The *principles* upon which this undertaking will be conducted are as comprehensive as the nature of the object suggests that they should be. In the execution of this plan it is proposed to embrace the common support of Christians at large, and to invite the concurrence of persons of every description who profess to regard the Scriptures as the proper standard of faith.

From England, Wales and Scotland, messages of approval and support pour in to the Society's Secretaries. The Presbytery of Glasgow and the Synod of Glasgow and Ayr direct that collections shall be made at all their places of worship. In Wales, the Bishop of Bangor recommends the Society to his flock. Thomas Charles records that there are "none of our poor people willing to live and die without contributing their mites towards forwarding so glorious a design".

Officials and friends of the Society begin to build up a clearer picture of the dearth of Scriptures in Britain and abroad. The Society places an order with Cambridge University Press for a large number of English Bibles and Testaments and 20,000 Welsh Bibles and 5,000 Testaments.

Swabia, south–western Germany, 18 October 1804

A priest writes of the Bible as "the best preacher in the world"

Karl Steinkopf quickly gets in touch with religious leaders and Christian organisations on the continent of Europe. In Germany and Switzerland the formation of the Society is greeted with delight by many, including some Roman Catholics. A Roman Catholic priest in Swabia writes the following letter to Steinkopf:

I had the pleasure to learn…[of] the great number of zealous friends of the Bible in London who are filled with a noble desire to send out the pure word of God as the best preacher into the world. This account excited in my breast the most heartfelt joy and gratitude towards that God…but I felt also lively emotions of unfeigned love and affection for you and for all the members of that venerable Bible Society; for whom I wish a thousand blessings. May the Lord Jesus, through whom all blessings are communicated to us, be the beginning and end of that praiseworthy undertaking! And may his name be glorified for it to all eternity!

What particularly induced me to write was your question, Whether the Bible was still prohibited to the Catholics? Being convinced thereby that you were mindful even of the poor Catholics, I was particularly moved and edified; for indeed nothing is more affecting than that love which embraces all without the least distinction; "for God is love; and he that dwelleth in love dwelleth in God, and God in him." I felt myself therefore constrained to thank you in the name of all honest and well-disposed Catholics for these your fraternal sentiments.

In answer to your question, I observe, properly speaking, the Bible has never been prohibited to the Catholics. The Council of Trent only states – *Indiscriminata lectio Sacrae Scripturae interdicta est.* Well-informed Catholics took this always in that sense only: that not all books of the Bible, *promiscuously*, should be put in the hands of the common people; referring chiefly to some books of the Old Testament. Besides, this prohibition of the Council of Trent has never been admitted as binding by the whole body of the Roman Catholic clergy in Germany; but so much is true, that all blind bigots of our church have always spread the opinion that it was entirely forbidden for all laymen to read the Bible: and this prejudice is alas still deeply prevalent among the greater part of the people. There are, however, at present among our clergymen, both in Swabia and Bavaria, [those] who strongly recommend the reading of the Bible, chiefly of the New Testament; and do everything in their power to promote it. I have for my own part distributed many New Testaments, and some Bibles, among better-enlightened Catholics; and several of my dear brethren in Christ do the same.

We are however not able to satisfy all the demands for Bibles...

I feel a very great desire to witness the formation of a similar Bible Society amongst the Roman Catholics, and indeed I will make some attempts though I foresee many difficulties... Your question, however, respecting the Catholics inspires me with the hope that your Society is desirous to extend its beneficial influence likewise to the Catholics...

I cannot express in terms sufficiently strong the fervency of my joy and love towards all who, throughout England, heartily believe in Jesus Christ as their only Saviour, and zealously endeavour to extend the Redeemer's Kingdom. I embrace them all as the beloved and elect of God, as friends and brethren in Christ, let them be of whatever name, or belong to whatever church or denomination... Truly God has a numerous *Army of Reserve* in England who do not bow before the Baal of the age, nor sacrifice to the God of the times....

This letter so encourages the General Committee that they place a thousand German New Testaments at the priest's disposal for distribution among Roman Catholics in Swabia and Bavaria.

Re-enter Granville Sharp

In the earliest months, the Committee adopts the idea of forming a biblical library so that, in the words of the minute, "the Society might never be at a loss for a standard edition and the means of collation whenever an occasion should arise for printing an edition on its own account". They instruct that copies of every translation, and of each edition printed under the Society's auspices, shall be sent to the library. The Committee invites the public to help in establishing the collection.

First to respond is Granville Sharp, who presents 39 volumes, including some very old and valuable ones. Other friends of the Society also respond generously so that by the end of the 19th century the library contains about 5,000 volumes of printed books and manuscripts. By this time the Society will have acquired other important private collections and the library will include versions of the Bible in more than 150 languages.

Britain, 1804 and eight months of 1805

Napoleon waits for an opportunity to master the English Channel and invade. Many people go to sleep afraid they will be woken by the sound of drums or the glare of beacon fires. Farmers bring lengths of bunting for their daughters to turn into signals to be flown from church towers at the first news of a French landing. In at least one great house in Norfolk, the horses are kept ready to carry the women and children at short notice into the depths of the Fens when the enemy arrives. An armed escort stands ready with 30 wagons to hurry the treasure of the Bank of England to the crypt of Worcester Cathedral, and a sentry stands beside the big gun on Edinburgh Castle to start a chain of beacons and church bells throughout Scotland.

The price of bread rises to 1 shilling and four-and-a-half pence for a large loaf and, to make matters worse, the 1804/5 winter is exceptionally severe with snow in January lying ten feet deep on high ground between Cheltenham and Oxford.

Through all this, the General Committee of the newly formed Society continues its work steadily. And then a chain of events begins in September 1805 which will end in bells ringing throughout the land.

Off the coast of south-west Spain, September to October 1805

Enter Admiral Nelson off Cape Trafalgar

At the end of September, Napoleon orders Admiral Villeneuve to leave Cadiz and land troops at Naples to support the French campaign in southern Italy. On 19–20 October his fleet slips out of Cadiz, hoping to get into the Mediterranean without having to fight. However, the British Admiral Nelson, already a national celebrity, catches up with Villeneuve off Cape Trafalgar in southern Spain, not far from the Straits of Gibraltar, on 21 October.

Villeneuve orders his fleet to form a single line heading north, and Nelson orders his fleet to attack Villeneuve's line from the west. By noon a squadron led by Admiral Collingwood in the *Royal Sovereign*, has engaged the rear ships of the French–Spanish line. Nelson, in the *Victory*, signals his famous message, *England expects that every man will do his duty*. Then his squadron attacks the rear and centre of Villeneuve's line, shattering his ships. Admiral Collingwood completes the destruction of the rear, and the battle ends late in the afternoon. Villeneuve is captured and his fleet loses 19 or 20 ships, which he surrenders to the British; 14,000 Frenchmen are taken prisoners of war. Nelson is mortally wounded by a sniper, but he dies certain of his complete victory. About 1,500 British seamen are killed or wounded, but no British ships are lost. Trafalgar shatters forever Napoleon's plans to invade England. British naval supremacy is established for more than 100 years.

The Times for 7 November 1805 reports that the joyful news of the recent victory has been given to King George III – but adds that "His Majesty wears a green shade constantly over his eyes, after candle-light; and we are sorry to say, he cannot distinguish any person except he be very near, and with the assistance of a glass".

Trafalgar is a great victory over the French but not the final one, and until Napoleon arrives in St Helena ten years later, the history of Bible Society continues against the background of the continued threat of war. Lord Teignmouth writes a poem, published anonymously, on *The Death of Nelson* which includes the lines:

Thus wept, thus honour'd in his grave,
Now Nelson sleeps – yet Britons! Know,
'Twas Heaven the power to Nelson gave;
'Twas God, through him, subdued the foe.

Lord Teignmouth's friend, Captain (later Admiral Sir Henry) Blackwood, who also distinguishes himself in the battle, presents a copy of the poem to each of the crew of the *Victory*.

FIRST FOREIGN VERSIONS

In 1804 there are only about 70 languages into which some part of the Bible has been translated. Most of these are languages of Europe and the Mediterranean area. Only one of them is from tropical Africa and two from the Far East. To this list, which has hardly been added to since the time of the Reformation, the Society will contribute nearly 800 more languages in the course of the next 150 years, and the work of other Societies will bring the total number of languages in which some portion of Scripture is available to over 2,300 by the beginning of the 21st century.

The first ever use of Bible Society funds to produce a foreign version of the Scriptures under its own direction is made with a grant for 2,000 copies of a Mohawk–English Gospel of John. The Mohawks are one of the six Indian tribes, or nations, making up the Iroquois Confederacy who live mainly in what is now New York State. During the American War of Independence the Mohawks were pro-British under their leader Joseph Brant and followed him to Canada.

Lord and Lady Teignmouth's home in Clapham

The Mohawk–English Gospel is translated by Tyonenhokarawen, a chief of the Mohawks, whose father is a Cherokee who has served in the British army. The chief himself has been a captain in the army and usually assumes the English name of Norton.

Captain Norton (to use his English name) does most of the translation work while staying as a guest of the Teignmouths in

Clapham. He sometimes appears at his host's table in Mohawk dress and performs a war dance, tomahawk in hand, to the astonishment of other guests. On returning to America, he will distinguish himself, at the head of his tribe, in the war against the United States in 1812 and will obtain a major's commission as reward for his services. He will revisit England, accompanied by a young Indian bride.

The principle of "without note or comment" is first and firmly put into practice with this translation. Captain Norton writes a lively introduction to the Gospel in the form of a spirited address to the Six Nations – but as soon as the Committee discovers this they order it to be withdrawn as incompatible with a fundamental rule of the Society.

Since the trigger for the founding of the Society is a shortage of Welsh Bibles, the Society is anxious to do what it can to improve the supply of Scriptures for Wales. In July 1806 it begins to distribute 10,000 copies of the Welsh New Testament and has 20,000 Bibles nearly ready to be circulated. Both Testaments and Bibles are edited by Thomas Charles and printed for the Society by Cambridge University Press.

Bala, September 1806

A week before the Welsh Testaments arrive, the people of Bala and the surrounding districts hear they are on the way. The news is on every lip and the atmosphere is electric. As dawn breaks on Thursday 25 September, news comes that the load of Testaments is approaching the town. Crowds from the town and surrounding countryside rush to meet it. A group of sturdy young men remove a tired old mare from the cart shafts and run with the load of Bibles to the town where they receive a rapturous welcome from a crowd which lines the streets.

Charles arrives back in Bala the day before the New Testaments come, after a preaching tour with Rowland Hill. He has no time to unload the Testaments and check them before they are sold. He gives one copy to his baby grandson, who goes on to become President of Trevecca College in South Wales and will recall the incident at one of the Society's jubilee meetings.

Young people in Bala read the books late into the September evening and when night falls they turn the pages by the glimmer of dim lamps. Next morning, labourers carry them into the fields and open them during their rest periods.

In her old age, Mary Jones will tell how she and others used to walk overnight to Bala in Thomas Charles's day to the communion services there, of the prayer meetings held on the way, of the preaching on the green at Bala during Methodist Associations in the town, and of the spiritual rejoicing on such occasions. *Mary was aged 21 on that memorable September day when the Testaments arrived in Bala. Was she there? Did she help pull the cart into the town?*

For the next ten years, the Society distributes a yearly average of 11,000 copies of the Welsh Scriptures.

Scotland, 1805–1816

Although the National Bible Society of Scotland will not be formed until 1861, work in support of Bible Society, and the Bible cause generally, begins in 1805 and is associated with the name of the philanthropist David Dale of Glasgow. As soon as the formation of BFBS is known in Glasgow, Dale sends a generous subscription and drums up interest among his friends. The Secretaries of the parent Society in London come to regard Dale as their Treasurer and general agent for Glasgow and the west of Scotland.

The earliest of the Scottish Auxiliaries, the Edinburgh Bible Society, one calling itself the Scottish Bible Society, and the East Lothian Bible Society, are established in 1809. By 1816 47 Auxiliaries will be formed in Scotland and send nearly £35,000 (£1,405,600 today) to the parent Society in London.

Although the Scottish Auxiliaries develop their distinctive ways of doing things, they are in the early years staunchly loyal to London. As the Committee of Edinburgh Bible Society tells its members, "Our connection, as a society, with the British and Foreign Bible Society, has been a source of continued satisfaction... During the foregoing year (1810–11) the sum of £700 has been remitted to the parent institution, making a total of £1,500 since the commencement of your society."

Early work in Scotland also reflects well the non-sectarian spirit which so characterises the work in England. When a Roman Catholic priest applies for help, the British and Foreign Bible Society sends Bibles and New Testaments to the Glasgow Bible Society for distribution in Roman Catholic schools.

Sadly, relations between London and the Scottish Auxiliaries will turn sour within 20 years of their formation.

Ireland, 1808–1817

The Dublin Bible Society, or the Hibernian, is founded in 1806 on the same principles as the parent Society. The Society in London says the Society in Ireland can obtain Scriptures at the cost of production and sends a grant of £100 (£3,800 today) the following year. In the same year, the Society also sends £100 to the newly founded Cork Bible Society. The Hibernian Bible Society soon establishes branches in other parts of Ireland and by 1813–14 the number of branches increases to 53.

Enter Joseph Hughes, Thomas Charles, Dr David Bogue and Samuel Mills touring Ireland for the Society

Thomas Charles records that the poor in their primitive Irish huts are polite and responsive but quite ignorant of the Bible. He doesn't think you can spread religion in Ireland without Bibles, preaching in the language of the people and establishing schools where people are taught to read Irish. "We have not met," he writes, "a single person who could read Irish and there are no elementary books in the language. Itinerant schools would do wonders here."

In its annual report for 1815, the Sligo Branch of the Hibernian Bible Society speaks with pride about the schools it has opened with a roll of 17,000 children. An inspector at one of these schools tells how he is invited to take a seat at the altar after Mass in a Roman Catholic church and to lend the priest his Irish New Testament. The priest reads a chapter from Matthew's Gospel and then addresses his flock:

"You have now heard in a language you all understand what I before read in the Mass, in your hearing, in a language you didn't understand. You all seem to be highly pleased with what I have read. Now this is one of the good books taught in the free school opened for the instruction of your children in this chapel, and supported, free of expense to you, by good people in England.

"The English books also provided by the Society for your children are good – very good. One of them, the Testament, is the Word of God; and if you wish to know the difference between the Catholic Testament and the English and Irish Testaments provided by the Society, it is even the same as if I should say 'Four and two makes six', and you should say 'Two and four makes six' – which you all know is the same in the end. I therefore not only permit these schools, but command you all to send your children to them and to be thankful. I shall be much displeased with the man who neglects such a blessing provided for his family."

Until the Irish potato famine of 1845–49, Irish is the language spoken by half the population of Ireland. The first 2,000 copies of the Society's Irish Testaments are distributed so quickly that three more editions are printed by 1817. In the same year, 5,000 copies of the whole Irish Bible are issued. The text used is the translation by the saintly Bishop Bedell who was appointed to the diocese of Kilmore and Ardagh in 1629.

Act 8

"Great things for God"

From its start, the story of Bible Society is intimately entwined with the work of missionaries. The Society quickly establishes links with a famous group of missionary translators in Serampore (today's Shrirampur) and Calcutta, of whom William Carey is the most remarkable. Carey was born in Northamptonshire and left school at the age of twelve to become a gardener's boy and then an apprentice cobbler. Caught stealing one day at work, his master sent him to church to repent. The punishment worked: the church he became attached to was Baptist, and Carey, who as a boy treasured a leather globe and a copy of Captain Cook's *Voyages*, in time became a Baptist minister. For many years Carey continued his cobbling by night, while running a school by day and acting as pastor of a church. For good measure, he somehow found time as well to teach himself Latin, Greek, Hebrew, Dutch and French.

Northamptonshire, England, 1785 A GROUP OF BAPTIST MINISTERS WAIT TO HEAR WHAT A 24-YEAR-OLD SPEAKER HAS TO SAY

Enter William Carey

After a brief introduction from the elderly Chairman, Carey introduces his subject: "Whether the command given to the Apostles to teach all nations ought not to be obeyed by all ministers to the end of the world". The audience receives his talk well for a while until an increasingly irritated Chairman intervenes.

"Sit down, young man! When it pleases God to convert the heathen, he'll do it without your help, or mine."

Three years later, a wealthy merchant gives Carey £10 to write and publish *An Enquiry into the Obligations of Christians to Use*

Means for the Conversion of the Heathens. In this pamphlet, which is published in 1790 when he is 29, Carey argues from a wide range of Bible passages to impress the urgency of missionary work on his readers: "For whosoever shall call on the name of the Lord shall be saved. How then shall they call on him, in whom they have not believed? And how shall they believe in him who shall not have heard? And how shall they hear without a preacher? And how shall they preach except they be sent?"

Carey put the facts starkly: the world population is reckoned to be around 730 million. Only something like 174 million of these are Christian. He quotes Cook's observation that the most barbarous of people "appear to be as capable of knowledge as we are". The Gospel needs to be spread just as it once was brought to English people. He vigorously refutes arguments that heathens are too uncivilised, or too far away, for any good to be done. Consider what merchants have managed: "It only requires that we should have as much love for the souls of our fellow-creatures, and fellow-sinners, as they have for the profits arising from a few otter skins."

As a result of his pamphlet, the Baptist Association invites Carey to address them at their 1792 meeting in Nottingham. The title he gives his talk becomes a famous watchword: *Expect great things from God. Attempt great things for God.* After his talk, and fearing that it has had little effect, a frustrated Carey grabs a Baptist leader as he leaves the hall.

"What, and again do nothing?" he asks.

But his talk has made an impact and four months later, at the Northamptonshire town of Kettering, the Baptist Society for Propagating the Gospel among the Heathen is formed (now BMS World Mission). It is agreed that Carey will lead the first mission.

Dr John Thomas, who has recently returned from Bengal, addresses the Kettering meeting.

"I know of ways," he tells the assembled Baptists, "of getting round the East India Company's ban on missionaries using British ships. If we are determined enough we can take the Gospel to India." Thomas offers to accompany the first mission to Calcutta himself. Eleven months later, Carey arrives in Calcutta with his wife, sister, three sons and Dr Thomas on a Dutch ship pretending to be an indigo planter looking for land.

Thomas's idea is for Carey to settle his mission at the Danish trading base of Serampore where he believes that Danish officers will not object to the setting up of a station. Thomas, however, turns out to be unreliable, irresponsible and in debt. He runs through Carey's mission funds within a few weeks. Stranded without money, Carey is forced to live up to his pretended identity as a planter.

Deep in the interior of India, the British authorities are offering untilled jungle land rent-free to planters for three years. Carey travels there with his family, none of whom – including his wife – are as enthusiastic about evangelism as he is. His sons grow increasingly unruly. Tigers, alligators and snakes make the jungle exciting but scary. Carey gratefully accepts an offer to move 300 miles further inland (but out of the jungle) to run another farm. Here the whole family is struck down by chronic dysentery. When Carey's five-year-old son dies, the family cannot find an Indian willing to help prepare the grave, so Carey, with dysentery himself, digs the grave on his hands and knees. On seeing how ill he is, two Indians come to help him – at which Carey weeps with gratitude.

Serampore, India, 1800

Money reaches Carey from England and he is able to leave the jungle and begin his mission in Serampore. Serampore was originally a Danish settlement called Frederiksnagar – today it is Shrirampur, in West Bengal state, north-eastern India. There Carey, Joshua Marshman and William Ward, collectively known as the "Serampore trio", establish the mission described by William Wilberforce as "one of the chief glories" of the British nation. In five years Carey translates the New Testament into Bengali and visits 200 villages. When Fort William College opens in Calcutta for educating Indian ministers of the Gospel, Carey is appointed Professor of Sanskrit, Bengali and Marathi – a position he will hold for 30 years.

A "corresponding committee", which Carey and his missionary colleagues form at the suggestion of the General Committee, provides a channel which enables Bible Society in London to assist in the publication of translations which are already proceeding in Hindustani, Persian, Marathi and Oriya, to which Sanskrit, Bengali, Telugu, Kanarese and Gujarati are added. Other languages follow within a few years. The General Committee places £1,000 (worth over £35,000 today) at the disposal of the translators, a grant which they repeat and add to in succeeding years. This paves the way for Auxiliary Bible Societies in Calcutta, Bombay, Colombo and Batavia.

Carey completes a translation of the whole Bible in Bengali (1809) and is also responsible for translating the Scriptures in whole or in part into 24 other languages and dialects. He publishes grammars and dictionaries in Sanskrit, Marathi, Punjabi and Telugu. Not content with this, he and Joshua Marshman edit and publish three volumes of the Hindu epic poem *Ramayana*. Carey comes to be called the "father of Bengali" prose.

WILBERFORCE, CAREY AND THE END OF SUTTEE

Carey's agitation is largely responsible for the abolition in 1829 of the Hindu rite of suttee, the ancient custom that has meant the death of every widow at the time of her husband's funeral. He saw his first suttee in 1799, watching in horror as a widow climbed on to a pyre of her own accord and was then held down by bamboos. Everyone around screamed to drown out the woman's cries.

In 1813 William Wilberforce reads to the House of Commons Joshua Marshman's horrifying account of a suttee ritual. Carey, Marshman and Ward have collected evidence of 300 suttees which have taken place in six months within 30 miles of Calcutta. Thanks to their detailed reports, Wilberforce and the evangelical lobby win the Commons debate and from 1813 Christian mission work in British India (which the East India Company has forbidden) is legalised. The concession causes hostility in the press and in Parliament. The Anglican columnist Sydney Smith attacks what he calls the "consecrated cobblers" in the *Edinburgh Review*, a reference to Carey's humble background, asking what Britain is doing, allowing "uneducated enthusiasts" to jeopardise Anglo-Indian trade.

Even as Smith writes, in India Carey, now a college professor, and his colleagues are translating the New Testament into twelve Indian languages with the enthusiastic support of the Society. By 1817 the General Committee sends over £33,000 to the "corresponding committee" in Calcutta, while grants to Madras, Bombay, Ceylon, Java and Malacca bring the total to £46,000 (£1,610,000 at today's values).

Carey has extraordinarily wide interests. He edits and publishes two works of the horticulturist William Roxburgh and helps to distribute prose texts for use in schools. In 1820 he helps to form the Agricultural Society of India.

In August 2003 the General Secretary of the Bangladesh Bible Society, James Halder, told me that Bible work in Bangladesh has a rich heritage which dates back to the work of William Carey. The Bangla Bible translation was his first Bible translation project. "To accomplish this task, he developed a very deep knowledge of the Bangla language. He not only spoke the language fluently but composed Bangla literature and songs, and taught at the University as well. His great scholarship and missionary drive resulted in his remarkable achievement: a Bangla grammar, the first Bangla dictionary, the invention of the Bangla printing press, and a superb Bangla Bible translation that is still in use over two centuries later. As the result of this legacy, Dr Carey is often referred to as the 'father of the modern missionary movement'. We Christians in this country are proud of these beginnings and their impact on the history of evangelism in the rest of Asia."

In her *The Book and its Story* (1854) Ellen Ranyard claimed that "the British and Foreign Bible Society has afforded assistance to Dr Carey and his associates, and to the various Bible Societies of India, to the amount of more than two hundred thousand pounds!" This is an extraordinary figure which I have not been able to check — if it is accurate the amount in today's values is £10,600,000! This is despite disagreements over how to translate the word for "baptise", which Carey, being a good Baptist, wants to translate as "immerse".

Two or three days before he died in Serampore, aged 73, in 1834, Carey was carried downstairs in a state of extreme exhaustion. He had worked in India for 40 years. The revised sheets of the last language into which he had translated the Scriptures lay upon the table. His work was done.

BEGINNINGS IN CHINA

South coast of China, 1807

Enter Robert Morrison

The 29-year-old son of a Scottish minister in Newcastle, Robert Morrison arrives on the south coast of China in 1807, the only Protestant missionary in an Empire of more than 300 million people. The leaders of the London Missionary Society are well aware, when they send Morrison to Macao, that the most urgent need is for a Chinese translation of the New Testament which will incorporate some of the old Mandarin translations which have been made by the Jesuits. In 1582 the Jesuit Matthew Ricci reached China and began a mission whose success was due to his skill in mathematics and astronomy and his knowledge of, and respect for, Chinese culture. Ricci and a colleague undertook a staggering journey on foot from the south of the country to Beijing which took them 17 years. After presenting two clocks to the Emperor, Ricci was allowed to stay in the capital as a clock maintainer and map maker. But after Ricci's death in 1610, the Jesuits lost their influence in China.

Two hundred years later, Morrison is a rather introverted man. On arrival in the Portuguese territory of Macao, he is stripped and interviewed and then refused permission to land. But Morrison has a letter of introduction to the small Anglo-American merchant community in Canton (Guangzhou) and manages to pass himself off as a clerk.

"You are lucky to have got this far," the merchants tell him. "You should give up any hope of making contact with the

Cantonese. The Government has forbidden any Chinese subject to teach Chinese to a European on pain of death."

However, the head of the American "factory" in Canton offers Morrison a small room in which to live. There he can pass as an American – they are less resented than the British – and attempt to learn the language. So Morrison lives in a tiny room, eagerly reading whatever Chinese literature he can lay his hands on. He grows his nails in the local style, lets his hair grow into a pigtail (as Hudson Taylor will do later) and wears Chinese clothes and shoes. He prays constantly. After he has attained a degree of fluency, he ventures out and tries to persuade the Chinese to speak to him, paying three street children to have tea in his room.

Morrison's incredible perseverance wins him the grudging respect of the European traders, and in 1809 the East India Company in Macao hires him as a Chinese translator. The post gives him a salary and the opportunity to study the language openly since the company is allowed to have translators. Then he marries the daughter of an English merchant. For the next four years Morrison continues to learn Cantonese and Mandarin – painstakingly compiling his own grammar and dictionary.

In 1812, on learning of this project, Bible Society votes £500 (£14,700 today) in support of Morrison's venture and makes further grants to a total of £3,000 (over £100,000 today) for the completion of the work. In 1814 Morrison publishes a Chinese grammar and a translation of the New Testament, based partly on an old Jesuit version. In 1818 he will finish a translation of the Old Testament, and in 1818 establish the Anglo-Chinese College in Malacca. His Chinese dictionary will appear in 1821 and remain a standard work for a long time. He follows this in 1823 by publication of the whole Chinese Bible in 21 volumes. He also translates the Book of Common Prayer and a large number of hymns and tracts. There were giants in those days.

Act 9

Good news for the Treasurer

William Wilberforce reckoned that the upper limit of the Society's income would be £10,000 a year. How wrong he was! One of the reasons for his mistake was that he failed to foresee the rise and phenomenal success of Bible Society Auxiliaries (not until the 1970s was the name changed to "Action Groups"). In essence, Bibles and New Testaments came to be supplied by the Society to Auxiliaries at fixed prices. The Auxiliaries sold Scriptures in their own areas and, after meeting local expenses of administration, sent the profit they made, together with any contributions they had collected, to the London Committee.

The General Committee of Bible Society encourages Christians in other parts of the country to follow the example of the two Associations in London (July 1805) and Birmingham (April 1806). On 28 March 1809 the first regular Auxiliary Bible Society is formed in Reading, with Nottingham following two days later. The constitution of the Reading Auxiliary stated that "this society adopt as far as possible the rules and regulations of the parent Society". Sadly, at the time of writing, there is no Action Group in Reading.

In Nottingham they lay it down that "one half of the amount of the funds of the society shall be subscribed to the British and Foreign Bible Society, and the remainder appropriated to the discharge of the expenses of the society, and to purchase Bibles and Testaments of the British and Foreign Bible Society to be distributed for the benefit of this town and neighbourhood".

Provisions on very similar lines form the basis of all the Auxiliaries which now begin to spring up in rapid succession until, in 1814, Richard Phillips, a member of the General Committee, and C S Dudley, a former member of the Committee and a future agent of the Society, introduce uniform guidelines for the establishment of Auxiliaries which last until they are slightly revised in 1852.

The birth of the Auxiliaries is hugely significant for the future success of Bible Society. They first appear in the annual accounts for the financial year 1809–10 as raising £5,945 (not far short of £200,000 today) out of a total income of £14,284 (£468,000). Already, income from the Auxiliaries exceeds in this financial year that from any other single listed source.

Five years later, the situation is even more dramatic with income from Auxiliaries (in 1814–15) bringing in a remarkable £61,848 (the equivalent to over £2 million today), dwarfing income from annual subscriptions, collections, donations and legacies.

With the formation of the Herefordshire Auxiliary in August 1814, every county in England has allied itself with Bible Society and the future looks bright. It isn't just the huge rise in income generated by the Auxiliaries that is important. They cooperate with the parent Society in the home distribution of Bibles to an extent that could never be achieved in any other way. They know just what the needs are in their areas.

In 1811 Richard Phillips investigates the system used by the Auxiliaries for distributing Bibles and decides that they have no proper way of stimulating the "humbler classes" to help themselves and to cooperate according to their means in promoting the general objects of Bible Society. The Auxiliaries also haven't yet settled on a principle which will come to be seen as important in the Bible Society story – that it is usually better to sell Bibles, even at low prices, than to give them away (though there will always be exceptions to this norm).

Richard Phillips decides that they should think of the poor not simply as likely recipients of Bibles but that it is possible to interest them in the Bible Society cause itself. And so Phillips draws up rules for Auxiliaries and Associations: his rules say that members should subscribe not less than a penny weekly and that neighbourhoods should be divided into districts. A sub-committee should be appointed to each district to drum up subscriptions. The sub-committee should enquire into the needs of each district and supply them with Bibles and Testaments at cost price, reduced prices or free, according to circumstances. Any residue from the funds should be sent to the Auxiliary or Branch in aid of the parent Society. The General Committee accepts Phillips's recommendations.

LADIES' ASSOCIATIONS

The first Ladies' Bible Society directly connected with BFBS is formed in Westminster in August 1811 and leads, in the following year, to the formation of the Westminster Auxiliary. Another Ladies' Auxiliary is formed in Guildford in July, and one in Godalming in April 1814. C S Dudley draws up a code of rules and by-laws which becomes the model of all future Ladies' Associations.

When, in May 1817, the Ladies' Liverpool Branch of Bible Society is founded with the Countess of Derby as patron, over 600 women busy themselves in the systematic investigation and supply of nearly 350 districts. In less than three months they chalk up over 7,000 subscribers, issue over 1,300 Bibles and Testaments and raise nearly £1,000. After a year they have drummed up over 10,000 subscribers and collect over £2,500 of which over £500 is sent to the parent Society for its general fund. More Ladies' Branches are quickly formed in other parts of the country.

Oxford, 25 June 1813

A speaker at the meeting to launch the Oxford Auxiliary has a sense of history.

"It was in this city," he says, "that the morning star of the Reformation, the immortal Wycliffe, first rose upon the world, and opened the treasures of the New Testament. It was in Oxford that three of our venerable reformers laid down their lives in support of the principle of our church – and I will add, in support of the principles of the British and Foreign Bible Society. It was in Oxford that one of those reformers, the venerable Latimer, uttered the memorable address to his fellow-martyr, 'Be of good comfort, Master Ridley, and play the man. We shall this day light such a candle, by God's grace, in England, as I trust shall never be put out.'"

Act 10

New societies for the continent of Europe

Bible Society work in Europe grows in a similar way to that in Britain, with multiplication of small independent local organisations which are generally known on the continent not as Auxiliaries but actually as Bible Societies. Only a few of these have maintained uninterrupted independence. Others have experienced regional groupings and modifications to take their place among the national Bible Societies which now exist in the countries of western and northern Europe.

As early as 10 May 1804, Ascension Day, the first Auxiliary on the continent, the German Bible Society, is founded at Nuremberg. The London Committee places 1,000 copies of the German New Testament at the disposal of the Catholic priest who has written to it, for distribution by sale or gift among Roman Catholics in Swabia and Bavaria. They make another grant of £200 to the Nuremberg Society towards distribution of the Lutheran Bible.

BASEL BIBLE SOCIETY

On 31 October 1804 Johann Rudolf Huber, pastor of the Reformed Church in Basel, and two friends of Karl Steinkopf, join with others to establish the Basel Bible Society.

Basel has been famous for its printing since the late 15th and early 16th century. It is also the centre of the German Religious Society which is influential in Germany and Switzerland and promises actively to assist Bible Society. Even before the foundation of the Basel Society, the London Committee has sent sums of £50 to the Secretary of the Religious Society so that he can distribute Bibles among the poor of Lausanne, Besançon, Montmirail and Strasburg and investigate supplying the valleys of the Cevennes as well as Nîmes, Bordeaux and even Paris. With the founding of the Basel Society, the London Committee votes a further grant of £300.

Napoleon has imposed an embargo on everything related to England and during 1807 only one letter reaches the London Committee from Basel. The letter says that a large edition of the New Testament is being printed in April and that the Old Testament is about to be sent to press.

In October 1808 the Committee receives a second letter from Basel, this time from Dr Hertzog, the 80-year-old Professor of Divinity in the University of Basel. He tells the Committee that the New Testament has been in circulation for some months and has met with unqualified approval. The Old Testament will be ready at the end of the year. They have received so many orders that the first edition will be practically sold out on publication – but they hope to proceed with a second and third edition. Dr Hertzog also has good news about distribution of a new edition of the New Testament in France.

On hearing this, the London Committee orders that a set of plates of the French Bible be despatched to Basel. After receiving further letters, the Committee sends another £600 to Basel for the purchase of Bibles and Testaments so that the large congregations in the traditionally Protestant area of Languedoc in south-west France can be provided with Bibles either by sale or free of charge as appropriate.

THE FIRST ROYAL DONATION

In Berlin, encouraged by the success of the Auxiliary which has begun in Nuremberg, a minister of the Bohemian Church secures the cooperation of several noblemen and forms a Society in 1805. The new Society sends a stirring address to Christians in the Prussian States. When King Frederick William of Prussia reads this he replies: "It is with real satisfaction that I discover from your letter of 7 February and the enclosed address the laudable endeavours of the Prussian Bible Society for the gratuitous and cheap distribution of the Bible to the poor of my dominions; and whilst I render justice to your particular merit in promoting such a useful institution, I transmit to you at the same time twenty Fredericks d'or as an addition to its funds." The London Committee sends an initial grant of £250 to Berlin plus further grants in later years to help in the publication of Polish and Bohemian Bibles.

Abergynolwyn village, Wales, 1806

Enter Mary Jones and her mother

Mary and her mother have enjoyed the (Methodist) Society meetings in William Hugh's home. They are pleased when in 1806 the Methodists build a chapel at Cwrt – the northern part of Abergynolwyn village. Gradually, all the meetings are held there; during the period Mary attends it, the chapel is very plain with an earth floor and no pews.

"If the members of the little church were poor of this world," a contemporary tells us, "they were rich in faith. There were, at Cwrt, a lot of extremely good old people who excelled in religious zeal, in faithfulness in attending the means of grace and in earnestness of prayer. The old women were not only more numerous, they were also more patriarchal in their way than the old men who were there. The women would be to the fore with the singing, and Mari Siôn would lead the singing. They would sing a verse over and over again, moving like a forest blown by the wind, going backwards and forwards, all together, completely regular in their movements, but with individuals shouting and ejaculating as they sang." The Mari Siôn referred to is Mary Jones's mother. In 1877 the chapel will be closed and converted into three houses – now holiday homes.

Mary, who is now 22, seems frequently to attend preaching meetings beyond Cwrt and quarterly Methodist Association meetings. She goes a number of times all the way to Associations meetings at Llangeitho (where Thomas Charles was converted) and sees and experiences "great and mighty things" there. On such occasions she often sees Thomas Charles and, as far as we can tell, both make a point of meeting and talking to one another.

Act 11

Scotsmen to Scandinavia

Edinburgh, 1804

Born into a poor home in Old Kilpatrick, near Glasgow, John Paterson begins in 1800 to study in Dundee as a candidate for the ministry. In 1804 two Congregational churches in Edinburgh invite him to go to India as their missionary agent. He chooses Ebenezer Henderson from Dunfermline as his colleague.

Henderson has worked as a boot maker and watch smith and has attended the same college as Paterson. In August 1805 the two men sail from Leith Docks, Edinburgh, aboard the *Fame* to Elsinore in Denmark, on their way to Serampore in north-east India. At this time, the East India Company is still hostile to missionaries, fearing that if they try to convert Indians to Christ Britain may lose its Indian Empire. It isn't until 1813, following persistent efforts by Wilberforce, Charles Grant and Josiah Pratt of CMS, that provisions to establish a church in India and the removal of obstacles to evangelisation are included in the renewal of the Company's charter.

Enter Paterson and Henderson

The two men begin their journey east aboard a Danish ship. When they arrive at Copenhagen, they find they cannot continue their journey until the following spring. Autumn and winter lie ahead of them. On their first Sunday in the Danish capital they form an impression of almost empty churches and listless congregations drowsing through lifeless sermons.

"There is as much need for a missionary here as in India," says Paterson.

On their second Sunday in Copenhagen, they preach in the home of an English captain. Their congregation grows rapidly and within months Henderson is also preaching in Elsinore. Over the winter, Henderson and Paterson decide not to travel on to Serampore but to do what they can to make the Bible available in Denmark. At London's request, the two men begin to supply information about the state of religion in areas which now comprise Denmark, Norway, Sweden, Finland, Lapland and Poland. They support themselves by giving English lessons to Danish families.

The Swedish Bishop, Edvard Rohde, says of Paterson: "No particular refinement or elegance could be traced in his nature. He was a taciturn character, and not a very good speaker either. His native Scottish acuity [sharpness], not to say shrewdness, made it possible for him to thoroughly understand and adapt to new conditions, and to shape them according to his will."

Iceland, 1807–1808

Justiciary Thorlekin, an Icelander, gives Paterson and Henderson detailed information about the condition of his country where, among a population of 47,000 with 300 parish churches, there are no more than 40 or 50 Bibles. An old printing press no longer works. And yet no people anywhere are fonder of reading: only one Icelandic child in 100 cannot read or write.

After an exchange of correspondence with the Bishop of Iceland, the London Committee votes a grant of £250 so that the Danish Evangelical Society can extend the printing run of an edition of the New Testament. Two thousand copies will be sent at the Society's expense to contacts in Iceland who can help in their distribution. The Committee promises a further grant to help in the production of an entire Icelandic Bible. Paterson sees the work through the press, the books are printed in Copenhagen and 1,500 are sent to Iceland in the spring of 1807.

In 1808 Paterson and Henderson travel over 2,000 miles through Norway, Lapland and Finland and, after exchanging letters with the London Committee, gain the Society's support for the publication of editions of the New Testament in Finnish and Lapp.

Finland, 1811

On 26 August Paterson sails out of Stockholm harbour in a small ship and arrives three days later at Turku, Finland's oldest city at the mouth of the Aura river and at this time the capital. Just two years earlier, Finland passed from Swedish to Russian control. Eventually, Paterson meets Bishop Jacob Tengström. The Scotsman describes to the Finn the religious revivals in England and Wales which have produced the British and Foreign Bible Society, and explains what the Society is trying to do.

Tengström and the newly appointed Governor General, Fabian Steinheil, are impressed.

"It is clearly essential that a Bible Society should be founded in Finland," they tell Paterson. "But first we must seek the permission of the Emperor."

Paterson is disappointed. Surely there is no chance that the Russian Tsar will approve! But his fears are misplaced. Tsar Alexander not only gives his permission but is also willing to become patron of a Bible Society in Finland. Moreover, he donates 5,000 gold roubles from his personal funds to be used to distribute the Bible among his new Finnish subjects.

The Finnish Bible Society is founded as one of the earliest independent national Bible Societies on 24 March 1812. By 1814 it has almost 1,000 donors, both men and women. It is today the oldest church-related association in Finland and the oldest publishing house to have continuously operated in the country.

The Finnish Bible Society faces an enormous challenge. Although the first Finnish New Testament was published in 1548, and the first full Bible in 1642, only 25,000 Bibles have been circulated since that time. The price of a Bible in 18th century Finland is the same as that of a horse. And yet there is a real hunger for God's Word. During its first 100 years, the Finnish Bible Society, with substantial support from the Society in London, distributes 1.8 million Bibles and New Testaments through a network of Auxiliaries.

Sweden, 1815

After Paterson leaves Sweden for Russia, the Swedish minister in London, Gustav Brunnmark, becomes the BFBS contact. He travels to Sweden and persuades the Minister of Justice, Mathias Rosenblad, to become Chairman of the Evangelical Society which has been established in Stockholm, on Paterson's initiative, to distribute tracts. Later, Brunnmark persuades the Swedes to form a Bible Society (1815) on the same lines as BFBS, with Rosenblad as its Chairman until 1847.

Bible Society charges Paterson with the responsibility in 1812 of visiting St Petersburg to see what can be done to develop its work in Russia. In July 1812 Paterson, Henderson and Steinkopf meet in Helsingborg, Sweden, and share experiences and plans.

Act 12

Royal patronage in Russia and Europe

Russia, 1812

John Paterson reaches St Petersburg in July 1812. As early as 1806 the President of the Society, Lord Teignmouth, and the Russian Patriarchate have exchanged letters about the Society's aims.

Enter Robert Pinkerton

Dr Robert Pinkerton, who will later succeed Steinkopf as the Society Secretary, is in Moscow to greet Paterson on his arrival from St Petersburg late in the evening of 2 September. Paterson and Pinkerton are two of the last Britons to see Moscow's old Tatar wall and high brick towers, the sacred red gates of the Kremlin, the green spires of the churches, and the cross and crescent glittering over the domes and cupolas of silver and gold.

It isn't a promising moment, since Napoleon's armies, which in the previous three months have driven across central and eastern Europe, have set fire to Smolensk's massive walls and towers and then abandoned the town. The armies are approaching the capital itself. Moscow is half deserted. It is dangerous to walk the streets. Princess Galitzin and her sister, Princess Metschersky, give the two men tea, but see no hope of forming Auxiliaries at this time. Paterson cannot succeed in getting any other royal or Government officials to listen seriously to him.

After three days in Moscow, Paterson and Pinkerton are forced to leave. At the point where the Smolensk road crosses the road to St Petersburg, 50 miles west of Moscow, the two men find the highway packed with wagons, carts, crowds of walkers, sheep and cattle, all fleeing from the French army. Amid them all, they see the Bishop of Smolensk in his coach, taking precious icons of the Virgin Mary to a place of safety. They arrive back at St Petersburg on 13 September. Next day, a huge fire breaks out in Moscow which destroys much of the town.

Enter Prince Galitzin

On 6 December 1812, the day when the great frost which will devastate Napoleon's army sets in, Paterson puts to Prince Galitzin, Minister of Public Worship, the plan he has drawn up for a Bible Society in St Petersburg. Someone describes Galitzin as a handsome little man with large penetrating eyes.

"Your proposal will be presented to the Tsar at the earliest opportunity," Galitzin tells Paterson.

Enter Tsar Alexander I

The Tsar is on the point of joining the army but postpones his departure in order to examine the scheme he is asked to approve. He has already generously supported the setting up of the Finnish Bible Society. In his early life he was cool towards Christianity, but Alexander has since been through some profound religious experiences and has become a regular Bible reader. The devastation of Moscow has deepened his sense of yearning for God. He has learned to pray.

"Never, even in my darkest moments," the Tsar tells Archbishop Tengström, "do I rise from my knees without the assurance that the Lord will bring about the deliverance of this nation."

His Majesty examines the proposal on 18 December and writes on the document, "So be it. Alexander."

As he writes, the last feeble remnants of the Grand Army struggle across the ice of the Niemen river. 125,000 Frenchmen have fallen in battle. 132,000 have died of exhaustion, hunger and cold in temperatures 30 degrees below zero. 193,000 are taken prisoner. Napoleon no longer constitutes a threat to the Russian Empire.

On 14 January 1813 the imperial edict authorising the

establishment of the St Petersburg Bible Society is made public. Jews as well as Christians, Russians and Armenians, Protestants, Catholics and Orthodox all welcome the news. On 23 January the Society is inaugurated in the palace of Prince Galitzin. Archbishop Ambrose, Metropolitan of Novgrod and St Petersburg, Seraphim, Archbishop of Minsk, the Metropolitan of the Roman Catholic Church, the confessor to the Tsar, several Ministers of State, nobles, clergy of different communions and a galaxy of VIPs turn up for the occasion.

As soon as the London Committee hears the good news about the forming of the Society, they send a donation of £500 (£14,500 at today's values). By the end of March, contributions received at St Petersburg come to 60,000 roubles, including a gift of 25,000 from the Tsar who asks to be considered a member with an annual subscription of 10,000 roubles.

Meanwhile, Pinkerton works hard to establish an Auxiliary in Moscow. London approves his plan and on 16 July 1813 the Moscow Bible Society is instituted in the presence of the Archbishop and hierarchy from church and state, as well as aristocracy and gentry. Paterson leaves St Petersburg for a tour of the eastern provinces of Russia where he finds Bibles are even scarcer than he has expected.

Meanwhile in Wales...

Tal-y-llyn, Wales, February 1813

Enter Mary Jones and Thomas Lewis

At the foot of Cadair Idris, the sound of bells echoes across the water at the south-west corner of Tal-y-llyn lake as Mary, now 28, marries Thomas Jones. Everyone calls the bridegroom Thomas Lewis, since Lewis is his father's name. He is a linsey and flannel weaver; throughout their married lives both Thomas and Mary work as weavers. For the first seven years of their married life, the couple live at Cwrt a few steps away from the chapel they both attend.

Before the year ends, Mary gives birth to the first of their six children. Only one of her children will survive her. They give the first baby his father's family name of Lewis; he will live until he is 18. Mary's second child, Mary, is born two years later and dies when she is two. Her third child, Jacob, is born in 1818 and will live until he is fifteen.

And in Paris…

Napoleon's broken armies have been decisively beaten at Leipzig and on 30 March 1814 Paris surrenders. Twelve days later, Napoleon signs an unconditional abdication. That night, he attempts to commit suicide but the prussic acid he always carries with him has lost its strength.

"God did not will it," he says, when he recovers.

St Petersburg, 20 January 1814

In his palace study, Prince Alexander Galitzin dictates a letter.

"Address it to Lord Teignmouth in London," he says to his Secretary. "Write this: My Lord, the Committee of the St Petersburg Bible Society has charged me, on the occasion of the departure of the Rev. John Paterson for England, to write to your Lordship, to express their most unfeigned gratitude to the British and Foreign Bible Society for having sent hither this worthy Member, whose attention and cares have been so hearty and so successful for the benefit of the Bible Society in Russia.

"The first year of the existence of this our Society has been already signalised by very numerous and considerable enterprises and actions. Besides the distribution of the Holy Scriptures in different languages throughout several countries of this extensive empire, the Committee have partly begun, and partly undertaken, to print them in the Slavonic, the German, Finnish, French, Polish, Armenian, and Kalmuck, or Mongol dialects. The number of Members and Benefactors in this salutary work increases daily. The most distant provinces of Russia are emulating the nearest in the active contribution to the success of it. The light of the Word of God begins to illuminate the cottages of the poor, the asylums of the helpless, the hospitals, and the prisons. The prisoners of war partake of it. Even the Heathens and Mahomedans begin to receive and feel it. In the meantime, the happy effect of the establishment of the St Petersburg Society and its Committee was the production of similar Committees, or rather parts of our General Committee. In several cities of Russia, such as Moscow, Riga, Yaroslaw, Dorpat, Revel, and Mittau, we entertain the most sanguine hopes, from the co-operation of these partial Committees in our general undertakings.

"The Committee, while they prostrate themselves before the Almighty Giver of all good, who with one hand hath delivered Russia from her outward enemies, and with the other planted in her bosom an institution for disseminating more effectually his word, acknowledge, with heartfelt satisfaction, the instruments of His holy decrees. The British and Foreign Bible Society have acquired a sacred right to the everlasting gratitude of the Society at St Petersburg; which cannot, at the same time, but give solemn testimony to the indefatigable co-operation of their member, the Rev. John Paterson, in their splendid successes.

"Accept, my Lord, the assurances of my esteem and most unfeigned respect for your person.

I have the honour to be
     Your Lordship's most humble
     And obedient Servant,
     PRINCE ALEXANDER GALITZIN"

On 28 September the St Petersburg Bible Society holds its first annual meeting. The chief dignitaries of the Greek, Catholic, Armenian and Georgian Churches attend plus "ladies and nobles of the first rank in the Empire". Five Archbishops and three Metropolitans from the Roman Catholic and Orthodox Churches become Vice-Presidents. The Society is given the title Russian Bible Society.

London, June 1814

After the Treaty of Paris brings peace in Europe, Tsar Alexander and the King of Prussia visit London and receive delegations from Bible Society. The meeting with the Tsar, on Sunday evening 19 June, is attended by Lord Teignmouth, the Bishops of Salisbury, Norwich, Cloyne, Admiral Lord Gambier, Nicholas Vansittart, Chancellor of the Exchequer, William Wilberforce, Vice-Presidents and the three Secretaries.

Enter the Tsar of Russia

Alexander I is strikingly handsome, tall, and carries himself well. His manner is charming.

The representatives of Bible Society thank him for his patronage of the Bible cause in Russia. The Tsar talks to them at length about the work of the Societies in Britain and in Russia.

"I believe the Bible will prove a blessing to our Empire," Alexander says.

He shakes hands with each representative of the Society. Karl Steinkopf seems carried away by his emotions.

"May the most high God bless your Imperial Majesty," he says as the Tsar shakes his hand, "for what you have done for my native land, and may your name go down to posterity as the father of your country and the benefactor of mankind!"

The Tsar beams. Of all countries at this time, Russia gives to the Society the most generous facilities and the warmest welcome. Not long after the meeting with the Tsar, free travel permits are granted to the Society's representatives; one colporteur travels 3,940 miles at a cost of less than £7. By the end of the 19th century, Russia will become the most important of the Society's foreign Agencies, and for over 70 years an average of one volume in every twelve the Society circulates is sent to some part of Russia.

Enter King Frederick William III of Prussia

The King of Prussia, now 44, is reinvigorated after his army's decisive victory against the exhausted French at Leipzig but unaware that Napoleon is not quite beaten yet. He receives the same Society representatives on 21 June.

"Your Majesty was the first monarch to patronise the object of the Society," the deputation tells him.

"We will do the utmost in our power to protect and favour the cause," he replies.

Re-enter Napoleon

Next year, the French recall Napoleon for 100 days. On 18 June 1815 the combined forces of the Duke of Wellington's Allied army of 68,000 (with British, Dutch, Belgian, and German units) and about 45,000 Prussians finally defeat Napoleon's 72,000 troops outside Waterloo village, south of Brussels.

"It was a damned near-run thing," observes the Duke with commendable honesty.

A small detachment of Cossacks escorts the Emperor to Fréjus in south-eastern France and an English frigate takes him to Elba. Thus ends a 23-year period of recurrent warfare between France and the other powers of Europe.

In 1813 a Bible Society Auxiliary was established on the island of St Helena. During his exile on the island, Napoleon will read and annotate a copy of the French New Testament which the London Missionary Society published in 1802. The preface was written by a Society supporter and friend of Thomas Charles, Dr David Bogue of Gosport.

Through these years, the dominant British feeling has been a mixture of fear, fascination and hatred of Napoleon – but not hatred of the French people. And in the 19 years that follow the Battle of Waterloo, the British people contribute £76,000 (over £4 million at today's values) to be spent by Bible Society in spreading the Scriptures among the French. Twenty years later, the armies of England and France will fight side by side in the Crimea.

THE NETHERLANDS BIBLE SOCIETY

After returning to England for a few months, John Paterson and Robert Pinkerton leave for Russia again in the summer of 1814. Pinkerton's journey takes him through Holland where already the minister of the English Reformed Church in Amsterdam has founded an English Bible Society. Its aim is to spread the Bible among needy members of the English Church and to establish a Dutch Bible Society. This is successful.

On 29 June 1814 Robert Pinkerton represents the London Society at a meeting in the English Reformed Church in Amsterdam at which the Netherlands Bible Society is founded. The Dutch Minister of Interior is President and the Governor General of Holland is one of the Vice-Presidents. It is reported that at least half the population of Holland are in need of a Bible. Most members of the Reformed Church possess one, not so many Lutherans and very few Roman Catholics.

Soon many places in the Netherlands establish their own Bible Societies. At first they give the Bibles away but later decide that people should pay as much as they can afford. Relations between the new Society and BFBS will not always be a story of sweetness and light. The present General Director of the Netherlands Bible Society (NBS), Haaije Feenstra, tells me, "In 1843 NBS had to compete with BFBS, which started spreading their own printed Dutch Bibles. This made NBS decide to publish its own Bibles. Cheap editions of the Bible appeared, as well as editions in which the language was adapted. By the way, these latter editions were not always approved of: deviations from the text raised distrust and suspicion of Bible forgery."

Turku, Finland, 1815

Enter Paterson and Henderson

Tsar Alexander is so delighted with the early success of the Finnish Bible Society that he nominates John Paterson for an honorary Doctorate of Theology at the University of Turku on the occasion of the 300th anniversary of the Reformation in 1815. Paterson is reluctant to receive the honour – perhaps due to Christian humility and uncertainty about the implications of accepting an award like this from the Russian Emperor. Jacob Tengström, promoted to Archbishop since the foundation of the Finnish Society, persuades Paterson to accept the nomination although he is not able to be present in Turku for the academic ceremony.

Four years later, Paterson and Henderson visit Turku and call to see Archbishop Tengström. Men awarded Doctorates from the University of Turku are entitled – and normally are proud – to wear the Turku doctoral cap with its stiff brim and soft velvet top with coloured cord and tassels.

Enter Archbishop Tengström

"Why are you not wearing your doctoral cap?" Tengström asks Paterson with a twinkle in his eye. "Do you want to give the impression that you do not value the honour conferred on you?"

"Well, I paid the fee for the cap more than a year ago," Paterson replies, "but I haven't yet received it."

"In that case," says Tengström, "I will give you one of mine which you can wear during your stay in Turku!"

Europe, 1812

Enter Karl Steinkopf

During its earliest years, Karl Steinkopf, the Society's Foreign Secretary, can only spread the news of its foundation and plans when his letters succeed in evading Napoleon's blockade of Britain. In June 1812, however, it becomes possible for him to sail for Gothenburg in Sweden and from there to travel via Copenhagen through Germany and Switzerland for a six-month tour. He extends the work, as is being done in Britain, by the formation of small, independent local organisations which are generally known on the continent not as Auxiliaries but as Bible Societies.

While not quite equalling the vividness of George Borrow's writing 25 years later, Steinkopf sends back to London some good accounts of his travels and achievements. On his journey from Zurich to Basel he follows the romantic bank of the river Limmat "whose pure streams had mingled with the blood of so many brave soldiers, who fell in the famous battle fought between the combined Austrian and Russian armies, and the French troops under Massena". He thanks God that the war is over in that part of Europe and that peace and plenty have returned, the shouts of the reapers are heard again, farmers are carrying home their corn, cattle are grazing in the meadows, marks of prosperity are reappearing. "My soul was joyful in the God of my salvation," he says.

He admires a chain of glaciers and then, after taking the road which has been cut through the Hauenstein mountain, he goes on foot, better to enjoy the view. Arriving in a valley he goes to the house of "an excellent clergyman, a man of genius, and a friend to religion and humanity". Here a number of former friends from his days as Secretary to the Christian Society in Basel have travelled distances of up to 20 miles to meet him. "I found not only the same faces, but also the same hearts, the same affection and confidence."

Steinkopf attends the committee of the German Bible Society. In the absence of Professor Hertzog, now 86, Emmanuel Merian, a mere 82, takes the chair.

"Please be kind enough to give the committee an account of the operation of the British and Foreign Bible Society," says Merian.

Steinkopf does this as concisely as he can and records that "they listened to my relation with the utmost attention; and at the close loudly praised God for all that he had done on behalf of his people, particularly through the instrumentality of England". For their part the Basel-based committee present Steinkopf with a written statement of the proceedings of their Society. Steinkopf tells the committee that London has decided to double its grant of £500 towards their work. In addition, Steinkopf gives instructions for specified numbers of Bibles to be sent to various parts of Europe.

Steinkopf makes five European tours between 1812 and 1823. These are pioneer days and his successors at times envy the freedom of action he enjoys. The London Committee has given him powers to take in its name those measures which he thinks will achieve the Society's objectives. He spends over £2,700 in encouraging the formation of Bible Societies, making grants in aid and in supplying Scriptures where they are most needed. He collects on the ground from the best-informed people the information which will guide the future operations of the Society.

Vienna, 12 August 1816

Robert Pinkerton reaches Vienna and four days later explains the objects and methods of Bible Society to Prince Metternich, Foreign Minister (soon to be Chancellor) of the still huge Austrian Empire. Metternich invites Pinkerton to dinner.

"I will put your proposals for a Bible Society to the Emperor," he says. "In a Roman Catholic country a measure of this kind has many difficulties to encounter which it would not meet with in a Protestant country. But I will do everything in my power to bring the matter to the desired conclusion."

On 23 December Pinkerton's proposal to Metternich for a Bible Society in Vienna is rejected. An edict is issued prohibiting throughout the Austrian dominions both the establishment of Bible Societies and the circulation of the Bible, either free or otherwise, by foreign Bible Societies. Consignments of Scriptures are seized and the Hungarian Auxiliary at Pressburg is abolished. The Nuremberg Branch is suppressed. Seven years later the edict is withdrawn.

Mixed news for the
Turkish Bible

During the course of his tour of the continent of Europe in 1814, Robert Pinkerton visits Leiden in the western Netherlands and examines the manuscript of a Turkish version of the whole Bible. Among other oriental treasures, this has been gathering dust in the archives of the university for 150 years.

Ali Bey

The translator of this Bible was the remarkable Albertus Bobowsy – better known as Ali Bey – who had been born in Poland early in the 17th century. Kidnapped in childhood by the Tartars (inhabitants of Tartary in Asia, members of any one of numerous tribes, chiefly Muslim, living in Russian Europe), he was sold to the Turks at Istanbul, where, after 20 years' training, he adopted the Islamic religion and was appointed an interpreter to Muhammed IV. An educated man, he could speak 17 languages – including English, German and French fluently.

Ali Bey's most important achievement was to translate the Bible on the instruction of Levin Warner, Dutch Ambassador at the court of the Grand Sultan. When Ali Bey finished his translation sometime around 1666, Levin Warner sent it to Leiden to be corrected and prepared for printing. But it was never printed – the manuscript was put into the university library and forgotten. As for Ali Bey, his work apparently led him to believe in the truth of Christianity but it seems likely that he died before being baptised.

When he had satisfied himself that the version would be useful to Bible Society, Pinkerton managed to borrow the manuscript and make arrangements for it to be copied and revised in Berlin. He gave this task to Baron Von Diez who had at one time been Russian Ambassador in Istanbul. Von Diez, an expert in the

Turkish language, was now elderly and ill health prevented him from making rapid progress with the task.

Berlin, April 1817

The Secretary of the Prussian Bible Society finds Von Diez weak and suffering badly. He is resting his head on his writing desk and only able to say a few words.

"I still indulge a hope that God will restore me that I may finish the Turkish Bible, but, if he should have otherwise ordained it, his will be done. I can say with Paul, 'If I live, I live unto the Lord, or if I die, I die unto the Lord.'"

Well, he dies unto the Lord on 8 April, having only revised four books of the Pentateuch.

The Society then invites Jean Daniel Kieffer, Professor of Oriental Languages in the Royal College of Paris, and Interpreting Secretary to the King of France, to take up the task which death has prevented Von Diez from completing. The French Government gives Kieffer permission to visit Bible House in London to discuss the project with the translations committee. He then travels to Leiden and makes arrangements for the manuscript of the Turkish Bible to travel to Paris – the French Government helpfully allows the paper and type to be imported duty free. The cooperation of the Royal Printing Office in Paris is secured and Professor Kieffer, assisted by a French aristocrat, begins to prepare the New Testament for publication. This is completed in time to be presented to the Society's annual meeting in 1819.

London, April 1819

But here's the rub. Despite the care which has been taken with the editing of the text of the Turkish New Testament, it is not free of various kinds of error. Ebenezer Henderson, who is travelling in Russia with John Paterson, writes to the General Committee about this. The Society invites Professor Kieffer to rectify the mistakes, which he does apparently conscientiously: he draws up a list of the minor mistakes and cancels the pages where there are errors of more importance. Since fewer than 100 copies of the New Testament have been issued, the General Committee takes the view that this is the only course of action which is needed.

Paterson and Henderson, however, do not agree that this is all that needs to be done. In their view, the entire New Testament needs to be suppressed and withdrawn. The General Committee takes advice from leading scholars on the vexed question. The experts advise the Committee that it is not necessary to take the step Paterson and Henderson have requested.

Paterson and Henderson resign

In 1822 Ebenezer Henderson and John Paterson resign as agents of the Society. The General Committee is naturally shocked to lose such loyal servants and in the spring of 1823 it suspends circulation of the translation. The Committee takes advice from Oriental experts in France and elsewhere as to the gravity of the errors in the Turkish New Testament.

Earl Street Bible House (see Act 17), 15 December 1823

The translations sub-committee meets in the smaller committee room. On the table in front of the members are a whole series of relevant documents. The Orientalists give their opinion that, while in a future edition of the Turkish New Testament several alterations would be desirable, the version as it stands has no major defect. The sub-committee makes its decision: there is no sufficient reason to suspend the circulation of the Testament any longer. The committee's decision is confirmed by the General Committee on 29 December.

Ebenezer Henderson will not let the matter rest. In 1824 he publishes an "appeal" to the members of the Bible Society "containing a review of the history of the Turkish version, an exposure of its errors, and palpable proofs of the necessity of its suppression". Samuel Lee, Professor of Arabic and Hebrew at Cambridge, writes a reply. The following year, Henderson returns to the fray with "The Turkish New Testament Incapable of Defence", which

Samuel Lee also answers.

Meanwhile, Professor Kieffer not only revises the New Testament text but proceeds with his edition of the Bible. In 1828 he completes the work. To whom do you think he should send the proof-sheets? Henderson, of course.

Henderson pronounces himself totally satisfied with Kieffer's work.

"I pray," says Henderson, "that God will bless the labours of an institution in the service of which I spent many happy years of my life, and which I will rejoice still to aid to the utmost of my power."

Henderson is by this time a theological tutor at the London Missionary College at Hoxton and will go on to become a tutor at Highbury College until 1850. In 1853 he will revise for the Society a Danish Bible and superintend another revision of the Turkish New Testament and a Turkish Genesis and Psalter. He dies at Mortlake on 16 May 1858, aged 74.

You should not feel too sorry for John Paterson. Following his resignation from the Society, Prince Galitzin and other friends in St Petersburg invite him to conduct the affairs of the Russian Bible Society. The Emperor Alexander grants him an annual salary of 6,000 roubles.

However, on the death of the Emperor who has been such a good friend to the Society (and is honoured with a portrait on the walls at Earl Street), his successor and younger brother Nicholas I issues, in 1826, an edict suspending the operations of the Russian Bible Society, placing it under the control of the Orthodox Church. Paterson leaves Russia, but the new Emperor treats him kindly and grants him a pension for life. Bible work in Russia will now be undertaken by agents, correspondents and colporteurs under direction from the Society in London.

Stephen Batalden is the Director of the Russian and European Studies Centre at Arizona State University and an expert on Bible Society's work in Russia. He tells me: "The British and Foreign Bible Society routinely encountered conflict owing to its Protestant and specifically evangelical roots. In the Russian instance, this meant that, even though the publication of Bibles and Testaments in multiple languages in St Petersburg was initially welcomed, there always lurked behind the surface the fear that the Bible Society effort would spawn a type of 'sectarianism' in Russia parallel to the nonconformism of England.

"The principled position that Bible Society took on such matters as added lectionary material, deutero-canonical texts, or capitalised pronominal references to Mary could not help brand the Bible Society effort as Protestant and, for many arbiters of religious culture in Russia, threatening."

Stephen thinks that, to a greater or lesser extent, this problem accompanied BFBS work elsewhere in Europe, as well as in Africa, Asia, and Latin America, and was intrinsic to the nature of the Bible Society movement. The finest BFBS overseas agents instinctively were sensitive to this issue, and sought to position Bible Society in a more open and understanding way, often at odds with the home office.

More generally, Stephen believes that one of the problems confronting the operation of BFBS in its overseas activities was the potential for misunderstanding between its very able and talented overseas agents and the London home office — and this accounts for Paterson and Henderson's resignations.

Despite resigning as a salaried agent, however, Paterson undertakes a tour through Scandinavia on behalf of the Society in 1832 and visits Berlin for it in 1836.

Returning home, he settles in Edinburgh and serves for many years as Secretary for Scotland of the London Missionary Society and acts as Chairman of the Committee of the Congregational Union. Until 1850 he also acts as agent and special correspondent in Scotland for his old Society. Then he moves to Dundee, does a bit of preaching, and dies at Kincaldrum, Forfarshire, on 6 July 1855, aged 79.

Act 14

Support from high society

Both the General Committee in London and the local Auxiliaries and Associations attach importance to securing the patronage of nobility, Bishops and the gentry. The Society's list of Vice-Presidents between 1805 and 1816 includes seven peers, four knights, one Vice-Admiral, fifteen Bishops, four Deans, and four MPs including Nicholas Vansittart, a former Tory Chancellor of the Exchequer who will become Lord Bexley in 1823. The Bishops include some who will do little to help evangelical initiatives within the Church of England but who are happy to add their names, influence and sometimes practical help to the work of the Society. Patrons of the Auxiliaries include the Princess of Wales, royal Dukes and Duchesses, Marquises, Earls and Countesses, Viscounts, Barons, Baronets and knights.

Not everyone approves of this feature of the Society's life. Dr John Randolph succeeded the sympathetic Beilby Porteus as Bishop of London in 1808. When invited to become patron of the Colchester Auxiliary, Randolph replies by declaring himself disgusted with the "pomp and parade with which the proceedings, and indeed all the meetings, of the new Society are set forth in the public papers; and the more so when he compares it with the simplicity and modesty of the old society" (SPCK, founded in 1698).

Cambridge, 1811

When the Master of Sidney Sussex College proposes the formation of a Bible Society Auxiliary in Cambridge, the Master and Fellows of Trinity College respond with a donation of 50 guineas to the Society's funds. However, not everyone approves of the idea – and this opposition comes from a totally opposite point of view from that we have seen from the new Bishop of London.

"We have at present two very extensive Bible Societies," Dr Marsh tells the University Senate, "the one founded in 1698 (SPCK), the other 1804. Both our archbishops, and all our bishops, with the Prince Regent at the head, are members of the former. Neither of the two archbishops, and only a small proportion of the bishops, are members of the latter. Our encouragement of the ancient Bible Society must contribute to the welfare of the Established Church, whereas our encouragement of the modern Society not only contributes nothing to it in preference to other Churches, but may contribute even to its dissolution."

Nicholas Vansittart writes a letter answering this charge which is full of good sense and moderation. He admits that patronage of Bible Society by the Bishops doesn't equal that of which SPCK can boast, but he questions whether the older Society was in such a short time "honoured with the support of so large a body of the prelates". He expresses the hope that "the time might not be far distant when the two Societies might equally flourish under the general patronage of them all". Vansittart welcomes the absence of distinction between Churchman and Dissenter in the new Society.

Bible Society, says Vansittart, is an establishment which has done more to spread Christianity than has ever been done in a similar period since apostolic days. To get rid of it would "be putting out one of the eyes of Britain". "If we cannot reconcile all opinions," says Vansittart, "let us endeavour to unite all hearts." This stout and eloquent defence of the Society will not be forgotten when the Society has to choose its second President in 23 years' time.

The Duke of Gloucester, Chancellor of the University, recommends that Vansittart's letter be distributed to those who attend the meeting to discuss the formation of the Cambridge Auxiliary. Wilberforce also intervenes, Charles Simeon takes up the cause from the pulpit at Holy Trinity, and Cambridge gets its Auxiliary.

Staffordshire, 1811

When the Staffordshire Auxiliary is to be launched in 1811, Viscount Anson suggests that Thomas Gisborne should be the keynote speaker. Fifty-three-year-old Gisborne was the fifth wrangler of his year at Oxford in 1780. A lifetime friend of William Wilberforce, he has written the book *Principles of Moral Philosophy* (1789) as well as writing about the slave trade, the duties of women and collections of hymns, poems and sermons. He has served locally as a curate in Staffordshire before being appointed Prebendary of Durham.

At the launch of the Staffordshire Auxiliary, Gisborne rises to the occasion and delivers a witty address. Warming to his task, he turns to a controversial subject.

"The charges advanced against the British and Foreign Bible Society," he tells the meeting, "at different periods of its progress, were they not to be occasionally mischievous, might furnish considerable entertainment. At one time it was clamorously alleged, 'Note and comments and interpretations will be inserted in your Bibles; you will undermine the Church of England by the expositions which you will interweave into the sacred volume.' 'It is impossible,' replied the Society. 'It is a fundamental law of our constitution that neither note nor comment shall ever be added.' Then succeeds an accusation from another corner of the sky, 'Why do you send forth the Scriptures without an interpretation? The Established Church will be ruined by your dispersion of the Bible without note or comment!' I leave these two classes of objectors to settle accounts each with the other. For the overthrow of the Bible Society both are equally anxious."

The Staffordshire audience smiles and feels better for Gisborne's spirited defence of the cause it supports.

Norwich, 1811

Enter Joseph Gurney

The wealthy Quaker banker and merchant, still a young man, sits at his desk at the Gurney country seat at Earlham Hall after the launch of the Norwich Auxiliary and writes a lively account of the day's proceedings. So many turned up for the meeting, they had to relocate to St Andrew's Hall.

"The Mayor looked magnificent," Gurney writes, "with his gold chain, in the chair. The Bishop [Henry Bathurst] first harangued, and admirably well, upon the excellence of the British and Foreign Bible Society, its objects, constitution and effects. He then introduced the Secretaries. Steinkopf, a most interesting German and Lutheran, and as far as I can judge from an acquaintance of three days, a remarkably simple and devoted character, first came forward. He told the tale of what the Society had done in Germany and other parts of Europe in broken but good English, and by degrees warmed the meeting into enthusiasm.

"He was followed by Hughes, the Baptist Secretary, an eloquent, solid, and convincing orator. The company were now ready for the resolutions. The Bishop proposed them, I seconded them [his first public speech], and after I had given a little of their history and purport they were carried with great acclamation. This was a great relief, as we trembled at the idea of a discussion. The Bishop was thanked for his liberality. It was really delightful to hear an old Puritan and a modern bishop saying everything that was kind and Christian-like of each other. The Bishop's heart seemed quite full... Owen closed the meeting with an unnecessarily splendid but most effectual address. More than £700 [over £23,000 today] was collected before the company left the hall.

"We had a vast party at Earlham, and a remarkable day, a perfectly harmonious mixture of High Church, Low Church, Lutheran, Baptist, Quaker! It was a time which seemed to pull down all barriers of distinction, and to melt us all into one common Christianity. Such a beginning warrants us to expect much."

Another of those present will long remember sitting down

Manor House, Little Sodbury, Gloucestershire, where William Tyndale began to translate the first printed English New Testament, Act 1.

St Michael's Church, Llanfihangel-y-Pennant, Merionethshire (since 1974 Gwynedd), where Mary Jones's parents were married and she was baptised, Act 2.

Monument at Tyn'y-ddôl, the ruins of the cottage where Mary Jones grew up and from where she set off on her walk to Bala, Act 2.

Mary Jones in popular imagination, Act 3.

Thomas Charles of Bala,
Acts 2–16.

Memorial plaques
at the house in
Bala High Street
(now a bank)
where Thomas
Charles lived and
presented Mary
with her three
Bibles after her
walk from
Llanfihangel in
1800, Act 3.

Old Swan Stairs where a committee meeting of the Religious Tract Society (RTS) in December 1802 agreed a Bible Society was needed, Act 14.

The Rev. Joseph Hughes.

Joseph Hughes, Act 4.

Granville Sharp,
Act 4.

Karl Steinkopf,
Acts 4–20

John Owen, Acts 4–5.

The Rev. John Owen

Clapham about 1800, Act 6.

Lord Teignmouth,
the first President,
Acts 6–21.

Ebenezer Henderson,
Acts 11–13.

Earl Street Bible House, Act 17.

Ellen Ranyard, Act 17.

M.ᵣˢ Ranyard

to dinner at Earlham Hall at five that afternoon. There were 34 people from different denominations and "words fail to express the delightful harmony of our feelings". This guest recalls that after the dinner things had been cleared away, Elizabeth Fry, Joseph Gurney's sister who had travelled from London for the occasion, "knelt down, and in a most sweet and impressive manner implored the divine blessing upon the company present, and for the general promotion of truth upon earth".

Two miles out of Norwich, Earlham Hall has been the family home of the Gurney family for some years. (It is now used by the School of Law at the University of East Anglia.) Old John and Catherine Gurney stood out among the plain Friends (Quakers) of Norwich Meeting because of their brightly coloured clothing, fashionable manners, visits to the theatre and to operas, and other practices frowned on by most Friends of that era. But two of their children, Elizabeth, who will marry the London Quaker merchant Joseph Fry, and Joseph Gurney, become among the most prominent Friends of the 19th century, as well as passionate supporters of Bible Society. Both of them travel widely and become active in the cause of social reform.

Elizabeth Fry will become very widely known in wider society. Her evangelical zeal and Christian compassion lead her to work with prisoners (as we shall see), the mentally ill, and the homeless. She is internationally renowned for her work, and even today there are Elizabeth Fry Societies devoted to prison work. She is also an eloquent preacher. Joseph Gurney will play a key role among Quakers, with one wing of Friends becoming known as Gurneyites.

Earlham Hall, Norfolk, 1818

As an agent of the Society in Russia, Portugal and Spain, George Borrow will play a major part in our story. Years before he becomes linked to the Society, when still a boy of fifteen, he sits fishing on a bank of the river Yare. He has his back to a low hill which slopes down from Earlham Hall and his float is in the water.

As he catches some fish, he takes them off the hook and flings them on the grass beside him. Then he hears a voice.

"Can you answer to your conscience for pulling all those fish out of the water, and leaving them to gasp in the sun?"

Borrow looks around to see a tall man, dressed in what strikes him as curious clothes but made from good materials. He looks young and vigorous with handsome features which are calm and kindly. He wears a hat "of finest beaver with broad drooping eaves" and his voice is as "clear and sonorous as a bell".

"Surely this is a very cruel diversion in which you indulge, my young friend," the man continues.

"I am sorry for it, if it be, sir," says Borrow, standing up, "but I do not think it cruel to fish."

"What are your reasons for not thinking so?"

"Fishing is mentioned frequently in Scripture. Simon Peter was a fisherman."

"True," replies the man, "and Andrew his brother. But you forget: they did not follow fishing as a diversion, as I fear you do. Do you read the Scriptures?"

"Sometimes."

"Sometimes? Not daily? That is to be regretted. What profession do you make? I mean to what religious denomination do you belong, my young friend?"

"Church," replies Borrow.

"It is a very good profession. There is much of Scripture contained in its liturgy. Do you read anything besides the Scriptures?"

"Sometimes."

"What do you read besides?"

"Greek and Dante."

"Indeed! Then you have the advantage over me. I can only read the former. Well, I am rejoiced to find that you have other pursuits besides your fishing. Do you know Hebrew?"

"No."

"You should study it. Why don't you undertake the study?"

"I have no books."

"I will lend you three books, if you wish to undertake the

study. I live yonder at the Hall as perhaps you know. I have a library there in which are many curious books, both in Greek and Hebrew, which I will show to you whenever you may find it convenient to come and see me. Farewell! I am glad to find you have pursuits more satisfactory than your cruel fishing!"

George Borrow watches as Joseph Gurney walks briskly back to his home. Years later, Borrow will take Gurney up on his invitation to visit Earlham Hall. "There I saw his gentle partner and his fair children, and on the morrow he showed me the books of which he had spoken years before by the side of the stream."

THE CALM AND WISE PRESIDENT

In July 1808 the Teignmouths leave Clapham and move into 4 Portman Square, London, where they live for the rest of their lives. Portman Square is a stone's throw north-west of where Selfridges is today. The Grants and Wilberforces also leave Clapham at this time. Lord Teignmouth becomes an active member of Marylebone Parish Church where the rector takes to seeking his advice on parochial affairs. He persuades the rector to introduce evening services into the churches of the parish and joins a number of charitable bodies.

But Lord Teignmouth's main concern is running Bible Society. He has grown to love it and delight in its work. He styles it "a new constellation" which "under the favour of Providence, has risen to illuminate the darkness of the moral world". Karl Steinkopf recalls Teignmouth's long years as President.

> In all his official and private intercourse with the Members, the venerated President never evinced the smallest partiality towards this or that particular class or communion. When any measure was proposed in the Committee, or any question was discussed, he listened to every speaker with the most perfect candour and the kindest attention; often giving to the arguments and reasoning [for] or against any proposition a far more deliberate consideration than was supposed by the party from whom those arguments proceeded.

He was possessed of an admirable calmness and composure of mind, not to be disturbed by any heat in the debate, or any accidental warmth of expression. Even when complicated and delicate subjects were brought under consideration, and differences of opinion arose, he still retained his self-possession.

Often I have watched his countenance, and every feature still expressed the placidity of his mind; nor do I recollect a single instance in which even a symptom of impatience betrayed itself. After calmly listening (sometimes for several hours) to everything advanced on one or the other side of the question, he might be seen making some memorandums: after which he would propose a Resolution, so adapted to the occasion, and so wisely and discreetly worded, that it was not infrequently adopted at once by all parties.

For many years, Lord Teignmouth spends three hours every day in prayer. He adjourns to his study at five in the afternoon to begin his evening devotions. From these secret times with God he will appear again to join his family, in the words of his son-in-law "like the Jewish lawgiver of old, with brightness in his face, as well as with the Law of God in his heart; and showing, by that heavenly-mindedness which marked his whole conversation, how earnest had been his prayer, that the same mind might be in him which was also in Christ Jesus".

At the age of 60 (in 1812) he tells Wilberforce, "I am perfectly contented that my name as once Governor General of India should sink into oblivion. But I hope that it will be remembered, by my latest posterity, as President of the British and Foreign Bible Society. I bless the Providence that has added this character and designation to my name, and pray that I may be enabled to discharge the most gratifying duties annexed to this situation."

Act
15

Bad news for the Northampton Auxiliary

Spencer Perceval was son of the second Earl of Egmont and educated at Harrow and at Trinity College, Cambridge. After a career as a lawyer, he entered Parliament as MP for Northampton and distinguished himself by his speeches in support of Pitt's administration. Perceval was a vigorous debater, especially good at thinking on his feet. His thorough mastery of all the details of his subject often gained him victory over his opponents. After serving as Attorney General and Chancellor of the Exchequer, he became Prime Minister in 1809.

Despite the demands of his job at 10 Downing Street, Spencer Perceval found time to be an active supporter and friend of Bible Society. In 1807, when he was Chancellor of the Exchequer, he lived for some months in Lord Teignmouth's house in Clapham while His Lordship spent the summer and autumn in Broadstairs. The date for the founding of the Northampton Auxiliary in 1812 was fixed to suit Perceval's diary. Meanwhile in Cornwall...

Scorrier House, Redruth, Cornwall

On the night of 2 May 1812 a Mr Williams, who lives near Redruth, dreams three times in succession that Perceval, "a small man, dressed in a blue coat and waistcoat", will be murdered by a man "in a snuff-coloured coat with metal buttons". Williams is inclined to go to London to warn the Prime Minister, but his friends dissuade him on the grounds that his warning will not be taken seriously.

On 11 May Perceval arrives at the House of Commons and enters the members' lobby. A shot rings out and the Prime Minister lies dead on the floor. The trigger has been pulled by John Bellingham, a bankrupt Liverpool broker who applied to Perceval in vain for redress of a personal complaint against the Government. A subdued inaugural meeting of the Northampton Auxiliary goes ahead on 27 May, attended by Secretaries John Owen and Joseph Hughes and presided over by the Duke of Grafton.

At his trial, Bellingham's lawyer pleads insanity on behalf of his client, but the plea is set aside and he is hanged.

A reshuffle of Government Ministers following Perceval's assassination means that Nicholas Vansittart, who was made a Vice-President of the Society the previous year, becomes Chancellor of the Exchequer. He still finds time to speak for the Society on platforms usually at Freemasons' Hall and later at Exeter Hall.

On 6 August 1812, in the Egyptian Hall of the Mansion House, on the formation of the City of London Auxiliary, Vansittart refers to the tragic events of the early summer. "In the very sanctuary of our laws," he says, "we have seen one of the best of men and most upright of Ministers, one of the brightest orna-ments of our Senate by his talents, and of society by his virtues, snatched away by violence – a man whom we are this day pecu-liarly bound to deplore, as a steady friend and firm supporter of the Bible Society, and a man warmly attached to the religion of his country, and living under the constant influence of its principles. But that such a crime should have been committed I am bound especially to lament, as I cannot but remember, with impressions of unceasing awe and regret, that a black deed of assassination has been the means of placing me in a situation so difficult and ardu-ous that the peculiar blessing of Providence can alone enable me successfully to fulfil its important duties."

Act 16

Words of hope for prisoners

England, 1806–1813

By 1811 there are nearly 50,000 foreign prisoners of war in England – French, Spanish, Italian, Dutch, Danish and Norwegian. The Government hardly knows what to do with so many. Many prisoners are held in the hulks of ships moored in the Thames and in harbours around the country. In theory they are waiting to sail for Australia under a sentence of transportation, but in practice many of them serve their whole sentences in the hulks and are released without ever leaving the country. At first, prisoners of war are drafted to the hulks in naval harbours, but as the war goes on, the Government decides that the presence of such a formidable force of trained fighting men in British ports represents a danger in case of invasion. So it is decided to send large contingents inland.

Dartmoor Prison is built at Princetown. Its seven severe blocks of granite buildings are ready in March 1806 to be occupied by between 7,000 and 10,000 prisoners. "For seven months in the year," writes an angry Frenchman, "*c'est une vraie Sibérie*, covered with melting snow. When the snows vanish the mists appear. Conceive the tyranny of *la perfide Albion* in sending human beings to such a place!" Many never leave Dartmoor alive and are laid to rest in the French cemetery.

Even before Dartmoor Prison opens, Bible Society's General Committee agrees to make its first grant to prisoners two days before Christmas in 1805. Immediate supplies are bought, but arrangements are made to print large editions of the French New Testament and of the whole Bible. Every year until Napoleon is finally defeated, large sums are spent on the spiritual needs of French prisoners. According to contemporary accounts, the prisoners receive the Bibles with thanks, with tears and with joy. They form reading parties and in some cases establish circulating Scripture libraries. Bibles are lent, sold very cheaply or given away.

Bibles for prisoners "have contributed," writes a French officer from a ship in the Medway, "to sweeten the bitter cup of which an inscrutable Providence has condemned us to drink deep for so many years". Another writes to the Society, "I should not do justice to my sentiments did I not declare my regret that my present situation does not permit me to have the honourable title of a member of such an institution."

When the United States declares war on Britain in 1812, many American prisoners come to share the same fate as Frenchmen. The General Committee decides to send a special consignment of 500 Bibles and 1,000 Testaments to Dartmoor for American prisoners. Many American and French prisoners take their Bibles back to their own countries at the end of the war.

Newgate Prison, London, 1813

Elizabeth Fry is delighted that her brother, Joseph Gurney, is so involved in the work of the Norwich Auxiliary and that the establishment of Bible Society gives her easy access to Bibles. She began to show an interest in prison work in Norwich when she was fifteen, and in 1813 begins visiting Newgate, London's chief prison from the 13th to the 19th centuries where many well-known criminals, including the thieves Jack Sheppard, Jonathan Wild and Captain Kidd the pirate, were held. In the year that she was born, 1780, the place was destroyed by a mob in the Gordon riots. After it is rebuilt, London's public executions are held there until 1868 when they are stopped. Newgate will finally be pulled down in 1902 to make way for the "Old Bailey" (Central Criminal Court).

When Elizabeth Fry first visits Newgate she finds that women, criminals and girls who haven't been proved guilty of crimes are all herded together and live in terrible, overcrowded conditions. Some of the women have children who are allowed to mix with the worst criminals. She begins her work by giving the poorer women clothes and then setting up a school for the children. She finds useful things for the prisoners to do. Then she begins the practice of reading to them from the Bible.

"To most of the prisoners the Bible was entirely new," Janet Whitney tells us. "They listened to it with unfeigned rapture. Mrs Fry's readings were to them a theatre and a concert, a church and a superior family circle, all rolled into one. Drama and poetry, exciting stories and sublime thoughts, came new and fresh to their ears. The unusual powers of imagination stirred within them. They glimpsed the moving pillar of fire and cloud, they thrilled to the blast of trumpets and the shout that brought down the walls of Jericho, they saw the angels' ladder bright and near, and they touched the hem of the seamless robe whose wearer had shown mercy to a prostitute. In their raw and crude fashion they worshipped, and some of them were profoundly changed."

One eyewitness describes hearing Mrs Fry reading from Isaiah 53 in Newgate Prison. The witness thinks that the chapter is in itself one of the greatest pieces of prose in the English language ("All we like sheep have gone astray; we have turned every one to his own way; and the Lord hath laid on him the iniquity of us all.") "Never till then, and never since then, have I heard anyone read as Elizabeth Fry read that chapter – the solemn reverence of her manner, the articulation so exquisitely modulated, so distinct, that not a word of that sweet and touching voice could fail to be heard. While she read, her mind seemed so absorbed in the passage of Scripture and in nothing else. She seemed to take to her own soul the words which she read and to apply them to herself; and then she raised her head and, after a pause, she spoke to the wretched women before her."

Bala and Kensington Gore, October 1814 TWO FOUNDERS DIE

You will remember how, in 1800, old Robert Owen prayed that Thomas Charles would have fifteen years added to his life. The end of this period is now drawing near. Charles has been ailing for three years and in the spring of 1814, in his 59th year, he grows worse. He edits and prepares for the press a new edition of the Welsh Bible which is published by the Society in the same year.

"Now I have nothing to do but die," he says.

On Wednesday 5 October he wakes shivering.

"Well, Mr Charles, the day of tribulation has arrived," a caller says to him – the sort of visitor some of us may feel we could do without.

"There is a refuge," Charles replies.

He dies later in the day. He has set up a printing press in Bala. Between 1805 and 1811 he has issued his Bible dictionary in four volumes; this remains the standard work of its kind in Welsh. He has edited a Christian quarterly magazine in Welsh. He has established day schools and Sunday Schools. He has toured Ireland. He was one of the makers of modern Wales. Most of all, he will be remembered as the man who presented Mary Jones with three Bibles and whose energetic pleading in London on behalf of many like her led to the foundation of the British and Foreign Bible Society.

In the same month, Henry Thornton MP, the Society's first Treasurer, falls seriously ill. He moves to live with his friend William Wilberforce, now living at Kensington Gore, where he dies on 16 January 1815, aged 55. Lord Teignmouth says of him: "Religion in him was a prevailing, active principle: it was the rule of his conduct; and showed itself in the undeviating probity of his life, the purity of his morals, and the benevolence of his actions. God had entrusted to him many talents; and he employed them to the glory of his Master, and to the benefit of his fellow-creatures. He had his imperfections; but they were few and light indeed, when compared with his virtues. What mortal is without them?"

Henry's nephew, John Thornton, takes over from his uncle as Treasurer both at Bible Society and the Church Missionary Society.

Act 17

A home of its own for the Society

Until 1816 the Society had no headquarters. The General Committee usually held its early meetings either at the room in Old Swan Stairs where RTS (Religious Tract Society) had hit on the idea of the Society in the first place; public meetings were held either at the London Tavern where the Society was founded or at the Freemasons' Hall in Great Smith Street. The library and depot had been in one place and the Accountant's office in another. In June 1816 the Society took possession of 10 Earl Street, built within the precincts of the old monastery of the Blackfriars – a building which has since been demolished to make way for Queen Victoria Street. The Society bought the house at a cost of £5,400 (over £216,000 at today's values) but the addition of a warehouse and other improvements brought the total cost to £12,000 (not far short of £500,000).

The front of the house looked towards the river. At the west corner at the back, a flight of steps led into Printing House Square, the headquarters of *The Times*.

Blackfriars, London, June 1816 A ROYAL BED

Enter Miss Enderby

Daughter of the previous owner, Miss Enderby was born in 10 Earl Street before the Society bought it. A remarkable woman, she will still be alive at the time of the centenary celebrations in 1904. She is proud of the fact that inside the house at the time of the sale is a four-poster bed with carved and painted ornaments and an inscription at its head which reads:

> Henri, by the Grace of God, Kynge of Englonde and of Fraunce, Lorde of Irelonde, Defendour of the Faythe, and Supreme Heade of the Churche of all Englonde. An. Dni. M.CCCCC.XXXIX.

Below the inscription, on each side, is the King's motto *Dieu et mon Droit* with the initials of Henry and his mistress (later Queen) Anne Boleyn. I have not been able to discover what the Society did with that bed.

Enter the General Committee

The General Committee soon begins to feel at home in Earl Street. It meets in a room with a long table in the middle, covered with a purple cloth. At one end the President, Lord Teignmouth, sits in a raised chair. Along the sides are rows of fixed benches, each one slightly higher than the one in front, as in a cinema, and filling the whole room. The room has been fitted out to provide enough room for the 36 members of the Committee and the staff who assist and advise them. They work hard, meeting on every alternate Monday in every month and more often as necessary. Six members, according to the Society's constitution, always have to be foreigners, living in or near London; fifteen are required to be members of the Church of England; and fifteen are from other denominations. All the Committee members are laymen (no women at this time), though they are assisted by staff members who are ordained. Any ordained person who becomes a member of the Society, by paying his subscription, is entitled to attend and vote at all meetings of the Committee.

From the middle years of the 19th century, the case of Bibles which will be exhibited at the Great Exhibition in Hyde Park in 1851 is always on display in the General Committee room. All these Bibles are displayed open, with a small ticket attached giving the language in which the verses are written and the number of Bibles the Society has published and printed in that language.

Over the fireplace, beneath the clock, hangs a magnificent map showing the countries of the world in many colours, pointing out where Bibles have been circulated, how many copies, and in what language, along with other statistics. There is a portrait of William Tyndale and, by the middle of the century, Lord Teignmouth and Lord Bexley, the first two Presidents.

On the table is a large, loosely bound book with raised characters. This is a version of John's Gospel for the blind, not yet in Braille, but in the system invented by Moon of Brighton and (costly to produce) on sale for eight shillings.

Next to the General Committee room is the smaller committee room where the sub-committees meet. Each member of the General Committee sits on a sub-committee for which he is best qualified: this may be the depository committee, which looks after the printing and binding of Bibles, or the agency committee which directs the work of the Society's agents in many parts of the world, or one of a series of finance committees.

By the middle of the 19th century, the walls of this smaller committee room are decorated with portraits of the Society's first three Secretaries – John Owen, Joseph Hughes and Karl Steinkopf – and others who have played a major part in the formative years: William Wilberforce, Granville Sharp, Admiral Gambier, the Bishop of Winchester, Thomas Charles of Bala, Broadley Wilson, Adam Clarke with his Buddhist priests, Oberlin, the pastor of the Ban de la Roche, William Greenfield, Tsar Alexander I, Emperor of Russia who encouraged and supported the Society, and a portrait of a Belgian colporteur.

EARL STREET LIBRARY

As the Society establishes itself in its Earl Street premises, the most interesting room becomes the library. Here, you will find at least one copy of the Scriptures in every language in which they have so far been printed, and in many cases several editions of each. There is a copy of John Wycliffe's New Testament, printed in 1810 – 426 years after the reformer's death. Wycliffe and his team of helpers laboriously wrote out the Bible in manuscript – it was never printed in his day or during the Reformation. There is a copy of Tyndale's Bible, printed in 1534, in which John 1:1–5 reads:

> 1 In the beginnynge was the worde, and the worde was with God: and the worde was God. 2 The same was in the beginnynge with God. 3 All thinges were made by it, and without it, was made

nothinge, that was made. 4 In it was lyfe, and the lyfe was the light of men, 5 and the light shyneth in the darknes, but the darknes comprehended it not.

There is a copy of Miles Coverdale's Bible, dated 1535, the first complete English Bible to be printed in England, and dedicated to Henry VIII. A copy of the Bishops' Bible, published in 1568, has been given a new binding. You will see the first Welsh Bible ever printed – the version of Dr Morgan, later Bishop of St Asaph – dated 1588.

An old Swedish Bible in the library is remarkable for its binding. A picture has been painted on the edges of its pages which you cannot see when the book is closed, but when the covers are opened and the pages slightly separated, you can see a picture of Bunyan's Christian on his journey up the straight and narrow valley to the heavenly city.

There is a display of "Polyglot" Bibles – printed in many languages at once in separate columns, for instance, Hebrew, Greek, Latin and English – an almost indispensable tool for Bible translators. One Dutch Bible, weighing 40 pounds, with brass clasps, is bound in boards of solid wood.

Martin Luther's German New Testament of 1524 and his whole Bible of 1567 are there, reminding us of how the German reformer gave the Scriptures to Germany in a homely and vigorous style which appealed to popular taste. When Luther, working with a team of scholars, revised his first translation they would sometimes spend up to fourteen days considering a single line, even a word.

It was in Bohemia (then part of the Austrian Empire, now forming much of the Czech Republic) that printing was first used for the more general distribution of Bibles in 1488. The Earl Street library includes a Bohemian version of the Scriptures dated 1596.

The Persian New Testament translated by Henry Martyn and published by Bible Society, in 1827 and twice again, is held in the library.

The library of Earl Street Bible House includes, by the middle of the 19th century, a present from the Director of the Imperial Printing Office in Vienna – a specimen of the Lord's Prayer written in every known language of the world at the time, and in every dialect of the language through successive ages. So, for example, you can read the Lord's Prayer in English as it was written in 1160, 1370, 1430, 1526, and so on with slight variations up to the year 1800. The Austrian Emperor donated money which was used to pay for this item.

In the manuscript library, next to the main library, the Society keeps in locked and numbered cases all the hand-written versions of the Scriptures it holds – some of them not yet printed, and some treasured originals from which Bibles circulated by the Society have been printed.

All these Bibles and manuscripts are still held in the Society's priceless collection at Cambridge University library.

Enter Ellen Ranyard

Earl Street Bible House includes a warehouse. When Ellen Ranyard visits this at around the middle of the 19th century, she is intrigued by the variety of Bibles she finds. In one compartment she comes across some beautiful English Family Bibles which sell at one sovereign (£1 then, £42 today) each. At the other extreme she finds Diamond Bibles, with marginal references, bound in best leather and with gilt edges on sale for one shilling and three pence – the same book handsomely bound in morocco sells for one shilling and eleven pence, its cost price. As well as "Diamonds", Bibles were printed as "Pearls" and "Rubies".

Climbing the stairs from the ground to the first floor of the warehouse, Mrs Ranyard watches a large iron crane which lifts bundles of Bibles to a wagon below, waiting to transport Scriptures to the docks or (by the middle of the century) to an early railway station. *No other crane in all London lifts such true riches!* she thinks.

Close to the trapdoor into the first floor, she sees a pile of Italian Bibles. A warehouseman with strong views which coincide with her own sees her looking at them.

"Those don't move now. Since the Pope has come back to

Rome, he won't let Bibles into Italy! That lot, too, are Spanish, and this, Malagassy – they're both very dead. English Bibles are lively, and move away as fast as they're ready. We sent out 9,000 of these Diamonds last month."

Ellen Ranyard picks up a Chinese New Testament and examines it. The words are not arranged across the page, but in columns from top to bottom. The paper is very thin, and printed only on one side, with the plain sides of two pages folded together like an uncut book. The paper for these Testaments has been made, and the books printed, in China. The cover is also Chinese, made of yellow paper, like silk, impregnated with gold dust. They have been printed from wooden blocks, on which the characters have been cut, like woodcuts. She comes across other Chinese Bibles which have been printed in England on English paper on both sides of the page and bound in the English way. She thinks that the Chinese may find this attractive.

Mrs Ranyard sees more piles of books of all sizes and another whole floor of them: Swedish, Portuguese, French, Russian, Amharic, Tahitian, Malay and so on.

"This stack of English came from Oxford this morning," the warehouseman tells her. "Those boxes have 20,000 Bibles and Testaments for Toronto in them. Yesterday we sent almost as many to Ireland, chiefly for the use of the schools in the Hibernian Society."

After the warehouseman leaves, Ellen Ranyard stands quietly with a friend among the great piles of Bibles. They were, she thought, *alone with all those written voices of God – the voice that answered Job out of the whirlwind, that thundered in the deserts of Sinai, that spoke by the prophets, and in the sweet harp of David; the voice that clothed its majesty in tenderness from the lips of the Redeemer of the world, and through evangelists and apostles is come down even to us – to our homes, to our hearts, and daily lives.*

A "LARGE, AIRY AND WELL-WARMED ROOM"

Printing an English Bible requires a licence from the crown, and in the 19th century Bible Society had its Scriptures printed either by presses of the Universities of Oxford or Cambridge or by (after 1837) the Queen's Printers, Eyre and Spottiswoode, in Shacklewell, north-east London. In the middle years of the 19th century, Eyre and Spottiswoode employed 150 people printing Bibles: compositors, pressers, readers, gatherers, revisers, collators, correctors, folders, bookers, lookers-over, hangers-up and tiers-up.

The Society never supplied any Bibles to anyone in sheets: every Bible was bound to prevent the so-called apocryphal books appearing within the covers of a BFBS edition and to avoid a preface or note or comment being added. All Society books were bound by contract, and in the middle of the 19th century the contractors were a firm owned and run by a Mr Watkins.

North London, 1840s

Re-enter Mrs Ranyard, on a visit to the bookbinders to the Society

Ellen Ranyard visits the contractors. She finds herself in a large, airy, and well-heated room, with long tables, at which sit some "neat, healthy and happy-looking girls" aged from twelve to 18.

The girls work for ten hours a day. Watkins pays them according to the quantity of work they get through and Ellen Ranyard thinks this tends "to make them industrious". He has introduced checks on the way the girls do their jobs, and the Society's contract with him states that he has to replace at his own cost any Bibles which turn out to be badly bound. If his girls fold or stitch badly, Watkins fines them.

"But," Watkins tells Mrs Ranyard, reassuringly, "among a staff of 200 workpeople fines amount to less that five pounds a year."

Ellen Ranyard watches the girls at work, folding pages and then sewing them. The Bibles are printed in large sheets, sometimes 64 pages in a sheet. Each folder sits by a table on which she spreads out the large sheets. In her right hand she holds a small ivory or bone folding-knife with which she flattens the folds of the sheet. Mrs Ranyard notices how quickly and accurately the girls do this – they have to match the first and last lines of print evenly with the opposite page. Of course the girls don't (normally) read the sheets they fold but look for the *signature* at the bottom of each page – which most readers never notice.

A girl takes up first a sheet marked with the letter A, folds it down the middle, and then across, and also once more down the middle. Then she takes up the next sheet, letter B, folds it in the same way and lays it on top of letter A. She carries on in the same way right through the alphabet until beginning again, except that she will attach the second A to a small a, the second B to a small b and so on. After the folded sheets have been put through a rolling-press, someone gives them to a collator, usually a man working in a separate room, who takes them in his hand to see if they are in the proper order, that no sheet is missing and that the folding has been done correctly. The collator does this expertly, holding the sheets in one corner and allowing them to spring back, one after another, while he checks all the signature letters.

Then the Bibles have to be sewn. A girl, sitting sideways against a table on which the sheets are laid, first picks up one marked A, and places the back of it against three strings or tapes, fastened in a sewing-press, then passes a needle, filled with strong thread, through the sheet. From the inside she brings it out at the back and carries it over one of the tapes, pushing the needle through the paper again from the outside – this causes the thread to embrace the tape. She reaches with her left arm around the press and returns the needle from one side to the other. In this way, sheet after sheet gets fixed to the tapes.

The girls work at great speed, expertly steering their needles in and out and over the tapes with the skill acquired after many weeks of performing the same task – and spurred on by the thought that their wages depend not on the number of hours they sit at the press but on the number of Bibles they sew.

"How old are you?" Ellen Ranyard asks one of the apprentices.

"Thirteen, ma'am," replies the girl.

"And how long have you worked here?"

"Three months."

"And how much do you earn?"

"One shilling and three pence, yesterday, ma'am," the girl replies.

"She's naturally quick," observes her forewoman, intervening, "a steady child, if ever I saw one!"

Mary Jones would probably have been glad of work like this with steady and reliable pay. The Earl of Shaftesbury, the Society's third President, will introduce legislation to reduce the hours worked by young people and raise the minimum age by which they can legally be employed.

After the Bibles are sewn, they are taken to the re-collating room to be examined. Here a second collator looks at every sheet to see if it has been torn by accident, or carelessly or improperly stitched.

"The collator has to fix his mind entirely on his job," says Watkins, "for the least distraction may cause him to overlook an error."

If no faults are found, the Bibles are carried to another building where only men work. Here the men pile the Bibles up, with a sheet of zinc or iron between each book, in a hydraulic press where they are left for a while before being taken to the cutting room where a man deftly cuts the whole pile of books with one stroke of a knife.

Next, the gilder receives the books, screws them into a powerful horizontal press, and scrapes the edges with a mixture of red chalk and water. Then he takes a camel-hair pencil, dips it into a cup containing egg white beaten up with water, and paints it on the still damp book's edge. He takes leaf-gold from a leather-covered cushion and applies it to the three edges of many books in succession, all squeezed tightly in the press to produce a solid and even surface. After a few minutes, the gold is sufficiently dry and set for polishing – a process which you would think would rub off every trace of gold, but doesn't.

The gilder holds in his hand a long-handled burnisher, to the lower end of which is attached a very smooth, straight-edged piece of agate which he places on the gilt surface. With his left elbow resting on the workbench, and the handle of his burnisher resting on his right shoulder, he rubs the gold vigorously: little gold is rubbed off but the end result is a shiny, highly polished appearance. The gilders can produce a variety of styles of edging as required.

The Bibles are then hammered one by one to produce a rounded shape before being passed to a case-maker who dresses them in sheep, calf or morocco covers according to the price at which they will be sold. The case-maker cuts the leather half an inch larger than the book all round and pares the edge with a sharp knife. He gives the morocco bindings a granulated appearance by rubbing the leather against itself. The Bibles are stamped or embossed by machine.

Someone calculated that each Bible needs fourteen people to make the paper, 21 to print it and 19 to bind it – 54 in all – and the Society sells them at an average of a shilling each. About 3,000 Bibles arrive at Earl Street Bible House from the binders every day. Here a trained team gives them another examination and any defective copies get sent back to the binders to be made good.

All in a day's work of making Bibles.

Act 18 A flying start for the Americans

Until 1782 every English Bible that Americans owned had been brought across the Atlantic by colonists from Britain. From 1775 the Revolutionary War disrupted trade, and the Declaration of Independence by thirteen American colonies the following year removed the need for a licence from the British Crown to print the English Bible. On 12 September 1782 the Continental Congress (the body of delegates who spoke and acted collectively for the people of the colony-states) approved "the pious and laudable undertaking" of Robert Aitken (1734–1802) of Philadelphia in preparing an edition of the Bible. It is the only instance in history of the Congress recommending a Bible.

Robert Aitken's Bible was an edition of the Authorised Version without the Apocrypha. He replaced the sonorous dedication to King James which introduced the famous 1611 edition ("Great and manifold were the blessings, most dread Sovereign…") with a preface issued by Congress. The Bible didn't sell well and brought its printer to the verge of bankruptcy. About 75 copies of the Aitken Bible are known to have survived.

In the following year (1783) Britain recognised the complete independence of the "United States", as the colonies had called themselves since 1776.

The example of the British and Foreign Bible Society is first followed in Philadelphia, William Penn's old city, where the Declaration of Independence was signed and the Constitution of the United States drawn up in 1777. On 12 December 1808 the Philadelphia Bible Society is established since, as the Society's report puts it, "it was immediately seen that the necessity for such an institution was the same as in Europe". The London Society immediately sends a donation of £200 and in addition, since Philadelphia needs Bibles in Welsh, Gaelic, French and German, sends out to America a consignment of these Scriptures at cost price.

In the following year (1809) six more societies are founded – in Hartford, Boston and Princeton and three in New York. By 1814 there are twelve Bible Societies in New York, eleven in Virginia, eight in Pennsylvania, seven in Massachusetts, four in New Jersey, three in Ohio, two each in Vermont, Maryland and South Carolina as well as societies in New Hampshire, Rhode Island, Connecticut, Delaware, Georgia, Kentucky, Tennessee, Mississippi Territory, Louisiana and the District of Columbia.

New Orleans, 1813

The Louisiana Society, based in New Orleans and founded in 1813, is the fruit of a missionary tour paid for by the Philadelphia, Connecticut and New York Bible Societies. The new Society operates among a population which includes many French and Spanish speakers, Roman Catholics and slaves.

Enter the Roman Catholic Bishop of New Orleans

The Bishop examines the Society's French New Testament, expresses his approval, and gives permission for copies to be distributed in a convent of nuns who educate the daughters of the principal Roman Catholic families in Louisiana. The Bishop doubts whether there are ten Bibles among all the Roman Catholics in New Orleans.

When the Philadelphia Society hears the news of the dearth of Bibles in the New Orleans area they resolve to print 6,000 French New Testaments for free distribution to the people of Louisiana; the New York Society resolves to do the same. Across the Atlantic in London, the British and Foreign Bible Society grants £300 for the same purpose.

Massachusetts, 1813

Although trade disputes lead to a declaration of war by the United States against Britain in 1812, Americans insist that they are "not at war with her pious and benevolent institutions". However, in 1813 a vessel armed and commissioned by the American Government captures a supply of Bibles and Testaments on its way from Bible Society in London to Nova Scotia, brings them into Portland, and sells them by auction.

"We are stricken with shame and regret," declares the Massachusetts Bible Society. It immediately appeals to the Boston public for subscriptions to replace the value of the books. In a day or two, twice the needed amount comes in and could be almost indefinitely increased. This is the same Boston where, less than 40 years earlier, as is well known, a band of patriots seized the tea ships, broke open the chests and flung the tea into the harbour. "The Christians of England are still our brethren, their generous spirit we are still bound to admire, and their efforts for the improvement of mankind we are bound to aid and promote," the Massachusetts Society tells its supporters. "By this act we shall do something towards repressing the animosities and antipathies which the present war has a tendency to generate between us and the neighbouring British Provinces."

Bible Societies continue to multiply in the United States, many of them assisted by grants from London. By the close of the year 1816–17, the British and Foreign Bible Society sends over £3,000 to 16 Bible Societies in many parts of America.

New York, May 1816 AMERICAN BIBLE SOCIETY FOUNDED

Enter Elias Boudinot

The Hon. Elias Boudinot, President of the New Jersey Bible Society, summons a convention of delegates from the different Societies of the Union. Thirty-three years earlier, as President of the United States Congress, Dr Boudinot signed the peace treaty which established American independence. Sixty delegates attend the convention representing 31 Societies. They meet in the Consistory Room of the Dutch Reformed Church in New York where they talk from 8 to 13 May.

Present at the convention are, in the words of William Taylor, "revolutionary patriots, soldiers, and statesmen; presidents and professors of colleges and theological seminaries; the most eminent surgeon of his generation; and plain untitled citizens". There are "Presbyterians, Episcopalians, Baptists, Reformed Dutch, Congregationalists, Friends" as well as "Roman Catholics among the rest". [The Roman Catholics are invited to join the new Society but decline.] However, "so great is the Christian harmony and love, that some of those least affected could not help crying out, 'This is none other than the work of God!'"

And so the American Bible Society (ABS) is founded with a constitution which is modelled on BFBS's "Laws and Regulations".

Enter Peter Jay

At the end of the six days of talks, one of the founders, Peter Jay, speaks at a meeting in the City Hall, New York. Peter is the eldest son of John Jay who was first Chief Justice of the Supreme Court of the United States.

"Our object," Jay says, "is to distribute the Holy Scriptures without note or comment. At this, no politician can be alarmed, no Secretary can be reasonably jealous. We shall distribute no other book, we shall teach no disputed doctrine. Laying aside for this purpose the banners of our respective corps, we assemble under the sole standard of the great captain of our salvation. We endeavour to extend his reign, and in his name alone we contend."

Due to poor health, Elias Boudinot isn't able to attend the convention he himself has called. He does however contribute $10,000 to its funds. For its part, the Society in London indicates its delight at the news from across the pond by sending a donation of £500 (£20,000 today) and a duplicate set of stereotype plates for the French Bible.

Boudinot is well enough to address the Society at its first annual meeting in 1817.

"Let it become a common proverb," he urges. "'See how these members of the American Bible Society love one another', though consisting of every denomination of Christians among us."

Enter Bishop Hobart

Evangelical clergy in the Episcopal Church, the American branch of the Anglican Communion, normally cooperate freely with ministers of other churches in the work of religious Societies. The high church Bishop John Henry Hobart challenges this practice when ABS is established. It was at his instigation, when not yet a Bishop, that the New York Bible and Common Prayer Book Society was founded in 1809. This Society differed from the Bible Societies in that it circulated the Book of Common Prayer with the Scriptures — never one without the other.

Bishop Hobart argues against Christian cooperative ventures for evangelism: the Gospel, he says, cannot be presented outside the context of some sort of church tradition. Hobart cannot conceive of Christian truth separate from the *form* of the Episcopal Church. On 3 April 1815 he sends a pastoral letter to "the laity of the Protestant Episcopal Church in the State of New York" in which he pleads with churchmen to support their own Society, arguing that it does all that the general Bible Societies do — and more. In circulating the Prayer Book with the Bible they fulfill "the general duty of diffusing religious truth more effectually than by the circulation of the Bible alone".

Bishop Hobart's plea to the laity is remarkable since some of the Bishops and many of the clergy have already associated themselves with Bible Societies all over America. Even the high church Bishop Theodore Dehon was one of the founders of the Bible Society in Charleston, South Carolina, and though he later resigned office because he differed from some of its policies, he still continued to attend its meetings. Moreover a lay member of Trinity parish in New York drafted ABS's constitution (with BFBS "Laws and Regulations" at his side) and delegates at the May 1816 convention included several prominent laymen of the diocese of New York and a future Bishop of Rhode Island.

According to Bishop Hobart, Bible Societies were founded on the principle of "the separation of the Church from the word of God – of the sacred volume from the ministry, the worship, and the ordinances which it enjoins of divine institution, and the instruments of the propagation and preservation of the gospel truth". ABS doesn't allow this charge to go unanswered. The cudgels are taken up by the distinguished churchman and lawyer, William Jay, another of the sons of Chief Justice John Jay. A rather unedifying pamphlet war between Jay and Hobart follows. ABS, however, will grow from strength to strength.

In 1817 the Society will make its first grant, giving 300 Bibles to the Steuben County Bible Society in Bath, New York. ABS will distribute Bibles to the crew of the USS *John Adams*, thus beginning a Scripture grant programme to the armed services which continues today.

Also in 1817 the ABS library is founded and will grow into a major world resource, highlighting hundreds of years of translation and printing history, and serving as a depository for new Scripture translations from around the world. Today it includes more than 55,000 titles, representing over 2,300 languages and dialects from the 13th century to the present.

In 1821 ABS elects John Jay as its President in succession to Elias Boudinot, and in the following year the Society moves to its first permanent home, 72 Nassau Street in Lower Manhattan. In 1823 ABS sends a gift of $1,000 to the now 62-year-old William Carey to support his continuing Scripture translation work in India.

Act
19

Harsh words from the Vatican

Enter Pope Pius VII

On 3 September 1816 Pope Pius VII addresses a brief to the Catholic Archbishop of Mohilev and Metropolitan of Russia who has recommended to his clergy the free circulation of the Scriptures among the people and support of the Russian Bible Society. The Pope's brief tells the Archbishop that "if the Sacred Scriptures were allowed in the vulgar tongue everywhere without discrimination, more detriment than benefit would arise". The Pope advises the Archbishop "to declare sincerely and plainly, in a fresh letter to the people, that Christian truth and doctrine, both dogmatic and moral, are contained not in the Scriptures alone but likewise in the traditions of the Catholic Church, and that it is solely for the Church herself to regard and interpret them".

In the same year, a Polish Bishop requests instruction from the Pope about the possible establishment of a Bible Society in Warsaw. Pius VII replies, opposing this. Lord Teignmouth tells William Wilberforce that he has a copy of the Pope's reply in Latin but that "we mean to keep it private, and by no means to suffer it, either in whole or in part, to get into print, for good reasons – we do not even wish it to be public that he has interfered. He calls the Bible Society – or, to use his own words – *Horruimus sane vaferrimum inventum quo vel ipsa religionis fundamenta labefactantur,* etc. – *Fidei labem gravissimumque animarum periculum.* The attempts to establish it *impias novatorum machinationes* and applies the terms *inimicus homo* to Pinkerton, without naming him. Thus we see the Roman religion retains its character."

Here is a translation of the Pope's Latin: "We are appalled by a quite cunning invention, by which in fact the very foundations of religion are shaken…by a most serious undermining of faith and endangering of souls…by the wicked contrivances of newcomers."

The term *inimicus homo* means "enemy" and is more or less consciously derived from the Latin text of Matthew 13:28 ("An enemy has done this") in which context it clearly alludes to the Devil!

Enter Pope Leo XII

In 1823 one of the first acts of Pius VII's successor, Leo XII, is to publish an encyclical in which he attacks Bible Society:

> You are aware, venerable brethren, that a certain Society called the Bible Society, strolls with effrontery through the world; which Society, contemning the traditions of the Holy Fathers, and contrary to the well-known decree of the Council of Trent, labours with all its might, and by every means, to translate, or rather to pervert, the Holy Scriptures into the vulgar language of every nation; from which proceeding it is greatly to be feared that, by a perverse interpretation, the Gospel of Christ may be turned into a human Gospel – or, what is worse, the Gospel of the Devil. To avert this plague, our predecessors published many ordinances, and proofs collected from the Holy Scriptures and tradition, to show how noxious this most wicked novelty is to faith and morals. We exhort you, therefore, by all means to turn away your flocks from these poisonous pastures, being persuaded that if the Scriptures be everywhere indiscriminately published, more evil than advantage will arise on account of the rashness of men...

Fortunately, today the relations between Bible Societies and the Roman Catholic Church are very different. The trustees of many Societies, including BFBS, include Catholics among their number and Pope John Paul II has warmly commended the work of the Bible Societies. You can read this happy story in Act 48.

Meanwhile in Wales...

A MOVE FOR MARY'S FAMILY

In 1820 Mary Jones, her husband Thomas and their two surviving children, Lewis (aged 7) and Jacob (aged 2), move down the valley to Bryncrug. The cottage where they lived still stands and when I was there in 2002, the owners were selling Mary Jones clocks made from the slate of the original roof which has recently been renovated.

Thomas serves as an elder in Bethlehem Chapel in the village. "He was rather a simple character," one writer says of him. The Calvinistic Methodists will bring him under church discipline in 1843 for an offence which apparently is not serious.

In the year the family moves house, Mary's fourth child, Ioan (John), is born. He will eventually emigrate to America and outlive his mother. I cannot tell you whether he ever makes contact with the American Bible Society. If he takes the third Bible presented to his mother by Thomas Charles with him, he doesn't appear to read it much. Mary will complain about the letters he writes to her from across the ocean.

"They have no religion in them," she says.

Act
20

Sad news for the Apocrypha

In one of the three Bibles presented to her by Thomas Charles, Mary Jones wrote a handwritten note which has become famous in Bible Society history. The Bible was a Welsh edition published by SPCK in 1799 and Mary wrote her note at the end of one of the so-called apocryphal books. The Apocrypha (from a Greek word meaning "hidden") is a term used by Protestants to refer to those books of the Bible which were included as part of the Greek version of the Old Testament but not included in the Hebrew Bible. The books were mainly written between 300 BC and AD 100. In the Septuagint (Greek version of the Hebrew Old Testament) they were not distinguished from the other books of the Old Testament.

During the 4th century, many Fathers of the church came to recognise a distinction between those canonical books written in Hebrew, and the rest — although Augustine and some other Fathers continued to consider all as equally canonical.

At the Reformation, many Protestant leaders refused to give the status of inspired Scripture to the Apocrypha, although Martin Luther included most of it as an appendix to his translation of the Bible and said that the books of the Apocrypha were "useful and good to be read". In the Thirty-Nine Articles, the Church of England said of these books that "the Church doth read [them] for example of life and instruction of manners; but yet doth it not apply them to establish any doctrine".

At the Council of Trent, the Catholic Church insisted on the full canonicity of all except three of the books of the Apocrypha. In 1611 the Authorised Version of the Bible did include the Apocrypha as a separate section between the Old and New Testaments. However, the more Puritan-minded Westminster Confession of 1646–47 declared that the Apocrypha was "not to be otherwise approved or made use of than other human writings".

Opinion in the Eastern Church varied until at the Synod of Jerusalem in 1672 it was decided that Tobit, Judith, Ecclesiasticus and the Wisdom of Solomon alone were to be regarded as canonical — although there is still not complete agreement on this amongst scholars of the Orthodox Church.

The common attitude to the Apocrypha in Britain, and favoured by Nonconformists, was one of rejection or at least suspicion. Gradually, the Apocrypha had come to be omitted from many, but not all, editions of the Bible sold in Britain.

The founders of the British and Foreign Bible Society failed to anticipate the grave problems the Apocrypha would cause the Society. They had not anticipated how rapidly the Society's principles and operations would be adopted abroad. Their knowledge of church affairs on the continent of Europe was good but not perfect — in particular they had not studied carefully enough the character of the versions of the Scriptures used by Protestants, Catholics and the Orthodox Church abroad. Or if they did, they did not think through the implications of their actions.

The Society founders had carefully guarded against the insertion of notes and comments in their constitution. However, since the omission of the Apocrypha seemed a natural thing to do in Britain, the Society's early General Committees failed to foresee the extent of the difficulties this would cause abroad.

The Society's Auxiliaries on the continent of Europe worked in countries where the Reformed Churches used Bibles with the Apocrypha included as a separate section and where the Roman Catholic and Greek versions included the apocryphal books interspersed among the other books. Gradually, the British attitude to the Apocrypha began to cause problems abroad.

As early as 1812 the General Committee attempts to persuade foreign Auxiliaries to take the same view of the Apocrypha as has been adopted in England. This leads the Auxiliaries in Berlin, Stockholm, St Petersburg and other places to send urgent letters to London. In June 1813 the General Committee agrees "that the manner of printing the Holy Scriptures by Foreign Societies be left to their discretion provided they be printed without note or comment".

This attempt at a solution to the problem causes problems in Britain and in 1820 the problem is brought to the General Committee for review. On the one hand, there are supporters who contend that to apply funds for the distribution of what they consider an "addition to Scripture" is a violation of a paramount rule of the Society. They strongly object to their money being used to circulate what they see as late Jewish legends, like Tobit, and Bel and the Dragon. On the other hand, there are those who argue that the term "Holy Scriptures" covers the "ecclesiastical Bible" (which even in the Church of England includes the Apocrypha) and that where a country's custom and familiarity lead people to insist on the Apocrypha this is a concession which may legitimately be made.

For two years the issue is repeatedly discussed at the Society's headquarters in Earl Street. On 19 August 1822 the Committee adopts a resolution which attempts to allow Societies receiving grants from London "to apply their own funds in whatever way, as to the printing and circulation of the Apocrypha, it may seem good to them". The resolution inflames an already tense situation. People criticise it as imprecise and evasive. They say that, although it attempts to restrict the way that funds from London are used abroad, grants from the Society will in fact help to circulate the Apocrypha. And so the hard-pressed General Committee has the issue put before it again in December 1824.

London, December 1824–1826

Lord Teignmouth, the now 73-year-old President, isn't well enough to attend the December meeting. He turns to prayer.

"Dear Father, give me the spirit of power, and of love, and of a sound mind that I may be able to speak and act with the wisdom which is from above."

Hardworking and painstaking to the end, he personally drafts a statement attempting to set out the arguments on both sides, but emphasising the fact that the question must be decided by reference to the Society's constitution.

On 20 December the Committee makes another attempt at solving the problem by passing the following resolution:

That no pecuniary grant be made by the Committee of this Society for the purpose of aiding the printing or publishing of any edition of the Bible in which the Apocrypha shall be mixed and interspersed with the Canonical Books of the Holy Scriptures; and that grants of money to Foreign Societies, which are accustomed to publish Bibles containing the Apocrypha, but separate and distinct from the Canonical Books, be made under an express stipulation, and the assurance of the parties receiving the same, that such grants shall be exclusively applied to printing and publishing the Canonical Books only.

A year of bitter controversy follows. In February 1825 the Edinburgh Bible Society sends to Earl Street a "firm and respectful remonstrance". The whole force of Scottish Presbyterianism is directed against the General Committee's resolution, while, from another perspective, in March 26 senior members of the University of Cambridge protest that the Society's resolution violates the fundamental principle of the Society that all Christian communities should work together in pursuit of the same goal. They object that the Society's stance will unnecessarily damage its promising work in Europe.

The Committee now withdraws its previous resolutions and attempts another compromise resolution which makes no reference to money grants but states rather ambiguously that it doesn't wish to interfere with the future distribution of the Scriptures in foreign countries "whether with or without the Apocryphal Books".

At this, the Committee of the Edinburgh Bible Society resolves to discontinue sending money to London till "friendly intercourse" can be renewed "by a removal of the circumstances which led to its interruption". Some Auxiliaries in England and Wales write to London expressing strong views, while others ask for clarification.

Enter a high-level task force

The General Committee now realises that no compromise will satisfy the anti-Apocrypha party. They appoint a special committee of 21 members including Lord Teignmouth, the President, five Vice-Presidents, the Bishop of Lichfield and Coventry, William Wilberforce and Lord Bexley. Lord Teignmouth is unable to attend the first meeting of this committee but sends a note setting out his views. He points out that the rules of the Society state that its "sole object" is "to encourage a wider circulation of the Holy Scriptures" and that it cannot, consistently with these rules, in his view assist the publication by foreign Societies of Bibles which contain the Apocrypha. Crucially and controversially, he doesn't think the Apocrypha can be classed as Holy Scripture. Nor does he think the fact that some English editions of the Authorised Version include the Apocrypha justifies including it in Bible Society editions.

"I urge you to come to a final and positive decision," Lord Teignmouth tells the special committee. "Uncertain and ambiguous resolutions have had embarrassing consequences."

The distinguished members of the special committee deliberate long and anxiously, eventually going along with their President's views. They agree to a recommendation which is accepted a month later by a General Committee meeting which is also attended by 70 members of the Society. The Committee's resolution bans the circulation of the Apocrypha by Societies supported from London. All Scriptures (whether Bibles, Testaments or portions) distributed by Societies supported by the British and Foreign Bible Society will have to be bound, and no books other than those regarded as Holy Scripture by the Society shall be bound with them. This will prevent any foreign Society circulating Bibles containing the Apocrypha from receiving support from London.

"There was no debating," Lord Teignmouth tells his son, "but there were some strong protests made. The resolution was, however, carried by a majority of at least four to one, and I think that the opinion of the country, as expressed in letters, remonstrances, and resolutions, was nearly in the same proportion."

Among those who dissent from the decision are Charles Simeon of Cambridge, Karl Steinkopf, and one of the Society's General Secretaries, Andrew Brandram. Brandram has a double first-class honours degree from Oriel College, Oxford and took over from John Owen as a Secretary of the Society in 1823. His opposition to the Society's line on the Apocrypha doesn't prevent him from remaining in post until his death in 1850 after 27 years of service. Of Steinkopf, Lord Teignmouth tells his son, "I felt for him. For he felt deeply the probable consequences of the resolution, and I love him in my heart."

Steinkopf resigns from his post with Bible Society, partly for reasons of health and partly because, as a Lutheran, he simply cannot agree with the Society's decision to discontinue circulation of Bible versions which include the Apocrypha. However, he will live to take part in the jubilee celebrations in 1854 and will give occasional assistance after his retirement to his successor, Robert Pinkerton.

After 1825, Auxiliaries and national Bible Societies formed in western and northern Europe will be supplemented by the establishment of Agencies of the British and Foreign Bible Society which restrict their own Scripture circulation to the Old and New Testament, and leave to national Societies the circulation of those versions containing the Apocrypha which the churches in their respective countries require.

One qualification for working with Bible Society, as for any organisation, is the ability to look on the bright side. Steinkopf will show the way by observing some years later that "upon the whole, a larger distribution of the Scriptures had taken place than in all probability would have been the case if the Apocrypha question had never arisen".

Pinkerton will look on the bright side from his different perspective. He will observe 16 years later (in 1842) that "a strong and extensive testimony has been borne by the labours of the Society against the improper use which has been made since the Reformation of those uninspired writings, and many individuals have attained to more correct views on this important subject".

In fact, the attitude of German clergy towards the form of

the Scriptures which they have been used to will on the whole continue unchanged. The ever optimistic Pinkerton will put a positive spin on this by observing later that "the energies of the continental Bible Societies have been called forth by our separation from them, to an extent which in all probability would not have taken place had they remained with us; and our Society, by entrusting the circulation of its Bibles and Testaments to individuals, has effected a greater distribution of the Scriptures than it would have produced on the former plan".

It is true that many thousands of Bibles without the Apocrypha in German, French, Dutch, Italian, Spanish, Portuguese, Hungarian, Bohemian, Danish, Swedish, Finnish and other languages will be distributed in Europe by agents and friends of the Society.

There is some concern that at the annual meeting of the Society on 3 May 1826 the controversy will surface again. Lord Teignmouth makes a special effort, despite his continuing poor health, to take the chair for two-and-a-half hours in the Freemasons' Hall. The resolutions putting into effect the decision on the Apocrypha are received and passed – if any disapprovers are present they are silent. Many English Auxiliaries send in resolutions approving of the decision.

The November 1825 resolution, however, does not satisfy Bible Society supporters north of the border. Scots supporters and committee members cannot forget that during the long course of the controversy, concessions have been made to foreign practices of which they disapprove. They assert that there has been a "tampering with the Canon of the inspired Scripture". Even the new resolution and the regulations putting it into effect are dismissed as "evasive or capable of evasion". Dissidents in Scotland encourage a distrust of the whole of the Society's administration in London and even speak darkly about mismanagement of funds.

Earl Street sends a deputation to Scotland to confer with Auxiliaries there. The President sends a letter to the Presbytery of Glasgow defending the course of action the Society has taken. But these attempts to restore the old spirit of cooperation fail. Trust between the two Societies has broken down. Scotland demands a change in the executive at home and abroad which would mean dismissal from the Society of all who have been involved in recent affairs, or are supposed to have been favourable to the circulation of the Apocrypha. A deputation from the General Committee nearly persuades Lord Teignmouth to agree to all its members resigning and leaving their re-election in the hands of subscribers. However, Lord Bexley intervenes to prevent what he considers would be an extreme and unnecessary course of action.

Sadly, the result is that nearly all the Auxiliary Societies in Scotland end their association with Bible Society in London. A pamphlet war continues to rage with a vehemence which is unworthy of a Christian cause. Happily, however, there are more moderate voices in Scotland and on 14 June 1827 a meeting in Edinburgh appoints 27 ministers and "other gentlemen of position" to form a "Committee of Correspondence" with the Society in London. They express their satisfaction with the regulations which the Society has drawn up following the November 1825 resolution and "their entire confidence in the integrity and uprightness of the men whose office it was to carry those resolutions into effect". They issue a statement explaining why they plan to resume friendly relations with London.

As time passes, the bitterness of the prolonged controversy fades, but from 1826 Bible work in Scotland will be carried on independently from London and the original relations between London and the Societies north of the border will never be restored. However at the Society's 50th anniversary, the Duke of Argyll, as President of the Scottish Bible Society, will attend the meeting at Exeter Hall on 8 March 1853. Referring to the differences of the 1820s, he will say that the two Societies have since learned to cooperate well. The National Bible Society of Scotland will be formed in 1861 and play a major role in the international history of Bible Societies.

Act
21

Bad news for the Guernsey Auxiliary

There is no reason to believe that any number of Unitarians (those who reject the doctrines of the Trinity and the divinity of Christ) have ever been members of the Society – certainly none served as officers, agents, or on the Committee – but there was nothing in the rules definitely barring them. So in September 1830 the Guernsey Auxiliary of Bible Society passes a resolution which it sends to Earl Street. The resolution declares that its members, "deeply impressed with the necessity of a simple dependence on the divine blessing, to be derived only through the Lord Jesus Christ, both God and man, pledge themselves to dis-countenance all union with Socinians [Unitarians]; and to pro-mote, to the best of their power, this most desirable object among all other Branch Societies, they earnestly recommend to the par-ent Society totally to withdraw from those who deny the divinity of our Lord". The Rugby Auxiliary sends in a similar resolution and some other Auxiliaries are known to agree with Guernsey and to hope that the matter will become an issue at the 1831 annual meeting. Yet other Auxiliaries tell Earl Street that they support the status quo.

As an initial response, the General Committee circulates a paper signed by the President, a number of the Vice-Presidents, including the Bishops of Winchester, Chester and Lichfield, Lord Bexley, William Wilberforce, the Treasurer, Secretaries and 32 members of the Committee. The signatories state that they object to the proposed alteration "of the fundamental principle of the Society, which admits of the cooperation of all persons willing to assist in the circulation of the Holy Scriptures". They object to the introduction of a "test" which would operate to bar any particu-lar group of people from assisting in the work of the Society. "The sound principles of Christian faith," they argue, "as well as Christian charity, are more likely to be promoted by an adherence to our present constitution than by any change which would occasion a breach in the Society."

Exeter Hall, The Strand, London, 4 May 1831

On 4 May 1831 the annual meeting is held for the first time in Exeter Hall on the north side of the Strand. Built the previous year for £30,000 (nearly £1.5 million at today's values), it is a remarkable building. The main portico opening on to the Strand is dominated (according to Sir James Stephen) by "twin columns, emulating those of Hercules". If we can believe the magazine *Punch* for January–June 1842 it has "staircases of highly polished marble, with banisters of cedar, curiously inlaid with gold". On the ground floor are offices (some later used as the headquarters of YMCA), committee rooms, and a room for "smaller" meetings of 800 people. The main hall, on the first floor can hold 2,500.

Exeter Hall has been built for religious and charitable meetings. Oratorios, especially *The Messiah*, are sometimes performed here. Until 1907 the building and its name will be associated with evangelicalism. In cynical mood, *Punch* tells us that "it is from this Hall that the good and pious, having voted a supply of religion to the black, depart for their own comfortable homes, having, to their exceeding content, indicated their Christianity by paying a pound, singing a hymn, and – taking care of themselves".

Difficult as it is to believe in the early years of the 21st century, the Society's 1831 meeting is the first public meeting in the history of the Society to which women are admitted. There is an unusually large attendance and a sense of expectancy that sparks may fly.

With Lord Teignmouth continuing to be frail, Lord Bexley takes the chair. The President sends a letter expressing his hope and prayer that the proceedings of the day will be characterised by gratitude to God and of expanded love to fellow men. "The basis of our union," he writes, "is the acknowledgment of the divine authority of the Holy Scriptures; and the simple object of our institution is to promote the circulation of them in the widest possible extent. It does not assume the authority of interpreting them; nor does it impose any test for the admission of its members."

William Dealtry, Chancellor of the Diocese of Winchester, moves the adoption of a resolution which has been prepared by the General Committee:

> That this Committee, feeling that it is their duty not only to confine themselves to the prosecution of the exclusive object of the British and Foreign Bible Society, but also to uphold the simplicity of its constitution, under which the contributions and assistance of all persons, without respect to religious distinctions, are admissible, earnestly, respectfully, and affectionately entreat the Committees of the Societies in question [Guernsey and Rugby] to reconsider the resolutions passed at their late meetings, with a view to their returning or conforming to the established principles of this Society.
>
> To the opinions thus expressed your Committee (with two exceptions) continue to adhere; and they are at liberty to state that in their opinion they have the concurrence of your President and many of the Vice-Presidents, together with that of the Committees of several important Auxiliaries, who have addressed them on the subject.

Captain Gordon speaks

Captain James Gordon, Royal Navy, a sturdy, no-nonsense man who was for a while the Member of Parliament for Dundalk, moves this amendment:

> That the British and Foreign Bible Society is pre-eminently a religious and Christian Institution; that no person rejecting the doctrine of a triune Jehovah can be considered a member of a Christian Institution; that in conformity with this principle, the expression "denominations of Christians" in the Ninth General Law of the Society, be distinctly understood to include such denominations of Christians only as profess their belief in the doctrine of the Holy Trinity.

Rev. Lundy Foot then moves another amendment which is designed to restrict the test to the Committee and executive of the Society. Captain Gordon then begins to make a long and rather rambling speech. He generates a lot of noise in the new venue and is frequently interrupted by the Chairman.

Daniel Wilson speaks

Finding that he cannot make himself heard above the din, Lord Bexley asks Rev. Daniel Wilson, the popular evangelical vicar of Islington who will become Bishop of Calcutta in the following year, to call for calm.

"I beg you all," Wilson pleads, "that neither approbation nor dissent be allowed to interrupt the calm, deliberate and Christian spirit in which such a discussion should be conducted."

Rowland Hill speaks

When Gordon finally comes to the end of his address, 87-year-old Rowland Hill stands up. He rebukes what he describes as "an unseemly display of party spirit".

"I wish that all Roman Catholics and Socinians in the world belonged to Bible Societies," he says, "for there they would find the truth to convince them of their errors."

With that, Rowland Hill walks out of the meeting.

William Dealtry speaks

William Dealtry speaks with some eloquence to a resolution he has proposed on behalf of the Committee and is listened to for a while but subjected to frequent interruptions. Those who can follow his speech hear him argue that in the sense in which the expression is used in the first amendment, Bible Society is not a "religious institution".

Luke Howard speaks

Dealtry is supported in a few quiet but effective sentences by Luke Howard, a Quaker chemist who was one of the Society's founders.

"The Society is not a religious body," he says. "It is a society for furnishing the means of religion, but not a religious society. In the Society of Friends we do not own Socinians – but then we are a religious society. I myself have taken some pains to exclude Socinians from these. But had we been engaged only in circulating the Scriptures we should not have felt it needful to exclude them. The moment you establish a Test I will leave you."

After Howard's speech, noisy confusion continues and Lord Bexley realises the danger that the day will pass with no resolution of the issue.

Andrew Brandram shouts above the din

Brandram, Secretary to the Society, moves to the front of the platform and shouts the question: "Whether the ancient law and practice of the Society should continue."

This question, which amounts to the adoption of the Ccommittee's report and resolution is carried on a show of hands by a majority of about six to one. Some amendments are put and not carried.

A messenger arrives at Lord Teignmouth's home in Portman Square to tell the 79-year-old President the result of the vote. He rises from the sofa on which he is lying ill and stretches out his arms.

"I thank God," he says, "for watching over the Society as he has done in our former trials."

Some supporters of the amendments will later mischievously put it about that Bible Society is in favour of Socinians being regarded as Christians. A number of Auxiliaries, however, make it clear to Earl Street that they do not favour a change in the law of membership.

On 7 December 1831 there is another meeting in Exeter

Hall. This time, those who took the view that the Society should have introduced "tests" designed to exclude Unitarians meet and form a new body – the Trinitarian Bible Society which is still active today. It is engaged in the publication and distribution of what its website describes as "faithful and trustworthy versions of the Holy Scriptures" in many languages throughout the world. I had a great-aunt who was a loyal supporter.

Rev. George Browne, historian and secretary of the British and Foreign Bible Society, who lives through these tumultuous days, will recall later that, "it was grievous to [the Society's] conductors and managers to have their motives impugned, their doings misrepresented, and their loyalty to the great Head of the Church brought under imputation and suspicion. It was especially grievous to see the Society deserted by some of its best and warmest and holiest friends – for such they were – who, for a time at least, withdrew their countenance and active aid, even though they did not all join the [Trinitarian] Society."

The story has a happier ending. The Society's next annual meeting, in May 1832, is one of the most harmonious and enthusiastic in its history. What is more, the Revs Gerard and Baptist Noel (the latter of whom seconded one of the test amendments) stand together on the platform and frankly retract the errors into which they say they have fallen.

"We publicly confess that we have done the Society an injustice," they say. "We now take our places once more amongst the friends and advocates of the Society, and as long as we have a voice to use and an arm to lift in its defence we shall assist it in its benevolent designs."

Meanwhile in Wales...

Bryncrug, Wales, 1831

In Bryncrug, the village a couple of miles from the sea where Mary Jones and her husband Lewis live, it is another sad year. Their first child, Lewis, and their sixth and last, Mary, die within days of each other. Lewis is 18 and Mary five. Jacob is still alive, at thirteen, but will die two years later. Ioan is eleven, will emigrate to America and outlive his parents. Ebenezer, if he is still alive, will be nine – but I am not sure when he dies, although we know that he does not survive Mary. It may be that, as so often in the 19th century, tuberculosis is the cause of the early deaths of five of Mary's children.

Mary soldiers on, like so many, especially the poor in these days, learning to live with death. Now in her late 40s, her faith holds. She is noted for her faithfulness at church, her punctuality at meetings, and her love of the Bible.

She reads her Bible daily as long as she is able – reading it right through four times during her life – and she learns large portions of it by heart, which is useful after she loses her sight. She can recite whole chapters of Thomas Charles's *Hyfforddwr* (The Instructor) – his catechism on the principles of the Christian religion – and is fond of the poems of the 17th century poet and preacher, Rhys Prichard. Often she follows visiting preachers from meeting to meeting for a whole day on their visits to the area, even when she is quite old.

Despite her poverty, she gives generously to her church as well as regularly to Bible Society. She is also a donor to her denomination's missionary society, and the first section to which she turns in her monthly magazine, *Y Drysorfa* (The Treasury), is the "Missionary Chronicle". Later in life, when her sight fails, she has to rely on others to read her Bible and favourite magazines to her.

To supplement her income, Mary keeps bees. Robert Griffith, her minister in Bryncrug in later years, remembered:

> She had only a small garden. It was full of various types of fruit, and innumerable bees. She would be there on a fine day in summer like a princess in their midst, and she could pick them up in her hands as if they were corn, or oat flour, without one of them stinging her.

She keeps the income from selling the honey for herself, but divides the income from the sale of the beeswax – which can be a quite considerable sum – between Bible Society and the Calvinistic

Methodist Missionary Society. She believes the reason the bees never sting her, and that their honey and wax are so plentiful and of such good quality, is that the bees know that she dedicates part of the income to their Creator.

Although we know that she met Thomas Charles from time to time until his death in 1814, we are not sure how she regarded her role in the Society's foundation.

Kensington Gore, July 1833

William Wilberforce is now 74 and seriously unwell. His old Quaker friend Joseph Gurney visits him and Gurney later reports that Wilberforce seemed delighted to have an unexpected visitor. They have a long conversation and Gurney will never forget Wilberforce's last words to him.

"With regard to myself," he says to Gurney, "I have nothing whatever to urge but the poor publican's plea, 'God be merciful to me, a sinner!'"

As he lies dying in July, messengers come to tell him that the Emancipation Bill has passed its final stages in Parliament. In addition to the slave trade, slavery itself has now been abolished in the British Empire.

"Thank God! Thank God!" he says, "that I have lived to see this day!"

4 Portman Square, London, 14 February 1834 DEATH OF THE FIRST PRESIDENT

Enter Lord Teignmouth

In the summer of 1833 Lord Teignmouth begins to recover from a serious illness. As he regains his strength, he is told of the death of his long-time friend William Wilberforce. Lord Teignmouth grows silent and introspective. He dictates an apology to the Wilberforce family for not attending the funeral and then looks at his secretary.

"I have myself recently been at the point of death," he says.

The secretary is not sure how to reply.

On Christmas Day, he suffers a relapse in health from which he never properly recovers. He does regain some ability to engage in conversation with friends and is inclined to relate anecdotes from his long and active life. But, his son will recall later, "his favourite and frequent theme was the mercy of God, in preparing him, by a protracted illness, for another world".

His last official act as President of Bible Society is to receive the newly appointed Secretary of the Bible Society, the Rev. George Browne, the Society's second historian.

Early in February 1834 Lord Teignmouth makes a curious prediction to a group of close friends and family.

"I shall die on 14 February, the date of our 48th wedding anniversary."

He proceeds to give this dismayed group detailed instructions for his funeral which he insists must only be attended by immediate relatives – unlike the major occasion which has marked Wilberforce's passing some weeks earlier.

The following Sunday he tells his wife and family, "I feel that I am resting upon the right foundation. I can leave you all rejoicing."

When 14 February arrives, Lord Teignmouth has what is described as a hearty breakfast. Feeling weak, however, he returns to bed. As his son Charles makes him comfortable, he falls asleep.

Exit Lord Teignmouth

The scene at his deathbed transports us back to a different age. Besides his immediate family, three servants sit and watch him sleep: one has served him for 34 years, another for 31 and the third for 28 years. The first President of Bible Society breathes his last at ten minutes to ten. He is 82.

Lord Teignmouth is buried in the parish church of St Marylebone. The epitaph on a monument to his memory records no more than his title, age and the fact that he has been

President of the British and Foreign Bible Society
From its foundation to his death, a period of thirty years.
And formerly Governor-General of India.

None of the friends who erect the monument has any doubts about the achievement which has been closest to his heart.

Lord Teignmouth quietly used the prestige of his rank and previous distinguished career, his wisdom and administrative experience, to guide the Society through its crucial formative years. He set an example of catholicity of spirit, rare in those days, and simple Christian piety. For 30 years he paid relentless attention to almost every detail of the Society's affairs and drafted the early annual reports himself. Only once until 1830 had he been unable to take the chair at the annual meetings. Even when declining health meant he could no longer attend meetings he kept in close touch with the Society's staff and sent them copious memos. He prayed constantly for the work. The Society's troubles and difficulties weighed upon his heart and mind as if they had been in his own family. Lady Teignmouth died five months later.

LORD BEXLEY TAKES OVER

Following Lord Teignmouth's death, the leaders of the Society unanimously agree to invite Lord Bexley to be his successor. We have already met Bexley, defending Bible Society against criticism at the formation of the Cambridge Auxiliary, speaking about the assassination of Spencer Perceval and trying to control the noisy annual meeting which debated the "tests" issue. Now, a deputation of the most distinguished Vice-Presidents of the Society are authorised to interview the 68-year-old former Cabinet Minister and offer him the position. He accepts.

Nicholas Vansittart (as he was known before being elevated to the peerage) was born in April 1766. His father, Henry Vansittart, was Governor of Fort William, Bengal and his mother was the daughter of a Governor of Madras. Vansittart was educated at Christ Church, Oxford, and was called to the bar in 1791. Five years later he was elected Conservative Member of Parliament for Hastings and continued to sit in the House for the next 26 years.

Westminster, January 1801

On a Saturday at the end of January in 1801, Vansittart is present at a reception held by the Speaker of the House of Commons. He soon becomes aware that something momentous has happened but doesn't know what. After some time, Spencer Perceval takes him aside.

"You seem not to realise what has happened," Perceval says. "I wish you would let me take you home to Lincoln's Inn in my carriage."

Once inside the carriage, Perceval says, "Mr Pitt has resigned and the King has sent for the Speaker, who is to be Prime Minister. He will send for you tomorrow morning. I am authorised by Mr Pitt to tell his friends that he wishes as many of them as think with the King on the Catholic question to take office under the new Administration. I hope you will have no difficulty in doing so."

"I think," Vansittart replies, "that the circumstances of the country are so critical that every man who can make himself useful ought to accept any appointment, however difficult or disagreeable."

Henry Addington, the new Prime Minister (later made First Viscount Sidmouth), summonses Vansittart the next morning and offers him the position as one of the Secretaries of the Treasury. Shortly afterwards he is sent to Copenhagen to conduct negotiations with the Danish Government. From Denmark, he joins the English fleet off the coast of Sweden and has a long conference with Admiral Nelson, while Sir Hyde Parker writes despatches which Vansittart takes back to England.

Vansittart becomes a Vice-President of Bible Society in 1811, and, the following year, after the assassination of Spencer Perceval, Lord Liverpool makes him Chancellor of the Exchequer, a post he holds for twelve years, making him the longest continuously serving Chancellor in British history. Only Gladstone, another Bible Society supporter, serves longer (twelve years and four months) but Gladstone is Chancellor in four separate spells. From 1801 to 1828 Vansittart holds Government office for all except two years.

He came to office as Chancellor at one of the most difficult periods in Britain's financial history after long years of costly war which continued until 1815. His opponents pretended not to understand his financial statements, but he was justly able to boast that he took over Britain's finances when they were in deficit and left office with a surplus revenue of £7 million. He had a reputation in Parliament of being an able administrator, a mild-mannered man but somewhat ineffective in debate. He was created Baron Bexley in 1823.

Anniversary meeting, Exeter Hall, The Strand, 7 May 1834

Enter Lord Bexley

Every eye is on the former Chancellor of the Exchequer as he stands to give his first speech as President of the Society.

"For twenty-three years," he begins, "I have been more or less engaged in the management of the concerns of this Society and the defence of its cause. I have never lost sight of its great and glorious object, and have never ceased to pray and wish for its success. I hope to be favoured, in answer to your prayers, with a portion of that Spirit from on high which your late worthy President possessed."

One of Lord Bexley's first duties is to assist in the development of a plan to give a copy of the New Testament and Psalms, clearly printed and well bound, to every freed slave in the British colonies in the West Indies who can read. Distribution of the books begins in August 1834.

Bexley is conscientious in carrying out his responsibilities as President, seldom missing a meeting either of the General Committee or of the more important sub-committees. He will take earnest part in the discussions.

During his long retirement from politics (he will live till he is 85) he will assist in the founding and promotion of Kings College, London.

Bexley died on 8 February 1851 having been an active supporter of the Society for over 40 years and its President for 17. It was said of him that "the primitive simplicity of his character procured him many friends, and his white hair and unworldly gentleness acquired the sort of reverence men are accustomed to feel for a saintly priest. Above all, his perpetual good-nature secured a patient, even half-affectionate attention." There are many surviving portraits of him including one in the hall of Christ Church, Oxford, and a crayon drawing in the National Portrait Gallery.

Act 22

Red tape and red wine for George Borrow

W e have already briefly met George Borrow, perhaps the most colourful character ever to work for Bible Society. As I write, the bicentenary of his birth on 5 July 1803 in East Dereham, Norfolk, is being celebrated by the George Borrow Society which enthusiastically keeps alive the memory of his unusual skills as a writer, his vivid descriptions of life in Britain in the 19th century, his love of gypsies, his linguistic abilities, and his incomparable accounts of his work for Bible Society in Russia, Portugal and Spain. His father, Captain Thomas Borrow, was an army recruiting officer and, with his mother Ann, in Borrow's childhood they constantly shifted home in Scotland, Ireland and many parts of England.

After attending Norwich Grammar School, Borrow was in 1819 articled to a solicitor in Norwich. However, his thoughts turned to literature as a profession. In 1824, on the death of his father, and now six foot two inches tall, he moved to London and started work as a hack writer. In *Lavengro* he described his experiences in London, including humorous accounts of working for the publisher Sir Richard Philips. Then he left London and, as he put it, for a considerable time "lived a life of roving adventures" which he wrote about both in *Lavengro* and *Romany Rye*, in some years outselling the works of Dickens.

His first contact with evangelical Christianity was when he got to know the Skepper family of Oulton Hall, Norfolk. Bible Society first heard of Borrow in 1832 when the Rev. Francis Cunningham wrote to Secretary Andrew Brandram about him. Cunningham was vicar of St Margaret's, Lowestoft, an Evangelical and warm supporter of the Society. Borrow described himself as "a zealous, though most unworthy member of the Anglican Church". A colourful correspondence between Borrow and the Society's Secretaries developed in which Borrow expressed his unbounded confidence in his own abilities at languages and in many other spheres as well.

On one occasion, Society Secretary Joseph Jowett concluded a letter to Borrow with the suggestion that "there is occasionally a tone of confidence in speaking of yourself which has alarmed some of the excellent members of our Committee. It may have been this feeling, more than once displayed before, which prepared one or two of them to stumble at an expression in your letter of yesterday, in which, till pointed out, I confess I was not struck with anything objectionable, but at which, nevertheless, a humble Christian might not unreasonably take umbrage. It is where you speak of the prospect of becoming *useful to the Deity, to man, and to yourself.* Doubtless you meant *the prospect of glorifying God….*"

Borrow walked overnight from Norwich to London for his first interview with the Society's editorial sub-committee. The minutes of the meeting record that the committee expressed to him "the necessity of confining himself closely to the one object of the mission, carefully abstaining from mingling himself with political or ecclesiastical affairs during his residence in Russia. Mr Borrow assured them of his full determination to comply with this admonition, and to use every prudent method for enlarging his acquaintance with the Manchu language".

Eventually, the General Committee accepted a recommendation that Borrow should go to St Petersburg at the Society's expense and be paid a salary of £200 a year to assist in editing the Manchu New Testament. On 31 July 1833 Borrow sailed from London to St Petersburg, armed with letters of introduction to various influential people in Russia.

With his characteristic enthusiasm and colourful turn of phrase, George Borrow wrote to Society Secretary John Jowett in February 1835 from St Petersburg, where he was in the final stages of editing and arranging printing of the Society's edition of the Manchu New Testament: "I am ready to attempt anything which the Society may wish me to execute; and, at a moment's warning, will direct my course towards Canton, Pekin, or the court of the Grand Lama."

Borrow returned to England in September and on 2 November 1835 the Committee "resolved that Mr Borrow be requested to proceed forthwith to Lisbon and Oporto for the purpose of visiting the Society's correspondents there, and of making further enquiries respecting the means and channels which may offer for promoting the circulation of the Holy Scriptures in Portugal".

Andrew Brandram wrote ahead to the Rev. E Whitely, British chaplain at Oporto, introducing Borrow to him as "having proved by experience that he possesses an order of talent remarkably suited to the purposes of our Society... With Portugal he is already acquainted, and speaks the language".

Losing no time, Borrow sailed from London on 6 November and five days later, having made slow progress, the steamship *London Merchant* passed Cape Finisterre in rough seas and lost sight of land.

Deck of the steamship *London Merchant*, off Cape Finisterre, 11 November 1835

Enter George Borrow

Borrow stands on the forecastle talking to two sailors. One of them, who has just got out of his hammock, is 27, the only son of a widowed mother, and considered the best sailor on board.

"I have had the most frightful dream," he tells Borrow, pointing up to the mast. "I dreamt that I fell into the sea from off the cross-trees!"

Several members of the crew hear the sailor say this to Borrow.

Shortly afterwards, Captain Whittingham realises that the wind is increasing.

"Take in the topsails!" he orders.

Some sailors climb the masts and loosen the sails. As they are hauling them down, a gust of wind twists a sail around violently, knocking one of the sailors into the now raging sea.

Borrow watches in horror as, after a few moments, the

sailor's head emerges on the crest of a wave. He recognises him as the man who has told him of his disturbing dream. Borrow will never forget the sailor's agonised look as the ship ploughs on.

The alarm is raised. During the two minutes it takes to stop the steamship, Borrow keeps his eye on the struggling man.

The crew lowers a boat but cannot find the rudder. Two oarsmen try desperately to reach the sailor in huge waves.

When they eventually get to within ten yards of the man, Borrow loses sight of them. At last the small boat returns to the ship. Only two men are aboard.

"We saw him below the water," they gasp, "sinking deeper and deeper, his arms stretched out and his body stiff. There was nothing we could do to save him."

Soon afterwards, the wind drops and the waves subside. *It is almost,* Borrow reflects, *as if the sea is satisfied with the prey it has received.*

Lisbon, November 1835

The *London Merchant* ties up in Lisbon harbour. Portugal has just endured six years of fierce civil war which ended in the defeat of Dom Miguel. Queen Maria II began her reign the previous year at the age of fifteen on the death of the Regent, her uncle, Dom Pedro. Under Dom Pedro's Regency, the many monasteries and convents in Portugal have been closed and their property nationalised. Intrigues and uprisings continue.

Borrow searches for lodgings and eventually finds some dark, dirty and expensive rooms. He thinks Lisbon a noble town in its setting on seven hills on the west bank of the Tagus. On the whole he finds little interest in religion among the Portuguese. Normally acerbic in his comments on Roman Catholicism, he notes that "the people appear in general to have shaken off the old superstition and feel no inclination to bend their necks to another yoke".

At first, Borrow cannot find one person in Lisbon who has read the Bible or knows anything of what it says. When people assure him they can read, he tests their claim by taking a New

Testament in Portuguese from his pocket and asking them to read a few verses aloud. They usually pass the test.

He visits Colhares, a prettily situated village near the sea and asks to see the school. He is taken to a small upstairs room where he finds a master with about a dozen pupils standing in a row. After embracing Borrow, the master offers him the only chair in the room. He shows him the books he uses to teach his pupils — spelling books much like those used in English villages of the day and a book of Catholic teaching.

"Do you use the Holy Scriptures in your school?" Borrow asks.

"Long before the children are well enough educated to understand the Scriptures," the master replies, "their parents take them from school so that they can help them in the fields. They don't really want their children to learn anything, considering time spent in learning wasted time. All the village schools in Portugal are supported by the Government, but many of them have recently been discontinued. Schoolmasters find it difficult to receive their salaries."

"Do you have a copy of the New Testament?" Borrow asks the teacher.

"I do."

"May I see it?"

The book turns out to be an edition of the Epistles translated in the previous century by a Roman Catholic priest, with extensive note and comment.

"Do you think," asks Borrow, "that there's any harm in reading the Scriptures without notes?"

"There's certainly no harm in it," the schoolmaster replies, "but simple people would derive little benefit without the help of notes. Most of what they read would be unintelligible to them."

Borrow shakes hands with the man.

"There's no part of Scripture so difficult to understand," he says before leaving the little school, "as those very notes which are intended to elaborate it. The Almighty would never have inspired his servants to write what was unintelligible to the great mass of people!"

For some days, Borrow explores the area around Lisbon, riding into the fields and talking to country people at work. He reports back to Bible House in London that "notwithstanding many of my questions which must have appeared to them very singular, I never experienced any incivility, though they frequently answered me with smiles and laughter".

Borrow comes to the conclusion that two-thirds of the Portuguese have no knowledge of the Bible at all. He spends less than two months in Portugal and on 6 January 1836, after a five-day journey, he crosses the Guadiana river and enters his first Spanish town, Badajoz. Here he meets gypsies and begins his *gitano* version of the Gospel of Luke which will later be published.

If Borrow were alive today, he would be surprised to learn that in 1972 the Portuguese agency of BFBS gathered a team of interconfessional translators (Catholic and Protestant) and entrusted to them the task of working on a new version of the Bible in current Portuguese from Hebrew and Greek originals. The outcome of this work was the "A Boa Nova" (Good News) version of the New Testament in 1978. In 1989 the translation of the Old Testament was concluded and a new complete edition of the Bible was published in 1993. Over 150,000 copies of this edition have been published. Including all the various editions of this translation, the number of copies printed amounts to over a million.

Under the guidance of Augusto de Almeida Esperança, in January 1989 the Agency of BFBS was organised with a national constitution and a governing body made up of fourteen people from various denominations. In September 1997 Timóteo Cavaco took office as General Secretary of Bible Society in Portugal.

Madrid, February 1836

Borrow finally arrives in Madrid as a salaried agent of the British and Foreign Bible Society in February 1836, at the age of 34. He finds lodgings at 3 Calle de la Zarza close to the Puerta del Sol in the centre of the town. His hostess, a plump woman originally from Old Castile, shows him to his rooms, accompanied by her two daughters. The apartment consists of a huge living room and a small bedroom. The living room is cold and draughty, sparsely furnished with a few chairs, a table and an ancient sofa.

"Did you ever see a more magnificent apartment?" the woman asks. "Is it not fit for a king's son? Last winter it was occupied by the great General Espartero." Baldomero Espartero, after a colourful and successful career in the army, will become Prime Minister of Spain next August.

Borrow's main reason for visiting the Spanish capital is to try to obtain permission from the Government to print the New Testament in Castilian for circulation in Spain. But he carries no letters of introduction to people of influence. Although he trusts that God will grant him success, he is far from sure how he will achieve his objective.

The Prime Minister is Juan Álvarez y Mendizábal, a Jew who began his career as a contractor to the national army. He was forced to take refuge in England for thirteen years during the period of Ferdinand VII's dictatorial rule but had returned to Spain in 1835. Mendizábal appears to wield almost unlimited power, and Borrow decides that it will be vital to persuade him to support his objective of circulating a Castilian New Testament in Spain.

But first he decides to call on George Villiers, the British Ambassador in Madrid. Next year, Villiers will inherit the title of Earl of Clarendon and return to England to become Lord Lieutenant of Ireland and then Foreign Secretary.

Enter Ambassador Villiers

Villiers receives his visitor warmly.

"If you want an interview with Mendizábal," he tells Borrow, "I will endeavour to procure you one, but I must tell you frankly that I cannot hope that any good will come from it. The Prime Minister is violently prejudiced against the British and Foreign Bible Society and is unlikely to encourage any efforts which the Society might make for introducing the New Testament into Spain."

Borrow persuades Villiers to write a letter of introduction for him to take to Mendizábal. Early one morning, he makes his way to the palace where the Prime Minister has his office. It is bitterly cold and he can see a covering of snow on the Guadarrama mountains. For three hours, Borrow waits with several others shivering in an anteroom, hoping for an audience.

At last, Mendizábal's private secretary appears and, after putting various questions to the others, turns to Borrow.

"What is it that you want?"

"I am an Englishman, and the bearer of a letter from the British Ambassador."

"If you have no objection," the secretary replies, "I will deliver it to his Excellency myself."

Borrow hands him the letter from Villiers and the secretary withdraws. After several other individuals have been ushered into the Prime Minister's room in succession, Borrow's turn comes at last.

Enter the Prime Minister of Spain

Mendizábal is standing behind a table covered with papers which he reads apparently with intense interest. He takes no notice of Borrow. The Prime Minister is even taller than Borrow who is himself six foot two inches. His complexion is florid, his features fine and regular, his nose aquiline and his teeth splendidly white. Though less than 50 years old, his hair is grey. He wears a morning gown, a gold chain round his neck and morocco slippers. The Prime Minister's private secretary stands at one end of the table with papers in his hands.

After a quarter of an hour, Mendizábal suddenly looks up and focuses his eyes on Borrow.

Their interview lasts for nearly an hour. As Villiers has warned, the Prime Minister makes no secret of his contempt both for Bible Society and Christianity. Borrow, however, persists in his request and, to his surprise, finds towards the end of the interview that he has made some progress.

"After a few months," Mendizábal tells him, "the country will be in a more tranquil state after our recent upheavals. You should then be allowed to print the Scriptures."

Just as Borrow is about to leave, the Prime Minister says, "Yours is not the first application I have had. Ever since I have held the reins of Government I have been pestered in this manner by the English, calling themselves evangelical Christians, who have come of late flocking into Spain. Only last week a fellow found his way into my cabinet whilst I was engaged in important business, and told me that Christ was coming. And now you have appeared and almost persuaded me to embroil myself yet more with the priesthood, as if they did not abhor me enough already.

"What strange infatuation is this which drives you over lands and waters with Bibles in your hands! My good sir, it is not Bibles we want, but rather guns and gunpowder to put rebels down with, and, above all, money that we may pay the troops. Whenever you come with these three things you shall have a hearty welcome. If not, we really can dispense with your visits, however great the honour."

"There will be no end to the troubles of your country," Borrow replies courageously, "until the Gospel has free circulation."

"I had expected that answer," says Mendizábal, "for I have not lived thirteen years in England without forming some acquaintance with the phraseology of you good folks. Now, pray go. You see how busy I am! Come again whenever you please, but let it not be within the next three months."

And so Borrow is forced to wait in Madrid before making a return visit to the Prime Minister. He is encouraged when, in March, the liberal paper *El Español* publishes articles favourable to English Evangelicals. He gets to know one of the editors who supports the aims of Bible Society and becomes a subscribing member.

Borrow spends a good deal of time correcting proofs of the Spanish New Testament as well as being sociable with Madrid gypsies. Rev. William Rule, a Wesleyan missionary from Cornwall who is working in Spain at this time, will write later about meeting Borrow in Madrid during these weeks. "It was rather amusing to find him receiving a morning visit and taking wine with two gypsy ladies, whom he did me the honour to introduce, one as 'an accomplished highwaywoman' and the other as 'an expert pickpocket'!"

Borrow quickly falls in love with the Madrid of the 1830s. He admits that St Petersburg has finer streets, Paris and Edinburgh more handsome buildings and London nobler squares. But the population of 200,000 Spaniards he finds infinitely intriguing. He grows familiar with the water-carriers of Asturia, dressed in coarse duffel and leather skullcaps, sitting at the side of fountains on their empty casks or staggering with them full to the top storeys of tall houses. And then there are the carriage-drivers of Valencia, lolling lazily against their carts, smoking cigarettes while waiting for customers. The beggars from La Mancha, wrapped in blankets, sit at the palace gates crying out for his charity as he visits Government officials. Years later, he remembers valets from the mountains, house stewards and secretaries from Biscay and Guipuzcoa, bull-fighters from Andalucia, butlers from Galicia and shopkeepers from Catalonia.

Before three months elapse, Prime Minister Mendizábal falls into disgrace and resigns. A group of his former allies forms a new administration which is encouraged by the Queen Regent Cristina, though unpopular in Madrid.

In Borrow's view, the cleverest member of the new Government is a man named Galiano, whom he got to know soon after his arrival in Madrid. Galiano has spent time in England. He dislikes Mendizábal intensely.

Soon after the formation of the new Government, Borrow visits Galiano.

Enter Secretary of State Galiano

"Now or never is the time to make an effort on my behalf," Borrow tells the Minister.

"I will do so," Galiano replies, "but you must have patience for a few days. We are very busy at present. We have been out-voted in the Cortes, and this afternoon we intend to dissolve it. It is believed that the rascals in opposition will refuse to depart. Come along and you may experience a dramatic scene."

Borrow attends the session of the Cortes. After an hour's

debate, the parliament is dissolved. Galiano gives Borrow a letter to his colleague the Duke of Rivas who heads the Ministry of the Interior – the department with the power to give Borrow permission to publish and circulate Bible Society's New Testament.

Borrow walks to the Interior Ministry and without too much delay, he is shown into the Duke's office.

Enter the Minister of the Interior

Rivas is a handsome man, only about 30 years old, an Andalucian who has written a number of books. He receives Borrow affably and listens politely to his request.

"Go to my secretary, go to my secretary," he says. "*El hará por usted el gusto* (He will gratify your fancy)," and then he bows low to indicate that the interview is at an end.

So Borrow goes to the Duke's secretary, whose name is Oliban, an Aragonese, who (according to Borrow) is neither handsome, elegant nor polite.

Enter Secretary Oliban

"You want permission to print the New Testament?"
"I do."
"And you have come to his Excellency about it?"
"Very true."
"I suppose you intend to print it without notes?" Oliban asks.
"Yes," says Borrow.
"Then his Excellency cannot give you permission," says Oliban. "It was determined by the Council of Trent that no part of the Scripture should be printed in any Christian church without the notes of the Church."

"How many years ago was that?" Borrow asks. The Council of Trent met from 1545–63, introducing sweeping reforms into the Catholic Church and clarifying doctrine contested by Protestants during the Reformation.

"I don't know how many years ago it was," Oliban replies, "but such was the decree of the Council of Trent."

"Is Spain at present governed according to the decrees of the Council of Trent?" Borrow asks.

"In some points she is," Oliban answers, "and this is one. But tell me, who are you? Are you known to the British Ambassador?"

"Oh yes," says Borrow. "And he takes a great interest in the matter."

"Does he? That indeed alters the case. If you can show me that his Excellency takes an interest in this business, I certainly shall not oppose myself to it."

Borrow pays another visit to the British Embassy. Ambassador Villiers performs marvellously on behalf of Borrow and Bible Society. He goes to see the Duke of Rivas and speaks to him at length on the matter. The Duke is all smiles and courtesy. Villiers follows this up with a private letter to the Duke which he gives to Borrow and asks him to present to him on his next visit. He writes a letter addressed to Borrow in which he expresses his regard for him, saying that nothing would give him greater pleasure than to hear that he has obtained the permission he seeks.

Borrow returns to the Interior Ministry to see the Duke and deliver the letter.

Re-enter the Minister of the Interior and his Secretary

Rivas reads the letter, smiles sweetly, and extends his arms in a theatrical gesture: *"Al secretario, el hará por usted el gusto."*

Borrow, with a strong sense of déjà vu, hurries to see the Secretary, who receives him coldly. Borrow tells him what the Duke has said and hands him the letter the British Ambassador has written to him. The secretary reads the letter carefully.

"It is evident that his Excellency *does* take an interest in the matter."

The secretary takes a sheet of paper and sits down as if to write out the permission to publish and circulate the New Testament. Borrow is ecstatic. And then, suddenly, Oliban stops and begins to think. He puts his pen in his ear.

"Amongst the decrees of the Council of Trent is one to the effect…"

"Oh dear!" says Borrow and leaves.

When he has recovered himself, Borrow pays another visit to Galiano.

Re-enter Secretary of State Galiano

"A singular person is this Oliban," Borrow says to Galiano. "You cannot imagine what trouble he gives me. He's continually talking about the Council of Trent."

"I wish he was in the Trent up to the middle!" says Galiano in excellent English. "I wish he was there for talking such nonsense. However, we must not offend Oliban – he is one of us, and has done us much service. Moreover, he's a very clever man, but he's an Aragonese, and when one of that nation gets an idea into his head, it's the most difficult thing in the world to dislodge it. However, we will go to him. He's an old friend of mine and I have no doubt but that we shall be able to make him listen to reason."

Borrow calls at the Admiralty Office and goes from there with Galiano to the magnificent Ministry of the Interior where they are shown into Oliban's large office.

Re-enter Secretary Oliban

Galiano takes the secretary aside to a window of the office and holds a long whispered conversation which Borrow cannot follow. Eventually, Galiano comes over to Borrow.

"There is some difficulty with respect to this business of yours. But I have told Oliban that you are a friend of mine and he says that that is sufficient. Remain with him now and he will do everything to oblige you. Your affair is settled. Farewell."

Galiano leaves and Oliban begins writing something. When he has finished, he takes out a box of cigars, lights one and offers Borrow one. The English agent of Bible Society declines. Oliban puts his feet on the table and begins to speak to Borrow in French.

"It is with great pleasure that I see you in this capital, and, I may say, upon this business. I consider it a disgrace to Spain that there is no edition of the Gospel in circulation, at least such a one as would be within the reach of all classes of society, the highest or poorest, one unencumbered with notes and commentaries, human devices, swelling it to an unwieldy bulk. I have no doubt that such an edition as you propose to print would have a most beneficial influence on the minds of the people, who, between ourselves, know nothing of pure religion – how should they? Seeing that the Gospel has always been sedulously kept from them, just as if civilisation could exist where the light of the Gospel does not shine. The moral regeneration of Spain depends on the free circulation of the Scriptures, to which alone England, your own happy country, is indebted for its high state of civilisation and the unmatched prosperity which it at present enjoys. All this I admit, in fact, reason compels me to do so, but…"

Now for it, thinks Borrow.

"…amongst the decrees of the Council of Trent…"

Borrow retains his cool and slips away dejected.

Spring is now far advanced. The sides of the Sierra de Guadarrama mountains have lost their snow. The trees of the Prado are in full foliage, and all the open country around Madrid seems to Borrow to be smiling. The summer heat hasn't arrived and the weather is perfect.

To the west of Madrid is a canal which runs parallel with the Manzanares river and is set in pleasant and fertile meadows. The banks of the canal have been planted with beautiful trees and Borrow finds it a delightful place. As he waits to receive permission to publish and circulate the Spanish New Testament, he relaxes there for hours, watching the shoals of gold and silver fish which bask on the surface of the green sunny waters. He talks to the man who sells oranges and water by a little deserted water-tower opposite a wooden bridge that crosses the canal.

Borrow has more tiresome meetings with Oliban who influences the Duke of Rivas against him.

"The Duke," Galiano tells Borrow, "says that your request

cannot be granted. The other day when I mentioned it in the council, he began to talk of the Council of Trent and spoke of yourself as a pestilent fellow, whereupon I answered him with some acrimony. There ensued noisy argument between us, at which Istúriz [Mendizábal's successor as Prime Minister] laughed heartily. But why do you need a regular permission to print your Testaments, which it doesn't appear anyone has the authority to grant? The best thing you can do under the circumstances is to commit the work to the press, with an understanding that you shall not be interfered with when you attempt to distribute it. I strongly advise you to see Istúriz himself upon the matter. I will prepare him for the interview, and will make sure that he receives you civilly."

Istúriz held office in various liberal Governments from 1808 until 1823, and then – during Ferdinand VII's despotic period – was forced to escape to England until 1834. He will live to hold high office under Isabella II.

Enter Prime Minister Istúriz

Borrow goes to the Prime Minister's office at the palace. He finds an atmosphere of cloistered calm, quite unlike the bustle, noise and activity he found during Mendizábal's administration. To his surprise, there are no other candidates waiting for an interview and he is introduced to the Prime Minister almost at once. He finds Istúriz sitting on a sofa with his arms folded, looking at the carpet. He looks sad and depressed. He looks up at Borrow, smiles and receives him kindly.

"I have lived long in England," Istúriz tells Borrow. "The Bible is free there and I see no reason why it should not be free in Spain also. I am not prepared to say that England is indebted for her prosperity to the knowledge which all her children, more or less, possess of the sacred writings. But of one thing I am sure, that is that the Bible has done no harm in that country, nor do I believe that it will cause any harm in Spain. Print it therefore by all means and circulate it as extensively as possible."

Borrow leaves the palace pleased that he has received, if not written permission to distribute the Spanish New Testament, at least an understanding that his work on behalf of Bible Society will be tolerated in Spain. He desperately hopes that, if the present Government falls, a future one will not interfere with him or appoint a new ambassador who will not support him as valiantly as Villiers has done. Not only has Villiers smoothed the way for Borrow to see Government ministers but he now sends a message to his lodgings to say that he himself proposes to buy a good quantity of Testaments and send them to various British consulates in Spain.

Borrow makes a short visit to England to consult the London Committee. The members agree to print the Spanish New Testament as quickly as possible and that Borrow should be responsible for its distribution. He sails from Falmouth for Cadiz and, in a severe storm which he graphically describes in *The Bible in Spain*, his ship is nearly lost off Cape Finisterre. Eventually, he arrives in Cadiz.

Cadiz, November 1836

Borrow walks into a Cadiz bookseller's shop and produces a London edition of the New Testament in Spanish.

"How do you think a book like this would sell in Cadiz?" he asks.

The bookseller examines the Testament.

"Both the type and paper are exceedingly beautiful," the bookseller tells Borrow, "but it is not a work which is sought after and is very little known."

Borrow travels to Seville on a Spanish steamer which takes him up the Guadalquivir river, arriving in the ancient town at nine on a lovely moonlit night.

Seville and Cordova, December 1836

He visits the Gothic cathedral, climbing its tower, and the Alcázar – the ancient palace of the Moorish kings. He crosses the

Guadalquivir by its bridge of boats and visits the suburb where the *gitanos* (gypsies) live.

He travels on horseback to Cordova, beautifully situated in a loop of the Guadalquivir.

"Don Jorgito," his landlord in Cordova says, "I love the English. They are my best customers. It's a pity that there cannot be greater union between Spain and England and that more English do not visit us. Why should there not be a marriage? The King will speedily be at Madrid. Why should there not be a wedding between the son of Don Carlos and the heiress of England?"

"It would certainly tend to bring a considerable number of English to Spain," Borrow replies, "and it would not be the first time that the son of a Carlos has married a Princess of England." He is thinking of the marriage of Philip II, eldest son of Carlos I of Spain (the Emperor Charles V) to Mary of England in 1555.

The host muses for a moment and then exclaimes, "*Carracho*, Don Jorgito, if this marriage could be brought about, both the King and myself should have cause to fling our caps in the air!"

Madrid, Christmas 1836

On his return to Madrid, Borrow takes rooms on the third floor at 16 Calle de Santiago, near the palace. He greatly admires his 35-year-old hostess, Maria Diaz, leaving us with a vivid description of her good looks and fine figure. "During the remainder of my sojourn in Spain," he recalls later, "I found [her to be] a firm and constant friend, and occasionally a most discreet adviser. She entered into all my plans, I will not say with enthusiasm, which, indeed, formed no part of her character, but with cordiality and sincerity, forwarding them to the utmost of her ability... Her motives were of the noblest kind – friendship, and a proper feeling of the duties of hospitality: no prospect, no hope of self-interest, however remote, influenced this admirable woman in her conduct towards me."

Borrow visits George Villiers, still British Ambassador to Spain despite a turbulent and rapidly changing political situation.

Villiers receives him with his usual warmth.

"Do you think," Borrow asks, "that I might venture to commence printing the Scriptures without any more application to Government?"

"You obtained permission of the Government of Istúriz," Villiers replies, "which was a much less liberal one than the present. I am witness to the promise made to you by the former ministers, which I consider sufficient. You had best commence and complete the work as soon as possible without any fresh application. Should anyone attempt to interrupt you, you have only to come to me whom you may command at any time."

Borrow leaves the British embassy elated. Within three months he arranges publication of 5,000 copies of a Spanish edition of the New Testament. The Testament is printed in Madrid at a small firm owned and run by Don Borrego, a local author and newspaper editor. Bible Society's edition is of course free of any note or comment and produced in a handsome cover.

Borrow plans to leave copies of the Testament with selected booksellers in Madrid and then ride into Spain establishing depots in smaller towns. He will, as he records, "visit the people in secret and secluded spots to talk to them of Christ, to explain to them the nature of his book, and to place that book in the hands of those whom I should deem capable of deriving benefit from it. I was aware that such an undertaking would be attended with considerable danger, and very possibly the fate of St Stephen might overtake me; but does the man deserve the name of the follower of Christ who would shrink from danger of any kind in the cause of him whom he calls Master?"

He buys a horse and looks out for a servant. Don Borrego recommends a Greek to him, Antonio Buchini, who turns up at Borrow's lodgings for an interview.

Enter Antonio

The Greek is dressed in the French style and looks very young though he turns out to be over 40. He is just above middle height without an ounce of spare flesh. He has wiry black hair, a low forehead, and small, grey eyes which look subtle and slightly malicious – but hinting at a sense of humour. It becomes clear from what Antonio tells Borrow that he is hot-tempered and has worked for and then left a whole series of employers.

"I'm afraid," Borrow tells him, "that you are of a turbulent disposition, and that the disputes to which you have alluded are solely to be attributed to your bad temper."

"What would you have, Monsieur?" Antonio replies. "*Moi je suis Grec, je suis fier, et j'ai des principes d'honneur.* I expect to be treated with a certain consideration, though I confess that my temper is none of the best, and that at times I am tempted to quarrel with the pots and pans in the kitchen. I think, upon the whole, that it will be for your advantage to engage me, and I promise to be on my guard."

"But you say you are a married man," Borrow says. "How can you desert your wife? For I am about to leave Madrid and to travel into the remote and mountainous parts of Spain."

"My wife will receive half my wages while I am absent, and therefore will have no reason to complain of being deserted. My wife is too well instructed to complain. She never speaks in my presence, unless I give her permission! Am I not a Greek, and do I not know how to govern my own house?"

Borrow asks Antonio's terms. They are extravagant – but he agrees to work for half the figure he names.

"Then I will engage you," says Borrow.

Antonio seizes a tureen of soup on a table, places it on his forefinger and twirls it around above his head without spilling a drop. He fetches a *puchera* (pot for stew) from the kitchen and performs the same trick with this, before placing it on the table in front of the astonished Borrow.

The relationship between Antonio and Borrow works and he serves this remarkable Bible Society agent for many months with courage and loyalty, sharing his adventures. Antonio some-times refers darkly to his "affairs of Egypt" – Borrow later discovers that this actually means his involvement in smuggling.

In May, Borrow receives a visit from Henry Southern of the British embassy.

Enter Henry Southern, in self-important mode

"Ambassador Villiers has asked me to communicate to you a res-olution which he has come to. Being apprehensive that, alone and unassisted, you would experience great difficulty in propagating the Gospel of God to any considerable extent in Spain, he is deter-mined to exert to the utmost his own influence to further your views, which he himself considers, if carried into proper effect, extremely well calculated to operate beneficially on the political and moral state of the country.

"To this end it is the Ambassador's intention to buy a very considerable number of copies of the New Testament, and to despatch them forthwith to the various British consuls established in the different parts of Spain, with strict and positive orders to employ all the means which their official situation affords them to circulate the books in question and to assure their being noticed. The British consuls are, moreover, to be charged to give you, whenever you appear in their respective districts, all the protec-tion, encouragement and assistance which you should stand in need of."

Forgiving Southern his pompous language, the visit thrills Borrow who believes that it is the first instance of a British ambas-sador making the Bible Society cause a national one and favour-ing it so directly.

Borrow and Antonio travel through Old Castile, north of Madrid, selling the newly published Testaments wherever they can.

The Spanish side of the Portuguese border, early summer 1837

The two men enter the valley of Bembibre in the south of the region of El Bierzo, Leon. The area is mountainous with Alpine-like passes, trout streams, pleasant meadows and, in Borrow's day, groves of chestnut and walnut. They enjoy the scene: the sun is high in the sky, but there is some shade from trees and cool air rising from a stream, a tributary of the river Minho. Gentle breezes blow across the meadows. The Englishman and his Greek servant arrive at a plain where tall grass is waving and chestnut trees are in full blossom, spreading giant boughs.

Beneath the chestnut trees are many carts with tired oxen lying on the ground, the crossbars of the poles they support pressing heavily on their heads. Their drivers are either cooking a meal or enjoying a delicious *siesta* in the shade. Borrow walks up to one of the groups of men.

"Are any of you in need of the Testament of Jesus Christ?" he asks.

The men stare at one another and then at Borrow in silence. At last a young man lying on the ground with a rifle in his hand speaks.

"What is a Testament of Jesus Christ? Are you Catalan, for you speak hoarse and are tall and fair like them?"

Borrow sits down among the men.

"I am no Catalan. I come from a spot in the western sea many leagues from here to sell a book at half the price it cost to make. Your souls' welfare depends on your getting to know this book."

Borrow tells the men what sort of book the New Testament is and reads them the parable of the sower. The men stare at each other again.

"We are poor," one of them says, "and cannot buy books."

Borrow stands up and mounts his horse. "Peace be with you," he says.

The young man with the rifle stands up.

"*Caspita!* (Wonderful!) This is odd." He snatches the New

Testament from Borrow's hand and hands him the money he asks for.

Galicia, north-western Spain, summer 1837

At Lugo, the only town in Spain to be completely enclosed within Roman walls, Borrow finds a wealthy bookseller and hands him a letter of recommendation from Madrid.

"I will gladly undertake to sell your Testaments," the bookseller tells Borrow.

Borrow sells 30 New Testaments in one day. The Bishop of Lugo buys two copies for himself. Several priests speak well of the books and recommend them to others.

Borrow sets up a depot in Coruña, stocking it with five hundred Testaments, from which he intends to supply the principal towns of Galicia. He circulates adverts for the books and sells an average of seven or eight copies a day – not a huge number, but encouraging to Borrow who reflects that a few months earlier it was almost impossible to buy a Spanish New Testament anywhere in Spain.

Santiago de Compostela, summer 1837

Here, at one of Spain's most beautiful cities, built in a warm golden granite (and today a World Heritage site) Borrow meets a colourful character who will help him in the work of selling Scriptures. Rey Romero, about 60 and the town's bookseller, is comfortably off, respected, and takes up the Bible cause with enthusiasm. Citizens of Santiago come into his large and splendid shop in Rua da Azabacheria, asking to buy one of the popular storybooks of Spain.

"Why don't you buy this book instead?" Romero says. "It's a sacred volume which is better, more instructive and even more entertaining than what you have asked for."

He is often successful and customers leave his shop clutching one of the beautifully bound New Testaments which Borrow has had printed and Bible Society in London has financed.

Romero takes a liking to Borrow and regularly visits him in the evenings at his *posada* (small hotel). The two men spend many hours walking about the town and its surrounding countryside together.

Borrow's travels in the northern provinces of Spain occupy him for most of the year 1837. By the time he returns to Madrid, the New Testament is enjoying a quiet sale in the principal towns of northern Spain.

Madrid, autumn 1837

Back in the capital he takes an important step. He opens a shop for the sale of Bibles in the Calle de Principe, a busy and upmarket street near the Square of Cervantes, and furnishes it handsomely with glass cases and chandeliers. He erects a sign outside which reads *Despacho de la Sociedad Bíblica y Estrangera* (Office of the Biblical and Foreign Society) – rather an odd rendering of the Society's title! He hires a shrewd Gallegan, Pepe Calzado, to run the business and give him a weekly account of sales.

During 1837–38 Borrow finds time to translate the Gospel of Luke into the Spanish gypsy and Basque languages. Throughout his life, he takes an interest in gypsies in many countries and spends time with them. The first and second editions of his translation of Luke in Spanish gypsy are held in the Society's library in Cambridge.

Borrow runs into a good deal of opposition from some (but not all) Catholic priests who try to influence the Government against him. In January 1838 he receives an order to sell no more New Testaments. Sir George Villiers advises Borrow to write a description of Bible Society and its objectives in Spain. The Ambassador delivers this personally to the new Prime Minister, Count Ofalia.

"What a pity that this is a Protestant Society, and that all its members are not Catholics!" the Prime Minister comments when he reads Borrow's paper.

To Borrow's surprise, Ofalia sends a message to Borrow requesting a copy of his gypsy Gospel. Borrow arranges for a copy of his edition of Luke to be handsomely bound and takes it himself to the Prime Minister's office. He finds the Count to be "a dusky, diminutive person, between 50 and 60 years of age, with false hair and teeth", but courteous. He receives the Gospel warmly.

"With regard to your New Testament," Ofalia tells Borrow, "the subject is surrounded with difficulties. The great body of the clergy has taken up the matter against you. The civic Governor of Madrid has issued a prohibition against your selling the New Testament. However, be patient and peaceable. I will endeavour to devise some plan to satisfy you. I am afraid that the bishops hate a sectarian more than an atheist!"

By "sectarian", the Prime Minister means a member of a Christian denomination other than the Roman Catholic Church. Borrow notices that throughout their interview Ofalia constantly looks behind and around him, as if in dread of being overheard. The two men part on good terms, but Borrow wonders how such a timid man has become Prime Minister of Spain.

Cárcel de la Corte Prison, Madrid, May 1838

On 1 May Borrow is arrested by an over-zealous officer who has allowed himself to be excessively influenced by local priests. He is escorted to Madrid's Cárcel de la Corte Prison – where he is given the best room and allowed to have furniture, food and wine brought to him by Maria Diaz and his servant. The British Ambassador takes up the case and treats it as an infringement of the rights of an Englishman. The Spanish Government expresses its regret. Borrow records vivid descriptions of his colourful fellow prisoners and leaves the prison on 12 May vindicated and triumphant. The authorities offer to dismiss the police officer who has arrested him – but when Borrow discovers that the man is married with a wife and family to support, he asks that he may retain his post.

"Whatever I do in future connected with the Gospel," he writes, "is to have the sanction of the Government who have expressed a desire to cooperate with the Bible Society towards the civilisation of the country."

He has an interview with the Archbishop of Toledo which he describes as "satisfactory to a degree I had not dared to hope for" and the prospect seems brightening for him when a setback occurs.

An Irishman with some charm, but inclined to be reckless and insensitive, finding himself underemployed in Gibraltar, Lieutenant Graydon resolved to do all he could to bring the Gospel to Spain. Working with Bible Society, but without a regular commission, he has circulated copies of the New Testament as far north as Barcelona and has begun to print the New Testament in Catalan and an edition of the Spanish Bible. By the beginning of 1838, in addition to consignments sent from Bible House in London, Graydon has overseen the printing of Bibles and New Testaments from a Spanish printing press.

Enter Lieutenant Graydon

At Almeria, on the south coast east of Malaga, Graydon reports that many priests come and buy copies of Bibles and Testaments and seem, at first, content with what they read. However, after three days, they appeal to the Bishop to put an end to the sales, giving as their reason the fact that title pages of the Bibles do not reveal the place where they have been printed. The Bishop has the edition of the Spanish Bible compared word for word with the Vulgate and sends out a written order that Graydon's work is not to be interfered with.

So far so good, and at first Graydon's work is remarkably successful. However, he has less insight than Borrow into the unstable political situation in Spain, the suspicions, pressures and precarious position of political office holders and the hostility of many of the priests. The Committee in London doesn't seem fully to understand these sensitivities either. The problem becomes acute when Graydon goes public in Malaga with a document which unwisely sets out his opinions on Catholicism in a style which will inevitably generate opposition to the Bible cause. Sure enough, the Spanish Government prohibits all Bible operations within the country and orders the seizure of all Bibles and Testaments.

Enter the British Ambassador

Sir George Villiers, bends over backwards to be tolerant towards Graydon's hamfistedness. He sends a note to the British Consul in Malaga referring to a letter the Prime Minister has sent to Graydon. The Ambassador's note looks as if it has been drafted by Henry Southern. It is a classic example of an official of the British Government patiently intervening to pour oil on troubled waters following excessive zeal by a servant of Bible Society.

> You will communicate Count Ofalia's note to Mr Graydon, and tell him from me that, feeling as I do a lively interest in the success of his mission, I cannot but regret that he should have published his opinions on the Catholic religion and clergy in a form which should render inevitable the interference of the ecclesiastical authority. I have no doubt that Mr Graydon, in pursuit of the meritorious task he has undertaken, is ready to endure persecution, but he should bear in mind that it will not lead him to success in the country, where prejudices are so inveterate, and at this moment, when party spirit disfigures even the best intentions. Unless Mr Graydon proceeds with the utmost circumspection it will be impossible for me to defend his conduct with the Government, for no foreigner has a right, however laudable may be his object, to seek the attainment of that object by infringing the laws of the country in which he resides.

Borrow is of course much more outspoken in his letters to the London Committee. His annoyance is understandable. Although he manages to rescue all the books from his shop in Madrid, at Salamanca, Seville, Malaga and in other parts of the country, the precious depots he has taken so much trouble to establish are seized by the authorities. However, the situation is eased, and the authorities' prohibitions on Bible work lifted, when Graydon turns his attentions to France in June 1838. Well over a decade later (long after Borrow's formal connection with the London Committee has ended), Graydon is in 1851 appointed Agent of the Society with responsibility for its work in Switzerland and northern Italy where he will serve until 1860.

Four months later, after he has distributed 3,000 Testaments and 500 Bibles during the year, put the affairs of the Society in Spain in order, and recovered from a sharp attack of fever which is perhaps linked to one of his periodic bouts of depression, Borrow returns to England. He seeks to correct "misunderstandings" — Society spin for some very cross words indeed — which have arisen between him and Bible House over the Graydon incident.

Act
23

Cheap and godly books for sale

By December 1838 Borrow is back in Spain for his fourth and final visit, full of optimism. He is convinced that every village in Spain will show an interest in the Scriptures. In the summer of 1839, he and Antonio travel to the large village of Villa Seca (today it has a population of 30,000), south of Madrid, where they are entertained for some weeks by Juan Lopez, husband of his hostess in the capital, Maria Diaz (who has retained her maiden name).

Villa Seca, Toledo district, south of Madrid, early summer 1839

On the banks of the Tagus, Borrow visits a school at Villa Seca where nearly 60 pupils are given a basic education. The headmaster, a tall slim man of about 60, wears one of the peaked hats of Andalucia. Though it is intensely hot, he keeps his long cloak on throughout the day. Borrow shows him one of the Society's Spanish New Testaments.

The headmaster examines the Testament for a long time without speaking and then puts it down with a sigh.

"I should be very happy to purchase some of these books for my school, but from their appearance, especially from the quality of the paper and binding, I am afraid that to pay for them would exceed the means of the parents of my pupils. They have very little money, being poor labourers. I blame the Government for establishing schools without supplying the necessary books. In my school there are just two books to be used by all the pupils – and these contain little that is good."

"What do you think the New Testaments are worth?" Borrow asks.

"Señor Cavalier," the headmaster replies, "to speak frankly,

I have in other times paid twelve reals for books inferior to yours in every respect. But I assure you that my poor pupils would be unable to pay the half of that sum."

"I will send you as many as I can for three reals each," says Borrow. "I am acquainted with the poverty of the land, and my friends and I, in affording the people the means of spiritual instruction, have no wish to curtail their scanty bread."

"*Bendito sea Dios!* (Blessed be God!)" says the headmaster.

The delighted head buys twelve copies.

East of Madrid, summer 1839

Borrow approaches the village of Cobeña dressed in the style of the peasants of Segovia, in Old Castile, wearing a leather jacket and trousers, and a hunting-cap on his head. He leads a donkey with a sack of Spanish New Testaments across its back. On the edge of the village, he meets a young woman who is holding a little boy by the hand. He assumes they are brother and sister.

"*Vaya usted con Dios,*" he says, using the customary greeting.

"Uncle," she replies, "what is that you have got on your donkey? Is it soap?"

"Yes," replies Borrow. "It is soap to wash souls clean."

"What do you mean?"

"I carry cheap and godly books for sale."

"May I see one?" asks the young woman.

Borrow takes a copy out of his pocket and hands it to her. She begins reading the New Testament aloud and continues for about ten minutes, occasionally pausing to say, "*Que lectura tan bonita, que lectura tan linda!* (What beautiful, what charming reading!)"

"How much is the book?" she asks, when she has finished reading.

"Only three reals," says Borrow.

"Although what you ask is very little," replies the young woman, "it is more than I can afford to pay. There is little money in these parts."

"I'm sorry," says Borrow, "but I cannot dispose of the books for less than this."

He says goodbye. After he has walked about 30 yards, he hears the boy running behind him.

"Stop, Uncle, the book, the book!" the boy shouts, breathlessly.

When he catches Borrow up, the boy hands him three copper reals, takes the Testament and runs back to his older sister, flourishing the book over his head in glee.

When he reaches Cobeña, Borrow sees a group of people, mainly women, standing outside a house. He takes some Testaments out of the sack and arranges them so that the group can see them. Each person takes a copy and some begin to read them aloud. But after nearly an hour, he has only sold one copy.

"We are living through very hard times," one of the women explains to him apologetically. "But your books are wonderfully cheap and appear to be good and Christian-like."

As Borrow is about to repack his books and leave, the local priest arrives on the scene. He examines the books carefully and looks hard at Borrow.

"What is the price of these books?" he asks.

"Three reals."

"The binding is worth more," the priest replies. "I'm afraid that you have stolen the books. I think perhaps it is my duty to have you sent to prison as a suspicious character. On the other hand, the books are good, however you obtained them. I will buy two copies, please."

As soon as the villagers hear that their priest recommends the books and has bought two for himself, they hurry off to find the needed money. Very quickly, Borrow sells nearly 30 copies.

At the next village, Borrow shows one of his Testaments to a woman he meets.

"I have a child at school and would like to buy one for him," she says, after examining the binding of the New Testament. "But first I want to know whether this book will be valuable for him."

The woman goes away and returns later, accompanied by the village schoolmaster who is followed by all the children of his school walking in a neat crocodile line. She shows the Testament to the schoolmaster.

"Would this be something useful for my son?"

The teacher looks at the Testament and then at the woman.

"You are a simpleton for asking such a question!" he says to the woman. "I know the book well. *No hay otro en el mundo!* (There is no equal to it in the world!)"

"I will buy five copies for my pupils," says the schoolmaster, turning to Borrow. "I regret that I have no money to buy more, otherwise I would buy your whole cargo."

"I want four copies," says the woman to Borrow. "One for my son, one for my late husband, one for myself, and a fourth for my brother. I am expecting him home tonight from Madrid."

Borrow wonders how the woman's deceased husband will benefit from the Testament, but gladly sells the delighted woman her four books.

Madrid, summer 1839

Back in the capital, Borrow selects what he describes as "eight intelligent individuals", five of whom are women, and sends them out into every district of Madrid. In fifteen days they sell 600 New Testaments. Every house in the then wealthy Calle Montera, now a red-light area, and the Puerta del Sol takes a copy.

To Borrow's surprise and delight, the curates of two Catholic churches in Madrid teach about 20 children Bible stories using Bible Society's 1837 edition of the Spanish New Testament. The churches are San Ginés in the Calle del Arenal and the Chapel of Santa Cruz in the Concepcion Jerónima. He thinks that this development alone justifies the Society's expense in publishing and supplying the Scriptures to Spain.

The supply of Bibles from London and Spanish printing presses does not keep up with what Borrow sees as the demand. "Had I been possessed of 20,000 Bibles in the spring of the present year, I could have disposed of them without leaving Madrid."

Borrow now prepares to draw his work in Spain and

Portugal to a close. "When the Bible Society has no further occasion of my poor labours," he writes to Andrew Brandram at Bible House, "I hope it will do me justice to the world. I have been a faithful and zealous servant. I shall on a future occasion take the liberty of addressing you as a friend respecting my prospects. I have the materials of a curious book of travels in Spain; I have enough metrical translations from all languages, especially the Celtic and Slavonic, to fill a dozen volumes, and I have formed a vocabulary of the Spanish Gipsy tongue, and also a collection of the songs and poetry of the Gitanos with introductory essays. Perhaps some of these literary labours might be turned to account."

Before he left Spain, Borrow was for the second time illegally arrested and put in prison, this time in Seville. Although the chief magistrate responsible for his arrest was dismissed from his post, and Borrow was released, he decided that he would have no peace from the Spanish Government and clergy as long as he remained in the country. He looked back with satisfaction on his success in distributing the Madrid edition of the New Testament, "by far the greater part having been dispersed amongst the peasantry of Spain, and the remainder amongst the very poor of the towns, the artisans of Madrid and Seville, the water-carriers and porters. You will rarely find a copy of this work in the hands of the wealthy and respectable, but you will frequently light upon it in the huts of the labourers, in the garrets or cellars of the penniless, and even in the hulks and convict-prisons. I myself saw it in the prison of Seville. As for the few copies of the entire Bible which I had at my disposal, they have been distributed amongst the upper classes, chiefly amongst the mercantile body, the members of which are upon the whole by far the most intellectual and best-educated of the subjects of the Spanish monarchy".

So came to an end the period which Borrow later described as "the most happy years of his existence". In *The Romany Rye* (1857), published nearly 20 years after his connection with Bible Society ended, as he recalled his work in Spain (writing of himself in the third person) "the blood glowed in his veins – oh, the marrow awoke in his old bones, when he thought of what he had accomplished in the cause of religion and civilisation, with the colours of that Society in his hat". In four years he had circulated nearly 14,000 copies of the Scriptures in Spain. It used to be said that between 1837 and 1839 Borrow's letters to the *Morning Herald* in London often anticipated Government despatches.

T H Darlow said of Borrow's many vivid letters home to the Society that they revealed his "singular genius, with so much that was impulsive and inflammable in his temperament, acting with conspicuous ability, energy, and business tact". They will "convince every unbiased reader that Borrow, with whatever prejudices and limitations, had a fierce sincerity of faith. Perhaps he should have been called a 'Bible Christian' in the literal sense of the words. He believed passionately in the book he sought to circulate. His gorge rose against the Church of Rome because what he saw of its practical working in the Peninsula appeared to him a perversion and caricature of the religion of the New Testament".

The Life of Ramon Monsalvatge, the story of a Spanish monk who converted to evangelical Christianity, tells of Señor Calderon, an ex-priest who finds the Bible treasured in many homes in Madrid. In one family, in which the father is very ill, he talks to the man and then suggests that they pray. On rising from his knees, the sick man extends his hand and says, "Why, I see that you too have been saved by the blood of Christ."

"How did you learn that salvation comes that way?" Calderon asks.

"From a book which I have received. Here it is. I received it from an Englishman some time ago."

It was one of Borrow's Bibles.

Borrow arrived back in London on 16 April 1840 and on 23 April he married Mary Clarke, the widow of a naval officer whom he met in Spain. With the proceeds from the sale of his writings he completed the purchase of an estate in Oulton Broad. He allowed gypsies to pitch their tents on the estate, mingling with them as friends as he had done in Spain. The summerhouse where he settled down to write his best-selling books still stands in the grounds. Borrow died on 26 July 1881 in Oulton, Suffolk, aged 78.

"Great news" for the chief

In 1816, the London Missionary Society (LMS) sent Robert Moffat to South Africa where, in Namaqualand, he persuaded the Hottentot chief known as Africaner to become a Christian. This reconciled the chief to the British Government who proceeded to give Moffat official support. From 1821 to 1830 he worked among the Bechuanas and began a translation of the Gospel of Luke in Sechuana – the first of a series of translations.

Namaqualand (South Africa/Namibia)

When Moffat completes his Sechuana New Testament, he stands one day before a fierce Chuana (Tswana) warrior in all his battle dress. Opening the book at John 3:16, Moffat reads the familiar words to him in his own language: "For God so loved the world, that he gave his only begotten Son, that whosoever believes in him, should not perish, but have everlasting life."

The chief leans forward with eager attention and shouts out, "Read it again!"

Moffat reads it slowly and emphatically a second time. The warrior cries, "Read it again!" and the missionary reads it a third time.

Then, throwing his arms above his head, the chief shouts his response, "Ah! That is great news! Great news! *Our gods do not love.*"

Enter David Livingstone

Just as Moffat finishes translating the whole Bible into Sechuana in 1838, LMS sends David Livingstone to help him distribute them. Livingstone will become the most famous of all LMS missionaries. Bible Society funds the printing of an edition of 5,000 copies of Moffat's Testament and Psalms in 1841 and sends supplies out to the missionaries. Livingstone carries a consignment of 500 of these up country from Algoa Bay to Lattakoo. Africans pay for these Scriptures in corn, goats and sheep. Many of them are still unable to read but the missionaries begin opening schools.

There are already some African Christian teachers in Lattakoo. They receive their Testaments with delight.

"We have never heard of such a thing," they say. "Our fathers, who have died in darkness, could not tell us about it. We thought it was a thing to be spoken to – but now we know that it has a tongue, which speaks and will speak to the whole world. Here is the book, and it can talk where there are no teachers. If a believer reads it, it tells the same news. If an unbeliever reads it, the book is still the same. This book will teach, preach and tell the news, though there were no other teachers in the country."

All this convinces Bible Society that "the New Testament itself is the most evangelical of evangelists, the most energetic of reformers, the most ubiquitous of missionaries". But the Society will continue to pursue its work in vigorous partnership with missionaries all over the world.

In 1845 Livingstone marries Moffat's daughter Mary. The couple begin making exploratory treks northwards to search for what Livingstone calls "the fleeing tribes of the north". In 1849 David and Mary will cross the Kalahari desert and become the first Europeans ever to see the shores of Lake Ngami (north-western Botswana). In 1850, both alone and with his wife and children, Livingstone will explore the banks of the Zambezi River above the Kalahari, and in 1855, travelling east, he will be the first European to see the Victoria Falls.

Livingstone now speaks Sechuana fluently, but is unable to communicate with most of the tribes he meets north of Kuruman. However, they prove invariably friendly towards the Scots doctor-missionary-explorer and without their food and help he would die on his travels. When he returns to Britain in 1856 he will publish his *Missionary Travels and Researches in South Africa* and become a celebrity in Europe and America. His writings about the evils of the slave trade result in the establishment of Scots missions at

Blantyre and Livingstonia in what is now Malawi. The world will hear even more of David Livingstone in the years ahead.

What is the secret of Livingstone's power? We get one clue from an entry he will put in his diary on 3 October 1871: "I read the whole Bible through four times whilst I was in Manzuena."

Act
25

Best-loved man in the kingdoms

When Lord Bexley dies in 1851, the members of the General Committee have no doubt that they should invite the Earl of Shaftesbury (known as Lord Ashley until the death of his father in that year) to become their next President. Ashley has been connected with the Society since 1846 when he was made a Vice-President and spoke at the annual meeting. A deputation on behalf of the Committee, including the Marquis of Cholmondeley, the Earl of Harrowby and Sir Robert Harry Inglis, visits Shaftesbury to convey the invitation. At first, he hesitates to accept, and they renew the invitation a few days later. As they wait for his reply they may well have reflected on the man they were inviting to take over the helm of the Society.

Shaftesbury was educated at Harrow and Christ Church, Oxford (like his predecessor), where he gained a first-class honours degree in Classics. In 1826 he began his parliamentary career as a member of the Conservative Party. By birth an aristocrat, he spent his life fighting causes that neither his party nor his class always tackled with enthusiasm. He must be awarded the title of the most eminent social reformer of the 19th century.

While at Harrow he had been horrified by the sight of a pauper's funeral and had from that moment dedicated his life to the cause of the poor and underprivileged. After reading Scott's commentary on the Bible, he wrote, "I have a great mind to found a policy upon the Bible, in public life observing the strictest justice, and not only cold justice, but active benevolence." Charles Dickens was always a warm admirer of Shaftesbury and became his close ally in his reforming work. This reminds us that when his youngest son was leaving home to join his brother in Australia, Dickens wrote him a letter in which he said, "I put a New Testament among your books for the very same reasons and with the very same hopes that made me write an easy account of it for you when you were a little child – because it is the best book that ever was or will be known in the world, and because it teaches you the best lessons by which any human creature who tries to be truthful and faithful to duty can possibly be guided."

When, after prayer and reflection, Shaftesbury decided to put the cause of reforming the conditions in British mines and factories ahead of political ambition, he threw himself heart and soul into it. He made up his mind to see and hear everything himself, taking nothing for granted or on hearsay. He visited mills. He went down mines. He called on working men in their homes. He came to understand the operatives' ways of living and habits of thought. He got to know them in a way which few had done before. It was said that he came to be "the best-loved man in the three kingdoms".

A contemporary has left us a vivid description of his appearance and style of speaking.

> He is above the medium height, with a slender and extremely graceful figure, which might also pass for that of some classic statue attired in a fashionable English costume; and the similarity is not at all impaired by the rigidity of his muscles. His forehead has also much of the marble about it; his curling dark hair, in its thick masses, resembles that of a sculptured bust, and his fine brow and features are distinctly, yet delicately cut; the nose, perhaps a trifle too prominent to be handsome. He has light blue eyes, deeply set, and near each other; his mouth is small, retiring and compressed. To judge from the set form of his lips, you would say that he seldom, if ever, acted from an impulse in his life.
>
> As pieces of composition his addresses are faultless. His delivery is fluent, but not rapid; his voice fine and rich in tone, but not sufficiently exerted to be generally audible. When he addresses an audience he stands with his hand resting on the platform rail, and as erect as such a position will possibly allow; he looks his hearers coolly in the face, and with a very slight bowing movement, barely sufficient to save him from the appearance of stiffness, he delivers without a moment's hesitation, and with great dignity of voice and manner, a short, calm, serious address.

Shaftesbury pressed for reform of conditions in factories and mines in the face of bitter opposition. Hard-hearted and greedy employers opposed him bitterly. Those who were neither hard-hearted nor especially greedy were also against him. Prime Minister Sir Robert Peel, with whom he had been a close friend for many years, and in whose Cabinet he had served, tried to tempt him away from the path of reform by offering him a position in the royal household in 1841. Shaftesbury emphatically declined this, refusing to get into any situation where he could not be "as free as air to maintain and advance the interests of this great question".

"If Peel oppose me," he wrote in his diary, "nay, even if he does not support me, I will surrender interest and ambition to the cause; I will persevere in it, God helping me, through storm and sunshine; I will commit all to Christ, and trusting to Him, I shall never be confounded."

He successfully piloted successive Factory Acts (1847, 1850, and 1859) through Parliament, achieving the ten-hour day and the provision of lodging houses for the poor in the same year (1851) that he became President of Bible Society. His Lunacy Act (1845) achieved major reforms, as a result of the Lunacy Commission he chaired from 1834.

"The name of Lord Shaftesbury," declared Benjamin Disraeli, "will descend to posterity as the one who has, in his generation, worked more than any other individual to elevate the condition and raise the character of his countrymen."

In 1840 he had turned his attention to the condition of the many children and young women who were employed in mines, collieries and other industries in terrible conditions. When he made a speech on the subject in the House on 4 August 1840 he said that his first objective was to bring these children within the reach of education. Characteristically he added that, though he might be charged with cant and hypocrisy, he was bold enough to undertake the task because he must regard the objects of it "as being created", like himself and others, "by the same Maker, redeemed by the same Saviour and destined to the same immortality".

The Commission he pressed for produced a report which revealed conditions which were simply unknown to many people.

Young children, girls, growing women were employed in difficult jobs in dark, damp and muddy mines sometimes for twelve or fourteen hours a day. Children as young as six or seven were carrying loads of coal of half a hundredweight up steps that equalled, in one day, fourteen times the height of St Paul's Cathedral. They were receiving no education.

Based on the Commission's report, he introduced his Bill into the House on 7 June 1842. MPs listened to him with rapt attention as he spoke in his usual clear and forceful style. Later in the day he wrote in his diary, "Just before I opened my mouth, the words of God came forcibly to my mind: 'Only be strong and of a good courage' – praised be his holy name, I was as easy from that moment as though I had been sitting in an armchair."

Queen Victoria, who had been a member of Bible Society since 1838 and Patron of the Windsor Ladies' Bible Association, studied Shaftesbury's speech with care. Her consort, Prince Albert, wrote to Shaftesbury: "I have no doubt the whole country must be with you; at all events, I can assure you that the Queen is, whom your statements have filled with the deepest sympathy." Shaftesbury's Coal Mines Bill, prohibiting underground employment of women and of children under thirteen, passed the House of Lords in the early days of August 1842, and soon became law.

Osborne House, Isle of Wight, 1848

Enter Queen Victoria and her Consort

The Queen summons Lord Shaftesbury to the not yet quite complete Osborne House for an interview. They discuss his reforming work which the Queen has followed closely since reading his speech to the House in 1842.

"We are concerned about our young people in the mines," the Queen says, as a maid pours Shaftesbury a cup of tea from a silver teapot.

When the interview ends, Prince Albert invites Shaftesbury to walk with him in the newly planted gardens.

"How may I best assist towards the common good?" the Queen's Consort asks Shaftesbury.

"Now, Sir, I have to ask your Royal Highness whether I am to speak freely, or to observe Court form?"

"Speak out freely," Albert replies.

"Then, Sir," Shaftesbury continues, "my earnest advice is that you should put yourself at the head of all social movements in art and science, and especially of those movements as they bear on the poor, and thus show the interest felt by royalty in the happiness of the kingdom."

Few doubt that the Prince follows this advice, especially in his planning and management of the Great Exhibition in 1851. Not long before being invited to become President of Bible Society, Shaftesbury had a long interview with Prince Albert about the Great Exhibition. The General Committee had decided that the Society should have a stand at the Exhibition where it could display its various editions and translations of the Scriptures. However, many took the view that the Society had no right to a place at the Exhibition at all – including, for a while, Prince Albert himself, although he became a life Governor of the Society in 1850.

In his interview, Shaftesbury tries to change the Prince's mind.

"Quite apart, Sir, from the religious aspect, the Society is entitled to a place at the Exhibition from an intellectual point of view. Is it not a wonderful proof of intellectual power, that the Word of God has been translated into 170 distinct languages, enabling all those people to read it in their own tongue? Is it not proof of great intellectual power that the agents of the Bible Society have given a written character to upwards of 30 distinct languages?"

"You have proved your right to appear," the Prince replies. "It is a great intellectual effort, and I will do my best to secure for the Society such a position that their deeds shall be made known."

Before the Great Exhibition opens, Shaftesbury decides, on 5 May 1851, to accept the invitation he has received to become the Society's third President. "I should have been grieved," he writes in his diary, "had circumstances prevented my elevation to that high post. It is the headship of the greatest and noblest of the Societies: and I am not indifferent either to the honour or the utility of the position. Grant me, O Lord, thy grace, and uphold me in the work."

"Remember," the Earl of Carlisle tells him, "you are now about to be the centre of the largest and most salutary influence that was ever exercised upon the mass of mankind."

"I feel it, I acknowledge it," Shaftesbury replies.

Two days later, Shaftesbury takes the chair at the Society's annual meeting and will do so at every such meeting for the next 34 years until and including 1885, the year in which he dies.

Exeter Hall, The Strand, 7 May 1851

An unusually hushed audience of members and supporters of the Society waits with expectancy to hear what the new President will say.

Enter the Earl of Shaftesbury

"I have now the honour to stand before you as President of this Society," he begins. "I regard this as a very principal honour – one which would be an honour at all times, but which, in the circumstances of the present day, seems to me to wear an unusual dignity and importance. What office, I ask you, can be more glorious, even for the most powerful of empires, than to be, as it were, the colporteurs of the Word of God to every kindred and tongue and people? And what position can be more dignified than to be, as it were, the storehouse of the Word of Life, to be offered to every living and immortal being? And, moreover, to be offered, according to the language of our Article, 'in a tongue that is understood of the people'?

"We are not now making a death-bed bequest, but, by the grace of God, these efforts were begun in the prime and vigour of the nation's grandeur. And thence it is that, in the midst of surrounding ruins, this nation has stood erect, a living example to all mankind, that for time as well as for eternity, for nations as well as individuals, the revealed Word of God is 'the one thing needful' – that 'better part', which will not, and, so far as man can prevail, 'cannot be taken from us'."

Hyde Park, London, 1851

That same year, the Great Exhibition finally opens in Paxton's Crystal Palace – an attempt to show the world Britain's scientific and technical achievements. Following Shaftesbury's successful lobbying of Prince Albert, the Society takes its place as one of 7,000 exhibitors.

Mary Jones will almost certainly hear of the internationally famous exhibition and perhaps even meet, at one of the Methodist Association meetings, someone who has attended. One Society staff member at the stand at the Crystal Palace reports back on some of the comments from visitors to the Society's stand.

"This is a noble work indeed!"

"This is the glory of the whole Exhibition! And how it is hidden in a corner, when it ought to have had a place like the Kohinoor diamond!"

And some more partisan comments such as, "We are looking to England: France, Switzerland, all the nations are looking to England. The Pope has put his foot into England, but we look to you and your Bible!"

On 13 October, Prince Albert visits the Society's stand. The member of staff on duty shows him the various editions of the Bible, contrasting the price of Bibles published in 1816 with those of 1851.

"It is indeed a good work," the Prince says, remembering his conversation with Lord Shaftesbury.

DISTRICT SECRETARIES AND AGENTS

As the Society's first half-century begins to draw to its close, there are still districts where neither an Auxiliary nor an Association has taken root. There are others where, after the first vigorous efforts, the groups have grown half-hearted or almost totally inactive. And so the General Committee begins to employ District Secretaries assisted by local agents who visit every part of the country holding meetings, improving action plans, and stimulating friends of the cause to greater effort. The whole of England and Wales is mapped and divided into divisions which become the responsibility of representatives of the Society who are continually on the move, strengthening the old Auxiliaries, forming new Branches and Associations, supervising, cajoling, counselling, encouraging and energising.

A LOOK BACK AT THE FIRST HALF-CENTURY

In its first 50 years Bible Society issued nearly 28 million copies of the Scriptures in 152 languages and dialects. Of these, 54 were complete Bibles, 64 were New Testaments and 34 consisted of single Bible books published as individual portions. The majority of these versions were in the languages of Europe and Asia.

Even by 1854, the only living African language in which the complete Bible was available was Amharic, one of the two main languages spoken in the ancient Christian kingdom of Ethiopia (see Act 49). Although Livingstone began his travels in 1841, he didn't make the greatest of his journeys until the years 1853–56 in the course of which he discovered and named the Victoria Falls. It wasn't until the end of the 19th century that the Society did the greater part of its work in Africa.

However, the extent of the Society's achievements so far and the vision of immense future possibilities were sufficient to make 1854 a time of rejoicing and gratitude to God. Christians in many lands joined in the special jubilee services and events. There are records of celebrations in Australia, Canada, South Africa and the West Indies, in Constantinople, Calcutta and Columbo, Jerusalem, Madras, and Shanghai. The principal missionary Societies and the European and American Bible Societies sent messages of goodwill and congratulation.

London Tavern, Bishopsgate, 7 May 1853

On the day on which the Society enters its 50th year, an event is held in the very room at the London Tavern, Bishopsgate, in which the Society was founded. Of those who attended the first meeting in 1804, just one is present today – Karl Steinkopf in emotional mood. Others are present who have been members of the General Committee, or active supporters, for very many years. John Thornton is there, who joined the Committee in 1805, succeeded his uncle, Henry Thornton, as Treasurer in 1815 and by the jubilee year has completed 37 of his 46 years of service in that position.

Those who attend the meeting record their "deep and thankful sense of the good providence of God, which has watched over the Society from its institution to this present hour, raising it from small beginnings to unanticipated magnitude and eminence". The "eminence" is indicated by a look at the list of Vice-Presidents in the jubilee year which includes the Archbishop of Canterbury, 21 Bishops, the Duke of Manchester and thirteen peers.

Exeter Hall, The Strand, 3 May 1854

The Earl of Shaftesbury presides at the great jubilee annual meeting itself on 3 May 1854. By this time a dramatic project has been added to the otherwise conventional series of objects originally designated for the jubilee appeal. The new idea is a major initiative to provide Scriptures for China. Revolutionary changes in the Chinese Empire seem to open prospects for the evangelisation of China which would have astonished Robert Morrison and which will encourage Hudson Taylor to establish the China Inland Mission (later OMF International) in 1865. As a result of the Treaty of Nanking, which concluded the Opium War of 1840–42, five treaty ports are open to Western trade and access to China is further eased by the transfer to Britain of Hong Kong.

The Emperor who seized the Chinese imperial throne in 1852 seems to be so favourably disposed to Christianity as to make the rapid evangelisation of China a real possibility. During 1853, the Society considers this challenge and as a result sponsors a campaign to print and circulate a million copies of the Chinese New Testament. Auxiliaries and individual supporters all over Britain respond generously.

In Bryncrug, 71-year-old Mary Jones donates a half-sovereign. The cost of a million Testaments (about £18,000 – £750,000 at today's values) is fully subscribed by February 1854. Further contributions take the total to nearly £41,000 (£1,722,000 at today's values) by the end of the year and to over £52,000 when it closes.

The new regime in China fails, however, to live up to the hopes that have been raised and as a result the circulation of large numbers of Chinese Testaments and Bibles proves far more difficult than those who launched the campaign anticipated. As things turn out, the fund provides for the Society's entire expenditure in China for the next 20 years and full freedom for the organisation of Scripture distribution develops only gradually over that period.

THE "GRAND OLD MAN" AND BIBLE SOCIETY

The two longest-serving Chancellors of the Exchequer, though sitting on opposite sides of the House, are both active in their support of Bible Society. William Ewart Gladstone, a Liberal, is Prime Minister four times and Chancellor of the Exchequer four times during Queen Victoria's reign. The Queen herself, while acknowledging his abilities, complains that he speaks to her "as if she were a public meeting". She dislikes his solemn pomposity and prefers Disraeli's wit and flattery. Popularly (but not entirely correctly) thought of as "not amused", she will scarcely conceal her delight when Disraeli proclaims her Empress of India in 1876.

Gladstone, for his part, says of Bible Society, "We may justly borrow from the old mythologies to term the Bible Society the hundred-handed and the hundred-eyed."

He has in mind that to bring the Bible within the reach of every person so that they may read its message, the Society stretches out its hands far and wide. By the turn of the century it will maintain depots and warehouses in nearly a hundred of the chief cities of the world in 50 countries, and bookstores in many less important towns. The Society has depots in Madrid, Madras and Melbourne, Toronto and Tiflis, Budapest and Buenos Aires, Rome and Rangoon, Canton, Calcutta and Capetown, Valparaiso and Vancouver, Sydney, Shanghai and Singapore.

Gladstone reflects on the fact that even in translated form the Bible doesn't lose its power:

> In general, even a good translation is like a copy of some great picture: it does not readily go home to heart and mind. But who has ever felt, or has ever heard of anyone who has felt, either in reading the English or in other translations of the Bible, the comparative tameness and inefficiency which commonly attach to a change of vehicle between one tongue and another? Is it believed the Epistles of St Paul in English have seriously lost by submitting themselves to be represented in a version? At least it may be said with confidence, that there are no grander passages in all English prose than some of the passages of the translated Epistles... Such is the case of the Bible in its foreign dress. I am not confident to pronounce that it loses nothing. But it retains all its power to pierce the thoughts of the heart; it still remains sharper than a two-edge sword; it still divides bone and marrow. It does its work... It is still the sublime prerogative of the Holy Scriptures thus to reverse the curse of Babel.

At another time, he says of the Bible:

> Amid the crowds of the court, or the forum, or the street, or the market-place, where every thought of every soul seems to be set upon the excitements of ambition, or of business, or of pleasure, there too, even there, the still small voice of the Holy Bible will be heard, and the soul, aided by some blessed word, may find wings like a dove, may fly away and be at rest.

London residence of the Chancellor of the Exchequer, 9 May 1854

Gladstone, aged 45, is serving the first of his four terms as Chancellor (this one from December 1852 to February 1855) but has time to note in his journal what the Bible means to him in hours of crisis and strain and how particular passages help him.

> On most occasions of very sharp pressure or trial, some word of Scripture has come home to me as if borne on angels' wings. Many could I recollect. The Psalms are the great storehouse. Perhaps I should put some down now, for the continuance of memory is not to be trusted. (1) In the winter of 1837, Psalm 128. This came to me in a singular manner, but it would be a long story to tell. (2) In the Oxford contest of 1847 (which was very harrowing) the verse: "O Lord God, Thou strength of my health, Thou hast covered my head in the day of battle...

He goes on in great detail to list passages from the Bible which helped him at the time of the Gorham contest, when he delivered his first budget speech (April 1853), and when he had to present the Crimean War budget to the House. Gladstone will live on until he is 89, dying in 1898, three years before the end of Victoria's reign.

Meanwhile, in Wales...

Bryncrug, Wales, September 1862

Re-enter Mary Jones and enter Lizzie Rowlands

In September 1862, Lizzie Rowlands (née Jones) leaves Bala to become governess to the children of Griffith and Elizabeth Jones of Gwyddelfynydd, just north of Bryncrug. Mary Jones is now 79, blind, and has been a widow for at least eight years, possibly longer. When Mary hears that a new arrival to the area is from Bala, she asks to see her.

Lizzie, then 18, calls to see Mary on her way to a prayer meeting. She knocks on the door of Mary's little cottage and hears a weak voice.

"Come in."

Lizzie lifts the latch and goes in.

"I don't know who is there," Mary says.

Lizzie Rowlands will never forget her first sight of Mary Jones. Mary's features remain vivid in her mind for the rest of her life: she is thin, with a sad expression on her face, living in a small cottage with an earth floor, a small table with a rush candle on it, and two or three three-legged stools. She wears the old Welsh dress, a petticoat and bed gown, a blue and white gingham apron made of linsey and a long cloak and hood, a plain cap and kerchief on her head.

"I am the one who has moved here from Bala," says Lizzie, "and have come to visit you."

At the mention of Bala, Mary brightens up and begins to talk freely. From that day, Lizzie will visit Mary almost daily for two years. Mary is not entirely housebound. To go to Bethlehem Chapel, a few hundred yards down the street, she wears a "bird's nest hat", a blue homespun cloak with hood, and carries a stick in her hand. In the winter she carries a lantern, not to light her way because she cannot see – but so that others can see her.

At this time, Lydia Williams lives with Mary. Lydia is Mary's niece and the granddaughter of the Methodist preacher, William Hugh, through whom Mary became a Christian. Mary lives upstairs and Lydia downstairs. "I often went in silently on a winter evening," Lizzie recalled. "When very cold, Mary would stay upstairs by her own fire and Lydia downstairs. There I would find her in the dark, praying and repeating hymns and she was never tired of hearing them read or repeated. Other times I would find her knitting with a rush candle on the table ready to be lit. She had entirely lost her eyesight for many years, but knew her Bible thoroughly... I had much pleasure in her company. At the mention of Bala she would brighten up and talk of her memories of that town. Indeed the word Bala seemed to thrill her soul and body. She would become animated as she told of the old Association meetings and communion Sundays there, and especially the story of her journey there to receive her Bibles from Thomas Charles. Had I known I should ever have been asked anything about her I should have carefully stored her sayings. I often think I should like to see her in heaven.

"She had a son named John in America and heard now and

then from him. I wrote several times and read his letters to her. She complained 'there was no religion in them'."

Sometimes when Mary is depressed and concerned about her own sinfulness she repeats Job 23, especially Job's words "Oh, that I knew where I might find him" (verse 3, AV), with tears in her eyes. When feeling more cheerful, she asks Lizzie to read to her from John's Gospel, since it contains the words of the "Man" himself, as Mary likes to refer to Christ.

Shortly before Lydia dies of tuberculosis, in June 1864, she gives Lizzie one of the three Bibles Mary received from Thomas Charles. This Bible will eventually find its way to the National Library of Wales where it is today.

After Lydia's death, friends move Mary to be looked after by another member of Bethlehem Chapel, Mrs Jones at Gwyddelfynydd. Several members of the church help to care for her. Rev. Robert Griffith, her minister, will later recall one of the elders asking Mary in her final illness, "You think you will go to heaven, don't you, Mary Jones?"

"Yes, I believe I shall go there," Mary replies, "but I don't know how on earth they'll put up with me there!"

Gwyddelfynydd, near Bryncrug, December 1864

Exit Mary Jones

On 16 December, now very weak, Mary celebrates her 80th birthday.

A fortnight later, on 29 December 1864, Mary Jones, with a few friends from Bethlehem Chapel at her bedside, dies in the little hamlet of Gwyddelfynydd, just north of Bryncrug. The Bible presented to her by Thomas Charles which she has kept for her personal use is on her bedside table. She leaves instructions for it to be given to Robert Griffith. Griffith later gives the Bible to Robert Oliver Rees of Dolgellau to be repaired, before being sent to Bala College. This copy is now housed with the Society's collection at Cambridge University Library. You can read in the Bible what Mary wrote at the end of the Apocrypha.

Mary Jones was born 16th of December 1784. I bought this in the 16 year of my age. I am daughter of Jacob Jones and Mary Jones his wife, the Lord may give me grace Amen. Mary Jones is the true owner of this Bible. Bought in the year 1800 aged 16.

Robert Griffith conducts Mary's funeral service, taking as the text for his sermon the last verse of Psalm 17 (NKJV): "As for me, I will see Your face in righteousness; I shall be satisfied, when I awake in Your likeness." They bury her in the churchyard of Bethlehem Chapel, Bryncrug. Her grave, with a stone erected by those who wished to preserve her memory, is today well preserved in the neatly kept graveyard on the banks of a stream. Mary is still one of the better-known of all Welsh women, both within Wales and internationally.

Later in this history, we shall follow the twists and turns of the story of how two of Mary's Bibles arrive at their present locations; and learn how it gradually dawns on Bible Society that it has a best-selling tale on its hands.

Act 26
A new home for a new era

In 1864, the year in which Mary dies, the Metropolitan Board of Works in London informs the Society's General Committee that they plan to build a new wide road from Blackfriars to the Mansion House and to demolish any properties which stand in the way. The new road will become Queen Victoria Street, and – sorry! – one of the buildings which will have to be razed to the ground is 10 Earl Street. This has been the Society's headquarters since June 1816, but it stands across the entire width of what will become the new road.

The Board of Works awards compensation for 10 Earl Street of £17,500 (worth £787,500 today). The General Committee decides to buy a plot of land for a new Bible House on a prime site which will face south on to the new Queen Victoria Street. They will pay £24,000 for the site which measures 7,400 square feet.

Mansion House, London, 18 January 1865

The Lord Mayor of London (Warren Storms Hale) chairs a meeting of friends of Bible Society in the Mansion House. Those present resolve to open a special building fund so that no portion of the ordinary income of the Society will be channelled away from the work of publishing, translating and distributing Bibles. The top two names on a subscription list which is opened are those of the Society's treasurer, John Bockett, and George Moore, a well-known philanthropist, who each give £500. The meeting appeals to the public for £30,000 (£1,320,000 at today's values) for the erection of a new Bible House.

The General Committee asks the architect Edward L'Anson, who has designed the Royal Exchange Buildings, to draw up plans for the new building. By November, workmen have cleared the site of 146 Queen Victoria Street, but it will not be until the following April that the contractors move in and begin to build.

Queen Victoria Street, London, 11 June 1866

The sun shines brightly on a huge tent, with room for 2,000 people, which has been erected on the site in Queen Victoria Street. Flags and flowers, most of which have been provided by the local parish authorities, add a riot of colour to the scene. By half past eleven the enclosure is totally full and crowds of spectators are huddled together in the street.

Enter the Prince of Wales

Shortly after noon, the 25-year-old Prince of Wales appears on the platform. The eldest son of Victoria and Albert (who had died aged 42 in the presence of the distraught Queen five years earlier), the Prince will serve another 35 years in apprenticeship before he becomes King in 1901. Sadly, the much-loved 22-year-old Princess Alexandra, who will later become Queen Consort to Edward VII, is not there. She married Edward three years earlier, and since she has already shown an interest in charity work, the crowd wonder whether a pregnancy has kept her from such an unmissable event.

The Archbishop of York, William Thomson, is there, the Earl of Shaftesbury, the Bishop of Winchester, the Bishop of Carlisle, Lord Russell, Dean Stanley, the Danish Ambassador, General Bülow, the Lord Mayor and Sheriffs of London, Sir Charles Trevelyan, the distinguished civil servant, and several Members of Parliament.

They sing Psalm 100. Rev. Thomas Binney reads a selection of Scriptures. Society Secretary S B Bergne turns to the Prince of Wales and reads to him an address briefly recounting the history and current objectives of the Society. The Earl of Shaftesbury then makes a short speech.

"An edifice will be raised for the glory of God," he says, "and for the promotion of the best interests of the human race."

He invites His Royal Highness formally to lay the foundation stone of what will be a magnificent Bible House, home of the Society for nearly 120 momentous years.

The Prince places in a prepared cavity a small Bible, a copy of the latest annual report, an inscription written on parchment, a copy of *The Times* (published in neighbouring Printing House Square) and several current coins. Then, with discreet assistance from brawny builders, the Prince lays the heavy block of granite. Those fortunate to be close enough can read what it says:

BRITISH AND FOREIGN BIBLE SOCIETY

Founded A.D. 1804

This Stone was laid June 11, 1866, by his Royal Highness
ALBERT EDWARD, PRINCE OF WALES.

ED. L'ANSON, *Architect.*	SHAFTESBURY, *President.*
RIDER & SON, *Builders.*	JOHN BOCKETT, *Treasurer.*
	C. JACKSON, } *Secretaries*
	S. B. BERGNE,}

"Thy Word is Truth," John xvii. 17.

"I have an hereditary claim to be here upon this occasion," Prince Edward says in his speech. "My grandfather the Duke of Kent, as you have reminded me, warmly advocated the claims of this Society. And it is gratifying to me to reflect that the two modern versions of the Scriptures most widely circulated – the German and the English – were both, in their origin, connected with my family. The translation of Martin Luther was executed under the protection of the Elector of Saxony, the collateral ancestor of my lamented father. Whilst that of Tyndale, the foundation of the present authorised English version, was introduced with the sanction of that royal predecessor of my mother the Queen, who first desired that the Bible 'should have free course through all Christendom, but especially in his own realm'."

He has been well briefed. The Archbishop of York then prays for God's blessing on the building project and the work of the Society. All eyes then turn to the Bishop of Winchester, 76-year-old Charles Sumner. Sumner was domestic chaplain to George IV and has already run the diocese of Winchester for 40 years. In a steady voice, he thanks the young Prince of Wales for the duty he has performed. The open-air congregation sing two verses of the national anthem, asking God to scatter Britain's enemies, confound their politics and "frustrate their knavish tricks". The Archbishop of York pronounces the benediction.

The ceremony over, Sir Benjamin Phillips, the second Jewish Lord Mayor of London in the city's history, entertains the Prince of Wales and principal visitors, the General Committee and secretaries at the Mansion House. The Earl of Shaftesbury presents the Lord Mayor with a Bible in memory of the occasion. And all day, the June sun has shone.

The building fund makes slower progress than the Committee hoped. Queen Victoria, the Prince of Wales and King William of Prussia each give £100 (£4,200 each at today's values). But 1866 is a calamitous year in which bank failures and commercial disasters are followed by virulent cholera, cattle disease, colliery explosions and widespread hardship experienced by working people during a severe winter.

By March 1867 nearly £29,000 has been given or promised but about £18,000 is still needed. And so the Committee issues a second appeal. It is said that children take a special interest in the fund. One Yorkshire clergyman organises a scheme for raising £1,000 among the young people of his district. A similar fund is launched in Wales to which Welsh school children in the United States contribute over £100. Someone estimates that of the £61,000 which the site and structure costs (over £2.5 million at today's prices), one-twentieth is paid for by the gifts of children. Early in 1868 the Society takes temporary offices at 12 New Bridge Street, Blackfriars.

10 Earl Street, London, 5 February 1868

Nearly every member of the Committee, the secretaries and staff, representatives of missionary societies and other friends attend a moving farewell service in the Earl Street building which has been home for 52 years.

This is a day for nostalgia. Old Josiah Forster, looking back to his early manhood, can remember the founding of the Society itself and can trace in his memory the whole course of its history through 64 years. Although no one is aware of this at the time, 1868 is a pivotal point in the Society's history. For in this same year, John Holland Ritson is born in Bolton, Lancashire. Ritson will grow up to become a colourful General Secretary of the Society and live on until 1953. Many people actively involved in the work of the Society as it approaches its bicentenary, including the present writer, can vividly remember the events of the coronation year, 1953. And so you can say that the entire history of the Society only spans three lifetimes!

After a service of prayer and praise, Committee and staff members take a last and at times tearful look at the rooms in Earl Street. The building brings back many memories and has been hallowed by the presence of godly men and women.

In the same year, George Browne dies in Weston-super-Mare aged 79. Browne succeeded Joseph Hughes in 1834 and served as Secretary of the Society until 1854. His *History of the Bible Society* was published in 1859 and he became an honorary Life Governor in the same year.

Central London, spring 1869

The new Bible House is finished just under three years after the foundation stone has been laid. The special fund is only a few hundred pounds short of covering the whole cost of the building. No lives have been lost during the construction and there have been scarcely any cases of serious personal injury. The Committee presents a Bible to each of the workmen who has been employed for any length of time on the building.

A new Archbishop of Canterbury, Archibald Tait, the first Scot to hold the post, has just taken over from Charles Longley. One of his first duties is to preach at a service in St Paul's Cathedral on 3 May to celebrate the completion of the Society's new headquarters. He chooses Ephesians 6:17 as his text: "Take the helmet of salvation and the sword of the Spirit, which is the word of God."

Next day, the Earl of Shaftesbury presides at a quiet devotional meeting in the new Bible House itself and dedicates the new Committee Room to God's service.

With its massive courses of granite set in impressive stone facades, its basement, ground and seven upper floors, its airy halls within, its elegant and spacious staircase soon to be lined with paintings under its domed roof, its columns and balustrades and panelling of brightly coloured marble, it is a swanky building. There are those who criticise and ask, as the disciples did in Bethany when a woman poured precious ointment on the head of Christ, "To what purpose is this waste?" (Matthew 26:8, AV).

In the Society's defence, Thomas Binney, the Congregationalist minister and author of the hymn "Eternal Light", points out that the expense hasn't come out of the income of the Society. Friends of the Society of all ages have given for the specific purpose of building a new Bible House. Most have given in addition to their ordinary contributions. "The house is a house of God," he says, "and though the plainest upper room may be a church, among a great people there should be some correspondence between their character and circumstances and the buildings which they erect for his service."

The General Committee invites the Society's continental agents to take part in celebrating the new building. On the platform of the anniversary meeting on 5 May sits Monsieur de Pressensé, for 36 years chief of the Paris Agency, Edward Millard, who has been driven out of Vienna in 1852, but is now controlling the Society's work in nearly every city of the Austrian Empire, and agents from Germany, Italy, Belgium, Holland and Denmark.

INSIDE LONDON BIBLE HOUSE

The flamboyant but serviceable Bible House at 146 Queen Victoria Street will become, over the 117 years that it is the headquarters of Bible Society, familiar to thousands of committee members, staff, missionaries, agents, church people, colporteurs, publishers, supporters, Bible readers and visitors. The building was still in use when I attended my first meetings of the General Committee (since renamed Board of Trustees) in 1985.

Imagine you are visiting London Bible House towards the end of the 19th century. First, you notice carved on an open book in the stonework above the main entrance, "The Word of the Lord endureth for ever." A short flight of steps takes you up to the central hall; on the right as you climb you read, "Heaven and Earth shall pass away, but my Word shall not pass away." On two tablets of black marble you see, inscribed in gold letters, the names of the first President, Vice-Presidents, Treasurer, Secretaries and Committee.

From the central hall you look upwards to the broad and elegant staircase which leads through successive floors to the top of the building. On the left, on entering the hall are the offices of the Accountant, Assistant Foreign Secretary and Assistant Home Secretary and on the right the Home Superintendent's room. In the Society's heyday about 40 members of staff reported to these four senior officials.

From the broad landing on the next floor you enter the large Committee Room on the right. This is the heart of the Society's operations where (until it is relaxed to monthly in the middle of the 20th century) the General Committee meets at least once a fortnight. On the walls of the Committee Room hang portraits of Presidents – Lord Teignmouth, Lord Bexley, Sir John Millais' portrait of the Earl of Shaftesbury, and the Earl of Harrowby. All these portraits now hang in the main corridor leading to Bible Society's collection in Cambridge University Library. Caleb Kemp, Chairman of the General Committee at the time of the centenary celebrations, will have the honour of seeing his portrait hung while he is still alive: "May we for many years to come have the pleasure of comparing the portrait with the original!" someone remarks.

There are also portraits of William Tyndale (now at the Swindon headquarters), Thomas Charles of Bala and Emperor Alexander I of Russia, that good friend to the Society in its early years.

If you attend a meeting of the General Committee, you are likely to hear a visitor from a foreign mission reporting on the work he is doing abroad (almost certainly the missionary will be male in the 19th century). The chairman will invite him to stand on a dais at his side while he addresses the Committee, his face perhaps bearing the unmistakable marks of many years spent overseas. Men like Steere, Hannington, Pilkington, Crowther, Moffat, Cristaller, Mabille and Cousins from Africa stand on that platform: Muirhead and Stewart from China, Macdonald from Alaska, Lawes and Macfarlane from New Guinea, Paton, Creagh and Langham from the South Seas and many others.

Opposite the Committee Room you see the rooms of the two Secretaries, the Chairman's room and the sub-committee room. In the latter the finance, publishing, home organisation and foreign committees meet – with others set up as required.

To the right of the next flight of stairs, you see a large and striking painting filling the wall space on the eastern side – Martin Luther reading the Bible in the library of the monastery at Erfurt, central Germany. The picture is the work of Royal Academy artist E M Ward and was presented to the Society by friends. It is a powerful scene with Luther, in his monk's dress, standing at a desk and bending over a large copy of the Bible with heavy rims and clasps and chained to the desk. The sand in an hourglass beside him has run out. The time for Reformation has come.

Coming to the library, the collection of Bibles shelved in the bookcases along the walls is now the most complete collection of its kind in the world, with between 10,000 and 12,000 books by the end of the century. There are now (towards the end of the 19th century) Bibles in more than 400 languages – not just Bibles published by the Society but many which have been presented to it, or purchased, from all over the world. In at least one case no one can read the book – a Bible for a tribe of "Red Indians", translated by John Eliot, and printed in 1665: the people and the language have died out.

The editorial sub-committee, which deals with all matters relating to new translations and revisions, meets in the library once a month. The committee spends many hours interviewing missionaries who are temporarily in England. They come either to present to the committee some precious manuscript on which they have long worked or to suggest changes to existing versions – improved use of words, or phrases which more accurately express the meaning of the original. One missionary, on improving his understanding of a language, finds that he has rendered the words "A crown of glory that fadeth not away" by a phrase meaning, "A hat that never wears out"!

The Great Bible issued in 1539 which Henry VIII ordered to be placed in all parish churches and secured by chain for the use of readers is there.

If you are in a mood for light relief while visiting the library, you will be shown the Treacle Bible where "balm of Gilead" appears as "triacle in Gilead", or the Vinegar Bible, the word being a misprint for "Vineyard", or the Breeches Bible where the clothes God makes for Adam and Eve are so described. Finally you may be shown the Wicked Bible in which the printer deliberately left out the word "not" in the seventh commandment so that startled readers are instructed: "Thou shalt commit adultery". He did this to discredit the King's Printer with whom he had complicated personal, financial and legal disagreements. A very cross Archbishop Laud fined the printers £300 for this grave offence – no mean sum in the 17th century. Not surprisingly, this whole edition of the Bible was as far as possible suppressed.

On the same floor as the library are the rooms used by the Editorial Superintendent, the rooms of the Literary Superintendent and his assistants, and the Metropolitan District Secretaries' room.

Going down the stairs again to the hall and turning right, you walk through folding doors into the warehouse. Here you find yourself in a workshop with noisy hammers at work. On the right is the Publishing Superintendent's room and the clerk's office. To the left you see the large and lofty packing room where over 6,000 books are packed and sent off every working day of the year.

In the morning, as soon as the orders are received and copied, they are handed to the clerks on the "bound stock" floor, immediately above the packing room. The ordered books are then picked out and placed with the vouchers on four tables which are lowered by machine to the floor below. You watch as the packers take the Bibles and quickly put them in cases or boxes, mark them with their addresses and send them through to the outer room for despatch. The packing has to be done carefully. Bibles are heavy in bulk and those for the tropics have to be watertight. For this reason many of the boxes are lined with zinc, which, after the books have been packed, is soldered down before the case is closed. In many foreign destinations – Madras, the west coast of Africa, South Sea Islands – cases of Bibles are landed through ocean surf and need this special protection.

In 1860 the Society sent a large case of Bibles, most of them in expensive bindings, to India. On the way the ship was wrecked and the case remained under water for several days. However, salvage operations secured the recovery of the case which was duly returned to Bible House. Warehouse staff opened the box to find every Bible dry and in good condition.

Climbing upstairs from the packing room, passing on your way the hose and buckets always kept full in case of fire, you come to the "bound stock" floor. Here, avenue after avenue of tall and deep shelves are full of English, Welsh and foreign Bibles – the Small Pica Bible in enamelled cloth selling for two shillings, sometimes known as the Poor Man's Family Bible, the complete Bible at sixpence, the Bible with Marginal References (but no "note or comment") at one shilling, the Penny Testament and Halfpenny Gospel, both bound in cloth.

Some books never get shelved. English Bibles for Sunday Schools and the Society's cheapest books come in one day and go out the same. Everyday, and often twice a day, the van from the Society's binders delivers the books completed the day before and then they are either stacked or placed on shelves. Three floors of the warehouse are filled with huge piles of printed books in sheets, waiting their turn to be draped in cloth or leather. Three clerks are employed full time working on the distribution of the Society's magazines – *The Monthly Reporter* and *Gleanings*. More than 80,000 magazines go out every month. In March each year, all the books are counted for stocktaking.

Bibles for the blind are printed on the fourth floor of the warehouse in two types — Moon and Braille — the first being ordinary letters in raised type, and Braille being the familiar system of dots.

You finish your tour by visiting the shop in the west wing of Bible House which is open to the public for the sale of Bibles in many languages and editions. I am afraid I cannot tell you whether you could buy a cup of tea or coffee in the shop — but I doubt it.

Mary Jones's married home in Bryncrug, Wales, as it is today, Act 19.

Lord Bexley (Nicholas Vansittart), Acts 15, 21.

George Borrow,
Acts 22–33.

Earl of Shaftesbury,
from Millais' portrait
of 1877, Acts 25–28.

The Jubilee Meeting in Caernarfon Castle, 1854, when the Society had 3,315 Auxiliaries and Branches in England and Wales. It had 5,726 in 1904, Act 25.

ER COF AM
MARY JONES,
YR HON YN Y FLWYDDYN 1800,
PAN YN 16 OED, A GERDDODD O
LANFIHANGEL-Y-PENNANT I'R BALA
I GEISIO BEIBL CYMRAEG GAN Y
PARCH. THOMAS CHARLES, B.A.
BU YR AMGYLCHIAD HWN YN FODDION
I DDWYN ODDIAMGYLCH SEFYDLIAD Y
FEIBL CYMDEITHAS
FRYTANAIDD A THRAMOR.

IN MEMORY OF
MARY JONES,
WHO IN THE YEAR 1800,
AT THE AGE OF 16, WALKED FROM
LLANFIHANGEL-Y-PENNANT TO BALA
TO PROCURE A COPY OF A
WELSH BIBLE FROM THE
REV. THOMAS CHARLES, B.A.
THIS INCIDENT LED TO THE FORMATION
OF THE BRITISH AND FOREIGN
BIBLE SOCIETY.

Mary Jones's grave at Bethlehem Chapel, Bryncrug, Wales, Act 25.

Bible House,
Queen Victoria
Street, Act 26.

Entrance to Bible House,
Queen Victoria Street,
Act 26.

The Bible House, Entrance Hall.

Entrance Hall to Bible House,
Queen Victoria Street, Act 26.

Marquis of Northampton, Act 30.

John Ritson, Act 30.

Centenary Service at St Paul's with Queen Alexandra, the Prince (the future George V) and Princess of Wales, and Archbishop of Canterbury (Randall Davidson), Act 31.

The Society's staff at the headquarters of the China Agency, Shanghai, in 1900, Act 31.

Bible Society headquarters, Shanghai, about 1900, Act 31.

Colporteurs in Mukden (Shenyang) in 1902, Act 27.

Biblewomen in Bengal in 1902 when the Society supported 650 Biblewomen working with over 40 missionary organisations in the Middle and Far East, Act 38.

Act
27

Seed sown in Korea

The rapid growth of Christianity in Korea was one of the remarkable phenomena of 20th century history. Translating the Bible into Korean was crucial in the conversion of the country. The whole tale is, on the whole, a happy story of cooperation between three Bible Societies. The translator W D Reynolds said in the 1950s that "the work of the Bible Societies has been the greatest single agency in the evangelisation of Korea".

The Chinese have for centuries regarded the Korean peninsula which lies between north-eastern China and Japan as a mountainous area of great beauty and cultural richness. For them, the word Korea literally means "land of the morning calm". The mountains of Korea are famous in China. They appear as those misty mountains you see in Chinese paintings.

Koreans are proud of their history and will tell you – and the museums bear them out – that the exquisite pottery of Japan originated in Korea. They practised the art of printing with separate type in Korea a hundred or more years before Gutenberg set up his printing press in 1452. Unlike the Chinese, the Koreans have an alphabet with fourteen consonants and eleven vowels.

In 1777, a group of Korean scholars who had been studying the writings of Ricci and other Jesuits sent Peter Ni, a young Korean of Seoul, to Beijing (Peking) to find out more. For more than 2,000 years the Koreans used Chinese writing in their literature and maintained cultural and political contact between Seoul and Beijing. When Ni interviewed the Beijing Jesuits on behalf of the Seoul scholars he began to study the Christian religion under their direction and was baptised – becoming the first Korean to embrace Christianity.

When Ni completed his investigations, he took back to Korea as many scientific and religious papers as he could, together with a large number of religious objects and crucifixes. He seems also genuinely to have had in his heart a burning conviction of the truth of the Christian Gospel. When he got back to Seoul he began to evangelise his friends. By the beginning of the 19th century, the church in Seoul numbered several thousands – but the authorities began to worry and issued an edict stigmatising Christians as "people who did not honour their parents [they rejected ancestor worship], and who loved a foreign power more than their own native emperor".

Although hundreds of people died in a persecution which followed, in 1857 there were still 15,000 Christians in Korea. The rulers of Korea made determined efforts to exclude all foreigners. Almost every stranger who attempted to enter Korea, or was shipwrecked on its shores, was killed. Charles Gutzlaff, an agent of the Netherlands Bible Society, succeeded in landing in 1832 and stayed a month, but then had to leave. The Koreans wanted no foreigners and no alien religion. Under the great bell of Seoul a stone bore an inscription calling on all Koreans to kill intruding foreigners. They forbade the distribution of Christian books on peril of decapitation.

When America proposed a treaty in 1871, the Korean authorities replied, "Korea is satisfied with her civilisation of four thousand years and wants no other." A civilisation which began 400 years before Abraham must have learnt something in the course of the centuries.

Yalu valley on the border between China and North Korea, 1874

The story of the translation of the Bible into Korean begins with the adventures of a Korean merchant who ventures in 1874 across the great Yalu river that forms the north-western boundary between North Korea and the north-east region (Manchuria) of China. In this beautiful area of pine forests in the shadow of the Great White Mountains, he crosses the river in a small boat containing *ginseng* and an assortment of other goods. *Ginseng* is a much-sought-after medicinal root which is said to have many qualities including bringing long life. A strong south-west wind blows up, the merchant's boat is wrecked and, although he escapes with his life, he finds that he is a penniless vagrant.

Enter Ross and MacIntyre

In his plight the merchant comes across a servant of Dr John Ross, a Scots missionary working for the United Presbyterian Church Mission, who has been posted at the Korean Gate looking for someone to teach his master Korean. Secretly, the merchant contracts to teach the missionary. Not even his relatives must know because if the Government finds out what he is doing they will both be thrown into prison and probably executed.

Dr Ross and his colleague, Rev. John MacIntyre, set to work energetically with this bankrupt merchant: their aim is to prepare literature, and particularly the Gospels, in Korean for distribution among anyone who ventures across the Yalu river. While on home leave in Scotland, Ross asks for help from the National Bible Society of Scotland in printing his translation of the Gospels. The Society readily promises such help.

Enter Saw Sang Yuin

Ross and MacIntyre select the Gospel of Luke and initiate Chinese printers into the mystery of working in Korean which, though simpler than Chinese, is new and strange to them. They need another assistant and he turns up through what Ross comes to think of as an act of God. Another Korean medicine dealer makes the trip across the Yalu with his cargo, but he proves to be such an inept salesman that he can barely pay his way with the proceeds. A rather dreamy man, he is down on his luck and Ross hears of him when he cannot pay his inn expenses.

Ross takes him on to help with printing Gospels. Though slow at his work, he proves reliable. In setting type he has to look carefully at what he is doing and grows interested. He begins to ask the Christian Chinese printers the meaning of this or that term or statement. When the Gospel of Luke is ready and printed, he asks to be baptised and Ross is surprised to find how well he understands Christian truth. His name is Saw Sang Yuin (sometimes written as Soh Sang-yuin). Some sources describe him as the first Protestant Korean convert.

The news leaks out that this work is being done and Koreans travelling to the Korean Embassy in Beijing begin to call in at the Scots mission in Newchwang (now Yingkou) to see what is going on. One of these men becomes interested and stays to assist in the printing. He proves so good at his job, and eager to work, that Ross releases the former compositor and sends him off to see how he gets on as a colporteur with a few hundred copies of the tentative edition of Luke in Korean.

Six months later, Saw Sang Yuin returns to Yingkou with some news.

"In a valley near the Yalu river," he says, "I found a large number of Korean refugees from a recent purge. I sold all the Gospels to them. Some of them want to be baptised after reading Luke's Gospel. I think you had better go and examine them."

Ross has such little faith in the dreamy man that he suspects he may be just coming back with a report which he thinks will please him. So he simply gives him another load of Gospels and sends him off again to keep in contact with the refugees. Six months later, Saw returns with more tales of people who have read the Gospel and want to be baptised.

Mukden (Shenyang), China, late 1870s

Ross and MacIntyre move to Mukden (Shenyang) and are deeply immersed in their translating and revising. They are surprised when one day a number of apparently well-educated men arrive at Mukden.

"We are former officials from Seoul who have taken refuge in the Yalu valley," they say. "There we met your colporteur and read his books. There are a number of us there now who pray to the God of Heaven."

And so Saw's stories are confirmed. Ross decides to embark on the long and difficult journey to see these new Christians. It is winter, snow lies thick on the ground, and only after great difficulty he reaches the Korean Gate. As soon as Ross arrives at his destination the Koreans begin making their way to the inn where he is staying. About 30 men, former Seoul officials but now rather well-to-do farmers with their wives, arrive to welcome Ross to the Yalu valley.

"We are believers," they tell him firmly, "and we want to be baptised."

Then, in another valley on the other side of a high mountain pass, nearly a hundred men from 16 to 72 years of age present themselves for baptism. Ross interviews them all. He decides that 85 may be baptised, but tells the rest they must wait for another occasion.

"We were informed," Ross writes later, "and from what we had seen we were now prepared to believe anything, that in each of the twenty-eight valleys which lay between us and the Great White Mountain, four hundred miles to the north-west, there were larger or smaller groups of believers waiting to be received into the Church."

Now Saw Sang Yuin makes another proposal.

"I want to take the books up to Seoul itself," he says.

Ross is not against the idea but first there is more translating to be done. By the spring of 1882 Ross's team have completed considered translations of the Gospels of Luke and John. Saw Sang Yuin prepares some of the first drafts himself. Bible Society in London supports the process, providing funds that enable the printing in September, although publication is by the National Bible Society of Scotland. BFBS now includes Korea under its newly formed North China Agency.

In the same year, treaty relations with Western powers are established but the effects of the new agreement are slow to percolate down to official level in Korea.

Saw Sang Yuin sets off for Seoul

In 1883, at the age of 33, Saw sets off. He takes with him a supply of Gospels in Korean and Gospels and New Testaments in Chinese. His objective is to try to reach the Korean capital. When he reaches Pong Wang Song, 40 miles south of the Yalu river, two policemen stop him.

"We must search your baggage," they say.

Quickly finding the Scriptures, the policemen arrest Saw and put him in prison.

"The penalty for having these books in your possession is death," they tell him.

Some years later, Saw will tell a member of the Society's staff (Thomas Hobbs) that at this moment he had no fear – he simply trusted in the power of God. Very fortunately for Saw, he finds that among the warders in the prison are two of his friends.

"You must escape," they whisper. "We will leave the door of your cell unlocked. We will take charge of the books and burn them publicly tomorrow morning."

"But the books are more precious to me than my life!" says Saw. "I must take a few copies with me."

After much pleading, the warders allow him to take ten books.

"You must be crazy," they say, "to want to take a book which will cost you your life if you are found with it!"

After dark, Saw makes his escape with ten Gospels and Testaments. After a journey of 370 miles he reaches Seoul. Ross manages to send him a box of Korean and Chinese Scriptures via Shanghai and Inchon on the coast, west of the capital. When the customs officials see the contents of the box, they report Saw to the Government who orders his arrest. Before this happens, however, one of the customs officials, a German, sends for him.

"I have received a letter from Dr Ross," the official tells Saw, "asking me to try to get the books through to you. I must tell you that my wife is a devout Christian and I am prepared to help you."

The official invites Saw to his home and he, and especially his wife, treat the colporteur kindly. After he has spent a year in Seoul he writes to Ross asking him to go there, as thirteen of his friends want to start a Christian church. A year later he writes to Ross again, urging him to make every effort to come to Seoul as there are now 79 believers. It is impossible for Ross to go at this time because the laws debarring foreigners are still rigidly enforced.

Leaving Saw in Seoul for a moment, I break off to tell you the interest which the Society and Christians from other Western countries are taking in the land to the south-east, across the Korean Strait.

Act
28

First contacts with Japan

Although for over a decade it has experienced an economic downturn, Japan remains today one of the wealthiest countries in the world – at least materially. Spiritually, the religion which is indigenous to the country is Shintoism, and over half the population claim some allegiance to "Shinto" which means "the way of the gods". An ancient system which expresses itself in nature and ancestor-worship, it is a religion in which doctrinal or moral codes do not feature. About the year 550, Buddhism arrived from Korea, bringing with it its combination of psychology, ethics and philosophy – a call to self-discipline, mind-development and unselfish conduct – which still has some appeal in the West. In an accommodating fashion, Buddhism received all the Shinto gods into its pantheon. Confucianism also crossed over from China and has had a good deal of influence, especially among educated Japanese.

Curiously, Christianity, which arrived in Japan much later than any of these ancient religions, had its effect on Buddhism. In the early years of the 20th century, Japanese Buddhists issued their sacred volume, the *Tripitaka*, in exact imitation of Bible Society's publications, with similar type and arrangement, morocco yapp binding, gold-red edges and silk tape, and with a folding map resembling that of Paul's missionary journeys, but illustrating the spread of Buddhism.

The first Christians to visit Japan were the Jesuits under Francis Xavier, one of the greatest of all Christian missionaries, known as the "Apostle of the Indies" and "of Japan". Jesuits reckon he was responsible for more than 700,000 conversions. Certainly in Japan the Jesuits gained converts quickly at all levels of society and it is said that images of Buddha "with a slight application of the chisel, served for images of Christ". But the Japanese Government put its foot down, stopped the propagation of the

Christian faith and practically exterminated all Christians. In 1637, 30,000 Christians were killed on the Shimabara Peninsula – some burned at the stake, some crucified, some scalded to death in boiling sulphur wells, some hurled from a rock into the waters of Nagasaki harbour.

For more than 200 years the Japanese authorities put it about that Christianity was associated with sorcery, sedition, political conspiracy, the corruption of society and the betrayal of the state. Children were taught to trample on the cross as a symbol of superstition and in every village public notice boards set out the rewards offered for informing against priests, catechists and converts.

It was perilous for a Japanese to confess Christ, and any European who was permitted to land in Japan read this edict:

> So long as the sun shall warm the Earth, let no Christian be so bold as to come to Japan. Let all know that the King of Spain himself, or the Christian's God, or the Great God of all, if he violate this command, shall pay for it with his head.

But things began to change in the middle of the 19th century. The Netherlands, the only European power trading with Japan, realised that, if Britain succeeded in forcing Japan to open the country, it would lose its monopoly. So the Dutch now planned to seize the initiative in opening Japan and thus to turn the situation to their own advantage. In 1844 the Dutch sent a diplomatic mission urging the military Government of Japan to open the country, but this suggestion was refused. Yet visits by foreign ships proliferated. In the 1840s, British and French warships visited the Ryukyu islands and Nagasaki to request commercial relations. In response, the military government strengthened Japanese defences and continued to make extensive military preparations against potential attack.

In 1846 Commander James Biddle of the American East Indian fleet appeared with two warships in Uraga harbour (near Yokohama) and held consultations with representatives of the Japanese military Government on the question of opening commercial relations. When this was refused, Biddle returned empty-handed. The United States, however, was anxious to gain access to ports for fuel and provisions for its Pacific merchant and whaling ships and wasn't willing to give up attempts to open up Japan.

But for two centuries the Japanese authorities had retained their political dominance through strict adherence to the policy of seclusion, and they could not muster up the resolution necessary to open the country. Opinion in the leadership was split between seclusion and opening the country. The opening of Japan was thus postponed until the last possible moment and had to be achieved unilaterally by foreign pressure, backed by massive naval strength.

This pressure was initiated on 8 July 1853 when four warships commanded by Commodore Matthew Perry, bearing proposals for a treaty of friendship and commerce from the President of the United States, dropped anchor in Uraga bay. Resistance was impossible, and in the following year the Shogun – the supreme military chief – signed the treaty which opened two of the Japanese ports.

In the same year (1854) that Western statesmen were trying to open up Japan to trade, a midshipman on board HMS *Baracoota* in the Gulf of Nagasaki accidentally dropped his New Testament overboard. The book sank but got caught up in the nets of a fisherman who took it to Wakasa Murata of Saga, a member of an aristocratic family who commanded the Japanese forces guarding the port. When he discovered that the book had been translated into Chinese, Wakasa sent for a copy from Shanghai. He read this and decided its pages contained the words of eternal life.

The Society's annual report for 1855 indicates that the eyes of the General Committee in London are already eagerly turning to the mysterious islands which (on a map of the world with Britain in the middle) are the first to see the sun rise.

In August 1858 Lord Elgin, on behalf of the British Government, secures a treaty with Japan which paves the way for better relations between the two countries. Early in 1859, the first Protestant missionaries – two Americans – begin to work in Nagasaki, on the extreme west coast of the country. In the following year, Bishop Smith, of the Anglican Diocese of Victoria in Hong Kong, visits Japan and gathers the materials for his vivid *Ten Weeks in Japan*. In May 1861 he holds his audience spellbound at the Society's anniversary meeting in Exeter Hall with the impressions of his journey.

When Roman Catholic missionaries are readmitted to Japan in 1858, they come across little groups of practising Catholics in Kyushu, the southernmost and third largest of the four main islands of Japan. They are the descendants of an early church planted in 1549 by Francis Xavier. James Robertson, who later will become the Society's secretary in Korea, used to keep on his desk a relic of this period in Japan. On one side was a very fine crucifix, on the reverse a Buddha. Visiting a Japanese home on one occasion, he noticed a wall plaque showing a cavorting warhorse. When he commented on it, his host took it off the wall, turned it around, and there was a crucifix.

In the grounds of the Katsura Detached Palace, Kyoto, the guides employed by the imperial household show you a Buddhist statue of the Goddess of Mercy. Two feet high, carved in stone, it has stood there since the 17th century. Look carefully, as the guide says, and you see the suggestion of a cross. Look more carefully, and you see that what you thought was Kwannon (one of the gods) is really the Virgin Mary.

An official Japanese delegation, making a tour of Western nations, arrives in London in the summer of 1862. The Society presents them with three copies of the Chinese Bible, together with a greetings message from the Committee. Before they leave England, however, the members of the delegation return the books with a polite acknowledgement and an explanation that acceptance might involve them in difficulties back in Japan.

As more missionaries arrive in Japan, naval officer Wakasa makes contact with one of them – Dr G F Verbeck of the Dutch Reformed Church in America. Wakasa, and other members of his family, put many questions to Verbeck who eventually answers to their satisfaction. On Whitsunday 1866, Wakasa, his brother and another close relative are baptised by Bishop Williams, also of the Dutch Reformed Church. In later years, Wakasa's daughter and niece will also become Christians – plus Wakasa's daughter's nurse who begins a Sunday School in which many children are converted.

No time is lost in trying to master the intricacies and complexities of the Japanese language. Like the Korean language, Japanese stands out as a sort of linguistic novelty. The Bibles the missionary translators produce, working with Japanese colleagues, have to use a special system of phonetics in addition to the 3,000–4,000 Chinese characters used in the literature of Japan.

Enter Jonathan Goble

An American Baptist, Goble was a marine on the Perry expedition trying to persuade the Japanese to open their country up to trade with America. He decides that he wants to return to Japan to spread the Gospel. After he has finished his education, he goes to Japan as one of the first Protestant missionaries. His translation of Matthew is dated 1871 and is the first Gospel to be printed in Japan, certainly since the 17th century, probably ever. He has to arrange for the printing himself. There are no modern presses. The text has to be cut in wood. The Japanese are not allowed to help foreigners produce such work, and so the blocks have to be cut secretly. Goble has the book printed by a man he describes as "probably too ignorant to know what he was doing".

Then the Gospels have to be distributed. Goble becomes the first colporteur in Japan. Together with another American Baptist, Nathan Brown, Goble completes the first Japanese New Testament in 1879. This is very much a first attempt. Much further work has to be done by teams of translators to make the Bible really accessible to the Japanese.

1872 is a significant year for the beginnings of Bible work in Japan. On 10 March, the first Protestant Japanese Christian congregation meets in Yokohama and takes the name of the Church of Christ. It is small – nine young men are baptised that day – and it is led by two Japanese teachers. In the same year, Dr J C Hepburn of the American Presbyterian Mission issues his version of the Gospels of Mark' and John in Japanese. A Bible depot is opened in a principal street of Kobe, one of Japan's leading ports. A Biblewoman begins to distribute Scriptures among the ships in Yokohama harbour and some new converts open shops for the sale of Christian literature.

A missionary convention meets in Yokohama, appoints a translation committee with members from American missions and proposes that BFBS and ABS should cooperate in Japan. In London, the General Committee discusses Japan and agrees that its objectives are the same as those of the Americans.

Enter Dr Bettelheim

The General Committee has earlier invited Dr Bernard Bettelheim to prepare a tentative edition of the Gospel of Luke in Luchu in parallel columns with Chinese. Bettelheim was the first medical missionary of the Loo Choo Naval Mission, which a group of British naval officers had founded in 1843. While working for the mission, Bettelheim lived with his wife in a house in the grounds of a Buddhist temple on the island of Okinawa, 4,000 miles south-west of Japan. In the course of a colourful life he assisted Commodore Perry in preparing his approaches to Japan on behalf of the Americans. Towards the end of his life, Bettelheim lived on a farm in Illinois and worked as a surgeon in the 106th Regiment, Illinois Volunteer Infantry. Before he died, he revised, with the help of Luchu speakers, his translation of the four Gospels and Acts and bequeathed his manuscript to Bible Society, sending the General Committee $400 towards the expense of printing.

Also in 1872, the Governor of Tokyo visits London Bible House and accepts a copy of the Chinese Bible and an English Reference Bible. Sadly, the Society has nothing in Japanese to offer him, but a few weeks later while the Governor and his delegation are still in Paris, the first copies of Bettelheim's translation of Luke's Gospel arrive from the printers and the General Committee sends one to the Governor in Paris. The Governor delightedly turns the pages of the book.

"It is very easy to read," he says.

A young Japanese member of the delegation who has become a Christian makes more detailed comments which are reported to the Society. This persuades the General Committee to press ahead with its work of translating the Scriptures into good Japanese.

The translations committee which was established by the

Yokohama convention issues the Gospel of Luke in Japanese in 1875, followed by Romans, Hebrews and a revised text of Matthew a year later. Then a row breaks out because the American Bible Society insists on the exclusive right to use the versions produced by the committee. Eventually, ruffled feathers are smoothed and a strategy for cooperation between the American, Scots and British Societies is devised. Work continues on translating the Old Testament.

In the summer of 1875 Alexander Wylie, the Society's agent for China, visits Japan to examine in some detail the possibilities for Bible work there. He meets the missionaries, and the translations committee receives him cordially.

"We are most anxious to cooperate with the British and Foreign Bible Society," they drawl in their mainly American accents.

A few months later, the first direct links between Japan and London Bible House are established by the time-honoured method of setting up a corresponding committee.

During the course of a second visit to Japan in 1876, Alexander Wylie holds useful discussions with the agent of the National Bible Society of Scotland and strengthens his relations with the missionary societies in Japan.

In 1878 the Church Missionary Society recommends to the Society its first colporteur and three get to work in the following year. Although their sales are not large, they encounter little hostility and the authorities do not interfere with their work. It looks as if a new day is dawning in Japan.

On 17 April 1880 the American Bible Society has the first edition of a revised "Standard" Japanese New Testament printed at Yokohama, and two days later an enthusiastic meeting, attended by representatives of fourteen missionary societies and of every Protestant Japanese congregation in Tokyo, takes place in Shinsakaya Bashi Church to celebrate the happy event.

Uyeno Park, Tokyo, October 1880

Famous for its cherry blossom in the spring, Uyeno Park, Tokyo, is the scene of a remarkable event. There are no official protests when, at an unprecedented meeting, Japanese and foreign Christians publicly testify to their faith in Jesus. The Christians take over spacious rooms and gardens on the edge of the park for the event. Several thousand people attend, including Buddhist priests and people from high positions in the Government. On a little island on the lake of Shinobazu stands the temple dedicated to the Goddess Benten. To the left you can see the temple of the thousand-handed Goddess of Mercy. Within a stone's throw to the rear sits a bronze image of Buddha, 20 feet high. In the middle of all this, a large and orderly crowd stands and listens as the Christian Gospel is preached.

At this stage, the work of BFBS in Japan is still small compared to that of the Americans and Scots. In 1881 the Society distributes fewer than 8,000 copies of the Scriptures, ABS over 68,000, and the National Bible Society of Scotland, with its 16 colporteurs, over 26,000.

In 1882 the Society employs twelve colporteurs in Tokyo and five other Japanese towns. But it is hard to find the sort of "spiritually-minded and steadfast" Biblemen that the Society is looking for. Mobs still sometimes grow hostile towards Christians in the more rural areas of the country, though Tokyo is regarded as more open and liberal in its attitude.

In 1883 the agents of the British, American and Scots Societies agree to divide among themselves the work of taking through the press the various books of the Old Testament as they leave the translators.

A remarkable transformation has occurred. Until 1853 Japan was vehemently hostile to Christianity. In 1883 there are 18 Protestant missions in 37 stations, 90 churches, 63 mission schools and 7 theological colleges. In the morning of 10 November 1883, while Europe sleeps, the 400th anniversary of Martin Luther's birth is celebrated in churches in Osaka and Tokyo. In hymn and prayer Japanese Christians thank God for the gift of an open Bible in a language they can understand.

"Already there are signs of a mighty revolution beginning," says J A Thomson, the agent responsible for Japan for the National Bible Society of Scotland. "Old fears, superstitions, and heathen practices are being discarded. Rich and poor are beginning to seek after God. Many fear that the crisis will be reached before we are ready. But we believe that Christ is with us, and we have courage to go on, looking to English Christians to strengthen our hands."

By now, students in all the higher schools of Japan regularly study English. Interest in the *Yeso kiyo Seisho* – "the holy book of the Jesus doctrine" – is growing. The cheapest textbook of which there is a Japanese translation is the English New Testament and when the stock in the Society's Japanese depot is nearly exhausted, an urgent telegram is sent to Bible House in London for fresh supplies. Sales of the English New Testament encourage sales of the Japanese translation.

Meanwhile, back in London…

Exeter Hall, The Strand, 6 May 1885

Enter Lord Shaftesbury for his last annual meeting

Since becoming President in 1851, Shaftesbury has not missed a single anniversary meeting. He is now 84 and has been unwell for some months. Committee members, staff and supporters watch anxiously as he walks very slowly to his usual chair.

"His very presence," the Archbishop of Canterbury remarked later, "was a speech."

The aged Earl stands up unsteadily and surveys his audience. Many of the faces are familiar to him.

"It has pleased God," he begins, "to lay me aside for nearly twelve months, and this is the first public duty I have been able to discharge during that time. I feel most deeply grateful to be able to do so, for it would have gone to my heart if now, for the first time in more than thirty years, I should have been unable to be present."

He goes on to speak with delight about the publication of the Society's Penny Testament. This was distributed free to school-children, and in addition nearly a million copies have been sold in less than nine months.

"My dear daughter has herself distributed 240 copies," he

says. "Now that I am feeling a little better I hope to start my round of visiting again. My prayer shall always be that I will die in harness."

Shaftesbury does make one more speech in June, putting the case for more help for suffering children. Then, following the advice of his doctors, he travels to Folkestone in July. He spends his last days in a room with a sea view. Almost his last words are, "The love of God which is in Christ Jesus our Lord. Yes, in his keeping – with him alone."

He dies on 1 October and, after a remembrance service in Westminster Abbey, he is buried in the Church of St Giles, at the family seat in Wimborne, Dorset.

In 1882, Shaftesbury had suggested that the Earl of Harrowby should succeed him. The Harrowby family had been in politics since Walpole's day in 1733. They had also been long associated with Bible Society – since 1816, there had always been a Harrowby on the list of Vice-Presidents. The second Earl had headed the deputation which invited Lord Shaftesbury (then Lord Ashley) to become third President way back in 1851. His son, the now 54-year-old third Earl, had been President of the Board of Trade from 1878 to 1880 and was now Lord Privy Seal.

A deputation invites him to take over from Shaftesbury.

"I will become your President," he replies, "on the understanding that I shall be free to resign after five years, without the slightest implication that my interest in the cause has diminished."

The condition is accepted and he is given a warm reception at London Bible House.

"Of all Societies," he says, "this is the nearest to my heart. The Bible Society has always been a watchword in our house. My grandfather was one of its earliest supporters."

In fact, he does not take up his option of resigning and will continue as President for fifteen years until his death in 1900. This will mean that the Society has only four Presidents (Teignmouth, Bexley, Shaftesbury and Harrowby) throughout the 19th century. If you want to enjoy a long life, become President of Bible Society.

Act
29

Good news for the publicity people

Apart from the unique nature and best-selling record of the Bible itself, Bible Society's most successful piece of publicity has been the tale of Mary Jones. Since it was first published at length in English in 1882, the story has never been out of print. By 1890 the English edition of the story had sold 95,000 copies and since then it has been translated into over 40 languages. The story has been told not only in books but in plays, musicals, film-strips, flannel graphs, tea towels and on the Internet. If you go to the house where Mary lived in Bryncrug you can even buy a clock partly made out of the original roof of her cottage!

It is ironic that this massive publicity should centre around a woman who was unknown outside a small circle when she died. Here is the intriguing saga of how it gradually dawned on Bible Society that its own foundation was wrapped up in a winning tale.

Just over two years after Mary's death, the Society publishes in its *Monthly Reporter* for 1 January 1867 an account of Mary Jones and her walk to Bala. Prior to this date, the Society has always attributed its foundation to the effect on Thomas Charles of an encounter with an unnamed Welsh girl who has walked several miles to read a Bible.

Eleven years later, in March 1878, Society Secretary S B Bergne writes to Robert Oliver Rees at Dolgellau (on the north side of Mary's mountain). Rees had been responsible for repairing the Bible which Mary had instructed should be given to Robert Griffith (who conducted her funeral). Griffith had passed the Bible on to Rees who had it repaired before donating it to Bala College. In his letter to Rees, Bergne writes: "It has occurred to us that the Library of this Society would be a most appropriate place for the Bible of the little Welsh girl whose history is identified in so interesting a manner with the origin of this Society."

Rees has the Society's letter discussed at a meeting of the North Wales Association in Wrexham in June 1878. Since it is already dawning on the Welsh, as well as to the Society, that there is something very special about Mary Jones, the Association refuses to hand over the Bible on the grounds that it is bound up with the history of Thomas Charles, Bala, and the Methodists. Later in the same year, the Religious Tract Society publishes an article about Mary Jones in its magazine *The Sunday at Home*. The article is based on research conducted by Rees. Rees turns his work into a booklet about Mary which is published in Welsh in 1879.

The Society then makes another attempt to get hold of Mary's Bible. The request is considered by the North Wales Association meeting in Dolgellau in June 1880. The Association deliberates long and hard and eventually comes to a decision. The Welsh will hand over the Bible to the Society on condition that another Bible "given to the same person [i.e. Mary Jones] at the same time" can be procured for Bala College. Two months later, the Society's magazine *Monthly Reporter* announces that William Coles has travelled to Wales on behalf of the Society to verify statements about Mary Jones. In the BFBS magazine *Gleanings* the following month, Coles reports that he has confirmed that Robert Oliver Rees's account of Mary Jones is substantially correct and that he has gleaned some further interesting reminiscences of her. The Society makes public the intention to erect the (present) memorial to Mary at her grave.

Penrhyndeudraeth, Wales, spring 1881

Lizzie Rowlands, who visited Mary regularly in the last two years of her life, now lives at Penrhyndeudraeth where her husband is head teacher. One day, after a Sunday School meeting, she has a visitor. It is Dr Lewis Edwards, representing Bala College. They have a conversation. On her bookshelf is one of the three Bibles presented to Mary Jones by Thomas Charles – it has been passed on to Lizzie by Mary's niece Lydia. "Gladly but sadly", Lizzie agrees to hand over the precious Bible to Edwards so that it may go to Bala College. Later, I will tell you how this Bible eventually finds its way to the National Library of Wales in Aberystwyth where it is today. The arrangement at last satisfies the Welsh and will allow Mary's personal Bible to be handed to the Society.

Monthly Reporter for May 1882 announces that William Jones has travelled to Bala to secure Mary Jones's personal Bible for the Society – the Bible will be displayed for many years at London Bible House and later go to Cambridge University Library where it remains in a magnificent new binding. In the same year, the ·Society publishes *The Story of Mary Jones and her Bible*, "collected from the best materials and re-told by M E R" – the first time the story has been published at length in English. The author is Mary Emily Ropes who has written many children's books and is sister of the librettist Arthur Reed Ropes. Her father William Hooper Ropes was a merchant in Russia and a Committee member from 1856 to 1869.

Meanwhile in Korea...

Re-enter Dr Ross

It is not until 1887, five years after the formal opening of Korea to the West that Ross is able to reach Seoul, landing at Inchon. Ross takes with him the first complete New Testament in Korean, published in Mukden, China (today's Shenyang). Bible Society in London has paid for the printing and the date of publication is 1887.

Roman Catholics are now also growing active in Korea and by 1890 have 17,000 members. They build a magnificent cathedral in the heart of Seoul.

Enter Dr Underwood and first Korean Protestant Church leaders

In Seoul, Ross meets Dr Underwood, another Scot who has recently arrived from Japan. On Ross's first night in the capital, Underwood takes Ross to the formal inauguration of a small community as a Presbyterian Church. Waiting till darkness falls, they make their way through the narrow alleyways of the town until they come to a small open courtyard.

They tap on the window of a house, are allowed to enter and find themselves in the presence of fourteen men – all, it seems, intelligent and well educated. They elect two of them – cousins of Saw Sang Yuin, the colporteur – as elders to be ordained the following Sunday. The men have been believers for six years and were among Saw's first converts. They discover that about 300 respected men of Seoul are believers, though not all of them are yet prepared publicly to proclaim their faith.

And so the New Testament, in the power of the Holy Spirit, has done its work before the missionaries arrived. Ross's translation of the New Testament, understandably, is not perfect. His first contact was with Korean refugees who were out of touch with the main streams of thought. Their language is dated.

The first Protestant missionaries to work in Korea set out to revise Ross's version into the speech commonly used in the neighbourhood around Seoul. Sharp differences arise among experts in the Korean language but eventually they manage to agree that they need to begin an entirely new translation. A Board of Official Translators is organised in 1893 which begins work on the New Testament in 1894. The first edition of the New Testament appears in 1900 with further revisions coming later. The 1906 revision becomes known as the Korean Authorised Version of the New Testament and will have a long and honourable history. There will still be those who cling steadfastly to it late into the second half of the 20th century despite the availability of later revisions and translations.

Three Bible Societies all played an important part in translating the Scriptures into Korean. The National Bible Society of Scotland assisted MacIntyre and Ross in their early work, and their later work was underwritten by Bible Society. The American Bible Society published the first attempts of a Korean named Ye Suchon to translate the Gospel of Mark into Korean. Ye Suchon also translated the Gospels and Acts into Sino-Korean – a form of Chinese with Korean endings – and these were published by BFBS in Yokohama, Japan, in 1884. The costs of the Korean translation work undertaken by the Translators Board were borne by BFBS and ABS dividing four-fifths between them and the Scots providing the rest.

As the Korean Church grows it needs to use the expressions and idioms of ordinary people. And so, as it is translated, the Korean Bible becomes more and more Korean, dropping its Chinese elements and gradually adopting local script. Finally, in 1952, a version is issued in Hankul which is approved by the Board of Education of the Republic.

The Bible Society's Secretary for north China visits Pusan, at the south-east tip of what is now South Korea in 1887. Later, he travels north to Seoul where he appoints Robert Turley to carry on the work.

By 1892, when E T Bryant retires as agent for north China, the Society has issued 78,000 copies of the Korean New Testament and six colporteurs are working in the country, distributing over 8,000 Testaments a year.

In 1893 the Society establishes a sub-depot in Seoul and a Chinese colporteur is put in charge. Two years later, Alexander Kenmure is made responsible for an agency for Korea which is established in Manchuria (north-eastern China). Kenmure arrives in Inchon, west of Seoul, in 1895 and in May 1899 Korea observes its first Bible Sunday, which becomes from then on a festival in the Christian year. On 28 December 1902, the authorities allow the Society and the Korean Tract Society to establish a library in the Seoul city prison.

The Society employs its first Biblewoman in Korea in 1896 and by 1903 she has 20 colleagues distributing nearly 4,000 Testaments a year.

In its "official-speak", the Society describes these women as "not always up to our ideals" but gladly pays tribute to the way they ford streams, climb mountains, and press on, weary and footsore "thinking how his feet were pierced with nails". Mostly, the Biblewomen in Korea are treated with respect but not always. They find ready listeners at funerals, weddings, birthday feasts, sacrificial holidays at the graves of the dead and at religious shrines. They go where men cannot go.

In the same year (1903), the Society employs 51 colporteurs

in Korea. Most of the 80 Protestant missionaries working in Korea in this year acknowledge that much of their success is due to the work of the colporteurs.

Between 1884 and 1904, the Society prints well over 300,000 copies of the Korean Scriptures.

In 1905, when poor health forces Alexander Kenmure to return to England, Hugh Miller (who joined the staff as an assistant in 1902) takes over from him. A great expansion of the Society's work in Korea will occur in Miller's time. He will carry on until 1938 when he retires and hands over responsibility to his colleague Thomas Hobbs who for many years has trained and supervised Korean colporteurs. In some years the Society employs over 140 of these men and by the outbreak of the First World War they are selling well over 300,000 copies of the Scriptures annually.

Meanwhile, across the Korean Strait...

Tokyo, 3 February 1888

Another of those memorable scenes in Bible Society history occurs in Tokyo on 3 February 1888 (2548 in the Japanese chronology). At a public meeting in Tokyo, Dr J C Hepburn, veteran translator of the American Presbyterian Mission, presides. The audience thrills as he takes the Old Testament in one hand and the New in the other. Reverently, he places them together.

"In the name of the whole body of Protestant missionaries in Japan," he says, "and of the whole church of Christ in America and England, I make it a loving present to the Japanese nation."

Two Japanese scholars have helped in the translation of the Old Testament and a revision of the New Testament to secure uniformity of style throughout.

When the first Japanese Parliament opens in November 1890, people are astonished at the growth of Christianity at all levels of society, including educated people. As well as several Christians in the Upper House, twelve of the 300 representatives in the Lower House are members of Protestant churches and, from the three people nominated for the office of Speaker, the Japanese Emperor selects a Christian.

A number of Japanese colporteurs work faithfully for the Society for many years. The Reverend Makoto Watabe, the current Secretary of the Japan Bible Society, has recently pointed out to me that Japanese colporteurs often walked a good deal further in a day than Mary Jones did! By the 1890s, the oldest, Nagasawa, is 75 and still hard at his work. Muraki, who has sold Scriptures for nearly fourteen years, has good news to report.

"I was persecuted when I began," he says, "but now all my relations are Christians!"

Montegi has another story to tell. On a sultry day in Tokyo, a stranger brings him a glass of cut ice. But in a little while, some people begin to throw stones at him.

"I am obliged to you for these," he says, picking up two of the stones, "but to an old man's teeth they are hard. I don't know who threw these, or who brought me the ice, but my heavenly Father knows!"

The people grow quiet then and listen as he tells them about the New Testaments he is selling.

A NEW ADDITION TO BIBLE HOUSE

When Menelik II is crowned Emperor of Ethiopia in 1889, he is set to become one of the country's greatest rulers (until 1913). The Society takes the opportunity to commission an Ethiopian, Gobau Desta, to take some handsome gifts for him, the Empress and the vassal-king of Shoa, Ras Makonnen, Menelik's nephew. Gobau Desta also takes with him a large Arabic Bible for the head of the Abyssinian Church.

Emperor Menelik II sends two elephant tusks to London Bible House

Menelik is delighted with his gifts and, in May 1892, he presents to the Society two large elephant tusks. In an accompanying letter, in beautiful Amharic script, the King writes:

> Your letter of greeting and the valuable portions of the Holy Scriptures have safely reached me, and I am greatly pleased with

all. May the greatest of all Kings give you an everlasting reward, inasmuch as you have remembered my country by your spiritual gifts and prayers... To express my heartfelt thanks for the present you have sent me, I forward to you two elephant tusks.

The largest of the tusks measures six feet two inches in length. The Society attaches them to either side of the wall at the entrance to the General Committee room. Many a visitor will think that a Bible House is a curious place for the exhibition of hunting trophies.

Although the King does not at this time allow missionaries back into his country, he allows Bibles in and in a subsequent letter to the Society he writes, "If you send a quantity of these books to Addis Ababa by a person, bearer of a letter from you, they will be received with pleasure, and I will see that they are distributed, and that a good price is paid for them." The General Committee accepts the offer with delight.

Keynsham, Bristol, 1896

Enter George Müller, the Society's longest standing supporter

Born a year after the Society was founded, 91-year-old George Müller's connection with the Society had lasted so long that no one could recall the beginning of it. There are few sagas in the history of the Christian church which can equal his story. In 1834 Müller decided that if he, a man of no means who had recently arrived in England from Germany, could raise the funds and support needed to found a home for orphan children, simply by prayer and faith without ever appealing for money, that would be something, in his words, to "strengthen the faith of the children of God, besides being a testimony to the consciences of the unconverted of the reality of the things of God".

His Bible was his inspiration. As he reflected on Psalm 68, one phrase gripped his attention, as he put it in his diary, "This word, 'a father of the fatherless' (Psalm 68:5, AV), contains enough encouragement to cast a thousand orphans, with all their need, upon the loving heart of God."

Following a public meeting (at which of course there was deliberately no collection) in Bristol in 1835 when he announced his intention, gifts in money and in kind began to be sent to Müller's home: furniture, cutlery, clothing and materials. In April 1836 he opened his first home in a rented house. Though he went quietly about his work, this little home amounted to a challenge to unbelievers to watch the work Müller had begun, to see if there was a God who would finance it. And here was a challenge to Christians not only to see what God would do, but to consider their response if he proved faithful.

Over the next 62 years, Müller received nearly £1.5 million. The various branches of his work included the care of 10,000 children, at first in four rented homes and then in five enormous buildings on Ashley Down which still stand today. In addition to the residential care of children, Müller sent thousands of pounds abroad to support hundreds of missionaries all over the world. He established schools in Spain, India, Italy, the Guianas and in many counties of England and Wales. Through the Scriptural Knowledge Institution which he founded and directed and which still exists, he circulated Bibles, books and tracts in many countries. He circulated an incredible 1,985,164 copies of Scriptures in all parts of the world in various languages.

In one of the letters he wrote to Bible Society, he referred in passing to the fact that he had read the whole of the Bible through "considerably more than one hundred times with prayer and meditation". In 1896 Society District Secretary Richard Perkins recorded that Müller appeared with him at "a delightful meeting" at Keynsham. George Müller died two years later and you can read his story in full in my book *George Müller: Delighted in God*.

Ten years earlier, Müller had visited Japan, attracting large audiences to hear him preach in Yokohama, Tokyo, Kobe, Kyoto and Osaka. That is a cue to return to our story of Bible Society's work in Japan.

Japan, 1890s

During the war with China in 1894–95, the Society gives away thousands of Japanese Scriptures to the troops and the fleet at Yokosaka and Hiroshima, and afterwards to prisoners of war and the sick and wounded in hospital. In an interview with the "field-agent", the Commander-in-Chief, Prince Komatsu, a cousin of the Emperor, warmly expresses his thanks to all the Bible Societies for the generosity they have shown to Japanese forces.

The growth of Christianity in Japan provokes a reaction of course. Buddhists, Shintoists, and other sects combine in mass meetings all over the country to attempt to ridicule the Bible and denounce its teachings. Circulation of Bibles falls – figures are lower in 1898 than five years earlier. However, a Christian printing company is established in Yokohama which openly prints Bibles. A chaplain is appointed to the prison in Tokyo. And the Emperor happily accepts a presentation to him by the British, American and Scots Bible Societies of an English Bible and the Japanese version in a handsome family edition which has just been published.

In 1898 150 daily newspapers are published in Japan, and, remarkably, 85 daily or weekly journals, including parish magazines, are registered as Christian. Translations of English books into Japanese include Bible commentaries, five *Lives of Christ*, various modern works on theology, and many books by devotional writers, from Thomas à Kempis to Andrew Murray.

Thirty-seven Protestant missionary societies are now at work in Japan. The Roman Catholics have one Archbishop, three Bishops, over 100 missionaries, 26 Japanese priests, about 50 monks and 120 nuns. There are over 50,000 Catholics, over 40,000 Protestants and over 25,000 Orthodox Christians in Japan. But the influence of the Christians is out of proportion to their numbers.

The Japanese political and legal establishment includes several Christians: one Cabinet Minister, two Justices of the Supreme Court, two Speakers of the Lower House, and two or three Vice-Ministers of State, to say nothing of heads of Bureaux and judges of Courts of Appeal. Many officers in the army and navy are Christians, and three daily papers in Tokyo are edited by Christians.

The Society now employs 26 Biblewomen who work under missionary supervision. The churches adopt a regular Bible Sunday and Japanese congregations begin to give regularly towards the work of the Bible Societies.

In 1903 the three Bible Societies agree a new division of their work. In future the American Bible Society will be responsible for the work in north-eastern Japan, with Yokohama as their headquarters. The British and Scots Societies will be jointly responsible for the work in the south-west, with F Parrott of BFBS as their representative in Kobe. The same price list will apply to all three Societies.

The three Societies try hard to prevent overlapping, laying the foundations for a greater and more lasting union later in the 20th century.

Baron Mayejima, ex-Cabinet Minister, addresses the tenth anniversary of the Young Men's Christian Association in Tokyo.

"We must have religion," he tells his audience, "as the basis of our national and personal welfare. No matter how large an army or navy we may have, unless we have righteousness as the foundation of our national existence, we shall fall far short of the highest success. And when I look about me to see what religion we may best rely upon, I am convinced that the religion of Christ is the one most full of strength and promise for the nation."

"You may think the Bible antiquated and out of date," former Prime Minister, Count Okuma, tells another meeting of young men. "The words it contains may so appear, but the noble life which it holds up to admiration is something that will never be out of date, however much the world may progress."

Act 30

A first-class mind for Bible House

John Holland Ritson was one of the most able and colourful characters of Bible Society history. I find it incredible to reflect that he was born less that four years after the death of Mary Jones, in the year that the Earl of Shaftesbury presided over his 17th annual meeting, became General Secretary of the Society five years before it celebrated its centenary, and lived on until the year of the Society's current patron's coronation!

Ritson was born in Bolton, Lancashire in 1868. He won an exhibition to Manchester Grammar School, and at the age of 17 gained an open scholarship in Natural Sciences to Balliol College, Oxford. Reading Natural Sciences just fourteen years after Charles Darwin published his *The Descent of Man* was an interesting experience – but that is another story. He graduated with first-class honours in Chemistry, resisted an attractive invitation to remain at Oxford as a demonstrator in the Balliol laboratory, and entered Wesley College, Headingley, Leeds in 1890 to prepare for the Wesleyan Methodist ministry.

The most famous of all Masters of Balliol, Benjamin Jowett, wrote a testimonial for Ritson. Jowett was the principal pioneer of the idea of "transfer of meaning" as the goal in translation; this was to be developed many years later by Eugene Nida. Jowett's testimonial shows an appreciation of Ritson's qualities which he was later to use with great success in the service of Bible Society.

> I have a very high opinion of Mr Ritson… He is gifted with considerable ability, and is very pleasing in character and manner. He tells me that he intends to become a minister in the Wesleyan body. He has a strong sense of duty, and I think him extremely well fitted for such a calling.
>
> B Jowett

After ordination, Ritson was appointed to the staff of Didsbury College, Manchester. In 1897 he moved to Blackheath, London, where in the following year he married Jane Sykes Lamplough, youngest sister of Williamson Lamplough. A leading Methodist layman, Lamplough had been a member of Bible Society's General Committee since 1894.

Enter John Ritson

In December 1899 Ritson is appointed one of the two General Secretaries of Bible Society. With admirable discretion, Lamplough offers to resign – not only because Ritson is his brother-in-law but also because Ritson is at the time minister of the Wesleyan Methodist Church in Blackheath with which the Lamplough family is closely connected. Maybe tongues are wagging and suggesting that Lamplough has exerted influence in Ritson's selection. The truth, however, is that Lamplough knows nothing of the negotiations which, at the suggestion of the Society's President, Lord Harrowby, have been going on to secure a Methodist minister for the General Secretary post.

According to Ritson himself – and this is surprising since Thomas Charles was a Methodist – "no representative of Methodism had held office on the staff of Bible House". In the event, Lamplough's offer to resign is not accepted – and in fact he becomes Chairman of the General Committee in May 1908, a position he will hold until 1922 when he becomes Treasurer. Unlike Lamplough's connection by marriage to the General Secretary, his positions as Chairman and Treasurer are subject to an annual vote. Relationships between the brothers-in-law are not always harmonious. On one occasion the two men are overheard arguing in Ritson's office in Bible House.

"No, Williamson," says Ritson, his voice raised in irritation, "I've quite made up my mind. We will NOT pray about it!"

Ritson spends a good deal of his time as General Secretary visiting the work of the Society in many parts of the world. In days when the fastest means of travel is by train, he will get to know intimately many of the countries where the Society he runs is active.

ONE HUNDRED YEARS ON

It is (in 1900) 100 years since Mary Jones walked from Llanfihangel to Bala to receive her three Bibles. In that time the Society has been busy. It has issued nearly 2 million Welsh Bibles, over 2 million Testaments and nearly 338,000 portions. A Welsh Bible costs ten pence and a Welsh Testament one penny. There are 356 Auxiliaries and Branches in Wales. She certainly started something.

Enter the Marquis of Northampton

The Society's four Presidents from 1804 to 1900 were all Tories. The fifth President, the Marquis of Northampton, who took over on the death of the Earl of Harrowby in 1900, had been a Liberal Member of Parliament from 1889 to 1897. All his predecessors had been far more than titular Presidents, having concerned themselves in detail with the Society's policies and, particularly in the case of the first two, committee work and correspondence as well.

The Marquis of Northampton will maintain this tradition of personal commitment to the Society's affairs in a remarkable way.

One colporteur, working on the French Riviera, hears a knock on his door one morning. He answers it to find a distinguished-looking English gentleman standing there.

"Good morning," the visitor says in excellent French. "I am the President of the Bible Society, and would like you to take me round and show me something of your work as a colporteur."

The startled colporteur spends one day in his life with the Marquis of Northampton as his companion as he works in his sunny French town.

When the Society celebrates its centenary, the Marquis will preside over many of the events in person and in the years to come will bring his political experience and diplomatic influence to bear on the Society's affairs. At this time the influence of the House of

Lords, in which he sits, is extensive, especially in foreign affairs. For a Society with international obligations, having a President who is able to intervene in situations requiring delicate negotiations is invaluable. When he dies, in 1913, the office of President will remain vacant for five years until the Duke of Connaught takes over at the end of the First World War.

Meanwhile in court circles...

That loyal supporter of Bible Society, and patron of the Windsor Ladies' Bible Association, had celebrated (in 1887) 50 years as Queen. A great jubilee was held for her. Wearing a black dress, with the ribbon of the Garter and a white feather in her bonnet, she drove through the streets of London, cheered by her subjects. They were prepared to forget her excessively long mourning over the loss of her dear Albert and their other grievances against her. They saw her not only as their own Queen – and few alive could remember any other monarch – but as the head of a great and expanding empire. In some ways the growth of Bible Society mirrored the growth of the British Empire.

Ten years later, in 1897, another jubilee was held to celebrate 60 years of her reign. Even as an old woman, Victoria remained interested in what was going on in the world. In 1900, when she was over 80, she visited Ireland. How much the country had changed since Thomas Charles and his friends had gone there in 1808! The Queen wanted to show her gratitude to the Irish for the way they had fought in the Boer War.

Exit Queen Victoria

Later that year, her health begins to fail. She moves to Osborne House, never to return to London. She drives out for the last time on 15 January 1901 and on the 22nd she dies in the presence of several members of her family. She is buried in St George's Chapel, Windsor, on 1 February, but as she wished to be buried near Prince Albert, the coffin is lifted three days later and taken to his tomb at nearby Frogmore.

This means that the Prince of Wales who has been serving his long apprenticeship for kingship since he laid the foundation of Bible House 35 years earlier, at last becomes King Edward VII at the age of 60, and the popular Princess Alexandra his Queen. When the Society celebrates its centenary in St Paul's three years later, the King will not be well enough to attend but Queen Alexandra will listen with rapt attention to the Archbishop's sermon.

Act
31

Unprecedented
global celebration

The Society begins to prepare early to ensure that its 100th birthday is appropriately celebrated. A centenary Grand Committee, chaired by Caleb Kent, the Society's Treasurer and soon to become General Committee Chairman, begins to meet regularly from 1 October 1901 and starts to send delegations to many countries.

PROGRESS TO DATE

The Society now has 5,875 Auxiliaries, Branches and Associations in England and Wales and 2,000 abroad. 850 colporteurs are employed abroad at an annual cost of over £43,000 (over £2,300,000 at today's values). Cumulative expenditure has risen to just under £14 million and over 180 million copies of the Scriptures have been issued. In one year nearly 6 million Scriptures are issued. The Society now issues Bibles in 89 languages; the New Testament in 74 more, and portions in 207 more. Revision of the Malagasi Bible (Madagascar) cost over £3,000. In preparing a new edition of the Lifu Bible for the French Loyalty Islands in the south-west Pacific, no less than 52,310 corrections were made.

By May 1903 centenary editions of the Bible and New Testament in the English Revised Version are in circulation and those of the Welsh Scriptures appear later. The Society presents nearly 10,000 Sunday Schools in England and Wales with a new desk Bible as a centenary memorial.

On 8 January 1904 the Society's neighbour *The Times* publishes a leading article headed, "Universal Bible Sunday". Note its tone:

The late Master of Balliol once remarked in his characteristic fashion that all Christians have two things at least in common – they have the Bible and they have Sunday. Certainly it seems a felicitous proposal to celebrate the 100th birthday of the British and Foreign Bible Society by observing the first Sunday in March this year as "Universal Bible Sunday". On that day the churches of every Reformed Communion throughout the world will hold special services of thanksgiving for the blessings which they possess in the Scriptures. In our own country the suggestion has been taken up with general enthusiasm, which is more noteworthy when we recall the acute forms which religious controversy has recently assumed in England.

There is one book, however, to which all Christians appeal, and one English institution which exists simply to make that book common. Ever since its foundation one hundred years ago the Bible Society has exerted a moderating and reconciling force amid ecclesiastical divisions. Organised on lines which appeal impartially to Churchmen and Nonconformists, this Society has been able to unify in common service multitudes of Christians who act together in no other religious cause...

The Bible Society acts as a chief partner and ally of every British foreign mission; and our great missionary societies, without exception, have joined hands to celebrate this day of common thanksgiving... Many of them have generously arranged to forgo their own sermons or meetings on March 6 in favour of the Bible Sunday... The Bible Society has achieved signal success in bringing together translators and revisers belonging to nearly all schools of theology and almost every communion of Christian faith. It has been able to combine and coordinate the ripest scholars and linguists in producing for each part of the mission field what becomes accepted as a standard Bible. Missionaries may well rejoice in the immense gain which they secure by escaping rival and sectarian versions. Nor do they forget what they owe to the agency which provides all the copies of Scriptures which they need, practically without cost to themselves....

London, March 1904...

The centenary celebrations themselves begin on Friday 4 March 1904 with a simple noon meeting for prayer at what is still known, even in the early years of the 20th century, as "new Bible House" in Queen Victoria Street. In the evening, the President of the Society, the Marquis of Northampton, and Caleb Kemp, Chairman of the General Committee, welcome hundreds of delegates and friends representing Bible Societies at home and abroad to the Hall of the Worshipful Company of Fishmongers, London Bridge – just a stone's throw from the memorable room at Swan Stairs where the idea of the Society was born.

On Saturday afternoon, 5 March, the Royal Albert Hall is packed for the first of two meetings there (the Guildhall is considered too small). The Lord Mayor and Sheriffs of London attend, complete with medieval sword-bearer, Sergeant-at-Arms and City Marshall. The late Queen Victoria's daughter, Princess Christian, cuts a huge birthday cake. The massive crowd sings the stirring centenary hymn written by Horace Moule:

> We thank thee for a hundred years
> Of mercy, Lord, and blessing...

led by a 1,500-voice choir.

...and around the world

Dawn on 6 March heralds the long planned-for, worldwide Bible Sunday. Several years of preparation have produced agreement that Christian communions from all over the world should unite in praise and prayer on the same day. The two English Anglican Archbishops have promoted the proposal on behalf of nearly all the Bishops. All nonconformist conferences and assemblies enthusiastically endorse it. It is adopted without exception by all missionary societies and worked hard for by churches in Europe, the British colonies, mission fields of Africa, Asia, the Pacific, Canada, the United States and Protestant congregations in Central and South America.

And so Bible Sunday is observed throughout the world on 6 March 1904: in Fiji, where only 50 years earlier there were cannibal feasts; in Korea; on the Yangtze river in China; on mail steamers in the Straits of Malacca and the Persian Gulf; at Blantyre in the highlands of Scotland; on board passenger liners; in Buenos Aires and so on.

In London, the day dawns bleak with sleet and rain, but St Paul's is crowded long before noon with worshippers from all over London and beyond. King Edward VII is unwell, but Queen Alexandra and the Prince (the future George V) and Princess of Wales and Princess Victoria (the late Queen's oldest child) attend.

The Lord Mayor and key office holders from the City of London, the Archbishop of Canterbury, the Bishop of London, the Dean and dignitaries of the cathedral, all in ermine, scarlet and gold, meet the members of the royal family on the steps of St Paul's Cathedral.

Archbishop of Canterbury Randall Davidson preaches from the text "Let there be light" (Genesis 1:3–4). He contrasts this Bible Sunday with Shrove Sunday of 1527, when leaders of the English Church watched from that very spot the burning of the English New Testament. In contrast, he says, princes, clergy and people are gathered today to thank God for the distribution of his Word to every nation under heaven. He describes true science and true religion as "sisters" and says that "nothing but disaster can arise from the petulant scorn of the one or from the timidity or the tyrannies of the other". This may be an echo of the evolutionary debates of the second half of the 19th century, although since around the time of Darwin's death in 1882 most educated Christians have accepted that evolution and Christian belief are compatible. Referring to Bible Society's long struggle against poverty, distance and language he says, "We look upwards and outwards and onwards: we thank God and take courage."

A clear photograph exists of Queen Alexandra and the Prince and Princess sitting listening to the Archbishop of Canterbury preaching his sermon. The service closes with an anthem by one of the musical Wesleys.

These celebrations in London are matched around the world. Lord Curzon, the Viceroy of India, attends the celebration in Calcutta. The Governor General of Australia turns up in Melbourne. In Washington the vast congregation at St John's in the centre of the capital includes President Roosevelt, members of the Diplomatic Corps, representatives of the Supreme Court, the Cabinet and Senate of the United States. There are services in cathedrals in Stockholm, Uganda, Bloemfontein, Shanghai, Singapore and provincial cathedrals in England and Wales. Nearly every school and mission station in virtually all Methodist circuits throughout the world observes the day. Someone says that "never in the Christian centuries have so many millions come so near to realising the dream and hope of 'one fold and one Shepherd'."

On Monday 7 March, after a quiet meeting for prayer at Bible House in the morning, the Marquis of Northampton entertains about 400 members of Christian churches and communions, including delegates from all over the world, at a lunch in the King's Hall of the Holborn restaurant. During the meal Bible Societies and churches from all over the world convey their greetings. In Wales that afternoon the schoolgirls of Bala decorate the statue of Thomas Charles and lay flowers on his grave. At 7 p.m. the Royal Albert Hall is packed for the second of the two Royal Albert Hall meetings, the "centenary meeting".

The Marquis of Northampton takes the chair with the Archbishop of Canterbury on his right. The Bishop of St Albans leads the prayers. The event certainly doesn't simply look back: the President of the Society challenges his audience with the needs of India where 450 million people are still without a Bible. In his address the Archbishop of Canterbury focuses on the twofold name of the Society (British and Foreign) and speaks of the deep undercurrent of Scripture which flows behind English speech and English life – "the Word of God, both in translation and the original has the same living power over the minds of men". Other speakers plead for the maintenance of the Bible in the home as the essential condition of our character and place as a Christian nation.

In Wales there is a procession to the ruins of Mary Jones's cottage at Tyn'y-ddôl. David Lloyd-George, MP and the future Prime Minister, chairs an enthusiastic Welsh meeting in Exeter Hall.

More important meetings follow on the Tuesday. At one, in the Queen's Hall, Langham Place, the United States Ambassador reads a message cabled from President Roosevelt which, amid an outburst of applause, conveys "to the British and Foreign Bible Society my hearty congratulations on their Centenary, and my earnest wish for the continued success of the good work". A delegate from the American Bible Society makes a speech vividly tracing the influence of the Bible in America from the landing of the Pilgrim Fathers in the *Mayflower* and the Puritan emigration from England to New England. To cheers, he speaks of the importance for the world of the United States and Great Britain setting an example as a moral influence – an example which other Christian nations should follow. Britain and the USA must cooperate in all good works for "we have one God, one Bible, one language, one destiny".

At the same meeting, the court chaplain to King Oscar II announces that the King of Sweden and Norway (he was King of both countries until 1905) has commanded him to express to Bible Society "his warmest thanks for the blessings vouchsafed through their work in Sweden and Norway during the century that is past. His Majesty regrets that, owing to a journey abroad, he is unable to celebrate, as it had been his desire, these memorable days together with his people". Representatives from Bible Societies around the world present gifts. A message from Prussia says that "by command of his majesty the Emperor, Bible Sunday was celebrated in all Protestant churches in Prussia". A telegram is read from the King of Denmark.

On the subject of the King of Denmark, I break off my narrative here to say that today (2003) the Bible Society with the closest relationship to their royal family is the Danish Bible Society. Daphne Bidstrup, of that Society, tells me that the Danish Bible Society has the right and responsibility to update and publish the Danish "authorised" version of the Bible. A Bible version is authorised when the King or Queen (at the moment Danes have Queen Margrethe II) acknowledges it. There are one or two other Bible versions in Danish but they are not authorised and hence not used in the state church and so are rare. In other words, the Danish Bible Society practically has a monopoly on the Bible. So there is a close relationship between the Queen and the Danish Bible Society. The Queen is also the patron of the Danish Bible Society and she has recently made illustrations for a Bible that was published in 2000 in Danish, Feroese and Greenlandic at the same time. It is entitled *Rigs – of slægtsbibelen* which Daphne translates as The Kingdom – and Family Bible. The illustrations were exhibited in museums in Denmark, Feroe Islands and Greenland. Recently they were also exhibited in northern Germany where it proved to be an unusually popular exhibition (probably, says Daphne because it was news to the Germans that the Queen is an artist – Danes have known that for a long time!).

Act
32

Trials of a translator

Enter Rev. W Millman

In 1904 the Society publishes Mark's Gospel in the Kele language of central Africa. The translation is the work of Rev. W Millman of the BMS Congo Mission at Yakusu, Stanley Falls. Millman is the first person to attempt a translation of the Bible into this language which is spoken from the Aruwimi river to the Stanley Falls. After completing Mark's Gospel, Millman presses on with the rest of the New Testament.

Millman persuades local boys to come in the evening to his bamboo house. Here they sit until midnight, teaching him to master the Kele language. As the equivalent for God, he adopts the Arabic word *Mungu*; he cannot use the word *Litiko*, which the Kele people use for their mythical personification of "fate" or "fortune", because the word also applies to diseases like smallpox.

For many colours the Kele people do not possess names, so Millman has to render "blue" by "like the sky", and "green" by "like the grass". He cannot find any word for "thanks" until on one occasion he kills a leopard which on the previous day had carried off a woman's little daughter. The mother leads a group of women to the mission house and thanks him with a local song. The first word of the song is *kelekele*. Talking about this afterwards, one of Millman's houseboys says, "She gave the white man *kelekele*", and that word is used locally from that time on for "thank you".

Sometimes Millman finds that the Kele translation has to be even more precise than the English, as in the case with the word for "brother" or "sister". You have to know whether the brother is an elder or a younger brother – or you have to guess and take the consequences!

Millman has to work hard to find words to translate specifically religious concepts. What word is he to use for "to bless"? One day he meets an old witch doctor to whom he has previously given some help. The witch doctor comes up to Millman, spreads out his hands, points to the sky and then spits in his face. One of Millman's boys is understandably afraid that the missionary will resent being treated in this way.

"That is his expression of good wishes for you," the boy says.

"What is?" Millman asks.

"This man is blowing on you."

"But he spat on me!"

"That is because he trusts you very much."

And so Millman learns that the witch doctor has blown him a blessing – the spit is part of him and the belief is that Millman can then work good or evil as a result. But he decides not to use this expression in Scripture. Rather than saying, "Isaac spat on him" he prefers to say, "Isaac spoke good things to him."

The Lokele boys make a suggestion to the missionary.

"If you can teach us to read what you have written down," they say to Millman, "then we will be better able to help you correct the words."

Millman readily agrees and the boys learn the vowels *a*, *e*, *i*, *o*, *u* in one night. They learn *s*, *m*, *n*, *w*, *y* a day or two later. Then they learn to combine the letters. At last, Millman writes a few sentences which need the only ten letters they know. His first sentence – it becomes the first complete sentence in the Lokele primer he writes – is *Masiya asowa owawa*: "Christ died, the innocent for the guilty." Millman has 20,000 copies of the primer printed and this becomes the first sentence which Lokele men and women learn to read.

A similar story could be repeated in many countries of the world.

In the early years of the 20th century, a missionary with more than 20 years experience in India wrote:

The Gospel is for all men, and its message is adapted to all men. It has an immense appeal to all men when it reaches their minds and hearts; but if the Gospel itself, and not a travesty of it, is to reach them, it must be presented not merely in a language of whose separate words and phrases they recognise the meaning, but in a language which moves freely in the terms of the life and thought, the feelings and aspirations, the tradition and the emotion of their experience. To know a language is not merely to be able to translate into its phraseology with considerable accuracy that which has been thought out in another language, but to think its words and to grasp the spirit and thought they focus.

And that task is ideally best done not by the missionary but by the men and women who have themselves grown up to speak the language into which the Bible is being translated.

Meanwhile in Wales, 1907...

At the ruins of the cottage at Tyn'y-ddôl where Mary spent her childhood and set out for her walk to Bala, Merioneth Sunday Schools erect a monument which, to this day, is well cared for. (Merionethshire has since become Gwynedd.)

> IN MEMORY OF MARY JONES, WHO IN THE YEAR 1800, AT THE AGE OF 16 WALKED FROM HERE TO BALA, TO PROCURE FROM THE REVD. THOMAS CHARLES, B.A. A COPY OF THE WELSH BIBLE. THIS INCIDENT WAS THE OCCASION OF THE FORMATION OF THE BRITISH AND FOREIGN BIBLE SOCIETY. ERECTED BY THE SUNDAY SCHOOLS OF MERIONETH.

(She was actually in her 16th year but hadn't reached her 16th birthday when she walked to Bala.) In October of the same year, Lizzie Rowlands enthrals the children of the Band of Hope, Llidiarde, with a talk recalling her visits to the elderly Mary Jones in the last two years of her life.

Slides and cake for Ritson

Kobe, Japan, 1907

Re-enter John Ritson

Confined to a narrow shelf of land between the Rokko mountains to the north and the sea to the south, Kobe is today a
part of the second largest urban and industrial complex in Japan.
When Bible Society Secretary John Ritson arrives there in 1907,
he acknowledges that Shintoism and Buddhism have enjoyed
something of a revival. But, always a man who knows his own
mind, he has no doubt that "these religions are doomed". In his
view the chief forces arrayed against the still young but growing
Christian Church in Japan are "indifference, materialism and
agnosticism".

Mr Parrott, who runs the Society's work in Japan, has
invited the 24 Japanese colporteurs who are within easy reach of
Kobe to meet Ritson at the Bible depot in Kobe. Since they know
they are going to meet the English Secretary of the Society by
whom they are employed, most of them turn up in European dress
for the occasion.

At a small conference to which others have been invited as
well as the colporteurs, the latest technology is used. Mr Lawrence,
the Society's sub-agent for Japan, controls a magic lantern fitted
with an acetylene light. The first slide is a hymn in Japanese
characters.

After prayer, led by Rev. C T Warren of CMS, Mr Parrott
gives a commentary on the slides. They are mainly tinted photographs from illustrations in the Society's popular reports. Magic
lanterns are as tiresome to use in Japan as they are in England. Poor
Lawrence, on show in front of the General Secretary of the mighty
British and Foreign Bible Society, puts in a slide showing a page

from the Latin Vulgate seven ways before he decides he has it right. This mishap reduces the colporteurs to giggles and Parrott is assured of a cheerful and receptive audience for the rest of his talk.

After the lantern show come the refreshments. Lawrence's team of helpers pour tea — Ritson dismissively describes it as a "weak, warm, green fluid" — into little cups without handles, served of course without sugar or cream or milk, and each guest is given cakes in a bag. According to correct Japanese etiquette, the cakes should not be eaten at once but saved. However, since the colporteurs are hungry after their long walks, and the time for their evening meal has passed, some of them adopt European habits and eat the lot there and then.

Several colporteurs then give talks. Maruyama, aged 40, when a Buddhist had emigrated to America and become a Christian under the teaching of Moody's Institute at Northfield, Massachusetts. Fired with a desire to give the Bible to his fellow countrymen, he has worked his passage back to Japan as a cabin boy and volunteered for service at Bible House. He conducted a house-to-house Bible campaign at Osaka in 1906 and now plans to do the same in Kyoto.

Colporteur Kogo, an older man, follows. An unmistakable member of the Salvation Army, he sings a poem he has written himself to a tune he has helpfully composed. Ritson finds it difficult to keep a straight face while listening to him.

"I sing in the streets and inns," Kogo says, "and always succeed in getting an audience."

Ritson believes it.

"After singing," Kogo continues, "I tell the people of their need of the Christ revealed in the Book I am selling."

"Every earnest man," observes Ritson, "has his characteristic *modus operandi*. And Kogo succeeds with his."

Ritson then gives a talk which Warren of CMS interprets. He speaks about the duty of supplying the Gospel of Jesus Christ to all men and women and about the joy to be found in suffering to attain that end. They sing another hymn and then there are more prayers.

Colporteur Fuji pleads for the increasing usefulness of the staff in extending the kingdom of God. His prayer is characterised by vivid imagery.

"As the Lord of hosts builds a castle in Japan for the defence of righteousness," he prays, "may we be used as the cement between the stones."

After expressing his gratitude for the conference, Colporteur Ikeno bows his head.

"I thank you, heavenly Father, for the privilege of being engaged in so great a work. I ask for an abundant blessing on the great committees directing Bible affairs throughout the world."

At the end of the conference, Ritson notices that it is difficult to get the colporteurs to go. They seem to want to continue in prayer and praise, although the hour is late. Maybe the spirit of the Korean revival is blowing east across the Sea of Japan.

With the rising tide of nationalism in the 1930s, Japanese leadership comes more to the fore, both in the Tokyo headquarters and in Kobe. Japan gets involved in her adventure in China and South-East Asia, and political relations with America and Britain grow strained. It seems wise to amalgamate the work of BFBS, ABS and NBSS in the Japan Bible Society. The American Bible Society hands over the splendid Bible House it has built in Ginza, the main shopping area of Tokyo, to the new Society. The spacious property of the British and Foreign Bible Society in Kobe is disposed of and the proceeds go into Bible work. A small local depot takes the place of Kobe Bible House. The Government officially recognises the new Japan Bible Society in 1938.

All through the war years the Japan Bible Society circulates the Bible and once or twice prints small editions of the Scriptures. Early in 1945, the Bible House is gutted in a great "fire raid" and all the stocks destroyed. No more Scriptures are available for sale until, under the American occupation, the American Bible Society acts with characteristic generosity. ABS makes a gift of 2.5 million Bibles and New Testaments in the immediate postwar period, leaving the Japan Bible Society to decide how to use them.

In 1952, the Japan Bible Society distributes 2 million copies of the Scriptures and is spending £3,000 (£54,000 today) a year on translating the Bible into colloquial Japanese.

In 2000 the Japan Bible Society celebrates 125 years of Bible distribution. The year marks the fourth of five years of special anniversary events. In May the Society holds a Bible exhibition in the city of Kobe that draws 25,000 visitors in five days. The Society exhibits fragments of the Dead Sea Scrolls, Mary Jones's Bible and other items.

In 2001, the Japan Bible Society publishes the *Biblical Original Languages Concordance* CD-ROM which enables the reader to search for Hebrew and Greek words in the Bible and will assist in future translation work. In 2002 South Korea and Japan co-host the football World Cup. The Japan and Korean Bible Societies work on a joint project to produce World Cup Scripture editions and work with a sporting events partnership to plan effective distribution during this major sport event.

In April 2003, in Kobe, following a Bible exhibition in 2002, the Bible House run by BFBS and NBSS between 1904 and 1937 is reopened by a group of pastors.

Act
34

The seed bears rich fruit in Korea

Re-enter John Ritson with Hugh Miller

In April 1907 Society General Secretary John Ritson arrives in Korea. He stays with Hugh Miller, but early in the visit the two men are invited for a meal in a Korean home where they are entertained by an interesting couple. Their host is approaching 70 and is not a Christian. His wife is only 22 and a member of the new and already rapidly growing Korean Church. For Koreans the couple are quite affluent – but it is a revelation for the Oxford-educated, middle class Ritson: the yard is alive with noisy hens and other animals, and the absence of drains creates a powerful smell.

Ritson and Miller sit cross-legged on the floor of a small room lined with oiled paper while their hostess serves them food on a table raised a few inches from the floor. The first course is boiled macaroni floating with bits of meat in a bowl of water. Quickly proving himself simply not up to the task of eating this with chopsticks, the wife gives Ritson a flat spoon. From time to time, his host places a piece of meat on Ritson's spoon with his chopsticks. The next dish is bean jelly, pickled radishes and *kimshi*, chestnuts and gritty sweet cake. Overall, Ritson observes that "for hospitality none can surpass the Koreans – in fact the rich are often reduced to poverty, by being literally eaten up by their relatives".

Although the American and Scots Bible Societies have been active in Korea, with the three Societies working in close partnership, by the time Ritson arrives, Bible work is mainly being undertaken by BFBS working on its own. Hugh Miller is cooperating with a strong and representative missionary committee which is responsible for selecting the members of the Board of Translators. Ritson hopes that the complete Korean Bible will be ready by 1909. When he interviews the Board of Translators they are working on the book of Ecclesiastes. They ask his opinion on the meaning of some passages, but he is acutely conscious of the inadequacies of his knowledge of Hebrew.

Ritson addresses a number of Korean audiences and this alerts the organisers of the tour to the problems which would be created if he were introduced as the "Secretary" of Bible Society. It is thought that this might give the impression that he sat, say on London Bridge, writing out visiting cards or letters for uneducated people. Then someone introduces him as "Chairman" of the Society, but he protests that this exaggerates his importance. Finally, he is announced as "Bishop of the Bible Society" – a title which he rather likes, commenting, with a twinkle in his eye, that it gives him "hope of Episcopal dignity".

At the time of Ritson's visit, the Society employs 68 colporteurs and 17 Biblewomen in Korea. The Biblewomen occupy themselves not just in selling the Scriptures but also in teaching Korean women how to read. In no country had the widespread circulation of the Scriptures done more to evangelise the people than Korea. Again and again, Bibles, New Testaments and Gospels, even in the absence of missionaries, have been the means of leading groups of villagers to become Christians. The Bible has been the pioneer of the Korean Church and nowhere has it been more fully recognised and followed up by the missionaries.

THE GREAT KOREAN REVIVAL

The year 2007 will mark the centenary of the great Korean revival. Many Christians in South Korea are praying that something similar will reoccur in the north of their peninsula.

Ritson arrives in Korea just as the revival has reached the peak of its dramatic power. As well as putting his own slant on the events, he has time for mature reflection on its significance. "It is generally admitted in Korea," Ritson notes, "that its awakening to religious life, which has so impressed the whole of Christendom, is due mainly to the seed sown by the Bible Societies." This is the story.

In August 1906 missionaries in Pyongyang (now in North

Korea), longing for a deeper experience of God's power in their lives, hold meetings for Bible study and prayer for eight days. Then they join with several hundred Korean Christians and all covenant to spend one hour each day in prayer for an outpouring of the Spirit of God.

The missionaries and the Korean Christians continue praying like this until 1907 when, in the first week of January, at a meeting in the Presbyterian church, the answer comes in an unexpected way. A number of Koreans stand up before the whole congregation and begin to confess their sin and cry out for God's mercy. In service after service scenes like this are repeated.

In episodes reminiscent of the early years of Wesley's preaching in England, and of some more recent charismatic meetings in many parts of the world, "many cast themselves on the ground in paroxysms of agony, many fell as if struck by thunderbolts, some became for a time unconscious; all cried for mercy". Services last in some cases for hours and are marked by powerful prayer, praise and thanksgiving as men and women make their peace with God.

In confessing their sins, those affected by the revival tell some extraordinary stories. One man says he has murdered his baby brother, committed to his care by his mother on her deathbed. Another has embezzled sums of money. Others have been guilty of theft and immorality. In Ritson's view, "confession and contrition, which all the instruments of torture known to the terrible penal code of Korea would have been utterly impotent to bring about, were produced by the power of God's Spirit".

Christian students in the Theological College and in the Union College and Academy come under the influence of the revival. They hold meetings for prayer, and in penitence some "beat the floor with hands and head: their screams and outcries were as though demons whose name is legion were tearing them".

One man has lived some years earlier in the north of Korea. He has never heard of Christianity but, living a hermit's life on a lonely mountain, he has given himself to prayer and fasting for two years, searching for truth. He fails and, abandoning his religious search, begins to live a wild life. He becomes a soldier and then hears the Christian Gospel for the first time. Returning to his father's farm and his own village, he wins converts for Christ. As the believers grow in number, they begin to build a church but have no funds to complete it.

And so these men and women begin to pray that God will send them the needed funds. When no answer seems to come, the man who has been a hermit sells the one ox which did the work on his farm – a fine animal which fetches a good price – and with the money he completes the building of the church. When a missionary visits the village he sees this young man – yoked with his brother to the plough – doing the work of the ox, while their elderly father holds the handles and follows the furrow. Surely a man like that will have no sin to confess!

But even he recalls much faithlessness and many acts of disloyalty to Christ. Humbling himself with a group of other Christians, he cries out for mercy and goes on his way, searching for a higher level of holiness.

This great movement in Korea is more than a revival among the Christians. It is a work of evangelistic outreach with large numbers of men and women convinced of sin and turning to Christ under the influence of the Holy Spirit. The General Secretary of the Bible Society, on his visit, is satisfied that it is not a case of members of a group following one another blindly. Nor is it limited to any one region: many are converted in Pusan, Chemulpo (Inchon), Taegu, Seoul, Kaesong, Wonsan and Pyongyang. And the revival has broken out spontaneously in places where missionaries have never been and even where local church leaders have lapsed into indifference or formalism.

Hugh Miller takes Ritson to a new and well-equipped hospital run by the American Presbyterian Mission where the Society supports a colporteur and Biblewoman. Ritson hears a sound which at first he thinks comes from the operating theatre. But it is a group of fourteen Koreans in a Bible Study being led by none other than Saw Sang Yuin himself. The group's singing of their opening hymn doesn't impress Ritson – "each singer composed his own tune as he went along and rendered it in a raucous screech" – but he is impressed by the enthusiasm with which they study the New Testament.

SIGNS AND WONDERS

John Ritson spends his first Sunday in Korea at Seoul. At the Methodist Episcopal Church in the morning 320 men sit on the floor on one side, dressed in their baggy trousers and white gowns, wearing stove-pipe hats, tied under the chin. The unmarried men have their hair in pigtails like the Chinese, but the married men have theirs cut off with their hair done up into a top-knot. About 300 women and girls sit screened from the men, the girls with bodices of pink, canary yellow and green.

Dr Reynolds, whom the Bible Societies have engaged to complete the translation of the Korean Old Testament, interprets Ritson's sermon. He finds the congregation eager and attentive. When he has finished speaking, a Korean pastor gets to his feet.

"I appeal to those of you who have questions on what our preacher from England has said to stand up."

Seventeen men and five women stand up, walk to the front and give their names and addresses. A team from the church visits each one in the following week.

In the afternoon Ritson preaches at a church the Koreans themselves have built – a low thatched building where 450 people have assembled to hear the English visitor preach. Saw Sang Yuin is there, giving Ritson a vigorous handshake, together with his nephew, the first member of the second generation of Protestant Korean Christians.

Ritson travels north by a new railway constructed by the Japanese during the war with Russia. After ten hours they reach Pyongyang, one of the ancient capitals of Korea, where the revival first broke out. He preaches at a student academy on "the joyousness of our God and his desire to make all men equally joyous through the gospel with which Christians are put in trust". After he preaches the students leave, some to their classes, others to prayer meetings where "spontaneously under the direct influence of the Spirit there arose a murmur of audible praise and pleading, without any confusion – the voices blending like notes from some great instrument of music".

Ritson goes to many prayer meetings and finds that "the

Spirit of God was present in power". That he thinks is the secret of the triumph of the Gospel in Korea – everywhere there is prayer. "Christians alike are acknowledging their sins before God and one another, and feeling their own weakness and insufficiency, are imploring – and not in vain – the baptism of the Holy Ghost" – these are Ritson's words, using terminology which has since proved controversial.

It isn't uncommon to find a thousand people turning out for a prayer meeting on a Wednesday night in Pyongyang. People pray daily and hourly, "some spending whole nights pleading for the salvation of human souls". "Can we wonder," Ritson asks, "that there is a revival among the living and a resurrection of the dead? All the world over, the Church's deepest need is such a sense of its sinfulness and its dependence upon God as will send it down upon its knees before the Almighty."

At the Methodist church on the Sunday in Pyongyang, between 700 and 800 people sit on the floor, the men and women separated as usual by a screen; in the front a crowd of small boys is packed tightly against the platform. Many of the women have their babies tied to their backs. Some of them have walked to church wearing straw hats over a yard wide, successfully screening their beauty from the eyes of the men. The women leave these hats in piles at the church door and hang their sandals on racks.

There are a number of enquirers at the end of the service – but Christianity in the growing Korean Church in the early years of the 20th century is a far from cosy affair. Even on confession of their allegiance to Christ the enquirers are not allowed to become church members without a period of serious probation.

"The missionaries do all they can to persuade them to become Christians," some say, "and when they consent they make it as hard as possible for them to enter the Church."

The probationary period can last for between one and two years. And sometimes the Korean church leaders are stricter than the missionaries. Hugh Miller tells Ritson that he visited one church where a small body of believers was examining some candidates for baptism. One was an 18-year-old young man who had read the Gospels, could repeat the Lord's Prayer, and had given good evidence of a changed life.

"He is all right," said the missionary in charge. "We will baptise him."

"No," said a Korean church leader, "I do not want this young man baptised. He is living with his old mother who sometimes loses her temper and beats him. When she beats him he gets mad with her. I do not want him to be baptised until he can take his beating without getting mad."

"Well," said an American present, "I am an elder of the Presbyterian Church in America, but if my membership depended upon answering the questions put by these Koreans, I would have to stay outside."

Ritson preaches in some churches where the congregations have grown so large that they have decided to hold separate services for the men and women. During the women's services the men are asked to stay at home and look after the children. After Ritson preaches to 1,500 men, eight come forward in response to the appeal from the Korean pastor.

Korean Christians are anxious to be self-supporting. A Presbyterian church holding 1,500 people was built entirely from Korean gifts, though an advance came from America to tide over the initial outlay. One Methodist church cost £800, with £400 given by Koreans; £100 was raised in a single collection – the average earnings of the members was about a shilling (five pence) a day. They give time as well, devoting a number of days every year to evangelistic work – going out voluntarily at their own expense, spreading the Gospel in the villages.

The missionaries, "plain, hard-headed, scholarly men", are amazed at what they believe to be a genuine work of the Holy Spirit. When Ritson congratulates a Korean pastor in Inchon on the success of a recent mission, he replies quietly, "It is the grace of God."

To those who suggest to the Bible Society General Secretary that the Korean revival is characterised by elements of hysteria, Ritson has his reply.

"It is a healthy hysteria which makes the impure pure, the

dishonest honest, the sinful holy. 'By their fruits you shall know them.' "

The revival is far more than superficial excitement – it is deep, real and widespread.

North Kando, Korea, 1913

Enter a Korean colporteur

In 1913, one Korean colporteur takes a journey in the north Kando region during the summer. On one particular day he walks many miles without meeting anyone. However, towards evening he arrives at a large village on the edge of a broad plain. Tired after his long journey, he sits down and talks to a man who is working in a rice field.

As the two men are talking, a dozen children between ten and twelve years old come out from the village.

"Are you in a mood to listen to what I have to say?" the Korean colporteur asks the children.

Some say they are while others say they are not.

"First wash your faces in that clear water over there," the colporteur says.

Some of the children do so while others refuse.

"Look how much cleaner the children who have washed are than you," the colporteur says to those who have refused to wash. Eventually, he persuades them all to wash.

Then he holds up a Gospel and begins to talk to them.

"Just as your faces were dirty but have been made clean by washing, so your hearts are unclean because of sin. But if you will believe in Jesus he will forgive your sins and make your hearts clean. The books I have to sell will teach you the way."

Each child, and the man who was working the rice field, buys a Gospel.

Then an old man wearing a *kwan* (a four-pointed hat worn by the Korean gentry) comes out from the village. He is smoking a long pipe.

"What books have those children got?" the old man shouts.

"We bought them from the visitor," the children say, afraid of what the old man will say.

"Return them instantly!" the old man demands. The children begin to do so until the rice farmer intervenes.

"Father, do not be alarmed. This visitor is teaching the children well. It would be good for us if we had one of these good men living in our village."

The old man, who is the father of the man who is working in the field, then allows the children to keep the Gospels. The colporteur looks up and sees the sun sinking behind the hills in the west. He has nowhere to sleep.

"Don't worry," says the rice farmer. "Come to my house and stay the night."

By 1925 the Society has published 10 million copies of the Scriptures in Korean, about five-sixths of them sold by colporteurs.

By the 1940s most fair-sized villages and all the towns have their churches, built by the Koreans themselves.

In the 1940s a first tentative constitution is drawn up for an independent Korean Bible Society. In 1941 the final step is taken and Bible Society transfers all its assets, except the Bible House, over to the Korean Bible Society. On the staff of the new Society is a Korean, Mr Chung, who has worked with BFBS people for over 30 years.

James Robertson is appointed Secretary of the Society in 1946 with Chung as his colleague. A resourceful and energetic Scot, Robertson began to work for Bible Society in Shanghai in 1926, served as an assistant in Hankou in 1929, and became Secretary for Manchuria in 1930. The difficulties of travel between Mukden (Shenyang) in China means that it is not until 1948 that Robertson is able to reach Seoul. In 1947 the Korean Government authorises the establishment of the Korean Bible Society which becomes a member of the United Bible Societies on 21 June 1949. In that year the Reverend Young Bin Im takes over from Chung as Secretary.

The Korean Bible Society asks both BFBS and ABS to

sponsor its work; ABS contributes greatly to the replenishment of the Society's stocks at the time of liberation and later when the Korean War begins. "The generosity of the American Bible Society," says James Robertson of BFBS at the time, "has been beyond all praise."

By the 1950s you have to search for Buddhist temples in Seoul, but the churches are obvious: there are over 40 in the capital alone. The port city of Inchon, where the first Protestant missionaries landed, has fourteen churches in 1950 and Pusan, where there was a temporary Bible House in the 1950s, has more than 20. Unlike the Buddhist temples, the churches are by then always crowded. At daybreak every morning, the bells of the churches peal out even in winter and you can see people moving towards their church with Bible and hymn book to begin the day with prayers. Sunday has become a high festival, when people seem to spend most of their time in worship or Bible study.

In contrast, most of the Buddhist temples are deserted and half ruined, subjects of picturesque photographs. At a commemoration meeting in 1952 when the new Hankul Bible is published, the Buddhist Minister of Education says, "I envy you Christians. Here you have the Bible in the latest system of spelling, but we Buddhists cannot issue our Scriptures in any form whatever."

As I write (in December 2003), the largest church in the world is in Korea – the Yoido Full Gospel Church in Seoul, with an incredible 700,000 members. The church building itself holds 25,000 people in the main auditorium, with a further 15,000 who watch on giant closed-circuit television screens in overflow chapels. During the 20th century Christianity in Korea grew from virtually zero to about a third of the population. John Ritson would be thrilled to think of the role the Bible played in the beginnings of such extraordinary growth.

Enter Young-Jin Min

The current General Secretary of the Korean Bible Society, Young-Jin Min, tells me that in preparation for the time when the

North and the South are reunified, the Korean Bible Society has been raising funds since 1990 to supply 1 million Bibles to North Korea, where channels for Scripture distribution are currently closed down. In addition, the Society is setting up a project to translate the Bible in such a way that it is readable by the people of both North and South. There are also plans to develop a children's Bible and scholarly editions to meet the varied needs of Christians in Korea. Along with Bible Society's functions of translating, publishing and distributing the Word of God, the Korean Bible Society will devote itself to helping Christians to practise the teachings of the Bible in their everyday lives through its development of Scriptures in a variety of new media.

Snapshots of a Siberian summer

Re-enter John Ritson with R T Turley

Returning from the Far East in June 1907, Society General Secretary John Ritson inspects the work of the Society in Siberia – that vast region of Russia which extends from the Ural Mountains in the west to the Pacific Ocean in the east and southward from the Arctic Ocean to the hills of north-central Kazakhstan and the borders of Mongolia and China. He travels part of the way with R T Turley, the Society's sub-agent responsible for Manchuria (Dongbei), the historic region of north-eastern China. Turley took charge of Manchuria in 1887 but had many years of experience of working for the Society even before that.

As long as the two men are in Manchuria, soldiers with fixed bayonets patrol their train from end to end every few minutes. Every two miles they see guard houses surrounded by loopholed walls and in each enclosure a pole covered with straw soaked in tar – this to be fired as a beacon if help is needed during raids of *chunchuses*, armed bands of outlaws who sweep down from the plains. Ritson and Turley break their journey at Haerbin, today the largest city in north-eastern China. In Ritson's day, the best hotels are primitive and law and order is conspicuous by its absence. Turley says farewell at Haerbin, but not before handing Ritson over to the tender care of Walter Davidson, the Society's agent for Siberia.

Enter Walter Davidson

Davidson, a Scots Presbyterian, joined the Society's staff in 1885, worked for a time in Russia and has, since 1895, been responsible for the Society's work in Siberia. In the 25 years of his service he has acquired an incomparable knowledge of the language, people and geography of this vast territory, one-and-a-half times the size of Europe. With his wife and son he has made his home in Ekaterinburg, where the Society maintains its principal depot. But he travels constantly by the recently completed Trans-Siberian railway which now forms a spinal column across Russia. The Society has established Bible depots along the entire route of the railway – with especially busy ones at Omsk, Tomsk, Irkutsk, Chelyabinsk and Ekaterinburg. But every city has some sort of depot with several resident colporteurs, whose travels form a record of incredible adventure.

Ritson has high regard for Davidson whose natural gifts and early training fit him well for his awesome responsibilities. A Bible Society agent needs to combine the gifts of bookkeeper, accountant, retail and wholesale bookseller, publisher – but most importantly he has to be an evangelist with side sympathies across the church spectrum. Though a Scots Presbyterian, Davidson worships with German Lutherans, sees the best in the Russian Orthodox Church and lives to bring men and women of all sorts and conditions nearer to God.

The Trans-Siberian Railway allows you at this time to travel from Vladivostok, the seaport in south-eastern Russia, to Moscow in ten days on a train with restaurant cars and drawing-rooms, with pianos, libraries and secretaries, and with the luxury of international *wagon-lit* carriages for the night. Scorning luxuries, however, Ritson and Davidson choose to travel on an ordinary Russian train. They stop at no fewer than 596 stations from east to west – Ritson counts them – and rarely reach anything which you could describe as speed. Ritson used to grumble at the train which took him every morning to Cannon Street before his brisk walk to London Bible House, but rarely will he grumble again after spending three weeks on a Russian train!

However, they cannot complain about the cost of the second-class tickets – between £4 and £5 each for the entire journey, and the intense interest of everything they see makes up for the inconveniences. The basin in the lavatory has no plug and you can only get a spray of water as long as you press the tap down.

Resourceful in every situation, Ritson keeps the tap down with his forehead while he washes his hands.

Ritson and Davidson take off their clothes

At Irkutsk, today one of the major industrial cities of Siberia, Bible Society's General Secretary and its agent for Siberia strip off to enjoy the luxury of a Russian bath in the glorious water of the Angara river from Lake Baikal. They bask in the steam from water thrown on heated bricks. They squirm as an attendant beats them with birch rods with green leaves still on them. They revel in the soapsuds from soft fresh water and emerge clean again – and all for about sixpence each.

Despite the length of the journey, no food is provided on the train. The two men get boiling water free at nearly all the stations, and make tea morning, noon and night, taking turns in washing up their enamel mugs. They feed on what they can get at station buffets and from enterprising individual Russians who sell food on the platforms. The great favourite is pickled cabbage soup with a chunk of meat in the middle.

One day, when Ritson is guarding their luggage from the attentions of beggars who board the train at most stations, Davidson arrives back from a shopping trip with half a rouble's worth of cold roasted wild goat wrapped in a newspaper. As they have a loaf of bread they are soon enjoying goat sandwiches.

Ritson wonders whether the Siberian climate is as terrible as many people think. Certainly, it must be extremely cold in winter – but it is dry and can you not actually enjoy snow under those conditions?

"You don't get any winter in England," Davidson's son tells Ritson. "You only get a period of bad weather."

The Russo-Chinese section of the line carries them over a great plain, green and flat with the only signs of life being the guardhouses. Then they cross a fertile mountain range, zigzagging their way down into a desert of sand dunes. The Trans-Baikal railway takes them over undulating and grass-covered land where flocks of sheep and herds of cattle are grazing. After another range of hills the landscape grows more beautiful.

They see clear streams, hills clothed with pine, fir and larch and plains carpeted with wild flowers – roses, lilies, daffodils, forget-me-nots, bluebells and buttercups. It is easy to forget that this land is sometimes held in the grip of hard frost and that bears and wolves abound.

The scenery is at its best on the Circum-Baikal Railway. Lake Baikal, in the southern part of eastern Siberia, is geologically the oldest freshwater lake in the world and the deepest continental body of water. At 12,200 square miles, it is also the world's largest freshwater lake, containing about one-fifth of the fresh water on the Earth's surface. For some years, passengers crossed it in trains on rails laid down on the ice in winter or on ferries in the summer. But by Ritson's day, the line has been completed around the south shore at a cost of £5 million.

Ritson never finds his long journey westwards dull: the train rattles for hours through vast, lonely pine forests, past great rivers of clear water, crossing the Kyrgyz steppes dotted with picturesque huts and tents of birch bark. He considers the Urals to be of surpassing beauty with some delightful scenery. Siberia in summer is very different from the popular perception.

Despite the beauty, over the whole of Siberia there is unrest. The authorities do not seem able to check the many acts of lawlessness. After sunset, highway robberies and murders are frequent; sometimes such crimes occur even in broad daylight. At one stopping-place they see that a crowd has gathered around a cottage.

"Two women and a man lie dead," someone tells them, "murdered for 30 roubles!"

They enter places of business where office managers sit with loaded revolvers on or in their desks. Some shopkeepers keep their doors bolted while they examine customers, peering through a small window in the door.

Twelve million people live in this immense area stretching from the Urals to the Pacific. There are immigrants from other parts of Russia, some of whom are in search of religious freedom, some who are economic migrants trying to make a living. There are the families and descendants of exiles. There are people whose ancestors have lived there for thousands of years, speaking a wide range of different languages. It isn't easy either for the Government to meet all the material aspirations of the people of Siberia, or for the church to supply their spiritual needs.

There is just one school for every 2,600 of the population, or one for each 2,200 square miles. Only twelve out of 1,000 can even get to school. There is one library for every 57,000 people.

Ritson is adamant that Bible Society should be not only tolerated but welcomed in Russia. All its Russian staff and colporteurs are members of the Orthodox Church and the church authorities generally approve of their work. Civil and military officials also have a high regard for them. The steamboat and railway companies grant free passes to the men, and free carriage to their Bibles in every direction.

The Society circulates the Scriptures in many languages. First there is the Russ Bible, then the Slavonic, either alone or in parallel columns with Russ. These books are printed on the presses of the Orthodox Church. After these two languages, the Society sells more books in Polish and German than any other language – but also sells Bibles in Hebrew, Yiddish, Kyrgyz Tatar, Estonian, Lettish, Georgian and about a dozen other languages.

The Society's depots stretch in an unbroken chain from the Pacific to the Baltic. Ritson visits those in Chita, a centre for trade with China, Irkutsk with its attractive embankments along the Angara and Irkut rivers, Krasnoyarsk standing on both banks of the Yenisey river where it is crossed by the Trans-Siberian railway, Omsk on the Irtysh river at its junction with the Om, Cheljabinsk and Ekaterinburg, the Society's Siberian headquarters and home for the Davidson family. Ritson finds all the depots in good order with stocks being carefully kept and the cash and other business books generally models of neatness and accuracy.

From the depots, the Society's colporteurs often make very long journeys. Siberia is full of military camps and barracks as big as towns. There are soldiers at every station, on the trains, everywhere. Ritson travels with officers who keep their revolvers within reach day and night. In Irkutsk his carriage is commandeered so that two soldiers, driven insane from sunstroke after a long forced march, may be taken into hospital. One day an officer is put on the train after being shot and severely wounded by a private. They never seem to be far from the point of a bayonet or the muzzle of a revolver.

Ritson thinks that the typical Russian soldier has many good qualities and that reverence for the Bible is almost universal among them. During the war with Japan, the Russian troops were paraded on the station platforms at Cheljabinsk so that they might receive from the British and Foreign Bible Society copies of the Gospels and Psalms. The little books were so treasured and read that on the return journey many soldiers bought whole Bibles. Officers encouraged the men to buy them. The Society now sells Bibles in canteens, on parade grounds and in barracks.

The Society places Bibles free of charge in the public libraries of Siberia. Each Bible has the inscription, "This book has been presented, in the name of love, by the British and Foreign Bible Society to the village of _____ People's Free Library, in order to give each resident in the village of _____ the opportunity of reading God's Word." Copies of the Society's New Testaments in bold type are chained to desks in railway stations where you can get supplies of telegraph forms.

Growing numbers of immigrants pour into Siberia, especially from the Far East – over 750,000 in 1908. Some of the Society's colporteurs have permits to work among them on the train and in the barracks built for their accommodation. These refugees travel in trucks, like covered goods vans, with notices which announce that they hold "forty men or eight horses". The immigrant trains have to stop for every other train and, at almost every station, the refugees lie about, waiting to move on.

Ritson and Davidson arrive at Krasnoyarsk, a city which stands on both banks of the Yenisey river. Early in the morning, they look into the third- and fourth-class station waiting-rooms. So many families are asleep on the floors that they find it difficult to pick their way through. They see fathers – some drunk with vodka – and mothers with deep lines in their faces telling a silent tale of hardship. There are boys and girls and babies covered in dirt and dressed in little more than rags. The families' worldly goods are rolled into bundles. A few are having a breakfast of dry black bread and weak tea. In a corner of one room they see a bookcase which the chief of the gendarmerie has lent to the Society: a notice says, "Here are sold copies of the Holy Scriptures." The Society's colporteurs board all the emigrant trains.

In Omsk, Ritson and Davidson are out after dark one evening. Hearing a "clink, clink, clink" Ritson asks Davidson what the noise is.

"Stand still and watch," Davidson replies.

The two men watch as a gang of prisoners passes by. The men are chained around the waist and manacled hand and foot – with some women in carts behind – all surrounded by a strong guard of soldiers with fixed bayonets and drawn swords who are ready to stop any attempt at escape or rescue. The prisoners are regularly marched from prison to prison so that no one can trace their whereabouts. Ritson and Davidson put 400 Gospels and Psalms in Russ and a few Testaments in other languages into the prison at Omsk.

"I cannot allow you to distribute the books yourselves," the prison governor tells them, "but I will ensure that they are given to the prisoners."

Bible House, London, 1908

Enter Eutychus Maslennikoff

Maslennikoff, the *doyen* of the Society's Russian colporteurs, visits London Bible House in the course of his first trip to England. With the assistance of an interpreter he gives a vivid account of a recent tour of northern Russia. One of his London hosts describes Maslennikoff, a devout member of the Orthodox Church, as "a short but thick-set man, who looked as though his life in the open air had made him as hard as nails, and his broad smiling face was tanned a deep ruddy brown by the wind and sun and rain".

He returns to his homeland and by 1914, Maslennikoff has put in 22 years of continuous work for the Society.

Until the revolution in 1917, when the Bolsheviks seize power, the imperial Government favours the Society and it works in harmony with bishops and priests of the Orthodox Church, who in general encourage their people to read the Bible. But Soviet Russia will become barred against the import of Scripture.

Act 36

Adventures for God's packmen

The French word *colporteur* means a pedlar or street seller. In the history of Bible Society, it means a man (and they were almost all men), who carries and sells Scriptures from person to person and from door to door. Though evangelists, they are still pedlars. Stories of their exploits all over the world bring a touch of heroism and adventure to Bible Society history – so much so that in 1928, when Edwin Smith writes an attractive little book of colportage stories for young people, he called it *Tales of God's Packmen*.

Scripture colportage first makes its appearance in the Society's records in reference to France. In 1830, or perhaps a little earlier, three French banking brothers from Toulouse named Courtois sent out colporteurs to sell Bibles on their behalf. In the early days they directed their campaign to villages in the foothills of the Pyrenees and they seem to have met with some success.

The system of colportage proved so effective that the Society and its Auxiliaries abroad rapidly adapted it, first to the needs of every country in Europe, and later to almost every country in the world. By the end of the 19th century, the Society in London directly employed over 900 colporteurs and some hundreds more worked for local churches and missionary agencies across the world.

Enter the men on whom the sun never set

From the closing years of the 19th century until the 1930s, the Society regularly employed about 1,000 colporteurs in many corners of the globe. God's packmen belonged to about 50 different nationalities, spoke in a wide variety of languages, dressed in many different fashions but they were, as Edwin Smith put it, "alike in loving the Book and in desiring that other people should read it and love it too".

Smith advised his young readers to look at their map of

Africa and find Khartoum, where General Gordon was killed. He wrote:

From this place the packmen ride on camels into the vast land of the Sudan, where there is so much desert. The camel can carry a heavy load, so the packmen can take away with them many books, and their food and their bedding, and stay away from home many weeks together. When night comes, if they have not reached a village, they spread their blankets on the warm sand and sleep under the stars. Nowadays some journeys in the Sudan can be made in motorcars. In this way, the packmen can travel in seven hours a distance which by camel takes as many days.

Far away in Asia, north of China, lies the great desert of Mongolia, where people live in queer, round huts. One of the Bible Society's men penetrates every year into that desert with a number of camels carrying loads of books.

In other countries, the colporteurs ride on horses, or on donkeys, or mules…

Where there are rivers, the colporteurs often travel in boats. Sometimes they go alone in a canoe, or with one or two paddlers. In South America they voyage hundreds of miles on the Orinoco and Paraguay, and other rivers, in Indian canoes, called *ubasd*, each one of which is made by hollowing out the trunk of a big tree. Other men travel on the mighty Amazon by way of its tributaries into the far interior of South America. This is where the Brazil nuts come from. Sometimes the packmen, when people have no money, exchange their food for Brazil nuts and come back with their canoes weighted down with nuts, which are afterwards turned into money.

In the Far East, the colporteurs travel along the rivers of Cochin-China in *sampans* – little boats with a canopy over them. On other rivers they make use of big public boats and sell their books to their fellow-passengers.

Of course, in all countries where there are railways, the packmen make use of them in journeying from place to place. Some railway companies are so kind as to give them free passes, so that they have not to pay for tickets. These men love railway stations, especially in the East, where people are content to camp for hours waiting for a train. Among these groups of travellers, who have plenty of time on their hands, they find many willing customers. Many men and women have reason to thank God for the hours they spent waiting for a train, because then they met a happy packman who persuaded them to buy a Gospel which brought God's light and love to their hearts. On board the train, too, the packmen find their opportunity....

Unlike missionaries, who were generally foreigners, the colporteurs were almost always nationals of the countries in which they worked. T H Darlow's description of them, written in 1920, may sound a little patronising to us today but it gives a good insight into how the Society regarded the 1,000 "wandering Biblemen" whom it employed around the world.

He moves among his own people, talking their homely mother tongue. He understands their ways of thinking and their quaint terms of speech, and his reports and phrases are racy, of the soil. But the colporteur is also a real evangelist. For he is chosen, not merely because of his gifts as a shrewd hawker, but because he has learnt to know and love the Book which he carries. Its power dwells in his heart and its message lives on his lips; and when he sells a Gospel he can add his own warm living words of witness to the Redeemer whom it proclaims. At the same time, it is no part of his duty to make proselytes or to detach adherents from any Christian communion. He has instructions to avoid controversy, as far as possible.

Darlow continued with a lyrical description of where the Society's 1,000 colporteurs went.

They visit palm-thatched huts in Java and lonely homesteads in Brazil, and crowded fairs in Spain. They win their way among Russian immigrants in Canada, among throngs of devotees at idol festivals in India, among coal-miners and schoolboys in Japan. One man rides with camels across the deserts of Central Asia. Another travels by motorcar in Western Australia. Another wades through swamps reeking with miasma in South Africa. Another ventures in a frail canoe down tropical rivers infested with alligators. An Italian colporteur plods along the footpaths of Umbria, making his centre at Assisi, fragrant with memories of St. Francis.

A Peruvian colporteur has his home among the snowy peaks of the Andes at Cerro de Pasco, which is described as the highest city in the world.

In Istanbul (Constantinople) in 1921, one of the Society's colporteurs had just sold a Turkish Bible in a coffee house at Galata when he overheard a conversation between two Muslims.

"You see that man?" one says. "He is God's policeman. He searches daily for those who have no Bible. When he finds such a man, he insists on his buying a Bible. If he does not buy, he reports him to God in prayer."

In China, the Society employs 300 colporteurs who travel the provinces selling Scriptures and, largely due to their efforts, circulate more than 3 million copies a year. Their salaries are tiny, usually five or six shillings a week, but they are usually glad to work for this sum. It actually compares well with the salaries paid by the 130 missionary societies then at work in China to their evangelists and lay workers. In fact the Society's colporteurs themselves are in effect employees of the local missionaries to whom the Society makes payment for their maintenance and by whom their travelling is directed and their supplies of books maintained.

A CHINESE COUNTRY FAIR

Enter a woman missionary with colporteur Fan Swenli

A woman missionary superintends the Society's colporteur Fan Swenli. When the two of them arrive at a Chinese country fair, they make their headquarters at the village chapel. An evangelist arrives with a pile of Scriptures and they are later joined by a Chinese Christian named Cheo with his concertina.

As the fair begins, all the country roads leading to it are lined with people of all ages. Actors are performing on the stage of an open-air theatre at the south end of the village. The river bank is lined with mule and donkey markets, while along the main street people are setting up stalls with all kinds of goods for sale. Near the theatre there are improvised restaurants selling hot cakes, meat dumplings and soup.

Candy men sell many sorts of odd-shaped sweets and delicious toffee for five coppers an ounce. An excited crowd of people hold out sticks of bamboo to receive the round balls of sticky sweetness rolled into shape by the nimble but sometimes dirty fingers of the candy men.

From the crowd, 80-year-old Grandpa Yin comes up to the missionary, colporteur and team, reciting "Jesus loves me" and he would quote the whole Catechism through to the end if they do not discourage him. Grandpa Yin is not a totally committed Christian though, for fear of his daughter.

"No food, no clothing from me," she tells him, "if you get baptised."

A Confucian scholar tells them he is familiar with the story of the Gospels and Acts.

"But I cannot understand why," he tells them, "if there is one true God, there are so many different kinds of churches — Roman Catholic, Baptist, Presbyterian and so on."

It is not an easy question to answer.

The team's village chapel is never empty from morning to night. Early each morning and late in the evening they meet for prayer and Bible reading. The colporteurs and evangelists are busy on the streets all day. Biblewomen go among a crowd of women below the open-air theatre. They rarely meet anyone who refuses to talk to them or receive a Gospel.

One of the Society's Chinese colporteurs is walking along with his barrow of books when a man approaches him.

"Do you have foreign books for sale?"

"I have."

"Do you have a book that tells about a dark valley that all men pass through and of someone who is willing to help us through and go with us in the dark valley?"

"Where did you hear of this dark valley?" asks the colporteur.

"Up in the city of Yancheng a few days ago, I heard a foreigner preach and he spoke about it."

The colporteur opens a copy of the Psalms and reads the 23rd Psalm. He tells the man of Jesus, the Good Shepherd.

The colporteur travels on many miles that day until, in the evening, another man approaches him.

"Do you have a book which tells about a great king who lived long, long ago and who was once a shepherd-boy?"

Once more the colporteur opens the Psalms and reads the 23rd Psalm.

"Where did you hear the story?"

"In the city of Yancheng, I heard a foreign teacher preach about this king."

"Pastor," the colporteur later tells his superintendent, a CIM missionary, "I thought you would be encouraged to go on, seeing how interested these two men were in the preaching."

Small Pearl Mountains, China, 1914

Enter Tschen Kin Kwong

Tschen was formerly a soothsayer and fortune-teller. When he became a Christian he joined the staff of the Society as a colporteur and worked for many years in the Shandong region of China.

In 1914 he visits all the villages, hamlets and market places south of the Small Pearl Mountains, part of the range which forms the watershed between the Yangtze to the north and the Pearl River to the south. He visits monasteries belonging to Buddhist and Taoist orders. The monks invite him in and give him meals. In response he gives them a copy of Genesis or Exodus. At one monastery the monks proudly produce the four Gospels they have previously bought.

At the chief market places, farmers from nearby villages meet every day. Tschen erects a platform and preaches before selling Gospels. On a good day he may sell 20 or 30 copies but often only ten. He reckons that about half the books he sells are genuinely studied, especially during the long winter nights or during heavy rains.

Often he walks for a whole day and finds it hard to sell a

single copy. In Hia Tschang he meets two old men who belong to his clan and are eager for him to explain to them the Christian Gospel. When he has done this, both join him for the rest of the day and help him sell about 100 books.

Sometimes he stands under a tree or by the wall of an ancestor-hall and begins to talk to the old and young men who are idling away their time.

"Dear brethren, come and listen to my message."

"Who are you? Are you selling medicine?"

"Yes, I am a medicine man."

"What disease can you heal, honourable brother?"

"I sell a medicine which is universal – the blind receive their sight, the lame walk, the lepers are cleansed, the deaf hear, the dead are raised up and the poor have the Gospel preached to them."

Now Tschen has the attention of his audience. He begins to speak of the Ten Commandments and tells them of the true God who shows himself as the true God by sending his Son.

"Buy one of these small books," he cries, "and you will find in it the description of your most hidden disease. You will also find in it the surest remedy which will even grant you life everlasting."

Tschen uses his experiences as a soothsayer to help him in his new calling as a Bible Society colporteur. You could earn a meagre living as a fortune-teller in China, where at the market places there were usually five or six of these men, each one of them claiming to have an insight into the future of their customers.

When he preaches, he enjoys the cut and thrust of banter with his audience.

"Sir, how is my *yün*?" someone shouts from his audience. Soothsayers say that the *yün* (destiny) shows itself in some dark lines in the face and on the palm of the hand.

"Brother," Tschen replies as a preacher, "the dark lines on your heart are more critical. Not an eternal fate is hanging over you, but an everlasting God is looking down on you, always ready to save you. What you need is a Saviour."

When he says that, he loses the attention of some. But others listen to what he says, think it over, and then take time to read a small yellow or red bound copy of a Gospel and perhaps invite him to have a meal with them.

A man lights his pipe, opens the Gospel and starts asking questions.

"What is the meaning of this striking passage? Who is it speaking about?"

On the Yellow Island, Tschen meets an elderly school-teacher who has been touched by reading a Bible Society Gospel. He has no relatives since no other member of his family is alive.

"I am alone in the world," he says. "As soon as I close my eyes I am a prey to all the powers of the world of darkness. Who will bring the spring and autumn sacrifices and burn the fires on my grave, and sprinkle some drops of wine on it and remember me?"

Tschen joins him in his small room and offers him a Gospel. They talk until midnight about all his questions. "I was able to pour light into his soul," Tschen remembers, "and comfort and hope from the Book of books, where I got my own comfort in the struggle of life. It was not at first the longing for a Saviour which filled his soul, but the unspeakable fear of that wandering and stumbling of the soul through all eternities from one place of horror and anguish to another, such as only the imagination of an Asiatic can picture. Today the schoolmaster is a different man, and he reads his Bible and finds in it and in prayer consolation and peace and joy."

"I HAVE FOUND A TREASURE!"

Rev. A Gracie, of Hudson Taylor's China Inland Mission (now OMF International), wrote to London Bible House in 1914 to tell the story of a successful visit one of the Society's colporteurs had made two years earlier to a little hamlet about 30 miles from his mission centre. The colporteur had sold a copy of the Gospels to a young man who began to read them eagerly. Every evening, late into the night, he sat under the light of this Chinese lamp, poring over Gospel stories.

"I have found a treasure! I have found a treasure!" he cries repeatedly.

"What sort of treasure have you found?" his father asks him.

"Why," the son replies, "these books tell me that there is a living God in Heaven who is our Father, and that there is a Saviour for men, who came to save us from our sins."

First the father and then the mother grow interested.

The CIM missionary visits the hamlet and baptises first the son and then the father, mother, daughter and daughter-in-law as well as several of their friends. Thirty people who became interested through the young man buy Gospels and begin to meet every Sunday in his house for worship and Bible study.

"As we sat round the table in that well-filled room," the missionary recalled, "reading and expounding the truths of God's precious Word, it was inspiring to see with what lively interest they listened. They have a real hunger for the Word of God. The work, as far as I can judge, gives great promise, and it has all grown out of that one visit of the colporteur selling the Gospels, and the conversation which followed between the colporteur and the young man."

By the 1920s, nearly a quarter of the population of the world live in China. The Society comes to see China as offering boundless possibilities for the spread of the Gospel. In the year 1919 the Society circulates 3,290,000 volumes – the highest figure yet recorded. The vast majority of these books consist of portions of Scripture, mainly Gospels, which are sold by the Society's colporteurs in Chinese cities, villages and hamlets.

It is not just BFBS which is busy in China. In the same year, the President of the Chinese Republic, Hsu Shih Chang, cables a message to the American Bible Society:

> The instruction concerning all virtue, as contained in the Holy Scriptures of the religion of Jesus, has truly exerted an unlimited influence for good among all Christians in China, and has also raised the standard of all my people along lines of true progress. I earnestly hope that the future benefits derived from the Holy Scriptures will extend to the ends of the earth and transcend the success of the past.

Act 37

Comfort for men in the trenches

In June 1914, at Sarajevo, a Serb nationalist called Gavrilo Princip fires a shot at the Archduke Franz Ferdinand, heir to the Austro-Hungarian throne. The Archduke's death triggers a rapid chain of events which lead tragically to the First World War.

The Society discovers that soldiers caught up in fighting speak around 50 different languages. It has already published versions of the Bible in all these languages – with just three or four exceptions in which it has printed the New Testament or at least a Gospel. In order to put the Bible into the hands of combatants, without distinction between friend and foe, the Society has command of resources and machinery of which no other organisation can boast. The Society therefore works hard to turn a huge emergency into an opportunity to spread the Good News of God.

For sick and wounded soldiers and sailors of every nation, the Society undertakes to present as many Testaments, Gospels and Psalters as are needed to all Red Cross organisations and field and base hospitals, whether in Britain or abroad. The Society also undertakes to supply these books, specially bound in khaki, in any numbers, free of charge and carriage paid, for prisoners of war, interned aliens, and civilian refugees. To its friends in any country who give away books to soldiers and sailors, the Society grants Testaments and Gospels at a war discount – in fact at a fraction of their cost of production.

This war distribution is arranged by the Society's agents from its depots in every corner of the globe. During the first two years of the war, the Society distributes over 5 million copies of the Scriptures in 50 languages to men and women caught up in the war in some way. The Society sends a consignment of New Testaments to Germany to be distributed by a German army chaplain.

"Although I am a Catholic priest," the chaplain writes to

London Bible House, "I am willing to undertake the circulation of the Testaments. In these hard times it is necessary that all Christians, whatever their confession, should stand together to build the kingdom of God." In a letter of thanks for a Bible one German soldier writes: "It was the right food, at the right time. May God reward you for it."

"MOUTH-ORGAN BIBLES"

The Society's India paper edition of the pocket Bible with a thumb-index to the different books proves a great hit with some British soldiers. "When I was in Egypt," a corporal writes from France, "I bought one of your Bibles. Now I want one for my chum and I enclose a postal order to pay for it. It is one of them mouth-organ Bibles that I want – the Bible with the alphabet running down the side." Another soldier asking for the same book describes it as "the Bible with all the chapters cut out down the side".

Soldiers certainly prize and read the books. "The Testament you gave me three months ago I have read through six times, and I am going through it again. I want to tell you that it has changed my life." Another writes, "I have lost my Testament – I can't tell how, but I do miss it… I never used to read it before, but I read it regularly now, and it does me good. I wonder whether you would give me another!"

An army officer from the Dardanelles (the narrow strait in north-western Turkey) reports that it is quite a common sight to see men quietly reading the Scriptures when resting after a battle. A British army chaplain tells the team at London Bible House, "I used to see men unostentatiously reading their Testaments as I passed their dug-outs."

A wounded man in hospital in Leeds describes an experience in Gallipoli, the scene of determined Turkish resistance to the Allied forces during the Dardanelles campaign. "A comrade of mine used to take out his Testament in the trenches and read it to us night and morning. He wouldn't miss a day. All in that part of the trench where he was, often a dozen men, would go and listen." A stretcher-bearer home from France speaks of wounded men reading their pocket Testaments while they are being carried to the dressing stations behind the firing line, where the men have their wounds attended to before being sent back to a base hospital.

An officer who takes part in the charge of the 10th Battalion of Anzacs at Gallipoli in April 1915 reports later that on the following day, men were sent out to retrieve overcoats which had been taken off to cover the wounded in the chill hours of early morning. These men found in the pocket of nearly every overcoat one of Bible Society's khaki Testaments.

They send a New Testament back to a mother in England. It has belonged to her son, a young soldier who died from injuries he sustained while fighting in the Dardanelles. She opens it and, through her tears, she sees what he has written on the inside cover: "To the best mother that ever lived – God be with you till we meet again."

On a battlefield in Flanders a British corporal and his comrade fall wounded and are still under fire. The corporal applies his first-aid dressing and then takes out his New Testament and begins to read. The two men lie side by side for hours, until a shell kills them both. They are found later, with the Testament still open between them.

A French soldier says, "I hear not merely the roar of cannons and rifles. I can hear in my heart divine words – passages of the Bible I love, on which my soul meditates. Yes, when I endure these terrible hardships, God through my Bible gives me strength and even joy. I carry my Bible in my soldier's knapsack. It is much worn now, and the rain has stained it. But I will not let it go. When I read it, I feel as if I were with friends who are praying for me far away."

A Canadian officer, home and wounded from the front, describes how in France he and his battalion found themselves in a perilous corner: they were under heavy fire and dared not move. He noticed a few of his men who had crawled into a group together. One of the men took out his knife and cut a Testament into half a dozen pieces and gave one section each to his comrades who began to read them.

Russia, 1915

The war gives the Society new opportunities to distribute the Bible in Russia. Soldiers on their way to the front, wounded men in hospitals, refugees from invaded or threatened provinces, and prisoners of war are eager either to buy Bibles and Testaments or accept them as gifts. Russian Christians visit the Society's depots to buy Testaments and Gospels for the troops at heavily discounted prices. In addition the Society gives away many thousands of books to soldiers.

In Moscow alone, during 1915, the Society gives away 14,000 copies of the Scriptures among sick and wounded soldiers and prisoners of war. Among those who carry out the distribution for the Society are ten priests of the Orthodox Church and three Lutheran pastors. The Society's colporteurs meet troops at railways stations when transport trains stop there. "The soldiers who have money buy the books and to those who have no money I give the Gospels and Psalters gratis," one colporteur who works at a railway station writes. "Many of them take off their caps when they have paid their money, cross themselves and kiss their books."

From the Crimea a woman who is working among Russian wounded soldiers writes to London, "It is indeed very touching to see how the invalids long to possess and read the Scriptures... A fortnight ago we gave a large quantity of Russian Gospels to a party of consumptive soldiers, many of them very weak."

ABS AND THE WAR

The United States enters the war on Good Friday, 6 April 1917. By April 1918 the American Bible Society has issued in its army and navy editions 2.25 million copies of the Scriptures. General Pershing, the commander of the American forces in France, cables Bible House, New York: "I am glad to see that every man in the army is to have a Testament. Its teachings will fortify us for our great task."

Armenia, 1915

The ancient city of Antioch, where the disciples were first called Christians, was also the Apostle Paul's departure point when he set out on his first missionary journey into Europe. Then in ancient Syria, now in south-central Turkey, the town lies a little inland from the Mediterranean. A broad, rugged mountain, Musa Dagh, rises between Antioch and the sea. On the slopes of the mountain stood six Armenian villages where nearly 5,000 people lived.

In July 1915 the Turkish governor of Antioch suddenly orders these villagers to prepare to leave within seven days. In terror they climb to the summit of Musa Dagh, taking with them their sheep and goats and whatever weapons they can find. They barricade themselves in on the crags of the mountain for nearly six weeks, holding at bay soldiers and an armed mob from Antioch. Musa Dagh falls away steeply to the sea.

After some time, French warships appear and answer desperate signals from the Armenians. With great difficulty they scramble down to the sea and leave the rocky shore in improvised rafts in heavy surf. The sailors help them on board their ships. The French take them to Egypt, at this time a British protectorate. The British Government organises a camp of over 500 tents where the refugees are given shelter and food.

The Government, with good sense, then commandeers a member of Bible Society's Egyptian staff to act as interpreter and storekeeper for the refugees. The Society distributes free Bibles, Testaments and Gospels in the Armenian and Turkish languages to every refugee who can read. It presents a Bible in the ancient Armenian version to their church as well as smaller Bibles to the Armenian priests.

Enter C T Hooper

The Society's agent in Port Said is one of the memorable characters in the Society's history who stamped his personality on the Bible House in the Egyptian port. Following the arrival of the

Armenian refugees, he receives a charming letter dated 1 November 1915, of which the following is a translation:

> By a cruel fate we had been thrown on the banks of the Nile, and there were left without a holy book to feed the human soul. Your honourable Society hastened to console us by presenting a Holy Bible to each family. It also supplied holy books and portions to our Holy Church and to me its servant. I beg hereby to express my best thanks and those of my people to your Society, which conceived and executed such a noble act. Glory be to Him and to His Word. Yours gratefully, VARTAN VARTERESSIAN.

Glimpses of Port Said's heyday

The Society attaches enormous strategic importance to Port Said, where two continents come together and East and West meet and mingle. It transfers the headquarters of its Egyptian agency there in 1912 because of the importance of the port as a redistribution centre for bulk consignments of Scriptures to the eastern Mediterranean and east Africa. At the entrance to the Suez Canal, the Society builds a magnificent Bible House and large warehouse.

Including Ismailia, Port Said has a population of over 90,000 people in the early 20th century and is perhaps the most cosmopolitan seaport in the world. From ships and housetops flags of all nations fly, many languages are spoken in the shops and many currencies exchanged. A collection is taken in a church in Port Said and the money given includes an English penny, an Australian sixpence, an Italian soldo, a French franc, an Indian quarter-rupee piece, a Turkish 40-paras, a Greek 10-lepta, a Belgian half-franc, a Tunisian 10-centimes, a Dutch quarter-guilder, a 9-piastre piece from Cyprus, an American dime, and a 20-cent piece from Ceylon, as well as copper coins from China and Brazil!

In 1919 the Society circulates 80,000 books in Egypt of which 34,000 are sold by its colporteurs. Port Said, which claims to be the largest coaling station in the world, is unique as a centre for Bible distribution. Port Said Bible House stocks editions of the Scriptures in 80 languages. Sales from the depot in one day in

1920 include books in Arabic, English, French, German, Greek, Italian, Japanese, Latin, Polish, Russian and Spanish.

The Society maintains a motor-launch in the harbour. Colporteur Harvey one day boards a ship and asks a British seaman if he would like a Bible.

"Thank you," the sailor replies, "I have one which I have had for thirty years. I would rather go on board without my shirt than without my Bible!"

Enter Markos: Ethiopian packer and colporteur

The Society employs an Ethiopian packer in its depot in Port Said called Markos. The agent in the port frequently calls Markos out of the depot to act as a colporteur among Ethiopian soldiers who pass through on Italian ships. Markos is a resourceful fellow: when he isn't allowed on board vessels, he sells Bibles from the BFBS launch alongside, ingeniously using a string and a basket. The soldiers on the decks pass coins down the string in a basket and the books are sent up in return. On one occasion, Markos sells 183 books, including 35 Bibles and 24 New Testaments in eleven different languages to the sailors on the same ship.

The Italians bring Ethiopian soldiers from Eritrea and land them at a transit camp at Port Said. When one day Markos visits this camp, a soldier runs up to him.

"Have you the New Testament in Ethiopic?" he asks breathlessly.

Markos produces one from his bag. The soldier kisses it many times and hands over the money. On one of these visits Markos sells 52 books in eight different languages and dialects then spoken in Ethiopia.

C T Hooper will live on until 1925 after 22 years in the Society's service, for 16 of which he is in charge of the agency in Port Said. It is widely recognised that Port Said Bible House was his monument, as he was its inspiration. "The Bible House," wrote one colleague, "was a place of good cheer, good fellowship, good living and good sense…there must be many in the days of war and since who blessed the Bible Society for putting C T Hooper at Port Said."

Following the devastation of Port Said in the 1967 war, the Society sold the Bible House which had seen so many colourful scenes in its history. The building itself is, however, in good shape and is now the New Regent Hotel, with the words "British and Foreign Bible Society" prominently displayed on an arched street entrance in a busy street. Today a salesman from the Bible Society of Egypt works in Port Said through the churches and sells products through bookstands. A church relations representative is responsible for fundraising in Port Said.

PROUD OF ITS CATHOLICITY

Writing in 1916, the Society's indefatigable Literary Superintendent, T H Darlow, demonstrated the continuing pride the Society took in its catholicity. "Hardly any organisation," he wrote, "can be more truly catholic in the Christian sense of that word. In Russia the presses of the Holy Synod print half a million books every year for our Society to distribute, while we have published various versions for the use of the missions of the Orthodox Church in Siberia and Central Asia. The Syrian, the Armenian, and the Coptic communities all benefit by the Bible Society's editions. Last year our depots supplied Greek Testaments and Hebrew Bibles to students and seminaries of the Roman Catholic Church in Spain."

THE BIBLE AND OTHER FAITHS

The attitude of Bible Society to the world of Islam during the first half of the 20th century is well captured in a section of its popular report *For the Healing of the Nations*, issued in September 1916. The report quotes approvingly from the writings of Samuel Zwemer (1867–1952), the scholar, preacher and evangelist who worked tirelessly to spread the Gospel in Islamic countries and to arouse interest in missions in the USA and Europe. From 1929 to 1937 he was Professor of Christian Missions at Princeton. Not all readers today will approve of his approach – but no one can doubt the clarity and vigour of his thought.

Zwemer is convinced (in 1916) that the distribution of the Bible has always been the best method of pioneering work by Christians in Muslim countries. He doesn't think that the results of the work of Bible Societies in the Islamic world have been sufficiently recognised. He writes:

For over a century, the Bible has been as leaven in the world of thought among Muslims. It has modified their outlook on life, changed their standards of ethics, challenged their conception of history, and compelled their readjustment of their judgment of Christ.

In all these particulars we may note that the disintegration of the old Islam and the attempts towards reform have been occasioned, if not caused, by the teaching of the Scriptures.

Translations of the Koran into a score of languages other than Arabic exist, but these translations are, as regards the common people, rare, expensive, and necessarily utterly inferior to the original in style and force. The Bible, on the other hand, has been translated into every tongue, and is the cheapest as well as the best-printed book in the Near East. Nor has its beauty and power been lost in the many excellent translations. The Arabic Koran, because of its obscure style, and archaic diction, is a sealed book even to the Arabic-speaking races, while the Bible uses the language of the cradle and the market place.

When we study the story of individual Muslim conversions, it is remarkable how in nearly every case the perusal of the Scriptures has led to the discovery of self and the desire to know the friendship of Christ. The Bible is at once our strongest weapon of conquest, and our most inoffensive method of constructive work. The Bible strikes at the very root of Islam by placing the sublime story of the life of our Saviour over against the artificial halo that surrounds the popular lives of Mohammed. No Muslim can read the Sermon on the Mount without seeing in it an indictment of popular Islam.

But in its internal documents, the Society's tone is more conciliatory. In 1923 it issues a 60-page book for its staff serving overseas. The book includes an admirably clear restatement of the simple aims of the Society. The second paragraph is headed "Catholicity".

and speaks of uniting Christians without asking them to surrender their personal convictions. Members of staff should carefully avoid any entanglement in politics. Under the heading "Attitude to the Religions of a Country" the handbook says that the Society's aim is "to propagate truth rather than to attack error". No one should denounce or ridicule existing systems of belief. This doesn't mean that the lips of the members of the staff are sealed: "Out of the abundance of the heart the mouth speaks, and nothing can better secure the object of Bible circulation than that those who have felt the power and sweetness of the Divine Word should testify of their experience to others; but there is an obvious difference between this and the language of controversy." And the attitude to other Bible Societies at work in the same field as BFBS, incidentally, should be to avoid the spirit of rivalry and to pursue strict observance of the principle of comity.

Enter Edwin Smith

By the time it publishes its popular report *The Seekers* in July 1925, the Society has a new Literary Superintendent, Reverend Edwin Smith, formerly a Primitive Methodist missionary. Smith is a distinguished anthropologist and a brilliant, if controversial, writer and lecturer. He is the author of the popular and delightfully written *Tales of God's Packmen* as well as a short 32-page history of the Society which is full of good sense. When he retires fourteen years later in 1939 at the age of 63, he will accept a long-standing invitation to lecture at the Kennedy School of Missions in the United States, also embarking on a long lecture tour across Canada on behalf of the Bible Society there. When he returns to England he will enjoy a happy retirement taken up with more anthropological and African studies. He died in Deal in 1957.

Unlike his distinguished predecessor, T H Darlow, Smith uses *Qur'an*, the strict transliteration of the sacred book of Islam. Smith includes a provocative section headed "Sincere Flattery" in his 1925 report. He writes:

It is a sign of the progress of Christianity when the devotees of other religions adopt Christian methods in defence of their faith. Muhammadans now imitate us by translating their Qur'an into languages other than Arabic – a thing that they would have regarded as blasphemy a few years ago. Moreover, they issue the Qur'an in a form resembling our Bible.

In Ceylon, the Hindus are making strenuous efforts to resist Christian activities and are opening Hindu schools on Christian models. In Japan "The Buddhist Salvation Army" has started. The name of General Booth's organisation is *Kyu-seigun*; the Buddhists have named theirs *Sai-seigun*: *seigun* meaning "world-army", and both *Kyu* and *Sai* meaning salvation. The Buddhists have adopted the Salvation Army's book of instruction for officers, only changing the words for God and Christ into Amida; and also its flags, drums and street preachings. For one of their hymns (translated by Miss A. Henty in the pages of her *Japan Quarterly*) we quote the verse:

> Peerless, aloft the peak of Fuji rises,
> Around our peaceful shores, wash quiet waves,
> And like the moon, on cloudless evening shining
> The Army of Salvation lights the world.

"The Buddhist army does not," Smith concludes sardonically, "according to all accounts, rescue the criminal and drunkard, nor bring help to the poor and suffering."

Enter colporteur-superintendent Oido

During 1924 Mr Oido, the Society's colporteur-superintendent in Japan, works with four other colporteurs in a district where the Buddhist Salvation Army is strong. They apparently meet with strong opposition. According to Oido, a well-known member of the Army, when invited to purchase a Gospel, retorts, "Clear out! It defiles my eyes even to see the outside of your books!" Notwithstanding this opposition, Oido and his team sell over 4,500 copies of the Scriptures in this area of Japan.

One missionary who supervises Society colporteurs says,

"Tibetans often tell me how, far away up in Tibet, Buddhist priests gather people round them in the long summer twilights and read aloud to them from the New Testament."

More recently, Society Vice-President and Bishop of Durham Tom Wright has written that "if the biblical narrative is true, the Muslim one is not, and vice versa; and the same for Hinduism, Buddhism and so on. The more open we make the Bible, the more we must expect that dialogue with our friends and neighbours of other faiths will include the clear statement of radically different world-views".

DISTRICT SECRETARIES 1905–1919: NICE WORK IF YOU CAN GET IT!

The Society's instructions to its Secretaries reveal something of the standing they are expected to maintain. They are required to travel by first-class railway coaches, but to avoid Sunday travel. They normally wear a frock coat and silk hat in the course of their Society engagements. There are records of occasions when they are met by the town band on arrival at their destination.

Among the District Secretaries, who are drawn from many Christian denominations, are certainly men of wide reading and culture as well as the capacity to work hard and to organise. The Rev. H K Marsden, MA, appointed to the West Riding of Yorkshire in 1910, has a particularly fine library. The Rev. Horace Cossar, MA, appointed to Cambridge in the same year, has coached the Queen's College boat for some years.

"I am prouder to be a Bible Society Secretary," he says, "than I would have been to become a Bishop."

Others too were colourful characters. Rev. W R Bowman was appointed District Secretary in 1897 and still works for the Society 30 years later. On the outbreak of war in 1914 a friend meets him and comments, "This is a terrible war, Mr Bowman."

"It's an awful war," Bowman replies. "It's spoiled two of my meetings already."

He is affectionately known as "Penny Bowman" because of his custom of urging local schoolchildren to save pennies regularly for the Society – at a time when the penny still has considerable purchasing power.

Rev. Crwys Williams, appointed to south Wales in 1914, is a distinguished Welsh poet and is crowned Bard at the national Eistedfodd on three occasions.

Act
38

Truth for India

The significance of Bible Society's work in India was emphasised by the increasing attention being given in the first quarter of the 20th century to the cause of education. The "reading habit" was growing to an extent undreamt of in the past. Among a people developing a taste for reading with very little literature available at a small cost, the Society had a great opportunity.

One woman missionary wrote to London Bible House in 1921: "I have never seen the people more ready to buy Gospels than they are now: during a bathing festival here last month we sold about 1,500 books. Even the *sadhus* in the temple were buying, and we had some of our best meetings in the temple court."

In districts of India where village schools had been established, the young people were eager to buy the Society's attractive little Gospels which sold for a farthing each.

BIBLES FOR STUDENTS

For many years it was the regular custom of the Society to offer the Scriptures to all students at the universities of British India. In 1918 the University of Calcutta alone had more undergraduates than Oxford and Cambridge put together. The Society offered each Indian student, when he or she entered college, a copy of the four Gospels and the Acts. Halfway through the course, the student was invited to accept a New Testament. When they graduated, the Society tried to arrange for all new graduates to leave with Bibles in their hands. Students were allowed to select for themselves which versions they preferred and, as it happens, they almost always chose English. During 1917 the Society gave away 10,300 volumes in this way – the students only received one if they applied and so we can assume they valued their Bibles.

A thoughtful Hindu, who did not call himself a Christian,

once said, "If I were a missionary, I would not argue. I would give people the New Testament and say *Read that*." A Brahmin, a member of the highest Hindu caste, told a missionary, "The Bible is a very good book, but people must not read too much of it, or they will have to become Christians." In Lahore, they did read the Bible and the Brahmin's warning proved to be all too accurate.

Lahore, 1917

The Bishop of Lahore gives the Society an idyllic picture of the faith of some Indian Christians settled in the Punjab.

> There is a little company who have banded themselves together to seek to prove the fullness of what Christ means. They meet daily, and sit sometimes half through the night singing and praying and exhorting. Their main purpose is evangelisation. There are Sikh villages around where they get a friendly welcome – I fancy largely because of their beautiful singing – and where there is a real movement towards Christianity…the part played by music in their religious life is, as far as my experience goes, unique. I have never been to a place where I felt so transported back into what I imagine must have been, from this point of view, the atmosphere of the Early Church… The Psalms in their Punjabi version are an integral part of their life, and when one remembers what the Psalms have been to Scotland, it seems impossible to exaggerate the hopefulness of the fact that every child knows large portions of these Psalms by heart, and that the village rings with them, almost literally by day and night.

In the south of India at this time the Society sells its Telugu New Testament for 4 old pennies – less than half of its cost of production. One young man buys one of these, reads it, and later comes into contact with Rev. Marshall Hartley, a missionary from the Wesleyan Methodist Missionary Society. Mr Hartley recalls that the young man came to a Christian event at a place named Aler. He attended the services, offered a subscription to the fund for a church in another village – not his own – and declared himself a Christian, though he had never been baptised.

"Why have you never been baptised?" the local Christians ask him.

"I have never seen a missionary until today," the young man replies.

"Then how did you become a Christian?" they ask.

"By reading the New Testament."

He explains that he has bought the Society's Telugu New Testament.

"I destroyed my own idols," he continues, "and mended a hole in the road with them. Then I went through my village of sixty houses reading the Testament from house to house. I persuaded the people to destroy their idols. Now I am looking for a Christian teacher who will lead them all into the way of truth."

The young man is baptised that day and a teacher duly despatched to his village.

Enter Sadhu Sundar Singh

Supporters of the Society who attended the anniversary meetings in the Queen's Hall, London, in May 1919, were rewarded by hearing a memorable address from an Indian Christian ascetic and evangelist who had become something of a celebrity.

Sundar Singh belonged to a well-known Sikh family in Rampur where his father was an extensive landowner. As a child the boy's mother taught him all she could of religion. She often spoke to him of a peace which must be sought before true happiness could be found. He read the sacred books of the Sikhs, Hindus and Muslims but without finding what he wanted. When he became a student in the American Presbyterian Mission School in Luhiana, he received an Urdu New Testament which he began to read eagerly. The teaching in the book seemed so subversive of all he had learnt that he tore it up in anger and burnt the pages in a fire. But still he was unhappy and later got hold of another Urdu Testament and studied it carefully.

One night he resolves that he will find peace before dawn. In Hindu fashion he washes and retires to his room, New Testament in hand. He begins to spend the long hours of the night in reading, meditation and prayer. Near daybreak it seems to him that a cloud fills the room and that from the cloud shines the radiant face of Christ. The peace which he has been searching for seems to fill his heart.

Neither persuasions nor threats can now deter him from going around speaking of his newfound faith. His family drives him out of his home, but in 1905 he is baptised at the Anglican mission in Simla and embarks on a course of theological training. He decides to lead the life of a wandering Christian *sanyasi* (religious ascetic) and to devote himself to spreading the Christian Gospel in Indian style.

Dressed in the saffron robe which is the badge of religious mendicants, relying on gifts for support, homeless and penniless, but carrying his New Testament in his hand, he travels on foot to villages from Tranvacore in south western India to Tibet. Wherever he preaches crowds flock to hear him.

As a speaker he is earnest, practical, convincing without excessive emotionalism. His sentences thrill his audiences. His supreme subject is Christ. He takes his illustrations either from the New Testament or from his own experiences – in no way embellishing them.

Queen's Hall, London, May 1919

When Sundar Singh appears at the Society's annual meeting in the Queen's Hall in London, there is a buzz of expectancy. Many have heard of him, but few have seen him in the flesh.

"I consider it a high privilege," he begins when it is his turn to speak, "to be here at this time to give my testimony to the wonderful power of the Word of God, and to the Bible Society by which the Word of God is being circulated all over the world. When I was not a Christian, I used to read the Bible, and I felt the power of the Word of God in those days. Of course I did not like it sometimes. I used to criticise it, and I used to tear up the Bible and burn it in the fire. But even then I must confess that sometimes I felt its wonderful power and attraction. Although I used to tear it up, I felt its power.

"Many others felt the power of the Word of God. They used to say, 'You must not read the Bible.' 'Why?' 'Because of its magic. You will become a Christian. Many of those who used to read the Bible became Christians. You must not read it.' Some of those who were opposed to Christianity realised that there was power in it. I used to feel in those days the wonderful power and attraction of the Word of God. Through the Word of God I was introduced to my Saviour. I knew Jesus Christ through the Bible. When he revealed himself to me in a sort of vision, I became converted, and I felt heaven on earth.

"When I was travelling in the Central Provinces, I was talking to some non-Christians in a compartment in a train. I asked them if anyone would like to read the Bible to know something more about Jesus Christ. There was a man there, an enemy of Christianity. He took a copy of St John's Gospel, he read two or three sentences, and afterwards he tore it up into pieces and threw it away.

"After two years I heard a wonderful story. The same day that this man took St John's Gospel and tore it up into pieces and threw it out of the window, a seeker after truth was going along the railway line. He was a real seeker after truth. For six or seven years he had tried his best to find the truth, but he was not satisfied. As he was going along the railway line and thinking about these things, he found the torn pieces of the Gospel, and he took them up and began to read. On one piece he saw the words: 'the Bread of Life'. He was anxious to know something about it. What was that bread of life?"

Sundar Singh told his Queen's Hall audience how the seeker after truth had shown the torn pieces of the Gospel to another man.

"Can you tell me what this book is? I am sorry that somebody tore it up."

"That is Christian. You must not read it. You will be defiled. You must not read such books."

At last the seeker said, "I must know something more. There is no danger in knowing about these things." He went to buy a copy of the New Testament, began to read it and became first a

Christian and then a preacher of the Gospel in the Central Provinces.

Sundar Singh described how he had met the chief Minister in an Indian State.

"It is rather difficult for me to confess openly," the Minister had told him, "but I believe in Jesus Christ. I came to know Jesus Christ through the Word of God."

The Minister showed Sundar Singh his New Testament.

"By reading this Word of God I came to know my Saviour, and I believe in Him. It is a precious heavenly treasure. I am surprised that this book is so cheap. Such a treasure must cost at least a thousand rupees for each copy, or five hundred rupees."

"The aim of the Bible Society," Sundar Singh told the Minister, "is not to make money, but to save souls."

JESUS CHRIST, THE GOAL OF HIS SEARCH

Another notable Indian convert was the poet Narayan Vaman Tilak. A stranger gave him a New Testament in a railway compartment. Tilak began reading it. When he got to the Sermon on the Mount he was transfixed.

"I could not tear myself away," he said later, "from those burning words of love and tenderness and truth. In these three chapters I found the answers to the most abstruse problems of Hindu philosophy."

Tilak said that he discovered in Jesus Christ the goal of his long search – that *sánti* (mental and spiritual tranquillity) which he had for long pursued in vain. In once sense he was a seeker, yet he always maintained that it was God who had sought and found him.

In July 1926 *The Statesman* of Calcutta reports Mahatma Gandhi's decision to teach for one hour each Saturday the students of National College, founded by him in the beginning of the non-cooperation movement. He meets them and asks them what he should teach.

"The New Testament," they reply.

THE SOCIETY'S DEPOTS

During the 1920s the Bible House in Queen Victoria Street is still the centre of an organisation which reaches out to almost every part of the globe. In the warehouse are stacked between 2 and 3 million Bibles, Testaments and portions as they are received from the printers and binders. Every working day during 1924, for example, an average of 9,500 books are despatched, 4,498 cases in all, weighing 434 tons.

But only 30% of the Society's books go out from London. As far as possible the Society's books are produced in the countries where they will be sold and read. Hundreds of thousands of copies are printed on the continent of Europe and in India, besides 649,000 in Korea and well over 4 million in China.

The Society maintains its own depots in about 100 of the chief cities of the world, and the sub-depots bring the total to over 200. These are dotted about in unfamiliar as well as familiar places. You will find the Society's depots in Barcelona and Baghdad, in Belize and Bandung, in Khartoum and Kerman, in Colombo, Callao and Changchun.

IN BORROW COUNTRY

During the 1920s the Society's colporteurs travelled to every part of Spain. When I visited *Sociedad Bíblica* in Madrid in April 2003, Lola Calvo produced a box of marvellous photographs of some of them. In the days before cheap package holidays, Edwin Smith was anxious to inform the Society's supporters that "Spaniards are reluctant to sleep at night in summertime". In Madrid, Smith continued, "you may hear one say at 10.30 p.m., 'It is cooler now, let us go home and dine.' After dinner they sit outside until the early hours of the morning".

The Society's colporteurs certainly take advantage of the opportunity offered by the relaxed Spanish lifestyle. Three of them take part in a special midnight campaign in Madrid. A well-known Spanish satirical writer makes fun of the campaign in a newspaper:

"Well-toasted and salted!" cries the girl with the almonds.

"Who will buy my cod-fish?" shouts a second hawker.

It is at this moment that the modern George Borrow makes his appearance, a Bible in his hand and a satchel full of them on his shoulder. "Who wishes to buy a good book?" he exclaims.

No longer, however, do Bible-sellers, except in the remotest country parts, experience the sort of opposition that Borrow contended with. In Madrid they are generally received courteously – even under the starlit skies outside *los restaurantes*.

A young Spaniard one day accosts the Society's long-serving colporteur, Señor Barri, in a Barcelona street. He calls out to the bystanders to listen to what he has to say.

"This gentleman sold me a Bible some months ago," the young man says. "Now I can say that it is a book for poor and rich, for the wise and the ignorant. It is not a Protestant book, nor Catholic, nor Muslim. It is God's book. I did not appreciate it at first. I neglected it for weeks. I found nothing in it, and indeed, meeting this gentleman again one day, I proposed to let him have it back at half the price I had paid for it. He advised me to keep and read it, saying it was the best book in the world. Now today I can say that I have found through the Bible the way, the truth and the life, as I came to know Christ crucified."

THE SOCIETY, MISSIONARY WORK AND *THE TIMES*

A leading article in *The Times*, published a few days after the Society's annual meeting in 1924, still demonstrates the classic British view of her Empire. But the leader adopts a thoroughly positive approach to missionary enterprise and the work of Bible Society.

> That we should come to races, barbarous or savage, a few years ago, uproot their customs, albeit substituting for them the most scrupulous justice, give them railways, motors, wireless and the rest, and yet withhold from them a knowledge which is open to

all at home to acquire, if it is not imparted in childhood, would be an unforgivable oversight. Nor is it only to the least enlightened races that the debt is due. Nations with ancient civilisations have equally a claim to expect that the common book of Christendom should in these days of vernacular presses be made accessible to them. Happily, as the Bible Society's statistics show, it is brought to them in great numbers. In the presentation of religion there is more than one element, but history plays an indispensable part in it; and a copy of the Scriptures, as faithfully translated as scholarship can render them, is one of the few things that change hands in this modern world of which it can be said without qualification that the giving is good and the gift perfect.

Debut for Bill Platt

No one had more influence on the direction of the Society in the middle years of the 20th century than the Rev. Dr William Platt. The first recorded contact between Platt and the Society was in a letter written by him from the Ivory Coast in 1918 where he was working as a missionary. In the letter, Platt scarcely conceals his impatience at the Society's delay in dealing with his request for some Bibles.

Born in 1893, Bill Platt entered the ministry of the Wesleyan Methodist Church from Didsbury College, Manchester, in 1916, and immediately volunteered for pioneer missionary work in west Africa. On the Ivory Coast, Bill followed up the work of the west African evangelist William Wadé Harris about whom he wrote an engaging book. "Prophet Harris" was the best known of the early 20th-century leaders of African mass movements for Christ. He belonged to the Glebo people of Liberia and was converted when he was about 20 through the work of Methodist missionaries. He baptised no fewer than 100,000 people and perhaps twice that number were deeply affected as a result of his work. The French colonial authorities, frightened at his success, imprisoned, mistreated and expelled him. White-robed, bearing a cross and a Bible, accompanied by women singers, and engaging readily in trials of strength with traditional priests and diviners, Harris conveyed a sense of immense spiritual power. Independent of the missions, and often alarming them, Harris encouraged converts to attend churches where they existed and appointed local leaders where they didn't. His preaching laid a foundation for all the churches, both Catholic and Protestant, of the Ivory Coast and for many beyond it.

Queen's Hall, London, May 1927

The Society expects Prime Minister Stanley Baldwin to chair its annual meeting in May 1927. Three times Conservative Prime Minister between 1923 and 1937, Baldwin headed the Government during the general strike of 1926, the Ethiopian crisis of 1935, and the abdication crisis of 1936. A good friend to the Society, he revealed his love for the Bible when he said: "The Bible is a high explosive. It works in strange ways and no living man can tell or know how the Book in its journey through the world has startled the individual soul in ten thousand different places into a new life, a new belief, a new conception, a new faith." (The Society tried to maintain balance in its political links: in May 1919, the Leader of the Labour Party in the House of Commons, the Right Honourable William Adamson, MP, addressed the annual meeting.)

When pressure of work prevents him at the last minute from chairing the meeting, Baldwin asks none other than the Marquis of Salisbury to deputise for him.

Enter Bill Platt

On the platform, waiting to be called by the distinguished Chairman, is the 34-year-old Mission Superintendent for the Wesleyan Methodists. Platt graphically describes the rapid growth of the church in west Africa following the energetic work of the now-ageing Prophet Harris. He injects some humour into his talk.

"So you can see that we are going to run the Bible Society into some great expense," he says. "To us the vital breath of our work is the work of the Bible Society. The Society has been described as the handmaid of the missionary movement. She is becoming the *mother* of the missionary movement. I am sure that the Ivory Coast movement – the salvation of those people and the permanence of the movement – depends on the Bible Society."

In 1930 Platt becomes the Society's Secretary for Tropical Africa and makes his headquarters in London Bible House. The building becomes his starting-off point for a series of tours which enable him to maintain the Society's numerous but scattered contacts in Africa. He sets off in December for a tour during which, in eight months, he visits Kenya, Uganda, Tanganyika, Zanzibar, Madagascar and Mauritius. He has acquired a good knowledge of French on the Ivory Coast and this proves invaluable in the French-speaking areas, many of which are now under his care for the Society's purposes.

In later tours, Platt visits the Congo, the Rhodesias and the whole of west Africa. He attends missionary conferences and services and arranges public meetings. He sets up advisory committees and encourages missionary bookshops to increase their Scripture distribution. He recognises the scale and significance of the challenge of Islam to Christian missionary work. Circulation of Bibles in Africa increases steadily during the period in which Platt is directly responsible for the Society's work there.

Platt focuses attention on the needs of Africa by his reports to the Committee in London and to a wider public by his deputation work at home. He writes a series of challenging articles for the Society's magazine in which he develops a number of themes. He emphasises the urgency of translations into African colloquial languages – making the Bible as easy as possible for Africans in their towns and villages to understand without sacrificing accuracy and reliability. In this he is strongly supported by Edwin Smith who, now in charge of the translations department, has himself been a missionary translator in Africa. Platt emphasises the importance of the Old Testament for the development of African monotheism – the belief in one God.

"Civilisation is descending upon Africa with the pace of an avalanche," Platt writes, "and she is expected to assimilate in two or three generations what Europe has evolved in two thousand years... We are at the end of a generation which has seen Africa awakened from her long isolation. We are at the beginning of an epoch which shall fix her destiny for hundreds of years."

In his articles, Bill Platt graphically illustrates his points from personal experience; a new generation of the Society's supporters at home find it all stimulating and inspiring. Platt, now 42, is the

General Committee's natural choice as Youth Secretary in 1935. He introduces vigorous and informal methods, including creating a new form of Bible Society fellowship for young people which will continue almost unchanged for nearly 30 years and will get hundreds of young people from a complete range of social backgrounds involved in the Society's work. It may be that a similar approach is needed today. Youth conferences become a notable feature of the Society's annual programme and a training ground for its staff in future years.

Platt never loses his concern for Africa in all the varying duties and responsibilities which fall to him in his long years of service for the Society.

But I must break off here to tell another important story with which Bill Platt will be intimately involved.

Act
40

Towards a new fellowship for the global family

From 1804 to the 1890s the British and Foreign Bible Society (BFBS) and the American Bible Society (ABS) were responsible for most of the Bible production and distribution throughout the world. With the British Empire at its height, BFBS regarded the world as its parish. ABS, although primarily concerned for the huge area and growing population of the USA, also tried to meet the needs of American missionaries in foreign parts. The National Bible Society of Scotland (NBSS) and the Netherlands Bible Society (NBS) were also important players on the global stage.

We have already seen in our story of Japan and Korea how, from the 1880s and 1890s, the biggest Societies cautiously attempted some cooperation. This was necessary since, by 1900, ABS was engaged in extensive operations not only in Korea and Japan, but also in China, and other parts of the Far East, as well as in Central and South America, Persia, and eastern Mediterranean countries.

In general, ABS didn't work in countries in the British Empire. However, there were certain countries where the two Societies (and in some cases other Societies too) worked in such close contact that there was the constant risk of confusion, duplication of effort and misunderstanding. For this reason, John Ritson attended a conference with officers of ABS in New York in 1911, before embarking on a second Canadian tour.

During these years, ABS withdrew from Korea and, as a *quid pro quo*, BFBS withdrew from the Philippines. ABS withdrew from Persia, BFBS from Central America and so on. ABS and BFBS agreed to share the work in Brazil, China and Japan by assigning separate geographical areas within these countries.

I have to say that Bible Society wasn't always cooperative in these early attempts by the big Societies to work towards closer union. As early as March 1919 ABS proposed a "World Federation of National Bible Societies". The proposed scheme was close to what would become the United Bible Society (UBS) 27 years later. BFBS responded snootily to the ABS suggestion: "From its very inception, [the BFBS] has been a World Society. The international character of our Society marks off its work from that of Societies which are limited to one country or section of a country, and with which you are proposing we should federate." BFBS at this stage preferred a suggestion from the Netherlands Bible Society of "occasional conferences of the leading Bible Societies for friendly and consultative purposes".

But, to anticipate, from roughly 1932 to 1946, the biggest Societies will generally coordinate their activities in a more orderly way. In this period an increasing number of "joint agencies" and independent Bible Societies will be created. Eric North (ABS) and John Temple (BFBS) will travel together to the Middle East to organise joint "Bible lands" agencies from Egypt and the Sudan in the south, to Greece and Bulgaria in the north. Others will follow in South America and the Far East.

Queen's Hall, London, 1931

John Dean, who became BFBS General Secretary in 1973, believes that Eric North of ABS was one of the giants of the 20th-century story of Bible Societies, highly regarded for the clarity of his thought.

Enter Eric North

In May 1931, North is accorded the rare honour of addressing the BFBS annual meeting. Although it isn't the first time that an ABS representative has spoken at the Society's annual meeting, it hasn't happened for over a century.

In his introductory comments, North refers to his predecessor's "sentiments of high appreciation" delivered a year after the founding of ABS in 1817.

"These are sentiments that I can repeat without a change,"

North tells the meeting. Later in his talk he emphasises an historic difference between the two Societies.

"An immense part of our efforts in the American Bible Society," he says, "have been necessarily directed to our vast immigrant population. For you, the expansion of your Colonial Empire opened at once doors to vast opportunities across the seas. For us, our Empire was within our own country."

North doesn't make specific proposals for closer cooperation between the various Societies on this occasion. He merely speaks of "new types of endeavour in order to achieve that which has been committed to us" and of the need for "new allies also".

He travels north to visit the Board of Directors of NBSS in Glasgow.

Enter John Temple and Arthur Wilkinson

In September 1931 the General Committee announces the appointment of the Reverend John Robinson Temple to join Arthur Wilkinson as Joint-General Secretary. Temple replaces Ritson who retires for health reasons (though he will still lead an active life until the 1950s). A Wesleyan Methodist minister, Temple has trained at Didsbury College, Manchester, and in 1910 went to China as a missionary. In 1917 he enlisted as a chaplain and served in France before returning to China at the end of the Great War.

No one – including Temple himself – would claim that he could match Ritson's intellectual abilities or skills as an administrator. His qualities are of a different order. "Charm" is the word most often used by those who know him best. Ritson, the man with a first from Balliol, never found it easy to suffer fools either gladly or in any other way. In contrast, Temple's capacity for tact and patient negotiation will be of great value to the Society in its negotiations with other Societies and as he leads it on the path towards the founding of UBS.

North (ABS) and Wilkinson and Temple (BFBS) will serve for many years and grow to appreciate each other. All three men will live to see the foundation of UBS. Wilkinson and North meet in London to discuss problems arising from competition between the two major Societies in China, India and other areas. They establish a rapport which lasts throughout their lives.

Meanwhile in Wales...

...some publicity is given to an assertion by Bob Owen of Croesor, a colourful and eccentric Welsh writer and self-taught historian, that "there is no truth in the Mary Jones story". He says, "It is said that Mary Jones's Bible is in the office in London. No doubt she had a Bible, but there is no certainty that there is any history to that Bible, any more than the thousands of other Bibles printed at that time to be sold in Wales." However, Owen's muddled statements are effectively answered by Dr John Owen of Morfa Nefyn who, in December 1936, publishes evidence which "proves conclusively the truth of Mary Jones's story". As we shall see, more evidence about Mary will emerge in the 1960s and we now know that it is John Owen who had the truth.

London Bible House, July 1932

On 26 and 27 July board and staff members of ABS, BFBS and NBSS meet in London Bible House. These "big three" Societies are at that time responsible for the bulk of Bible distribution throughout the world. John Temple invites staff from all three Societies for some meetings in his home. A warm atmosphere of Christian fellowship develops. The delegates discuss cooperative work by the three Societies.

The official communication reports, "We have just completed a Conference which we believe is not only unique in the annals of the three Societies, but also rich in significance for our future history." The ABS representatives conclude their formal report on an uplifting note: "In one of the opening prayers of the Conference we were reminded that the Master himself had entered the Conference Room before any of us. At the close of the Conference we were sure that he had been with us and brought an outcome far beyond our hopes."

The conference produces some revolutionary conclusions

regarding China. It recommends that the Societies should work together with a view to encouraging the formation of a China Bible Society. However, the outbreak of war between Japan and China in July 1937 means that from that time on, Bible work in China takes on the nature of a prolonged rearguard action. Another result of the conference is that instead of having three Bible Societies in Hong Kong (ABS, BFBS and NBSS), one Society, BFBS, is appointed as "administering Society" and the costs will be shared by all three.

Re-enter Bill Platt

In 1937 Bill Platt is appointed Home Superintendent, responsible for the work of the District Secretaries. Previously, this post has been held by a succession of Anglicans, since it has been reckoned that this helps the Society in its relationship with the Church of England. Platt launches an intensive campaign for new income, issuing 10,000 new collecting boxes through the Home Auxiliaries (today's Action Groups) at the average rate of 1,000 per month. These are decorated with a design which relates the English Biblical heritage.

At the annual meeting in 1939, the General Committee reports that the Society has circulated 11 million copies of the Scriptures during 1938 and has achieved a surplus on the year's activities of £433 – nearly £14,000 at today's values – the first surplus since 1934.

Woudschoten, Zeist, July 1939 A CHALLENGE TO ENCOURAGE THE *USE* OF THE BIBLE

The Netherlands Bible Society (NBS) celebrates its 125th anniversary in July 1939. It invites nine Bible Societies to attend a conference in Woudschoten, Zeist. Three are unable to accept but representatives from BFBS, ABS, NBSS, the Norwegian Bible Society and Bible work in France join the Netherlands Society.

Enter Professor Kraemer

Professor Hendrick Kraemer, a layman who has been to Indonesia as a translation expert on behalf of NBS, and one of the principal figures in the emerging ecumenical movement, makes the opening speech and issues a powerful challenge to the Bible Societies to cooperate with the churches to encourage the *use* of the Bible. Professor Kraemer

- acknowledges the important work of the Bible Societies in translating, printing, and distributing the Bible, but calls for a systematic and well-planned movement for teaching those who buy a Bible how to read and *use* it for private and family worship.

- notes that, while most Bible Societies issue the Bible only, some publish additional material. He suggests that more is needed: "All Bible Societies ought to include in their activities the preparation, printing, and distribution of books with collections of tales from the Bible."

These two proposals spark off lively discussion. Undeterred, Kraemer goes on to criticise the quality of translations, questioning the instructions given by the Bible Societies to their translators. For example, he doesn't like the requirement that "the translation of the scriptures, if possible without loss of idiom, dignity and beauty of phrase, should be made in a language that average people can understand without explanation". The logic of what he is saying seems to be leading to the proposal that Bibles should be issued with explanations. This cuts across a basic principle of Bible Societies that Bibles should be published "without note or comment". Some delegates think that Kraemer is asking Bible Societies to take on the task of the churches. All these issues will be much debated in the years ahead – indeed they still are today.

In a report, the Societies declare their agreement that the objectives of the Bible Societies "will be fully carried out provided that the Holy Scriptures circulated by the Societies neither contain nor have bound with them any matter of description which either in any way interprets, or attempts to interpret the inspired word, or can in any way be regarded as having a doctrinal bias".

The Woudschoten meeting represents a key turning point in the history of the Bible Society movement in that it recognises the need for a more nuanced understanding of the traditional "without note or comment" stance and foreshadows a revision which will be made in the 1970s.

However, the main concern of the Woudschoten Conference is to encourage cooperation between Societies. The Secretaries of the American, British and Dutch Societies speak encouragingly of areas where this is already happening.

Enter John Mott

Seventy-four-year-old John Mott, who nearly 30 years earlier chaired the Edinburgh Missionary Conference, addresses the Woudschoten Conference with a passionate call for common understanding and action.

"In face of the growing indigenous churches," he says, "we want the finest and widest cooperation possible, and your work is essential to undergird all other Christian activity. Moreover there is a danger of our getting out of step, for by government and education we are making literate millions of people every year. Can you therefore delay corporate action? This is a day of God's visitation not only for our sins, but visitation by God in that He is beckoning us on and drawing us closer in this cooperation."

After Mott's speech at Woudschoten, the delegates resolve to continue to work together and encourage in each country the formation of a Bible Society working on the same principles as they are. They even resolve to establish a "Council of Bible Societies" which would be something like the later UBS – but these plans are overtaken by the Second World War.

Act
41

Friends on opposite sides

In September 1939 the German invasion of Poland prompts an Anglo-French declaration of war against Germany. After the period of "phoney war", all the European countries except Portugal, Spain, Sweden and Switzerland are fighting. Japan and the United States join in later while China continues a struggle against Japanese invaders that began in 1937.

Within a few weeks of the declaration of war, the Society makes an edition of 300,000 pocket-sized New Testaments available, bound in khaki, royal blue, or air force blue for members of the services. In each copy a printed message from King George VI reads:

> To all serving in my Forces by sea, or land, or in the air, and indeed to all my people engaged in the defence of the Realm, I commend the reading of this book. For centuries the Bible has been a wholesome and strengthening influence in our national life, and it behoves us in these momentous days to turn with renewed faith to this Divine source of comfort and inspiration.

To the pocket Testaments, the Society adds an edition of the very popular Ruby Bible, which since it first appeared in 1933 has achieved outstanding success as the Shilling Bible. Gospels in khaki and blue paper covers are also issued. By the end of 1939 orders for the pocket Testaments exceed half a million and continue to come in. The Society opens a "Services Scriptures Fund" which is commended by Cosmo Gordon Lang, the Archbishop of Canterbury, who writes of the troops: "The Services New Testament will remind them of some of the deepest associations of their lives, and of the eternal verities which stand above and beyond all human conflict."

During the first full year of the war, there is a heavy drop in income from the Auxiliaries. In blacked out towns and villages it has become increasingly difficult to hold meetings after dark, while shortages of petrol and restricted public transport seriously limit the amount of travelling which District Secretaries can do.

It is time to meet a couple of women who will use their formidable talents to boost the Society's profile during the dark days of war and beyond.

Enter Mildred Cable and Francesca French

Mildred Cable went out to China just after the Boxer Rebellion of 1900, working for the China Inland Mission (now OMF International). She was then 21. For fifteen years she worked with Eva French in a girls' school in Shanxi province, where they were joined by Eva's younger sister, Francesca. Then the three of them set out as pioneer missionaries in the vast expanses of the Gobi desert, which they crossed no fewer than five times. When they returned to England just before the war broke out, Mildred settled in the Dorset town of Shaftesbury with Francesca French and their adopted Tibetan daughter, Topsy.

Bill Platt visits the trio in Shaftesbury in the autumn of 1939 and persuades Mildred to devote her remarkable energy and experience to Bible Society and its cause. Her work in China and her travels across the Gobi desert are still quite recent events and have given her something of celebrity status in the Christian world. In the course of her journeys in Asia she has spent a lot of time distributing Bibles, as well as personally witnessing, and has a fund of stories to tell. Here is a flavour of one of them.

A lama (either a Tibetan or Mongolian Buddhist monk) has come from the other end of China. Mildred and the two French sisters pitch their tent on a threshing-floor where crowds can conveniently gather for the preaching. The travelling lama knows nothing about this. He is tired after a long day's walk and sits behind a wall, looking around for the sign of a temple where he may spend the night. Mildred, Francesca and Eva leave the threshing-floor for a short walk and there they find him.

"Lama, you look tired. Have you come far?"

"I have walked for eight months to get here."

"And where have you come from?"

"I have come from the east, seeking the land where the sun sets, and where God is."

By now the three women and the lama are sitting together on a crumbling earth-mound, behind which rises a high city wall, golden in the rays of the setting sun. A turret guardhouse is silhouetted against the light blue sky, and the sentry leans over the battlement and looks down on them. Mildred speaks.

"If it is God you are seeking, why go to the land of the setting sun?"

"Because they say that he dwells there."

"Lama, God is not far from any one of us."

And the three women speak to him of Jesus.

Bill Platt, as Home Superintendent, sees the disruption caused by the war as a challenge. He realises the need to make preparations to meet the needs of Europe when the war eventually ends and to prepare for rapid advances in literacy in China, India and Africa. He realises that a new appeal to women is needed at a time when national service has deprived the Society and churches of so much male leadership.

Platt rallies the District staff, many of whom are his seniors in age and length of service. Much of his success in mounting an entirely new programme of recruitment and support for the Society is due to the inspiration and energy of Mildred Cable.

Under Platt's direction, the Society organises a series of intensive campaigns which are especially, but not exclusively, directed at potential women supporters. They are held in areas crowded with people who have moved there in the war to avoid the most vulnerable cities. Early in 1942, Mildred contributes an article to an economy wartime issue of *The Bible and the World*. Under the title "A Call to Women" she emphasises the message which she has begun to proclaim at many meetings.

"Whenever I have spoken about the Bible," she says, "and the place it should hold in our national life, I have found immediate response, and a deep concern lest, as a nation, we should undervalue our priceless heritage of an open Bible and our complete freedom to worship God."

This is just the sort of message Bill Platt wants to drive home to his flagging or lapsed supporters. In 1942, Mildred Cable together with Lady Mance and Lady Alexander become the first female members of the Society's General Committee. It has taken 138 years.

From 1940 hundreds of thousands of prisoners of war are locked behind barbed wire in camps in Germany. Since BFBS and its Agencies are cut off from these people, ABS sees an opportunity to work where Britain is no longer able to help. ABS General Secretary Eric North writes to the General Secretary of the World Council of Churches asking whether an office can be set up in Geneva to make Scriptures available to the prisoner of war camps.

Enter Olivier Béguin

Such an office is set up in Geneva, in neutral Switzerland, with Olivier Béguin (we shall meet him again) as its Secretary. Béguin represents the work of the churches and the two biggest Bible Societies through the remaining years of the war. He has a good deal of success in maintaining contact with Bible Society Agencies in Europe which are now out of contact with London. Then, when the Japanese attack Pearl Harbour, the main US naval base in Hawaii at the end of 1941, drawing America into the war, he manages to build links with Agencies which become cut off from New York.

Bibles and New Testaments continue to be produced and circulated during the war and some supplies do get into continental Europe from outside. In the early days of the German invasion, a bomb drops near the Warsaw Bible depot, blowing out the windows and doors. One little pane of glass only remains, on which are the words, "Heaven and earth shall pass away, but my word shall not pass away." These words remain on that small fragment, and through the long months and years, people as they pass by take off their hats, making the sign of the cross.

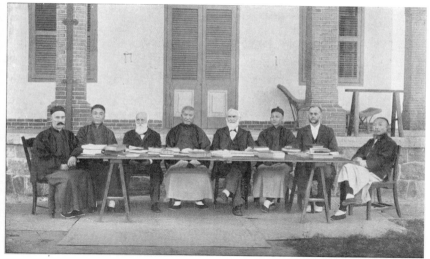

Revisers of the Mandarin New Testament in session in Chefoo, 1905, Act 31.

Korean family reading the
Scriptures, 1904, Act 34.

Depot staff and colporteurs, Kobe, Japan, 1908, Act 33.

Depot staff, Seoul, Korea, 1908, Act 34.

Colporteurs at Seoul, Korea, 1908, Act 34.

Colporteur Minenko at Taischet, Russia, selling Bibles along a train, Act 35.

The Society's colportage boat, Port Said, 1907, Act 37.

Port Said Bible House today, Act 37.

Karl Uhl, Act 42.

First UBS President Bishop
Eivind Berggrav, Act 42.

Uli Fick with his staff at Stuttgart in December 1985. Three years later the
World Service Centre was opened in Reading, England, Act 47.

Eugene Nida, who was present at
Elfinsward in 1946 and was the
brains behind the *Good News Bible*
and the dynamic equivalence
method of translation, Act 47.

The Opening of Bible House, Swindon, on 9 May 1986 by Her Majesty Queen Elizabeth the Queen Mother from a painting by Nigel Purchase, Act 47.

Bill Platt at the age of 95 attends the opening of the UBS World Service Centre in Reading in September 1988. With him are, left to right, Geoffrey Hill, John Dean, Steven Downey and Cirilos Rigos, Act 47.

James Catford, Chief Executive from January 2002, Act 49.

Bicentenary service at St Paul's Cathedral, Monday 8 March 2004. Colourful dance depicted stories of the Tower of Babel, the Incarnation and Day of Pentecost.

"It's a miracle," they say.

By the end of the war, Alexander Enholc, the Society's agent in Poland, reports that 266,000 Bibles, New Testaments, and portions have been distributed, despite great risk, and that 6,000 Bibles and 22,000 New Testaments have been printed.

The Society's tone and approach to the possibility of cooperation with other Societies changes now. The snootiness is a thing of the past. Now it is taking initiatives in that direction. In October 1941 Arthur Wilkinson, joint Secretary of the Society with Temple, writes a letter to Eric North at ABS. He expresses the hope that when normal Bible work can be resumed after the war "it should be so far as possible a cooperative work of the three main Bible Societies" (American, British and Dutch). A few months later Wilkinson writes again, hoping that when they get together to plan their postwar policy they can agree to the idea of a "*Federation* with the joint title and some simple form of Constitution which will express in words what is a growing reality – mutual cooperation".

While these important letters sit in Eric North's pending tray awaiting the end of the war, we must follow a dramatic tale on the continent of Europe.

Act
42

A telegram to the Führer

Enter Karl Uhl

Until 1939 the Society has one Bible depot in Germany and another in Vienna with Karl Uhl, who has been there since 1924, at the helm. Following the *Anschluss* (union) between Austria and Germany in 1938, and in view of the imminent retirement of the Society's long-serving head of the Berlin depot, Rudolf Haupt, the Society decides to give Uhl responsibility for Bible work throughout Austria and Germany. The plan is that the Bible depot in Berlin will be closed and Uhl will run the operation from Vienna.

Just as the operations are being reorganised, war breaks out. The German authorities designate the assets of BFBS as "enemy property", putting them under the administration of the Reichskommissar. The assets consist of 35 tons of Bibles, bound and unbound, and the necessary plates and matrices needed for printing.

Vienna, January 1941

Enter the Gestapo

On 25 April 1940 Karl Uhl is called up for service in the German army. On 17 January 1941 the Gestapo visit the depot in Vienna and speak to Erwin Schwartz who is in day-to-day charge in Uhl's absence.

"All the work of the British and Foreign Bible Society," the Gestapo tell Schwartz, "is forbidden in the whole territory of the Reich. The complete stock of Bibles, both in Vienna and Berlin, including printing and bookbinding material, has been confiscated and must be handed over for destruction."

Schwartz is alone in the depot. He is not going to give in easily.

"In the middle of the war," he asks, "have you nothing else to bother about than to destroy God's Word? That you cannot do – you have no power to carry it out. Will you ship out the whole stock, when no means of transport is available? Or will you seal the Bible depot?"

Schwartz receives no immediate answer.

On the staff of the Vienna Gestapo is a man who as a child had been a member of Uhl's Sunday School and then youth group. This man greatly respects Uhl and speaks well of him to the other members of the Gestapo.

"Uhl is honourable and dependable," he tells them. "His faith is genuine."

However, some time later Uhl's unit is transferred to the Pommern district and rearmed. He receives a letter addressed to him personally from the Berlin Gestapo and forwarded to him by their colleagues in Vienna. The letter says:

The Bible stocks in northwest Berlin which have become unusable will be transported and pulped, because the warehouse space is required for important war purposes. The cost of this will be charged to the British and Foreign Bible Society. Any objection to this order is inadmissible.

Karl Uhl is shocked. He decides to send a telegram to the Führer himself:

While I am in the service of Germany, someone is seizing the capital assets of my work in the homeland. My Bible stocks in Berlin are to be committed to destruction, and every right is denied me to find a favourable settlement by just means. Already at the end of January I sent a petition to you to request your decision with regard to the banning of our work. Without waiting for this, in the immediate future stocks to the value of 100,000 marks are to be destroyed. To be brief: I distribute always only the pure Biblical text without confessional or propaganda bias in nearly all the languages of the world. In spite of the existence of an English connection during times of peace, I have never acted otherwise than in the interests of my Fatherland. I know that bearing in mind many urgent matters, a definitive ruling on my case cannot be expected just at present. I ask you therefore for your protection, ensuring that in some way my Bible stocks and warehouse will remain permanently protected. This has to do with a holy and pure enterprise concerning the distribution of the Word of God in the languages of the world.

Karl Uhl

Uhl sends a message to Erwin Schwartz to come to Pommern from Vienna. The two men pray together and discuss a number of courses of action.

Uhl goes to see the captain of his unit, a bank official from Austria who, though sensitive in his dealings with others, takes his military duties seriously.

"I must go to Berlin to save the Bible Society's stocks," Uhl tells the captain.

"It is impossible," the captain replies. "There is a total ban on all leave."

"Captain," Uhl insists, "I must find some way to get to Berlin. The destruction of this considerable stock of Bibles must be prevented."

"It is simply not possible. But cheer up – think of the misfortunes that so many people suffer in these times. Families lose their fathers, and fathers lose their wives and children in their homes. Your case is a sad one, but it concerns materials which can possibly be replaced after the war."

The captain then adopts a gentler tone, switches from "Private Uhl" to "Herr Uhl", and looks kindly at Karl.

"Herr Uhl," he continues, "you know that I have frequently shown a detailed interest in your remarkable and really wonderful work. I respect the work of the British and Foreign Bible Society because it is of worldwide scope and radically transforms the lives of men. It encourages the call for peace on earth. I also know that the Bible is disregarded by the people who are presently in power. But then I know too that people who allow the spirit of the Bible to have an effect on their lives, even in our time, also are reliable citizens. They respect the powers that be even when their faith is held in contempt. I must tell you though that I see no possibility of letting you go to Berlin."

"Captain, I must go to Berlin."

There is a long pause.

"Private Uhl," says the captain, stiffening a little. "I will write a report and will send you with it to the battalion commander. My best wishes go with you."

UHL'S SECRET ASSIGNMENT

Karl Uhl is announced at the commander's office. The major, an East Prussian who is feared as a strict officer, reads the captain's report. Uhl salutes him as smartly as he can.

"Herr Major," he says, "I must without fail go to Berlin for a short while because there a large stock of Bibles, for which I am responsible, is to be destroyed. That must be prevented."

To Uhl's surprise, the major becomes friendly in a quite unmilitary way, offers him a chair, and asks for full details of the situation. Uhl tells him about the work of the Bible Society and how it has come to be viewed with hostility by the Gestapo. The major is quiet for a few moments.

"I am sorry," he says. "I cannot help you. There is a total ban on all leave. All troops are in a state of immediate combat readiness. There are no exceptions, not even for officers. Your situation is hopeless."

Then the major speaks less formally again.

"Our personal safety is more insecure than ever. I don't know, and you don't know, whether or not we will survive this war. We are not even sure of the next year, of the next month. Nevertheless we must perform our assigned duties and carry out the tasks which are required of us. But what is material loss when we are surrounded by such crying injustice? All material is replaceable, but you are not replaceable, and nor am I, if we lose our lives."

"Herr Major," Uhl replies, "for sure I don't know everything. But I do know two things: I will return home safely and then I will continue with Bible distribution as my life's task."

The major raises an eyebrow.

"Is what you are saying imagination or knowledge?"

"I know it," says Uhl simply.

The major shakes his head and says nothing for a few minutes.

"Your captain in his report," he says when he breaks his silence, "has described your military service as particularly conscientious. He has urged me to fulfil your request if at all possible. I cannot give you leave. That is simply impossible. Not even for a death, not even for the death of a whole family in a home, can I allow leave. But I will give you an official assignment. A secret assignment please! For this I will allow you three days: two days for the return trip and on one day you must do whatever is possible."

The major gets up and Uhl follows suit.

"Thank you," he says – and inwardly thanks God for an answer to prayer. He manages another smart salute.

Two hours later he reports backs to the captain.

"I have an official order to travel to Berlin!"

The captain beams with genuine delight.

Uhl sends Erwin Schwartz to Berlin in advance to prepare the way by visiting friends who are in a position to make the necessary appointments. Uhl, accompanied by his wife, arrives in Berlin late in the afternoon of 20 May. Schwartz tells them they can expect little help from contacts in the area, some of whom are already under suspicion for subversive activities.

Berlin, May 1941

Enter Erwin Schartz and wife

The next day Uhl, accompanied by his wife and Schwartz, walk to the offices of the Reichskommissar for the administration of enemy property.

"I have been in touch with the Gestapo," the Reichskommissar tells them, "but the news is not good. I suggested to them that at the end of the war the British and Foreign Bible Society would be able to make a claim upon the German Reich to make reparations for the losses incurred. They replied that after the war the English will be in no position to make any claims. I recommend that you ask for help from the Propaganda Ministry because I know that your telegram to the Reichskanzler has been passed to them. I know a secretary who is close to Dr Goebbels. I will speak to her in advance of your approach. We cannot help here. When the Gestapo decides something, nobody can do anything against it. The Gestapo is a state within the state."

Back at their Berlin hotel, the trio open their Bibles. "Fear not, I am with you; be not afraid for I am your God," they read in the Old Testament. And, "Blessed is the man who endures temptation, because after he has been tested, he will receive the Crown of Life, which God promised to those that love him," they read in the New. They kneel and pray that the Lord will protect and guide them as they make the most important visit of their lives.

"WHAT HAPPENED TO MY WORD IN BERLIN?"

Herr and Frau Uhl, with Erwin Schwartz, make their way to the Gestapo headquarters in Berlin. They do not find it easy to enter the building complex. After answering a whole series of questions, they are eventually ushered through a series of fortified gates and doors, all guarded by men in black. At last they arrive at the office of the head of the press department.

Uhl knocks on the door. The chief opens it personally.

"I knew that you were coming and I know what you want," he says. "But I want you to know that the matter is settled. We are emptying the warehouse. We are pulping everything. Later we will let you know what the whole thing cost and then you can pay the bill at your convenience. If the waste paper brings in more money than the expenses incurred, we will even put the extra money at your disposal. Heil Hitler!"

The press chief wants to shut the door but he is not quick enough. Uhl has his foot in the way.

"Herr Doktor," says Uhl, "you have the power and the opportunity to destroy my stocks of Bibles. But I must inform you of the fact that one day God will ask you, 'What happened to my Word in Berlin? Who condemned my Word to destruction?' How will you answer?"

The chief's eyes widen. He stops trying to close the door and invites the trio into his room to sit down. He waves Uhl to a soft leather armchair, his wife to his right and Schwartz to his left, before speaking again.

"For such an unnecessary object, for which nobody asks any more, one should not waste a word. Who today in the Third Reich wants a Bible? Nobody. Today everybody asks only for the word of the Führer, because he alone brings prosperity and order, already now in Germany, and later in the whole world. I simply do not understand that a rational man, such as you appear to be, can still be involved in such a business.

"You know that we are at war with England, and I consider therefore that you are committing a crime, when you know that you are protecting English Bibles. It would be wrong to reconsider this case. The decision has been made."

"Herr Doktor," Uhl replies, "the decision has not yet been made, at least not in your sense. The Bible is the most distributed, translated and also the most read book of our time. It has produced our civilisation and has become the basis of our culture. Much of our daily life in its many forms comes under the influence of this book. And we see that the situation is the same for other people. So this book is indispensable and the stocks held in Berlin must be protected and made secure. The Bible has absolutely no connection with England. It is no English invention and there is no 'English' Bible in the sense that you express it, Herr Doktor.

"And furthermore, if it was reserved for English Christians, by the founding of the British and Foreign Bible Society, to take the lead in establishing a special kind of missionary activity, then it must be added that from the beginning Germans, and citizens of many other countries, have participated in its leadership and have been invited to become partners in the work."

The press chief replies in characteristically Nazi style.

"The Bible is a Jewish book," he says. "It is therefore pernicious and must be forbidden in the Third Reich. It tells of the trickeries and crimes of the Jews. In addition the Bible will teach us only false humility and submissiveness, whereas it has now become clear that only we as a master race are given the task of saving the world and of expunging everything which is rotten."

"Herr Doktor," Uhl replies from his perspective, "I can see that you have neither read the Bible nor even skimmed through it. Otherwise you would have known long ago that the Jews have left the way that God led them, and have thus incurred much hard punishment from God. If they had stayed on the way that God had showed them, they would have become and remained a people of blessing for all mankind. But they did not want this, and they have become sufficiently punished. Now only we can be such a people of blessing, but also only when we are willing to follow obediently in God's way, and are ready to listen to his Word. If we don't do this, we too will perish. It is important, Herr Doktor, that you do not condemn these Bible stocks, but rather that you set them free."

The chief then shifts his tone and approach. He notices the decoration pinned to Uhl's chest. Mistaking the war service cross, second class (which it is) for the iron cross, second class (which it isn't – though Uhl will be awarded this later), the Doctor says: "Obviously you are a brave and efficient soldier. I can see that because you have already been awarded the iron cross, second class. I'm sure that you are also aware that the Führer has made it known that all exceptional soldiers shall after the victorious ending of the war be put into good and secure positions which will also be well paid. Certainly it will no longer be necessary for you and your family to earn your bread from such so-called missionary activity. On the contrary you are in line for a pleasant, quiet and carefree life."

"Herr Doktor," Uhl replies, "do not be concerned. Even if the future is hidden from me, I know quite well that I will return home safely, and will take up again my task of distributing God's Word, whether it is permitted or not permitted."

"If the materials are destroyed," the chief interrupts, shouting now, "when no printing press has permission to print Bibles, if it is no longer possible for you to collect or borrow financial resources, how then will the Bibles come again?"

"Then I will ask God," Uhl replies quietly. "And he will shower just so much gold from heaven as I need to initiate the production of Bibles. And for gold I will receive more Bibles, Herr Doktor!"

The seconds tick by in silence. Uhl's heart races. He senses that on either side of him his wife and Schwartz are praying.

"You will receive my written reply. Now you must go. Heil Hitler!"

On the way back to the hotel, Uhl is so weak that his two companions have to support and lead him. At the hotel, on their knees, they thank God for a safe return and trust him for the right outcome.

Uhl returns to Pommern and makes a report to the major and the captain. Four weeks later, his unit marches into Russia. The weeks pass.

One morning, a letter arrives for him. It is a copy of a memorandum from the Berlin Gestapo, forwarded to him by the Gestapo in Vienna. His heart leaps as he reads it.

> Karl Uhl is permitted to remove the Berlin Bible stocks within six weeks and to transfer them to another location. If this is not done the whole stock will be destroyed.

By the time he receives the permit, Uhl's wife and Erwin Schwartz have already requested and received from the Vienna Gestapo permission to bring the entire Berlin stocks to Vienna. The then President of the Lutheran Church, Heinrich Liptak, later President of the Austrian Bible Committee, puts some empty rooms at their disposal to house the Berlin Bibles and printing equipment.

The Württemberg Bible Society undertakes to buy as many Bibles as are needed to provide the funds needed for transport costs. With the help of the Kommissar for the administration of enemy property, and on the assurance of director Diehl that the Bibles will only be sold abroad, the Berlin Gestapo give their approval to the plan.

In Berlin, Erwin Schwartz visits a transport agent, hoping somehow to arrange for the large consignment of Bibles to be moved to Vienna. Speed is vital.

"Herr Schwartz," the agent asks, "how soon can the shipment be made?"

"I have got permission from the Gestapo that the stocks are to be transported to Vienna," Schwartz replies. "And I have already been able to find in Vienna the necessary warehouse space. The removal can and should be carried out as soon as possible."

"Wonderful!" the agent replies. "Tomorrow I was going to have to send three empty railway wagons to Vienna. We will start moving right away."

For the whole day and the following night, trucks run between the warehouse and the station. At 9 a.m. the following morning, all 35 tons of the Bible Society's Berlin stocks are on their way to Vienna.

Schwartz pays another visit to the head of the press department in the Gestapo complex.

"Herr Doktor, the Bibles are on their way to Vienna."

"I am beginning to believe in miracles!" he replies.

In Russia, at Christmas 1941, Uhl hears from his wife that the precious consignment has arrived in Vienna. He writes back to her: "Thank you, you conveyer of such happy news. Although I should not say it, I am surprised by the wonderful resolution of our difficulties, even though I knew and believed that it would happen. And now I rejoice that God has again marvellously intervened and helped us."

In August 1946 Uhl returns to Vienna from a Russian prisoner of war camp to find that Bible work there is re-established.

Looking ahead to September 1970, a meeting of the European Regional Committee of UBS in Vienna paves the way for the Austrian Bible Society to become autonomous. BFBS will hand over the Bible House, in an attractive part of Vienna, including all its stock and equipment.

Karl Uhl will live on until 1998 when he dies aged 91.

Meanwhile in London...

The Society holds its annual meeting in the Queen's Hall on 7 May 1942. Three days later the building is destroyed in an air raid. Meetings will now be held in the Kingsway Hall. On 5 May 1943 Viscount Sankey, a new President who has succeeded the Duke of Connaught, announces that King George VI and Queen Elizabeth have agreed to become patrons of the Society, a position which the Queen will hold with active interest until her death at the age of 101 nearly 60 years later.

In November 1944 John Temple makes a wartime journey across the Atlantic. At the headquarters of ABS in New York he discusses with the American Board, Eric North and his staff, the postwar development of Bible work in Europe. They discuss cooperation between Bible Societies, and a new attitude of trust between senior executives in ABS and BFBS develops.

In the same year, BFBS Auxiliaries in India become fully fledged as the Bible Society of India. As Dr B K Pramanik, the current General Secretary, has put it to me, "The umbilical cord may have been cut but the mother (BFBS) kept visiting the daughter (BSI), and relationships with other Bible Societies were also maintained and strengthened." Today the Bible Society of India is one of the biggest Bible Societies in the world with a central office in Bangalore which is supported by 15 Auxiliaries all through the country and a translations centre at Shillong in northeast India. The Society is looking forward to celebrating its own bicentenary in 2011.

On 25 October 1945 John Temple cables Eric North in New York: "We strongly urge calling early in May 1946 a conference in London of Bible Societies in connection with European work. Your presence essential. May we rely on it and use your name with ours in notifying other Societies?" The ABS Board considers this and approves both of the conference and North's presence at it.

A LEGEND'S BLESSING

With the war over, John Temple decides to go to Norway to see Bishop Eivind Berggrav, the Primate of Norway and President of the Norwegian Bible Society. Berggrav is an almost legendary figure, known in many countries as a man who resisted the Nazi occupation of Norway with spiritual weapons. Thanks to the intervention of two distinguished visitors to Norway, the aristocrat Count Helmuth von Moltke and the theologian Dietrich Bonhoeffer, he was not executed but put under house arrest. It is said that because of his loving concern for their welfare, his guards had to be frequently changed. Berggrav bore witness to what the Bible meant to him.

"In war time and especially in occupation time," he said, "the Bible explained itself to us. It is the usual experience all over the world that when a man is in need of God's Word, he gets it in the Bible, but when he is in no need, he finds the Bible a very difficult book."

In Bible House, Temple has a conversation with Platt before he leaves for Norway.

"If I can get Berrgrav's blessing," Temple says, "we'll go ahead with the foundation of the United Bible Societies."

Enter Bishop Berggrav

In Norway, Berggrav greets Temple warmly and eagerly gives his blessing to the idea of forming the organisation which will come to be called the United Bible Societies. He goes even further and agrees to Temple's suggestion that he should become President of the new organisation.

"I should like Norway to play a greater role in providing Bibles for the world," Berrgrav tells Temple.

Temple finds his meeting with the Norwegian Primate a profoundly moving experience. When the time comes for the two men to say their farewells before the General Secretary of the Bible Society begins his journey back to London, Temple speaks.

"May I ask you to give me your blessing in this work?"

Temple kneels. Berggrav prays that God will indeed bless the idea of forming a body which will coordinate the work of national Bible Societies throughout the world.

Act 43

A global fellowship for Bible Societies

The conference which will lead directly to the founding of the United Bible Societies (UBS) will be held at Elfinsward – the retreat centre of the Diocese of Chichester at Haywards Heath in West Sussex, England. The Rt. Rev. George Bell, Bishop of Chichester, will be the conference host.

Enter Bishop Bell

Bell was educated at Westminster School and Christ Church, Oxford. He has taken an interest in all things ecumenical since he went as part of the British delegation to the meeting at Oud Wassenaar (near The Hague) of the World Alliance for International Friendship through the Churches.

Bell has supported the "Confessing Church" in its struggle against the Nazi Government. The Confessing Church was a group of German evangelical Christians most actively opposed to the "German Christian" church movement sponsored by the Nazis between 1933 and 1945. At the end of the war, in 1945, leaders of the Confessing Churches met a delegation of the Provisional World Council of Churches led by Bishop Bell. They met in the upper room of the Württemberg Bible Society in Stuttgart. The leaders of the Confessing Churches made their famous "Declaration of Guilt" for failing to do more against Nazi tyranny. This action opened the way to a restoration of fellowship between the German churches and the World Council of Churches.

For his part, Bell was outspoken in his condemnation of what he believed to be indiscriminate allied bombing of German towns during the war. Bell's voice in the House of Lords, calling for a consideration of what these bombings were doing for the future, went unheeded. His opposition to the bombing was probably a major factor in preventing him from succeeding William Temple as Archbishop of Canterbury in 1944.

At Christmas 1945 Bell made a broadcast to Germany. "While all that can be done will be done to relieve distress and rebuild the physical structures of Europe," he said, "the crucial need is for 'the liberation of the soul of Europe'. This can only be done by a spiritual power from outside, by something which military forces can never supply, nor our mechanised civilisation provide from its own resources." Later, Bell's contacts with German and other churches after the war will facilitate the first meeting of the World Council of Churches in 1948.

Haywards Heath, West Sussex, England, May 1946

Delegates at the Elfinsward conference centre are from the four Bible Societies most active in promoting the idea of working together: BFBS, ABS, NBS and NBSS. There are also delegates from Czechoslovakia, Denmark, Finland, France, Germany, India, Norway, Poland, Sweden and Switzerland. The World Council of Churches is in the process of being formed and is also represented.

Enter Eugene Nida

In early May 1946 it is cold and rainy. But one young American delegate, Eugene Nida, whose name will become famous in Bible Society history and in the world of translation, recalls, "There was the warm glow of renewed friendship by old friends who had not seen each other during the long dark years of World War II. We had all come through London and had seen the sprawling wasteland of rubble in the centre of the city and realised it must be far worse in Rotterdam, Dresden, and Stanlingrad. In London, St Paul's Cathedral and the nearby Bible House were standing like symbols of hope."

Capturing the heart of what made Elfinsward so momentous, Nida continues, "We were all profoundly influenced by the sense of overwhelming urgency to meet the spiritual need of the churches in eastern Europe, the countless refugees in Asia, and the rapidly growing number of believers in sub-Saharan Africa. Colonialism was becoming a thing of the past, and the rise of two superpowers posed the threat of total economic destruction. Under such circumstances it was not easy to make plans, but it was also no time to be concerned about traditional ways of doing things. Old rivalries in Latin America and duplication of effort in Asia had to be forgotten." Nida's verdict is that "Elfinsward profoundly changed the Bible Society movement and radically changed my life".

Bill Platt's small job at the conference is to help John Temple and his secretary in the task of "bedding down" the distinguished delegates who come: one or two Primates and Presidents, Bishops, Moderators, leading church laymen, Bible Society committee men and women (there are a few women in the official photograph), officers and agents from many countries and leading representatives from Auxiliaries in what are now Commonwealth countries.

ELECTRIC MOMENTS AT ELFINSWARD

Enter Hanns Lilje

The conference has already convened when Dr Hanns Lilje of Germany, who will become Bishop of Hanover, comes into the hall. The legendary Bishop Berggrav is presiding. When Berggrav spots Lilje, he leaves his chair and walks down the aisle to embrace him. The two friends haven't seen each other since 1940. Both have been imprisoned. A year earlier, Lilje has been liberated from his prison in Nuremberg by American troops. During the session, he addresses the conference.

"I apologise for beginning on a personal note," he says. "During the war I was placed in a special prison in Berlin run by the Gestapo. Three times I was nearly killed by them, having the choice of dying from hanging or starvation or being shot. It is unnecessary for me to explain that during that time, with nothing to read or write, chained up night and day, unprotected from air raids, I relied on those things that I had learnt in my youth and they kept me and many others going.

"I discovered that a prisoner in a neighbouring cell had been a high-ranking Nazi official. We both understood Morse code and communicated by tapping out messages to each other. I managed to obtain a Bible for him. Some weeks later, before being led out to execution, he tapped on the wall, 'I am going out to life, not to death.'"

In his own address to the conference, Bishop Berggrav speaks of how the world's statesmen respect the message of the Bible. "Before going to his first conference with President Truman on the atomic bomb, Prime Minister Attlee said this: 'I am going with hope, because I have seen how St Paul's Cathedral is standing there above all the ruins of the centre of London, as a symbol of the spiritual values standing above all the ruins of mankind. I am going, not frightened in my soul, but taking with me these three: faith, hope and love, and the greatest of these is love.'"

When Bishop Bell addresses the conference as its host, he takes up the theme he has raised in his Christmas broadcast to Germany – the battle for the soul of Europe. "The Bible speaks today," he tells the delegates, "once the conscience can be drawn to perceive it, with an extraordinary clearness – speaks not for warning only, but for comfort and inspiration…. There is something in the Bible which is immensely objective and massive in its simplicity."

Another moment which few who are there will ever forgot occurs during a joint communion service led by Bishop Bell. During the service Martin Niemöller, the German Lutheran pastor and outspoken opponent of Hitler, spontaneously goes forward to embrace Berggrav – another example of two men who have been on opposite sides of the recent conflict united in their love of Christ and the Bible.

WHAT A CENTRAL OFFICE WILL DO

Enter A L Haig, Secretary for Europe

A L Haig, BFBS Secretary for Europe, gets down to specifics in his conference speech. He begins by paying tribute to the work which Olivier Béguin has done in Geneva during the war, citing this as an example of what a central office might do, avoiding overlapping as well as coordinating work done by various Societies in Europe. He sketches the way he sees the network of Bible Societies developing. "In some countries, there are already national Bible Societies," he says. "In others, the churches are not ready for them. Some will need to continue working as agents of the BFBS or ABS. All will need to be coordinated and developments carefully monitored. It will be difficult, if not impossible, to set up national Bible Societies before the full support of the churches in those countries has been secured. In recent years the BFBS tried to leave the work in Germany to the various German Bible Societies [there were 34 in all], but it was not possible to reach agreement before the war, and the Nazi regime made the position still more difficult."

Re-enter Eric North

General Secretary of ABS Eric North presents the conference with a summary of what a central office, if established and enlarged, could do for the Bible Societies:

- provide information to Societies able to contribute for the needs of others
- coordinate contributions to avoid duplication of gifts
- assist in exchange of experience in production, distribution, and promotion
- interpret Bible Society work to church leaders in countries without Bible Societies
- help the development of translation and publication for mission fields
- administrate supervision of special areas
- provide reports on editions available in various languages for the Societies which need them

Under the chairmanship of Sir Gilbert Hogg of NBSS, the conference passes this resolution:

The Conference of Bible Societies assembled at Haywards Heath, England, on May 6 to 9, 1946, moved by the need of the world for the Word of God and by the deep Christian fellowship of those who work together for its spread: resolves to recommend to the National Bible Societies and National Committees representing Bible Society interests and work: That upon approval of six of the bodies eligible to membership, there shall be formed the United Bible Societies.

It is thought that an Executive Committee, meeting annually, will be made up of one representative of each Society or committee in membership. By 11 July 1946, six Societies have approved this, and the Executive Committee is empowered to appoint officers. The conference has recommended that John Temple should be the first General Secretary working from his own BFBS office in London Bible House. The Executive Committee meets in Amersfoort in the Netherlands the following year and confirms Temple's appointment. The United Bible Societies has arrived.

Re-enter John Temple as General Secretary of UBS

As long as Temple remains General Secretary of UBS, Bible Society has no reason to criticise the way the infant organisation is developing. Yet there are many unresolved questions. Everyone agrees that UBS must not become "a super-Bible Society", greater than the sum of its parts. The original intention is that it should facilitate cooperation between the Societies themselves, not formulate policies or initiate action apart from them. However, UBS cannot avoid becoming an arena for negotiations which have been formerly carried on through confidential exchanges: in this new situation there is a danger that people not directly concerned with the issues at stake will pitch in to pursue the interests of their own Societies or Agencies.

Furthermore, some people frankly think there is an air of unreality in a situation in which newer national Bible Societies can participate on a basis of equality with the Societies upon whose subsidies their existence often depends. No Society has more to

ose in this respect than BFBS. Since 1804, as its title proudly proclaims, it has been an international Society to the core and now it
is under increasing pressure to restrict its outlook and approach to
being just another "national Bible Society". It has to learn to listen where it has been accustomed to speak, and to search for
agreement where it has been in the habit of giving instructions.

On the surface at least, the paradox of this new situation
does not weigh too heavily on Temple himself. His approach to
the whole problem is, as usual, pragmatic. From what we know of
the man, it is almost certain that he felt that it was a movement of
the Holy Spirit and as such should be followed and not resented.
UBS had been the fruit of much prayer and had been born of the
insight of men like Berggrav whose saintly character had been
proved in something near to martyrdom.

Re-enter Bill Platt

Bill Platt, for his part, is well aware of the need for Bible Society
to adapt to the new situation. In a revealing article looking back
on the years immediately following the foundation of UBS but
written a quarter of a century later, he writes:

> What, for instance, about the paternalism of the dear old BFBS?
> She still believed she was the salt of the earth, and not only the
> earth, but of all other Bible Societies! Then, across the Atlantic,
> there was the lively ABS – an economic giant now flexing
> dynamic muscles to the Nth degree but still willing to tread the
> corridors of dollar-power in other lands and in other Societies.
> There were also the shrewd NBSS men of Edinburgh, and the
> wide-eyed colleagues of the NBS in Amsterdam – both part of
> the "Big Four" and watching the new strategy of the "Bigger
> Two".

Platt will retain a vivid memory of Dr Rutgers, General Secretary
of NBS, in John Temple's office in Queen Victoria Street, in his
staccato, machine-gun English, "offering to him sugar-coated pills
for further cooperation"! All this may sound more like a council of

war than the setting up of a United Bible Society. Platt insisted they were all close friends really, but, he conceded, "I fear very human"

The way Platt saw it, there were two sorts of Bible Societies in 1946. There were the big four "missionary" Societies, with their headquarters in London, New York, Edinburgh and Amsterdam. And then there were the other Societies, most of which had been originally inspired by BFBS, and were almost as old. Bluntly, Platt said, "they had been content during a hundred and fifty years to supply Scriptures to their own kith and kin, their home churches – Norwegians, Swedes, Danes, Germans, French, Swiss. They had little or no world outreach. Now, the war over, for all of us it was a new Bible Society world we looked at, and in doing so, we came face to face with ourselves."

During his own travels for the Society, Platt stayed at wonderful Norwegian missions in Madagascar a dozen years before the Haywards Heath meeting. He saw marvellous Swedish missions at Mataldi and Brazzaville on the Congo. He encountered dedicated men of God from Bremen and Berlin working on Lake Victoria in Togo and in Ghana. He enjoyed the hospitality of Swiss and French missionaries in the Cameroons. But in almost every case the Bibles for these missionaries had come from London, subsidised by churches in Britain and the British Commonwealth. And so, in contrast to the "big four", he talked about the "non-missionary" Bible Societies. What were the churches in those Western countries other than England, Scotland, America and Holland doing about the Bible for their own missionaries overseas?

This question could not be separated from the questions: What is a Bible Society? What are its responsibilities? Is it just a printing press to provide Bibles for pews in national churches? Is it a sort of mail-order business or a benevolent "sales bookstand" funded by computer-like propaganda? Or is it, asked Platt, "really a personal living arm of the Christian churches?"

Platt never forgot as a young man meeting a prominent Methodist preacher, who, on reading an appeal from one of the Bible Societies, described them as "camp-followers of the churches" – outside organisations, always wanting money. He liked to think – and tried to encourage others to think – of the church and the Bible Societies as partners in a worldwide enterprise for the spread of the Gospel. At Haywards Heath, with Bishop Berggrav, President of the Norwegian Bible Society in the chair, meeting with the Bishop of Chichester, Dr Bell, as their host in his own diocesan retreat house Elfinsward, it had been easy to think of the churches and the Bible Societies as partners. How could they forget it when most Scripture translation work had been done by missionaries sent out by the churches?

After an extensive tour of Australia and New Zealand in 1946, Bill Platt is appointed Assistant General Secretary of the Society early in 1947. This is a new appointment which is intended partly to relieve Temple of an increasing volume of administration so that he can devote more time to UBS work. Another of Platt's duties is to conduct research into the numbers of Scriptures which will be needed in the postwar world. Platt does his sums – it takes him several months – and he produces an estimated figure of 48 million copies of the Scriptures required to meet the accumulated shortages of the war years.

Exit Temple

John Temple makes a rapid tour of the Far East in 1948 during which he discusses the implementation of a constitution for a China Bible Society. A few people in Bible Society circles know that Temple has been suffering ill health for several years. However, it comes as a great shock to many when, on his way back to England, Temple dies suddenly in Hong Kong on 30 November 1948 at the age of 63.

Temple has served the Society faithfully in all areas of its activity and has had just the qualities needed in establishing the human relationships which were required in steering the path to the foundation of UBS.

"His ability was great," Arthur Wilkinson wrote, "and his work will stand the test of time, but his personality was greater. His finest work was done through his personal contacts. He could win the affection and respect of others more quickly than any other I have known. He had a genius for friendship, which he used not as a mere means of increasing the number of his friends, but of gaining them for the service of his Lord... I have known men of greater endowments who have accomplished far less."

From his retirement in Kent, 80-year-old John Ritson, who preceded Temple as a General Secretary with a very different style, writes rather wistfully to London, "The need for the Bible in every land is so urgent that I have the deep belief that God who loves as we cannot will guide the Committee in their search for another man who will carry on the Society's work worthily. I shall continue to pray for you all – and I have time now."

Re-enter Bill Platt as General Secretary of BFBS

Bill Platt is the obvious choice to succeed Temple as General Secretary, and one of his first tasks is to go to China and pick up the threads of the work that his predecessor has been doing there. He encounters a dramatic clash of ideologies. Communism is sweeping the country. Platt does everything he can to ensure the provision of Scriptures for those parts of China where the next consignment to arrive may be the last. Until now, most Chinese Bible work has been conducted by the China Bible House in Shanghai (jointly administered at this time by BFBS, ABS and NBSS). It now becomes clear that China Bible House may not be able to continue to supply Chinese Scriptures for much longer, so Platt arranges for the establishment of an effective centre for the Society's administration in Hong Kong which can be used if contact with mainland China is lost.

On his return to England, Platt throws himself vigorously into every aspect of the Society's work. Nothing is too large or small for his attention. He continues to be one of the most sought-after speakers on behalf of the Society up and down the country. He has a remarkable ability to relate what the Society is doing to almost any contemporary situation. He can focus on some historical or political theme or event and transform it into an engaging tapestry of words in which the significance of the Bible always emerges in the brightest colour.

Platt seems to have inexhaustible reserves of energy which he devotes to the Society's cause. Whatever other interests he has are secondary to his devotion to BFBS. Most people find working for him a stimulating experience and that his enthusiasm brings out the best in them. Those in some form of distress discover that he also has a hidden reserve of personal kindness. The same man who enjoys the company of distinguished people to whom his position gives access also finds time to visit junior members of staff in hospital or to wait long hours at a railway station to welcome home an employee who is returning from an overseas visit.

It may not always have been so easy for those who had to work on equal terms with Platt. The Society's practice of having two General Secretaries of equal standing had long demanded a degree of trust and self-discipline which stretched those Christian qualities to their limits. Originally intended to provide a balance between the established and dissenting churches, the Society begins to wonder about it in the 1940s but will only abandon the practice in the 1990s.

In 1949 Mary Carter revises and rewrites the best-selling book *Mary Jones and her Bible*. It will be reprinted in most years until 1968.

MAKING UBS WORK

With Temple "promoted to glory", the responsibility for carrying on not only the existing policies of the joint Agencies, but also the results of Haywards Heath, falls upon Eric North and Gilbert Darlington of ABS, and Wilkinson and Platt of BFBS.

Enter Olivier Béguin, first full-time General Secretary of UBS

UBS needs a new General Secretary. Olivier Béguin's essential work during the war in neutral Switzerland has admirably prepared him for the task. Temple has done the job from the same desk in London Bible House from which he acted as joint General Secretary of the Bible Society.

Béguin accepts an invitation to become the new full-time General Secretary of UBS. It is an ideal arrangement. He comes from one of the neutral countries. He represents a smaller Bible Society and cannot be regarded as one of the big four. He speaks French, German and English and his wife Hungarian.

Béguin, with his colleagues in the Bible Societies in London, New York, Amsterdam and Edinburgh has to work out the implications of the infant UBS. In the years immediately following the Haywards Heath conference, Norway quickly begins to take a bigger interest in overseas work and it is suggested to the dynamic Berggrav that the Norwegian Bible Society might undertake the supply of Scriptures for Madagascar. This is arranged with great success, together with some responsibilities in Latin America. Then the Swedish Bible Society expresses an interest in supplying Scriptures to some of its own missionaries in India and provides £10,000 for that purpose.

Canada is already interested in overseas work and 50 years earlier, paid for the first Bible House to be built in west Africa, in Lagos, Nigeria – this was occupied by a Canadian agent. The Canadian Bible Society will now undertake responsibility for part of the work in the Caribbean, where she has extensive interests and later, under Canada's long-serving General Secretary Kenneth McMillan, will build the Bible House there. Moreover, Canada is invited (with her large French-speaking population) to take a further interest in west Africa, where French is the second language of millions of people who are within the French Colonial Empire.

Canon H H Arrowsmith, General Secretary of the Bible Society of Australia, visits east Africa, where (in what was then Tanganyika) Australian bishops and missionaries have worked for years. The infant UBS invites Arrowsmith to take a special interest there. Meanwhile, the Commonwealth Council of Australia takes responsibility for the work in New Guinea, and New Zealand undertakes to oversee Bible Society work in the Pacific Islands.

Act 44

Adapting to a new world

Like all human institutions, Bible Society has its faults. But it could never be accused of rushing too quickly to embrace change! It had never seriously contemplated changes in the structure of the General Committee, despite the fact that diminishing leisure time was making it more difficult to secure new members. Its meetings did become less frequent – monthly instead of fortnightly – but that was all. The practice of having two General Secretaries was beginning to be seen as no longer essential on the grounds of denominational considerations but was perpetuated until the closing years of the century.

New members of staff either learn the elements of their work from their colleagues – "sitting by Nellie" – or receive specific terms of reference which are identical to those of their predecessors but increasingly difficult to relate to changing patterns of life in the missionary movement as a whole, from which the Society at times stands magisterially aloof. The handbook still supplied to its overseas staff in the 1940s is dated 1923. While containing much admirable good sense, it is also full of anachronisms.

However, sensible change can only be embraced if the past is understood. Looking back on a career with BFBS and UBS which spanned a few months less than 45 years, John Dean has recently said that he doesn't now think that he and his colleagues did enough to ensure that committees discussed issues with sufficient awareness of what had gone before, other than in the recent past. He thinks that part of the training of every UBS consultant and of every Bible Society senior executive should be a formal course of study. They should be provided with online access to a suite of materials which he thinks should be called the "UBS Library". He dares to suggest that promotions and salary increases for UBS staff should sometimes depend upon the successful completion of a written examination, following the study of assigned materials.

THE KING GRANTS THE SOCIETY ITS CHARTER

The laws of the Society contained material which stood in considerable need of restatement at various points and modification in others. At last recognising this, a special meeting at London Bible House on 30 January 1944 agreed to authorise the General Committee to present a petition to the King in Council, requesting a royal charter.

Enter Viscount Sankey

Eighty-two-year-old Viscount Sankey presides over the meeting. A distinguished legal figure and educationalist, Sankey was educated at Jesus College, Oxford. As a judge of the King's Bench (1914–28), he was Chairman of the Coal Commission which in 1919 recommended the nationalisation of the mines. He served as Lord Chancellor in the Labour and National Governments of 1929–35. Lord Sankey took a strong personal interest in the objects of Bible Society, became its President in 1942, and made his wisdom and experience available to its officers. It was he who had announced that the King and Queen had consented to become patrons of the Society.

As his last great service to the Society before his death in 1948, he guides it through the intricate processes of law which the petition to the King involves. The motion in favour of seeking the charter is passed by 42 votes to five. The argument that since God has so richly blessed the Society in the past, its future usefulness is assured without altering its regulations, does not win the day.

At last, after four years of negotiations and legal formalities, a meeting of the Privy Council on 25 October 1948 authorises the granting of a royal charter to the Society. The charter gives considerable advantage to the Society in matters affecting the administration of estates and the holding of property. Until the Society was so constituted its properties, which at that time it held all over the world, could only be held by the Incorporated British and Foreign Bible Society Association, which was a registered Trust Association and still exists today but as little more than a formality. The royal charter means that the Society as a whole now acquires legal recognition and is better equipped to establish its identity in an increasingly complicated world.

The most significant changes made in the process of adopting a charter concern the privileges of the Society's members. Under its previous regulation provision was made for every clergyman or dissenting minister who was a member of the Society to be entitled to attend and vote at all meetings of the Committee. Under the new bye-laws attached to the charter this right becomes restricted to the ordinary annual meetings of the Society. The effect of this is to restrict the right to legislate for the Society to a much smaller body than in the past, a body which even at special meetings of the Society is from now on confined to the President and Vice-Presidents, the 36 elected lay members of the General Committee, and the honorary life Governors.

Provisions affecting those areas of the Society's work which within the next half-century will become increasingly discussed remain unchanged in the charter and bye-laws. "Note and comment", the Apocrypha, and the circulation of English versions other than the Authorised and Revised versions are still not permitted. However, in August 1951 a number of mainly technical changes are made to the charter – though one of more significance widens the permitted range of English versions in which the Committee may authorise copies to be circulated, thus making it possible for the Society to distribute the New English Bible (New Testament) when it appears in 1961. Further changes are made in 1968 and, in 1984, the fundamental change of including the word "use" in addition to "distribution" as one of the Society's main objectives. The revised charter also imposes an age limit of 70 on members of the General Committee.

London Bible House, 8 December 1949

Enter the King and Queen

It is a year since the Society has gained its royal charter. On 8 December 1949 King George VI and Queen Elizabeth visit Bible

House. Although the Society has long enjoyed the support o members of the royal family, several of whom, including Victoria and Albert, showed an active interest in its work, this is the firs time that a reigning British sovereign visits its headquarters. The visit lasts two hours and allows the King and Queen to see every aspect of the work of the Society and to meet most of the senior members of the Committee and staff. "They made very real to us," Bill Platt will write in the next annual report, "the fact that we work under their gracious patronage."

"If we rely upon our own strength either as an Empire or as individuals," the Queen herself says, "we shall indeed find the burden too great, but if, through prayer and Bible reading, we learn to live each day in the strength and power of God, we may well go forward with confidence and hope."

Sadly, just over two years later the King will die. The present Queen will accept the invitation to become a patron of the Society in addition to her mother.

Arthur Wilkinson

In his co–Secretary, Arthur Wilkinson, Platt has a colleague senior in years and experience. Their partnership had already been in the making for some years before they were called on to share the highest responsibilities in the Society. Wilkinson was due to retire in 1951, but despite frequent periods of ill health, he agrees to the General Committee's invitation to stay on until 1953, by which time he will have completed 24 years working for the Society, al of them as General Secretary. The friendship he developed with Eric North of ABS was a crucial feature of the years leading up to the foundation of UBS.

When he retires in 1953, Sir Graeme Tyrrell pays him a generous tribute. Tyrrell has had a long–standing interest in the Society's work having been President of the Ceylon Auxiliary from 1926 to 1935. He became a member of the Society's General Committee in London in 1937 and was its Chairman from 1942 until 1951 and a Vice-President from 1943 until his death in 1964 His long administrative experience in the Government's diplomatic service and his wise counsel was valued by the Society for nearly 40 years. He chaired the opening sessions of the Haywards Heath conference which brought UBS into being.

Of Wilkinson, Tyrrell says, "He was a prime mover in the policy in the formation of the national Bible Societies, which are now in being in China and Japan, India and Brazil. It was his vision which conceived the idea of the United Bible Societies, and he played a large part in bringing the idea to fruition."

Bill Platt pays generous tribute to his long-standing colleague, even if what he writes reflects his own burning convictions as much as Wilkinson's:

> He was never afraid of new ideas...throughout his years Wilkinson has never felt satisfied that to translate and circulate the book was adequate. He wanted to say "Behold the Book"; to work for its *use* and widespread study – and to speak to the Churches about these things... And in the campaign for Bible study and more expository preaching to be launched this autumn, under the leadership of the British Council of Churches, he is seeing some of his dreams come true.

The campaign Platt referred to was *The Bible Speaks Today* which was launched as part of the Society's third jubilee celebrations.

Two reasons to celebrate

Westminster Abbey, 2 June 1953

Enter Queen Elizabeth II

The coronation of Queen Elizabeth, the Society's present patron, on 2 June 1953 was the 38th in the present Abbey church and the 50th to have taken place in Westminster. The service itself had hardly changed for 1,000 years.

When Elizabeth arrives at the Abbey she first puts on a crimson robe and then enters the west door to be greeted by boys of Westminster School who have the ancient right of shouting "*Vivat! Regina Elizabetha!* (Long Live Queen Elizabeth!)." After the oath in which the Queen promises to govern according to the laws and to maintain and defend the Church, a key moment in the splendid service arrives.

The Archbishop of Canterbury, magnificent in his golden cope, and the Moderator of the Church of Scotland, austere in his Geneva gown, stand before the young Queen. The Moderator, Dr James Pitt-Watson, presents her with "the most valuable thing that this world affords". He tells her: "Here is wisdom; this is the royal law; these are the lively oracles of God." Ten years later, the same Archbishop – by then Lord Fisher of Lambeth – will become President of the Society.

To many Christians, not least in the Society and among its supporters, it seems right that the Bible should be so conspicuous in the coronation service in a country which owes more to the Bible than any other book. Many supporters are sorry that the clause in the Society's constitution forbidding the circulation of the Apocrypha prevents it from offering to provide the actual Bible presented to the Queen at the coronation.

However, the Society does acquire discreet publicity no

only from the biblical associations of the coronation service but also from its long association with members of the royal family. Never, in its long history, prone to miss a publicity opportunity, the Society issues a number of popular editions of the Bible in special bindings, with the Royal cipher embossed on the covers in gilt. The Society's circulation of 614,000 "Coronation" Scriptures represents one third of the total issued in Britain to commemorate the event. Other coronation editions include the popular Ruby Bible which has enjoyed immense circulation as the Shilling Bible of the 1930s, but is now four shillings and sixpence a copy for the standard edition.

Enter Queen Salote

Among the official guests at the coronation, none is more popular than Queen Salote of Tonga. Refusing to take shelter under an umbrella in a shower of rain, she gains universal admiration for her natural dignity and the warmth of her personality. Welcomed as the tallest Queen of the smallest kingdom, the Society is delighted that before returning to her homeland Salote finds time to visit Bible House. She has a strong Christian faith which gives her a sense of God's presence in times of trouble. And not only is she Queen of an island with which the Society has a well-established link, but she is actually Chairman of the committee engaged in the revision of the Tonga Bible!

Queen Salote's chaplain subsequently writes to the Society saying, "It is true that the British and Foreign Bible Society has rendered, and is still giving us most valuable service, and we cannot find words equal to the sense of indebtedness we feel." The Queen devotes much time to establishing networks within the Church which encourage Bible study and prayer. She ignores demarcations between churches and welcomes all who work for the welfare of her people in whichever church.

THE THIRD JUBILEE

At Bible House, discussions begin about the celebration of the forthcoming 150th anniversary as early as 1949. It is agreed that one aim of the celebrations will be to try to revive the traditional work among the Auxiliaries which still have not recovered from the disruption of the war years. Another will be to emphasise a "recall to the Bible", a rediscovery of the Book which has influenced so profoundly the life of the English-speaking world in particular.

In the years leading up to the celebration of the Society's bicentenary in 2004 there has been much talk of a campaign to influence an increasingly secular culture: there is nothing new under the sun. A theme of the third jubilee in 1954 is a campaign designed to make the country as a whole, and in particular people in the churches who take their Bible heritage for granted, more conscious of the relevance of the message of the Bible to their contemporary situation.

In the 1950s, involvement in such a campaign is a new departure for the Society and represents the furthest point to which it has extended its activities beyond circulating Bibles. The campaign also brings the Society into official cooperation for the first time, and publicly, with the British Council of Churches (BCC) which was set up in 1942.

Two Secretaries are made responsible for the promotion of the campaign – one representing BCC and the other the Society. Under the title The Bible Speaks Today the campaign is launched in St Paul's Cathedral on 20 October 1953 at an evening service of "worship and affirmation". Princess Margaret attends. In the course of the next six months more than 200 Bible Weeks will be held up and down the country. A travelling exhibition tours the country, illustrating the relevance of the Bible message to the conditions of the time: among those who visit the exhibition is the Queen Mother. A series of Sunday evening addresses, intended to form a basis for discussion, are broadcast on the old Home Service (now Radio 4) of the BBC between October and December 1953.

There are those who hope that the Society's third jubilee campaign will, as one writer expresses it, "be used as a means of deepening the spiritual life of the churches, and of pointing our people once more to the truth of God in Holy Scripture". Hopes are high that the third jubilee and its associated campaign will "be the occasion of a refocusing of thought and prayer on the Bible".

This is all well-intentioned, but there is a certain ambiguity to it which the Society will not entirely resolve in the years ahead and with which the trustees are still grappling as I write in 2003. Campaigning to make an impact on culture and society requires the concerted effort of all the churches – and this raises questions not only about the nature of the Society's relationship to the church, but also about how far it should trespass beyond the limited objectives of its founders. There were those who tried tentatively to think their way through this dilemma in the 1950s but the issue remained unresolved.

In addition to The Bible Speaks Today campaign, a variety of other events contributes to the build-up to the third jubilee celebrations. The jet-propelled aircraft is still a novelty, and when in September 1952 the first copy of the Bible in the new Union Swahili version is flown to Entebbe in a *Comet* of the British Airways Corporation, widespread interest is generated both in and beyond the ranks of the Society's supporters.

A series of initiatives to recruit new supporters for the Society is launched in the period preceding the jubilee, including some to increase interest in its work by women. The Queen Mother takes a personal interest in some of these appeals. One disappointment is that Mildred Cable's death on 30 April 1952 in Hampstead at the age of 75 means that she will be absent from the great events of 1954. Topsy, the little girl the Misses Cable and French had adopted in China, will live on and visit Bible House in Swindon a few years before she dies in January 1998.

England and Wales, December 1953 to December 1954

Sunday 6 December 1953 is the first official day of the thir
jubilee year. For the first time in its history, the Society employs
firm of professional consultants in public relations to help it pre
sent its programme to the press, radio and general public. This
a daring step at a time when most charities and missionary organ
isations are wary about retaining the services of PR experts. Ther
are those who raise an eyebrow but the experiment seems to mee
with some success.

With a whole string of events during the jubilee year an
many visitors coming from abroad, this is too good an opportu
nity for publicity for the Society to get wrong. Articles appear i
daily papers and magazines which up till then have rarely men
tioned the Society.

Enid Blyton, one of the best-selling children's writers of a
time, writes a book about the Society entitled *The Greatest Book i
the World* which will be widely read not just by the younger gen
eration. Sadly, Miss Blyton is unwell and unable to attend th
Society's annual children's birthday meeting on 6 March to whic
she has been invited as a special guest. The birthday party is hel
at the newly built Royal Festival Hall with Derek McCulloch
"Uncle Mac" of BBC's *Children's Hour* – as Chairman. "Mar
Jones" makes her inevitable appearance in Welsh dress and th
children tuck into a 930-pound birthday cake – a gift from friend
of the Society in Australia.

During April 1954, guests from the Society's oversea
Agencies, from other Bible Societies, and from churches on ever
continent begin to arrive. Many of the visitors represent nation
Bible Societies which have taken over responsibility from BFBS i
their countries. In many cases, the Society still subsidises them an
the work of translation still involves close consultation with th
translations department in London. The printed books, especiall
complete Bibles, are in many cases still printed and bound i
England and a whole range of other technical services are provide
by London Bible House. All these visitors are coming to celebrat
with what is still seen as "the mother of the Bible Societies".

Enter Young Bin

One of the most memorable visitors to come to London for the 1954 celebrations is Rev. Young Bin Im who took over as Secretary of the Korean Bible Society in 1949. A cheerful and ebullient character, Young Bin impresses all whom he addresses and meets by his evangelistic fervour and his astonishing command of unfamiliar English idioms. No one would think that he has recently endured the disasters and heartbreak of the Korean War. Three times since taking over as Secretary of the Korean Society he has seen the Society's headquarters and most of its Bibles destroyed, first in Seoul and then in Pusan. He has seen Korean roads choked with escaping refugees and been one of them himself.

Yet Young Bin has come through all these experiences with undimmed vigour, telling with glee the story of how an important text of the Korean Bible was carried to safety across enemy territory in a pickle jar.

All the Society's official guests return to London for the week of 1–7 May. Not since the centenary in 1904 – and perhaps not even then – has the Society held such meetings. The week begins with a reception of guests by the General Committee on what would otherwise be the occasion of its scheduled meeting. Arnold Clark, the Chairman, welcomes the guests and reads greetings from other Bible Societies. John Stirling presents one of the special publications financed from the third jubilee fund, his edition of the Authorised Version with line drawings by Horace Knowles. That evening, Lord Luke of Pavenham, a Vice-President, and Lady Luke act as host and hostess at a third jubilee dinner in the Connaught Rooms.

Next day, 4 May, the Queen Mother visits Bible House and unveils a plaque commemorating her previous visit with the late King in 1949 and accepts copies of the Jubilee Bible for her grand-children, Prince Charles and Princess Anne.

On the morning of 5 May, the 150th annual meeting of the Society is held in the Central Hall, Westminster, and chaired by an invited and well-loved guest: Bishop Berggrav of Norway, President of the United Bible Societies.

"I see this gathering," says the Bishop, "as a 'Guard of Honour' for the Word of God. We hold up our hands to God and thank him for all he has done through this Society."

The Archbishop of Canterbury presides over a spectacular evening event: representatives from Bible Societies in 40 countries, preceded by their national flags, move in six processions on to the platform of the Central Hall. The Westminster Choral Society sings excerpts from Handel's *Messiah*.

Among a series of speakers is Eric North of ABS, generous in his gratitude, praise and the gift he bears: he hands over a cheque from ABS of $100,000. The Canadians give £75,000, the Koreans £200.

"When I was struggling to save my life in that dreadful summer of 1950," says Young Bin of Korea in his talk, "I never dreamed I would know today... Faith is the God-given power by which one can see hope out of hopeless ruins, possibility out of utter impossibility, and encouragement out of black discouragement."

The Overseas Service of the BBC broadcasts edited versions of the 5 May events and also a series of talks about the work of Bible Society.

Next day, many of the guests visit Hampton Court palace. Bible Society visitors pay tribute to the memory of those who as a result of the Hampton Court conference of 1604 gave the world the most widely read of all Bible translations

On 14 May the London Symphony Orchestra, the Alexandra Choir and leading soloists perform a programme of choral works on biblical subjects in the Royal Festival Hall. The principal conductor is Sir Malcolm Sargent who has recently become a new Vice-President of the Society.

On 21 June *The Times* publishes a special supplement on the Bible which carries an article about the work of the Society in addition to articles by leading scholars on historical, social and literary aspects of the Bible. For many years *The Times* and the Society have been, and still are in the 1950s, neighbouring institutions in Queen Victoria Street.

On 6 December the Queen and Prince Philip attend a ser

vice of thanksgiving in Westminster Abbey to bring the Society's third jubilee year to a close. The congregation is so large that many have to be accommodated in the neighbouring Church of St Margaret to which the service is relayed. Bill Platt leads the opening act of thanksgiving. Prince Philip reads the lesson. Rev. James Stewart preaches from Psalm 119:162 (AV): *I rejoice at thy word as one that findeth great spoil* – the text has always been thought particularly applicable to the Mary Jones story.

"It is no use setting a tepid Christianity against a scorching paganism," Stewart tells his congregation. "I am pleading with you for a new resolve to use the Bible as the basic instrument of that world mission which we must espouse with all our heart."

After the service, the Chairman of the General Committee, the Treasurer and the two General Secretaries, Platt and Cockburn, are presented to the Queen at the west end of the Abbey. She gives them a commemorative copy of the Bible which was presented to her the previous year at the coronation service.

Act 46

A challenge for the world's Christians

UBS, in the 1950s, is still run from a few rooms in London Bible House. It issues a challenge to all Bible Societies, in addition to the "big four" plus Canada, Australia, New Zealand, Norway and Sweden, to become more missionary-minded, and to link their work closely with the life of the Christian communities in their own countries. It sends out a call to church leaders everywhere to make worldwide distribution and interest in the Bible one of their central activities.

Eastbourne, 1954

Since 1954 marks the 150th anniversary of BFBS, UBS decides to meet in Britain, at Eastbourne, for its Council meetings. Representatives and observers arrive from India, Pakistan, Ceylon, Africa, Brazil, Switzerland, Finland, France, Ireland, Iceland, Japan, Korea, Indonesia, in addition to the usual members of the Council. The new voices are far from silent.

It soon becomes apparent that Indonesia is asking to form a Bible Society of its own, as distinct from simply being an Agency, and to become a full member of UBS. Then Malaya asks the question: Why shouldn't there be a Malayan Bible Society?

So quite naturally, the question arises: What exactly is a Bible Society? The question has been asked many times since. Over many years both Indonesia and Malaya have been helped by European Bible Societies, one from Holland the other from Scotland. But the populations of both countries are predominantly Muslim, and the churches small minority groups. The UBS Council has to face the fact that whereas it is easy to build a Bible House or start a Bible Society Agency in any given centre, it is quite a different matter to launch an indigenous Bible Society. Basic questions arise when considering the formation of a Bible

Society: Is there an adequate Christian community? Is there a local church rooted enough in the indigenous community and strong enough to support a Bible Society and so to apply for UBS membership?

Therefore in 1954, under Platt's chairmanship, UBS sets out the categories and conditions of membership. The idea of "associate membership" of UBS emerges. The Council invites local advisory groups and Agency committees to look at the support they are receiving from their churches and the extent to which these are committed in interest and action to the translation and distribution of the Scriptures. If this develops and there is an adequate Christian community likely to give its support, then recognition for full membership of UBS may be a possibility.

The older Societies, including Bill Platt himself, claim that they want to steer clear of the spirit of paternalism. Eric North, of ABS, speaks at Eastbourne of a "global strategy" which would aim to bring closer together the activities of the Societies, older and younger, into a more integrated partnership. For several decades there has been much closer cooperation between the older Societies: it is now clear that in a shrinking world, in which the first Bibles have already flown from London to Africa by jet, more consultation is called for.

Exit Bill Platt; enter John Dean

In 1960 Bill Platt retires as General Secretary of the Society. Bill first spoke at a Society meeting way back in 1927. He will live on until he is 100 and turn up at Society and UBS events for many years to come. But for now, an extraordinary man leaves centre stage.

Less than four years earlier, a young man has arrived at Bible House. John Dean joined BFBS on 31 December 1956 as a junior clerk in the finance department. He will be appointed an assistant accountant in 1962 and be seconded to UBS as World Budget coordinator in 1967. He will go on to serve as General Secretary of the Society and as a UBS World Service officer. He enjoys Bible work to the full and has the ability and enthusiasm to write vivid accounts of his travels on Bible Society and UBS business. He will be around to play an active part in the events to mark the bicentenary of the Society in 2004. As through all the history of the Society, there is change and there is continuity. A good man goes. Another good man arrives.

The world will not be quite the same, though, after 22 November 1963. On the same day that President Kennedy is assassinated in Dallas, C S Lewis, the most gifted Christian writer of the 20th century who "made righteousness readable", dies.

DRIEBERGEN CONFERENCE, 1964

Leaders from the UBS fellowship meet church leaders mainly from western Europe in Driebergen, the Netherlands, in 1964 to try to enlist their support in the Bible cause. Among their conclusions is the important statement that the "conference encourages the preparation, in collaboration with all Churches, including the Roman Catholic Church, of a common text in the original languages, to be the one source of translation for all Christians, and expresses the conviction that by means of honest scholarship this is now a possibility". The conference also resolves to encourage "the exploration of the possibility of preparing, at least in certain languages, a common translation of the Bible that may be published either in common or separately as circumstances may require".

Significantly, too, the conference recommends the publication and circulation of the Deuterocanon/Apocrypha where there is a demand for this as well as editions with fuller readers' aids "to make the Scriptures more intelligible to readers". Uli Fick, a distinguished General Secretary of UBS, will later look back on this conference as marking a stepping stone to a new era of cooperation between Protestants and Roman Catholics.

Bala, north Wales, 1965: more revelations about Mary

The library at Bala College is being dismantled. Two members of the staff of the National Library of Wales, David Jenkins and Bryn Williams, come across a Welsh Bible, printed in 1799. Inside they find a manuscript note:

> Lydia Williams's Bible, Mary Jones's niece, who lived with her. On her deathbed, Lydia gave her Bible that is this one, to me, namely one of the three given to Mary Jones by Mr Charles. When the College gave Mary Jones's own Bible to the Bible House, Dr Lewis Edwards knew where this one was. When preaching in Penrhyndeudraeth, he called at my house and who was I to refuse Dr Edwards? I entrusted it to him, gladly, yet sadly.

The note is signed by Lizzie Rowlands. Mary gave one of her Bibles to her mother's cousin, Ann Richards, of Ty'neithen, Bryncrug. Her name appears in this Bible and Lydia was her granddaughter.

I have already told you the story of how Lydia handed the Bible to Dr Edwards. David Jenkins brings the Bible to Aberystwyth to be kept with the Calvinistic Methodist archives housed in the National Library of Wales where you can see it today.

The popularity of the Mary Jones story continues unabated and even in this year (1965) it is translated into Thai, one of 40 languages in which you can read the story.

There's more. In March 1965 a letter is published in the magazine *County Quest* from Lizzie Rowland's daughter, Mrs Margaret Dunn, aged 91. She says that her mother knew Mary Jones well and used to read the Bible to her: "My mother heard the story of the walk to Bala many times... Mr Charles gave her three Bibles. Lydia [Williams], Mary's niece, gave the third Bible to my mother." Mrs Dunn is unaware, but is later informed, that this Bible is held by the National Library of Wales.

In 1967 an article by Monica Davies is published in *The*

Journal of the Historical Society of the Presbyterian Church of Wales which gives previously unpublished information about Lizzie Rowlands and her connection with Mary Jones in her final years. I used this information when I told you the story of Mary as an old woman. All this adds greatly to our knowledge of Mary and strengthens the evidence that Thomas Charles presented Mary with three Bibles (the earliest Mary Jones stories popularised by the Society had him handing her just one).

Meanwhile, across the Atlantic...

City Hall, New York City, May 1966

ABS celebrates its 150th anniversary in New York. General Secretary Eric North delivers an address in the same room (the City Hall, New York City) in which the founders met to inaugurate the Society. Archbishop Donald Coggan later recalls "the biggest dinner party I think I have ever attended".

"When the Word goes out, the Church is born," Coggan tells the Americans in his speech. "And when the Church is born then healing begins in a broken society. Then the walls get broken down. And then God's plan for His world begins to take shape."

Enter the UBS World Service Budget

In the same year, a UBS regional structure is introduced and a World Service Budget established, amounting to $6,200,000. Next year, John Dean, who has worked for eleven years in the Society's finance department in London Bible House, is assigned to UBS as World Service Budget coordinator. He works from New York for two years, coordinating and developing UBS financial and administrative procedures.

In 1967 Bible Societies around the world distribute over 100 million Scriptures for the first time. Fourteen Societies are by this time contributors to the UBS World Service Budget.

A LITTLE RELAXATION FOR "NO NOTE AND COMMENT"

If you are not involved in the Bible Society movement, you may want to skip this section – but I hope you won't because the story it tells has wider implications. I will keep it as brief as I can. You can read about the issue in more detail in my chapter "Without Note or Comment: Yesterday, Today and Tomorrow" in the book *Sowing the Word* to be published in 2004.

The story about the relaxation of the Bible Society founders' rule banning "note and comment" from their Bibles began when the Netherlands Bible Society celebrated its 125th anniversary in 1939 and Professor Kraemer challenged Bible Societies to think about encouraging the use, as well as the circulation, of Bibles. In fact it is not unusual to read statements in the Society's publications in the first half of the 20th century to the effect that the work of the Society is not done when the Bible is delivered to its destination.

Then in 1958 Eugene Nida, of ABS, wrote a paper on "Reader's Helps" which set out to show how marginal notes in Bibles could provide helpful explanations and yet "avoid all doctrinal interpretation or emotionally charged accusations or innuendos".

Eight years later, ABS General Secretary Laton Holmgren wrote to BFBS General Secretary John Watson noting that, without any policy change, the ABS Board had in recent time authorised a variety of Bible readers' helps which he set out in some detail. He explained to Watson how the ABS Board now understood the "without note and comment" clause. And two years after that, in 1968, UBS/Vatican guidelines listed the following as helps for readers which would not contravene *the intention* behind the "no note and comment" rule: alternative readings or renderings, explanations of proper names, plays on words (e.g. the ability of the Greek *pneuma* to mean "spirit", "wind" and "breath"), historical backgrounds, cultural differences, cross-references and section headings. In addition, certain supplementary features, which Bible Societies had previously avoided, were cleared for use: indices, concordances, maps and illustrations.

In 1971, UBS adjusts the wording of its constitution so that the phrase "without note or comment" becomes "without doctrinal note or comment". Many other Bible Societies later make the same change to their key documents. The change is based on the assumption that it wasn't "notes and comments" in themselves that were the problem but doctrinal positioning or advocacy on issues where Christians were not in agreement. Readers' helps will enable Bible Societies better to serve the needs of their audiences, but the aim will be to provide them in a way that avoids interpreting texts along doctrinal lines or advocating divisive theological positions.

Writing in *Word and World* in 1977, Archbishop of Canterbury and UBS President Lord Coggan says, "As time goes by, the gap which yawns between the world in which the Bible was written and the world in which we live grows ever wider. It is not simply a matter of the passage of time. The difference is deeper and more subtle than can be measured in terms of centuries." He notes the difference between the pre-scientific world and the scientific world of today, the highly rural and pastoral context of the Bible and the high urbanisation of today, and a technologically simpler world in contrast to today. He argues that these changes justify the inclusion of non-doctrinally-divisive notes in Scripture publications.

But there are limits to the relaxation. In the same year (1977), the UBS Executive Committee (UBSEC) recommends to all Societies that they should not handle the English Living Bible, on the grounds that it is a paraphrase, straying too far in some places from the original Hebrew and Greek.

Meeting in Chiang Mai (Thailand) in 1981, the UBS General Assembly suggests that Bible Societies should examine afresh the fundamental "without doctrinal note and comment" principle to see what this means if construed positively rather than negatively. Instead of asking "How far can a Bible Society go (without contravening the principle)?" the question should be "What do readers need to know to be better able to use and understand the Bible?"

On 13 July 1984, BFBS takes a related step. A revision of its royal charter makes the fundamental change of including the word "use" in addition to "distribution" of Scripture as one of the Society's main objectives. This makes it possible for the Society's product range to be dramatically broadened and the Society becomes for a period as much a wholesaler of "Bible helps" as it is a publisher of Bibles. But at this time, too, the environment for Bible and religious publishing in the UK is becoming increasingly competitive, with the growth of Hodder & Stoughton and HarperCollins alongside the two traditional Bible publishers, Oxford University Press and Cambridge University Press. Wholesalers are continuing to grow, especially STL (Send the Light).

Five years later, now no longer Archbishop but still UBS President, Lord Coggan writes an article entitled "Without Note or Comment – Then and Now". In this he compares the idea of readers' appealing for helps in understanding the Bibles they read to the appeal of the Ethiopian official to the Apostle Philip for contexting help: " 'Do you understand what you are reading?' 'How can I understand unless someone gives me the clues?' " (Acts 8:30–31, New English Bible).

In 1989, UBS Europe–Middle East Region publishes guidelines entitled "What should Bible Societies Publish?" These guidelines allow "non-prescriptive" readers' helps which "assist readers in making up their own mind on how Bible texts should be interpreted".

On 9 March 1990 ABS issues a vision statement for the 1990s which includes the statement that "the Bible cause is more than production and distribution. It is the promulgation of effective Bible reading in terms of changed lives…."

In all this, the fundamental assumption is that the intention of the Society's founders was to avoid comment which was *divisive* thus hindering the fundamental objective of ensuring the widest possible collaboration of all Christians in the cause of distributing the Scriptures and making them heard.

In pursuing this interesting theme we have run ahead of ourselves in our story of the BFBS. So, to return…

Act
47

A retailer joins the admirals

We are now well into the "swinging 60s" – the world of the Beatles, the miniskirt and the white heat of Harold Wilson's technological revolution. But at Bible House, you are transported back to another age…

London Bible House, 1968

Enter Julian Smith

A 35-year-old walks a little anxiously along a busy Queen Victoria Street and arrives at No. 146. He is a member of the family which established and built up W H Smith, the famous British high street name with interests in retail, publishing and news distribution. Julian is here to attend his first meeting of the Society's General Committee. He glances up at the words carved on the open book in the stonework above the imposing main entrance: "The Word of the Lord endureth for ever."

He is the youngest person so far to join the Committee – a record since broken by Lady Jill Brentford who joined while in her 20s. Julian discovers that, among his colleagues, are a number of retired admirals and generals as well as several retired colonial administrators. There are Admiral Sir Guy Russell and Admiral Sir Peveril William-Powlett representing the Royal Navy and Brigadier Charles Swift representing the Army – he is the Committee Chairman. Given the rather Victorian tone of the proceedings he is not surprised that there are no retired RAF officers! The whole thing conjures up for him a vision of gunboats steaming up African rivers manned by sailors and soldiers with a rifle in the left hand and a Bible in the right, in order to subdue the natives by one means or the other!

In 1968 day-to-day management of the Society is in the

hands of three General Secretaries, one each for Home, Overseas and Administration. John Williams and John Watson, Home and Overseas Secretaries respectively, almost invariably wear black suits and dog collars. Bernard Tattersall, the first layman General Secretary, always wears a suit and tie.

The General Committee, at this time, always meets once a month starting with a sandwich lunch (about the only similarity with today) which is taken in a small and rather crowded side room. The members then adjourn to the General Committee room which is dedicated solely to that purpose. This room, both in layout and design, owes more to a court of law than anything else. The Chairman sits on a raised dais under a canopy and is flanked on either side by the three General Secretaries (also on the dais). Immediately in front of the dais is a table for other members of staff who need to attend the meeting. All the General Committee members sit in serried ranks of high-backed chairs facing the dais.

There is a predetermined seating plan and all Committee members have to sit in the same place at every meeting. If Committee members in the seats on either side of you, or even several seats to left and right, fail to attend, you are not allowed to move in order to sit next to somebody. Julian Smith always imagines that this is because the Chairman (and Committee members) have a seating plan and without it no one has any idea who anybody is!

However much paperwork a Committee member has to contend with, there is never any question of having a table to put it on. It just has to go on the floor under your chair.

At the time of Julian's arrival, the Society is in the throes of revising its Royal Charter and Bye laws. This is being done, not as with all subsequent revisions, by a sub-committee or even an individual, but by the whole General Committee in plenary session. This puts quite a strain on the brain of a newly appointed Committee member who has received little if any induction, and who comes into the revision exercise somewhere in the middle of its course! Julian has little clear recollection today of other business that is transacted at these meetings but he feels sure that it is mostly formal. There is a finance and general purposes committee that deals with a lot of the day-to day running of the Society in much the same way that the executive committee will come to do, but he doesn't recall that reports come to the General Committee for comment or debate.

THE CHANGING FACE OF THE GENERAL COMMITTEE AND MANAGEMENT

When Charles Swift retires from the Chairmanship, he is succeeded by Eric Starling (Starling and Smith were both members of All Souls Church in Langham Place). Eric initiates a number of changes, not the least of which is the major remodelling of Bible House. This leads to his resignation from the General Committee since he becomes the architect (his profession) to the project and, as such, cannot remain as a Committee member. This is a major undertaking which has a significant impact on the way in which business is conducted.

Now, members can put their papers on a table and are allowed to choose where they sit. The tables are arranged as a hollow square so that committee members can actually see each other's faces! At about this time the number of General Secretaries is reduced to two – John Weller (Overseas) and Neville Cryer (Home).

In 1971 Tom Houston becomes Communications Director, eventually to become Executive Director in 1977 responsible for the running of the Society. Tom operates in tandem (but first among equals) with Neville Cryer who takes on relationships outside the Society. During the 1970s and early 1980s, the running of the Society is a much looser and less structured operation than it is now. While doing a spell as Chairman of the Executive Committee, Julian is responsible for recruiting a new Executive Director to replace Tom Houston. He conducts this exercise almost entirely on his own although referring back to Committee members from time to time. This is considered entirely acceptable at the time and Julian doesn't remember any eyebrows being raised! The outcome is that Richard Worthing-Davies is appointed (he was already working as Publishing Director).

Julian Smith will retire from the Society's Board in 2004 after 36 years of continuous service. "For more than 150 years following its foundation," he reflects, "the Society concentrated on translation, production and distribution of the Scriptures. The Charter and Byelaws required this to be done 'without note or comment'. Hence it would seem that the Society had little real interest in what became of the Scriptures after they had reached their final destinations. However in the latter part of the 20th century this changed. Revisions to the Charter and Byelaws allowed the Society to produce and distribute helps to readers and, even more significantly, wrote into the Society's role the responsibility to promote the use of the Scriptures. These two changes brought about a major and highly important change in what the Society did and how it set about it.

"The Society stands in an unique position in relation to its role in promoting the widest possible distribution and use of Scriptures. It is not bound by any sectional dogma or set of beliefs or interpretations of Scripture. Hence it is able to function across all interdenominational boundaries and can talk with equal authority to all shades of Christian belief. This is a crucial standpoint in promoting the centrality of Scripture amongst all the Christian Churches of the world.

"In the light of the world in which we live and the point the Society has reached in its history, there can be little if any doubt that it is right that the Society should adopt a campaigning stance to further the spread of Christianity through the use and understanding of the Bible."

Since 1905 the Society has produced a magazine, *Bible in the World*, which in the 1960s and 1970s attracted some criticism on account of some articles which adopted a doctrinal stance on the interpretation of the Bible. Partly for this reason, in 1972 a fresh newsprint type of report called *Word in Action* is introduced – still flourishing over 30 years later and familiar to many thousands of Bible Society supporters.

MUSICAL CHAIRS AT UBS, ABS AND BFBS

By 1972 UBS has two World Service Officers with responsibility for specific regions – John Weller in London, based in London Bible House, with responsibility for Europe–Middle East and Africa, and Warner Hutchinson in New York with responsibility for Asia–Pacific and the Americas.

In 1973 John Dean, still acting as the Society's General Secretary for another four years, takes over from John Weller his responsibility for Europe–Middle East and Africa.

John Erickson succeeds Warner Hutchinson as UBS World Service Officer with responsibility for the Asia–Pacific and Americas regions. He is involved in the talks with the Amity Foundation which lead to the important "Bible Press for China" project.

The first Bible rolls off the presses of the Amity Printing Company in Nanjing on 17 October 1987. The 1 millionth copy is printed in 1989. On 4 December 2000 the Chinese Church celebrates the printing of 25 million Bibles and the figure today has exceeded 30 million. Geoffrey Hill looks back on the Nanjing Press as one of the most positive developments during his time of involvement in Bible Society work from 1978 to 1992 (as Finance Director of BFBS from 1978 to 1988 and of UBS from 1998 to 1992). He admits that BFBS was decidedly lukewarm on this project at first, while the Americans were enthusiastic from the start. The Americans were right. In 2003 representatives of Bible Society and a delegation from China, including Government Ministers, exchange visits.

In July 1976 the Society installs its first mainframe computer. Over the years computers have played an increasingly important role in the work of the Society as they have in most businesses and in our personal lives. In order to make good use of the benefits of advancing technology the proportion of the Society's expenditure on computers for both hardware and software has increased dramatically and it has affected all aspects of the Society's work.

GOOD NEWS BIBLE

n October 1976, after resisting the idea in the 1960s when the New Testament first appeared in America, the Society publishes he Good News Bible.

You cannot talk about either the Good News Bible or the more recent Contemporary English Version without referring to a man we first met as a young man at Elfinsward when UBS was founded – the American, Eugene Nida. In 1964 Nida consolidated research he had been doing for almost 20 years on the principles of translation, especially Bible translation, and published a new book on the principles of translation, entitled *Towards a Science of Translating*. He followed this with a series of other books.

For many years Executive Secretary for Translations at ABS, Eugene Nida has had a bigger impact on translation theory than almost any other person in recent history. Nida's starting point is to reject the traditional method of translation often referred to as "formal equivalence" – the method more or less used in the Authorised Version, Revised and American Standard Versions, Revised Standard Version, and New American Standard Version, to name but a few. Formal equivalence attempts a word-oriented translation, with emphasis upon preserving the features of the original language with respect to vocabulary, syntax and tone, so far as this is possible in the translated language.

By contrast Nida advocates what is called "dynamic" or "functional equivalence". Dynamic equivalence is defined by recognising that each language has its own characteristics, many of which cannot be transferred to another language without loss of effective communication. Nevertheless, advocates of dynamic equivalence believe there is nothing in one language which cannot be said in another. Thus the emphasis comes to be on the message rather than its form. It makes the assumption that the writers of documents, including the writers of biblical texts, expect to be understood by their readers. And what the translator attempts to do is to reproduce this meaning by finding the closest natural equivalent expression in the new language, whether it is English or a new language having the Bible translated into it for the first time. John Ritson's tutor at Balliol College, Oxford, a distinguished classical scholar and translator of Plato in the second half of the 19th century, was also an advocate of "transfer of meaning" as a goal in translation.

Not everyone agrees that it is either possible or valuable to make the attempt to transfer meaning in this sense in translation. Any translation which forces the translator to decide the meaning of a passage runs the risk of excluding viable options of meaning that may be better left ambiguous and subject to further consideration. And the translators of the New King James Bible stoutly defend what they call "complete equivalence" which seeks to preserve all the information in a text, while presenting it in good literary form.

Nevertheless, publication of the Good News Bible by the Society is a major milestone in its history, marking a shift in its strategy. The Bible's distinctive yellow dust jacket and Annie Valloton drawings mark a shift to a more professional publishing emphasis. Many see the impact of this version in helping readers more easily to understand the Bible as a major development in the work of Christian outreach. For some years the Good News Bible becomes the highest-selling Bible translation in the United Kingdom. Although its popularity has waned, as other translations using similar methods have appeared, the Good News Bible is still used extensively, not least in schools and by children.

BIBLE A MONTH CLUB

The Society launches Bible a Month Club (BAMC) in June 1977. The idea was well tested and improved in the USA, Holland and Germany before being adapted for Britain. It takes its BFBS organiser, David Longley, more than 18 months to prepare in detail. Longley sets a target of 1,500 members by December and another 1,500 by the end of 1978. The idea of the club, to encourage individual or group supporters of the Society to give a regular monthly sum to supply some part of the world with a new Bible or part of a Bible, is one which seems to appeal particularly to a new set of younger adults. By December 1977 the number of contributors is over 1,800 and the target has been exceeded.

This means there is a new source of income which is readily calculable and fairly predictable, though any contributor may withdraw at any time if in difficulty. BAMC has not only been a significant income-generator but the means of increasing prayer for the work of Bible Societies worldwide. Today over 300,000 people encounter the Bible every year as a result of the club.

In 1977, the General Committee approves a new management structure. John Dean resigns as General Secretary to devote himself fully to UBS work. Neville Cryer becomes General Director and Tom Houston Executive Director with responsibility for the overall operations of the Society. The Society's overseas committees are disbanded and the Society is less involved in UBS affairs except for its substantial financial contribution to the World Service Budget and limited involvement in UBS committees.

ABS continues to be more involved with UBS affairs with some staff continuing to hold dual roles. In July 1978 John Erickson becomes General Secretary and recording secretary of ABS while continuing to serve as UBS World Service Officer until 1988.

Warsaw, Poland, May 1977

I remember Neville Cryer, joint General Secretary of the Society with Richard Worthing-Davies when I joined the General Committee in 1985, for his energy, devotion to the Society, and exuberance as an after-dinner raconteur.

In May 1977 he is enjoying dinner in a modest hotel in Warsaw. A few hundred yards away is the great Vistula river which flows through the heart of the city. All around, the trees are full of leaves and the harshness of winter has gone. It is a time for the people of the capital to relax as spring gives way to summer.

Around the dinner table people are certainly smiling for it is a 160th birthday party. To celebrate, some 20 men and women have gathered from all over the city and some from other parts of Poland or even further away. They do not want to miss this party.

It is a remarkable gathering of Polish church leaders. There is the Primate of the Polish National Catholic Church in his many-buttoned black cassock with its edging of red silk. Alongside him is the Chairman of the Polish Methodist Church and another of his ministers. There is the pastor of the Reformed Church in Warsaw, whose building was one of the few not destroyed by Nazi flame-throwers. Next to him is the happy face of the Archbishop of the Polish Orthodox Church who will later make a presentation. Opposite Neville is the much-travelled representative of the Seventh Day Adventist Church and beside him sit two ministers of the Baptist Church.

In the midst of this array of church leaders, and in addition to the four senior members of the local staff and some from overseas, is the hostess and her husband: Barbara Enholc-Narzynska General Secretary of the Polish Bible Society, whose husband is Bishop Narzynsky, the leader of the Lutheran Church in Poland. Radiant and happy at this unusual party, Barbara rises to propose the health of the guests beside her. First, she refers to the Polish Government and the presence of one of its Ministers, the Director of Cults, who has agreed to share in this family event. Then she turns to the British Ambassador and his wife who are her personal friends and regular supporters of Bible Society.

"In you," she says, "I see reflected that close link between Britain and Poland which is so much part of our long history – the 160 years of history we are celebrating tonight."

Now it is the turn of the Director of Cults to speak.

"It is a very special thrill," he says, "for me, as a Pole, to mark something which has lasted for this length of time. Old as the race of the Polish people can claim to be, it is the first time that I have ever been able to be present in my country at the birthday of a Polish institution which has lasted so long. For me this is a matter of special pride. Although I am not a churchman myself I cannot but rejoice that it is a Christian body which has achieved this record in my country. For that alone I thank the Polish Bible Society. I wish it a long life and as many years again of service in the future."

When Neville discovers later in the evening that the Minister has turned up at the party even though he would quite like to have joined millions of other Poles in watching Liverpool play Muenchen Gladbach in the European soccer final, he particularly appreciates his presence!

Then one of the oldest present, a distinguished scholar, rises to speak. There is a hush of respectful silence.

"I am bound to say," he begins, "that I was at first opposed to a new and more popular translation of the Bible in the Polish language. But I am now wholly convinced about the need for such a work and will give whatever time and energy remains to me to help in the task."

After the speeches, the Orthodox Metropolitan comes round the table to Barbara, with a beaming smile on his face, to present to her his Church's gift. It is an icon, specially painted and blessed for this special occasion.

As he walks back to his lodgings that night, Neville reflects on the evening's events. He remembers how delighted Barbara was when she received the icon from the smiling Primate.

Walking by the ancient river Vistula in the May moonlight, Neville thinks it a little odd that when this Polish Bible work began in the land on which he now walks it was Russian soil – and at that point in the river, 30 years earlier, Russian troops crossed in boats to free Warsaw from another oppressor. His mind goes back even further to the days following the defeat of Napoleon, to a Poland which was just another province of a vast Russian Empire. It was across that frontier that Robert Pinkerton rode on horseback in March 1817 and successfully persuaded Tsar Alexander I (then in Warsaw) to become the first patron of the Polish Bible Society.

In 1944, in the Warsaw uprising, the Bible House at 15 Aleje Jerozolimskie Street was destroyed. BFBS paid for the rebuilding of a house at 40 Nowy Swiat Street, Warsaw, to replace the destroyed headquarters. The new building was opened in August 1947.

I am glad to say that, 27 years later, Barbara Enholc-Narzynska is still General Secretary of the Polish Bible Society. When I asked her to tell me how things are going, she spoke of how work began in 1995 on a major ecumenical translation of the

Bible by an interconfessional committee of translators from eleven churches – Roman Catholic, Orthodox, Evangelical and Pentecostal. By 2001 work on the New Testament and Psalms was complete after six years which had seen, in Barbara's words, some "dramatic and hot discussions". This edition is "a historic ecumenical, theological and cultural event, which contributed a lot to the unity of Christians in Poland".

Meanwhile, back in Britain…

GOOD NEWS FOR BOTH SIDES!

As the Society approaches its 175th anniversary a little remembered event in its history occurs – which may surprise some current Committee members, staff and supporters. Briefly, one Saturday night in March 1978, a large banner advertising the newly published Good News Bible is shown at the side of a football pitch during screening of the popular programme *Match of the Day*. Though the actual viewing time is only 59 seconds the rather prolonged exposure of the advert with its strap line *Good News for both sides* attracts some comment in newspapers. The BBC decides that such advertising is not permissible. However, the following year, the Society takes the unprecedented step of advertising the new Bible on the tube to Heathrow Airport. After six years with Tom Houston as Communications Director, the Society is determined to use every reasonable modern technique to promote the Bible cause.

Exit Bernard Tattersall

A sad event occurs on the 16th of that same month (March 1978) when Bernard Tattersall dies from a heart attack while sitting at his desk in Bible House. Bernard had left a successful career in banking to respond to a call from the Bible Society of India and Ceylon for a general manager. He was Director of Finance and Administration, the first layman to become a General Secretary of the Society, and had served as joint Treasurer of UBS and Chairman of its personnel sub-committee.

"Having worked for and with Bernard for over twenty years," John Dean writes at the time, "and having grown up in the Bible Society movement under his inspiration and leadership, I would like to express how very much I owed to Bernard's always-available, always-trustworthy, always-constructive experience, encouragement and objective criticism – at first as a great boss to work for, and later as a true friend to cherish."

With Neville Cryer, as General Director, and Tom Houston, now as Executive Director, working in tandem, the Society establishes a new publishing division in 1978 under the leadership of Richard Worthing-Davies. Richard has first-class qualifications in organisational management. The Society embarks on a radical review of its publishing and distribution operations, rapidly expanding its range of products following the change in the UBS constitution in 1971 to confine the prohibition on note and comment to "doctrinal" comment and anticipating the relaxation of its own charter in 1984 to allow it to work for an increase in the "use" of Scriptures as well as its distribution. The revised charter also imposes an age limit of 70 on members of the General Committee.

Since 1916, the Society has had a large purpose-built warehouse in New Cross, London. Since the lease on this is running out, the General Committee has to consider whether to move the whole operation out of London. After a detailed survey of possible locations, Swindon is chosen. The Committee does not feel ready to make a final decision on the sale of London Bible House but they agree to purchase a piece of land in Swindon that can accommodate both the warehouse and the office. They also set a time limit on when they will make a final decision on the office. The Committee approves the purchase of the property in September 1979 and the warehouse is relocated in October 1981. The office move to Swindon is approved in December 1983 when it is also agreed that the library will be placed on permanent loan with Cambridge University Library.

Swindon, 9 May 1986

The General Committee finally approves the terms of the sale o
London Bible House in February 1985. It means farewell to the
elegant staircase, the columns, the balustrades and panelling o
brightly coloured marble, which have been a feature of the
Society's life for 117 years.

During 1986, staff begin to relocate to a brand new office
building at Westlea, Swindon. None of us who were present on
9 May 1986 will forget the visit of the Queen Mother to open the
building officially. Her legendary charm (and unique ability to
make everyone she speaks to feel they are the only person in the
world) is on display to the full. We treasure Nigel Purchase's painting of the occasion.

As a result of the move from London to Swindon, the
Society loses some dedicated and skilled staff who sadly, for a variety of reasons, are unable to make the move. All of those seeking
alternative employment are able to find new jobs within a reasonable period of time. New members of staff who live in the area
or are prepared to travel or relocate, are soon busy at Stonehil
Green.

THE SOWER

John Dean worked for the Society from 1956 until 1978, the las
five years as General Secretary, before becoming a UBS World
Service Officer. In 1986 he asks archivist Kathleen Cann to do
some research into the Society's famous logo, the sower. Kathleen
who still works part-time at the Society's collection at Cambridge
University Library as well as being Secretary of the George
Borrow Society, discovers that the symbol of the sower appeared
for the first time on the cover of the Society's *Monthly Reporter* in
January 1889. The only previous logo was an open Bible, over the
motto "Search the Scriptures" which appeared in 1858. The
sower is based on a statue by the English sculptor Sir W Hamo
Thornycroft (1850–1925), completed in 1886 and erected in Kew
Gardens in 1922. (The statue was still there in July 2001 when

ohn Dean took a photograph of it.) The sower continues to be used on the cover of the *Monthly Reporter* and its successor *The Bible in the World* until the 1960s.

The sower continued to be the Society's logo until the late 990s, when he was at last replaced by a symbol which John disapprovingly describes as an "exploded firecracker"!

Budapest, Hungary, September 1988

t is a crucial time in the history of UBS. The structures are expanding, new global officers have been appointed, the global office is about to move to Reading in England. In the course of he closing worship service at a meeting of the UBS Council in Budapest, four men kneel at the front. They are Cirilo Rigos, vho has been appointed General Secretary (to follow in the footsteps of John Temple, Olivier Béguin and Ulrich Fick), John Dean vho will continue as a World Service Officer until 1992, taking on responsibility for the Americas, Geoffrey Hill who is replacing he American Charley Baas as Finance Officer and will establish he global office in Reading, and Philip Oliver who is replacing ohn Erickson as he becomes Chairman of the UBS Executive Committee.

Enter Donald Coggan

UBS President Donald Coggan addresses the Council.

"Dear sisters and brothers, we present to you these global taff officers, elected and appointed to serve the global fellowship of the UBS. It is your task to uphold them in their ministry with prayer and honest advice, and to assist them in applying all that they know and can do for the good of all. Are you ready to do so?"

The Council stands and responds, "I am."

Coggan then calls the four forward and addresses them.

"Cirilo, John, Geoffrey, Philip. Before God and in the presence of your co-workers, I ask: Are you ready to dedicate yourself entirely to the service of the Word of God, and, to that end, to the service of the world fellowship of the UBS?"

"With the help of God, I am," each replies.

As hands are laid on the four, Coggan prays for strength enlightenment, wisdom and understanding from God.

Of Coggan, John Dean says: "He was one of the fines Christians I have ever had the privilege of knowing and working with. He was the very model of Christian leadership, which he exercised with personal modesty and charm, and yet at the same time with unmistakable authority and seriousness." John has told me how pleased he was that Coggan laid his hands on him personally. Geoffrey Hill showed me a treasured file of press cutting and photographs of the memorable occasion.

Another highlight of the Budapest Council is the sermon preached by Uli Fick at the closing service. At the time that the conference at Elfinsward was giving birth to UBS, Fick was a young German prisoner of war reading a New Testament provided by ABS. He has been General Secretary since 1 January 1973 and he is always impressive on these occasions. He has an especially attentive audience to hear him bring his closing words to the UBS fellowship.

"The greatest experience which I take with me home from these 16 years with the UBS is that I could see Christ grow by what the Bible Societies are doing and by what the Holy Spirit did grant. Without the Bible there is no knowledge of Christ Without God we are lost. With him, however, there is life and clarity, joy and future.

"So joy is the first and last word. You will take many impressions home with you from this meeting. Each person who participated will take home a highly personal mix of memories, and different impressions, words, discoveries and sentiments which will be important to each one of you.

"You will take with you also a new commitment to the task Let us not see this commitment as a heavy duty, a burden which in addition to other things we must do, we have let ourselves be talked into at the Budapest meeting! See your commitment to the Bible cause with all joy which your hearts can hold… Be happy about being part of the work which gives honour to Christ. Be happy about seeing so many around you who share this joy."

But for now there is work to be done. Worldwide, Bible Societies are now distributing over 500 million Scriptures a year. Thirty-four Societies are contributors to the World Service Budget of which twelve are "net-supported" and 22 are "net-supporting". Geoffrey Hill and John Dean have already secured the floor of a modern office block at Reading to become the UBS World Service Office. Now they have the task of arranging for people, documents and equipment to move from New York, Stuttgart and London to suites of rooms just by the river Thames in Berkshire. Ninety-five-year-old Bill Platt turns up for the official opening and casts a critical eye over the offices. Here work will be done which was first undertaken by his colleague John Temple at his BFBS General Secretary's desk in London Bible House 40 years earlier. UBS work will no longer be overshadowed by any single national Bible Society.

Cirilo Rigos was previously a successful pastor and influential church leader in the Philippines. The job of General Secretary of UBS does not work for him and, in a reorganisation of the structure in 1990, Rigos resigns. He is succeeded in May by John Erickson who will serve in the post until December 1997.

Erickson is an ordained Lutheran who served as a missionary in Japan in the 1960s before joining ABS. He still takes an active interest in the Bible Society movement. "There is no question in my mind," he told me in 2003, "that the mission of Bible Societies is as valid today as it was in 1804: meeting the Scripture needs of people – that is, providing for the widest possible effective distribution of Holy Scriptures, without note or comment." John likes to quote Eric North: "The work of the Bible Society takes place when the man with the Book meets the man without the Book, and so witnesses to the power and help of that Book in his life that the person without the Book wants it for his very own."

In New York, the ABS has a new President, Eugene Habecker. Habecker asks John Dean, who has over 30 years' experience of Bible Society work since joining BFBS at the end of 1956, to serve as consultant to ABS, reviewing the work of the Society's international relations department and advising on ABS/UBS relationships.

In his report, John Dean highlights the fact that for a number of years, BFBS has had little involvement in UBS affairs other than through its substantial financial contributions to the World Service Budget. The situation is different with ABS, many of whose key staff still serve in UBS roles while continuing as UBS officers. The result is that ABS and UBS agendas are often synonymous – what is good for ABS is good for UBS and vice versa.

There is, however, a certain revival of BFBS involvement in UBS at this time. With the fall of the Berlin Wall in November 1989, opportunities for Bible work in eastern Europe are developing rapidly. Richard Worthing-Davies has personally been drawn into a roving international role, which increases his travel extensively. Richard becomes a member of the UBS Executive Committee, Chairman of the UBS Structure and Administration Sub-committee and a Director of the United Bible Societies Trust Association.

He visits Prague with Roger Russell, his marketing manager, and they develop plans for the Society to assist in the foundation of the Czechoslovak Bible Society (now the Czech Bible Society). To respond to Richard's increasing workload out of the country, the General Committee in June 1990 invites Neil Crosbie to take on the job of Operations Director.

In 1991 there is an attempted coup in Russia. Father Alexander Borisnov, President of the Bible Society of Russia, use this as a heaven-sent opportunity to do the work he loves to do: "I had the joy of distributing the New Testament to soldiers on both sides of the barricades as they sat on top of their tanks. When there was no one sitting on top, we climbed up to knock on the hatch and when it was opened we gave the soldiers a New Testament. I stood there in my priestly garments and with my Moscow City Council badge. Only one out of about 3,000 soldiers would not take the New Testament that I offered."

How this would have delighted Tsar Alexander I and Prince Galitzin 177 years earlier!

And through Philip Poole (at this time the Society's Finance Director) the Society also has substantial involvement with

Belarus. Modern Bible Society work only begins in earnest in that country in 1989–90 with the Minsk Branch of the newly forming Bible Society of the USSR. By 1991 the USSR is no more and the Minsk office becomes the fledgling Bible Society of the Republic of Belarus. It is legally registered as a religious entity by the authorities in May 1992. Philip makes his first visit in June/July 1992 and will make at least one visit every year for the next decade.

At first there is an explosive growth of Protestant Christianity, a Western (mainly anti-Russian) focus to national policy, and open doors to Bible work. New churches meet in public buildings, schools are open to Bible Society, and over a million Bibles are distributed from a standing start in this nation of 10 million people.

Once the Lukashenka regime comes to power in 1995, things start to change, national policy becomes more anti-Western, and the Russian Orthodox Church is advanced as the true representative of the national religious spirit. Things become rather more difficult for the Protestant Churches. However, the Bible Society of Belarus has a range of current projects which include providing Bibles for visually impaired people; helping people living in territories polluted with radiation from the Chernobyl catastrophe; assistance to children deprived of parental care; help for new churches and children's Christian summer camps; publication of the New Testament in Byelorussian translated by a Catholic priest; and the popularisation of Bible literature among different strata of Belarusian society.

Arthur Scotchmer

Arthur Scotchmer is the Society Board member with the most experience of UBS affairs in recent years. Arthur spent his career in the oil industry, until 1973 in Africa. He attended the first meeting of the Bible Society's General Committee in July 1974 and his first involvement with UBS came in 1991 when he was appointed to the Board of the European Production Fund. He was appointed a member of the UBS finance sub-committee in 1993.

The following year, when UBSEC established a capital project review committee, Arthur was appointed Chairman.

Arthur has always been an advocate of a system that would ensure that the top four or five contributors to UBS programme should automatically have a seat on the global Board but this ha never yet been accepted. He believes it is vitally important tha BFBS Board members should have the opportunity to learn mor about what is happening in the UBS world, and to ask questions Trust between the Society, and indeed all national Bible Societies and UBS is vital for the health of Bible work around the world.

Act 48

A change of tone at the Vatican

We saw in Act 19 how Pope Pius VII accused Bible Society of undermining faith and endangering souls, while his successor Leo XII spoke of it as "strolling with effrontery through the world".

The 20th century saw the Vatican adopt a new approach to the Bible, eventually welcoming the work of Bible Societies and wholeheartedly cooperating with them in their work.

As early in the century as 1919, the Archbishop of Bologna, soon to be elected Pope Benedict XV, did everything in his power to promote the circulation of the Bible. He ordered a weekly distribution in the churches of leaflets containing the Gospel for the day in Italian. When he became Pope, the Vicar General, acting on Benedict's orders, wrote to all the clergy in Rome exhorting them to intensify their work of expounding the Gospel and ordering that in all their churches at Low Mass the priest, after having read the Gospel in Latin as usual, should turn to the people and in a loud and distinct voice read it also in Italian. The Pope sent a letter to Cardinal Cassetta, of the St Jerome Society, in which he said, "May the Holy Book enter Christian families, and there be a precious jewel sought after and jealously guarded by all, so that the faithful, habituated to the daily reading and comment, may learn to live worthily, in all things pleasing to God."

On 15 September 1920 Pope Benedict XV issued an Encyclical Letter on "St Jerome and Holy Scripture" which concluded: "Our one desire for all the Church's children is that, being saturated with the Bible, they may arrive at the all-surpassing knowledge of Jesus Christ." At Christmas of the same year, he spoke of five plagues which afflicted the age and of the only solution to these dangerous tendencies.

"The sole remedy," said the Pope, "is a return to the light of the gospel. Let individuals and peoples, impatient of discipline and

subjection, return to the gospel, because from God all is power
Let them return to the gospel, and from it learn to return to
brotherly love. Let peoples return to the gospel, and find again tha
simplicity of custom and that virtue without which neither individual good nor family peace nor social progress can reign or
earth."

On 9 January 1963 Pope John XXIII asked a huge crowd o
pilgrims in Rome, "Every day you read papers and books, but do
you also take time to read the Holy Scriptures?"

The Second Vatican Council came the following year with
its declaration that "the Word of God should be available at al
times". "All the faithful" should have easy access to the Scriptures
in the liturgy, through the Scripture readings and the homily, and
also in the daily life.

Following this major change of tone, the United Bible
Societies and the Vatican Secretariat for Promoting Christian
Unity began to work together. In June 1968 they issued thei
"Guiding Principles for Interconfessional Cooperation in
Translating the Bible". In this epoch-making document UBS and
the Vatican expressed their agreement on the principles to be fol-
lowed for interconfessional (Protestant and Roman Catholic
Bible translations. By December of the same year, Olivier Béguin
(UBS) and Father Abbott (Vatican Secretariat for Promoting
Christian Unity) produced "Roman Catholics and the Bible", a
progress report on developments in this field.

In September 1969 the UBS General Committee, meeting
perhaps ironically in Edinburgh, adopted a statement about publication of some editions of the Scriptures containing the Old
Testament/Deutero-canonicals and Apocrypha. The Catholic
Church came to accept a compromise whereby the Deutero-
canonical books (the Catholic term for the Protestant Apocrypha
would appear as a separate section in front of the New Testament
Dozens of joint projects were set in motion, each involving
Roman Catholic, Protestant and in some cases Orthodox scholars
and experts in translation.

HOLMGREN SEEKS TO ANSWER
AMERICAN CONCERNS

Within a few years, some Evangelicals in the United States who are suspicious of collaboration with Catholics are criticising the new pioneering, interconfessional Bible translation effort. In response to this, ABS General Secretary Laton Holmgren addresses the ABS Senior Officers Council in May 1970. The important and well-informed paper he presents to the Council is designed to demonstrate how such partnerships with Roman Catholics are fully consistent with the history of the Bible Society movement since 1804.

Enter Laton Holmgren

"It was the view of the founders," Holmgren says, "that only if the Bible Societies can faithfully serve the 'whole church of Christ in the whole world' can they effectively fulfil their core-mission. They set the pattern at the founding to seek the involvement of all the major Christian traditions, and already at the ABS founding Roman Catholics were invited to join the enterprise [they declined]. ABS staff are drawn from the widest possible denominational spectrum. Our cooperation with the Vatican is not some recent drift toward ecumenism. Ecumenism in its best sense has always been the ABS posture.

"The Roman Catholic Church has always been one of the historic churches which the Bible Societies have included in their service posture – although I admit that Catholic audiences were not always served well until Vatican II opened the doors wide to vigorous cooperation in the Bible cause.

"However, within the cooperative mode in which Bible Societies work, no Evangelicals who are uncomfortable will ever be coerced into cooperative translation projects or the support of projects with which they do not wish to be involved."

At its meeting at London Bible House on 21 July 1980, the Bible Society General Committee appoints its first Roman Catholic members, and in 1982 Uli Fick, General Secretary of UBS, publishes the results of a survey which reveals that in 23 countries, Catholic representatives are on the Boards of Bible Societies.

By 1987, no less than 161 interconfessional Bibles and New Testaments are published.

On 26 October 1989 Pope John Paul II meets a team of UBS officials at the Vatican.

"Dear brothers in Christ," he says to them, "I am happy to welcome you, distinguished representatives of the United Bible Societies. We meet in the awareness that the life in Christ that we share is clarified and sustained in every way by the Word of God. It is therefore with joy and gratitude that I take note of the spirit of ecumenical collaboration which prevails in your work as you seek to make the Scriptures increasingly known and understood.

"I am confident that the United Bible Societies and the World Catholic Federation for the Biblical Apostolate will foster the fraternal collaboration which already inspires your efforts...

"Holy Scripture nourishes faith, strengthens ecclesiastical unity and is an important element of our common spiritual patrimony with Abraham's stock, our Jewish brothers and sisters...

"To penetrate the Scriptures is to enter into the very mystery of God...

"I gladly express the hope that members of the United Bible Societies will continue to participate, according to their gifts, in the proclamation of the gospel which calls for the conversion of all mankind to Jesus Christ in the Church."

Thirteen years later, a now frail Pope has an even more remarkable message for Bible Societies.

The Vatican, Rome, 22 April 2002

It is spring 2002 in Italy. Representatives of 37 Bible Societies have been invited to an audience with the Pope. One of the Societies represented, the British and Foreign Bible Society, has been accused by the Pope's predecessors in the early 19th century of undermining faith, endangering souls, and "strolling with effrontery through the world". What will the Pope say today?

Enter Pope John Paul II

"Dear friends in Christ," he begins, his voice clear, though showing the signs of the Parkinson's disease from which he increasingly suffers. "In the peace of Easter, I am happy to welcome 'you (who) have been born anew...through the living and abiding word of God' (1 Peter 1:23). The Bible Societies exist to open the inexhaustible riches of sacred Scripture to all who will listen: and that is a noble Christian service, for which I give thanks to God.

"For many years, your Societies have been engaged in translating and distributing the text of Scripture, an essential part of proclaiming Christ to the world. For it is not just words which we must speak: it is the Word of God himself! It is Jesus Christ, promised in the Old Testament, proclaimed in the New, whom we must present to a world which hungers for Him, often without knowing it. It was Saint Jerome who declared that 'ignorance of Scripture is ignorance of Christ' (*Commentary on Isaiah*, Prologue). Your work then is above all a service of Christ.

"The urgency of this task demands that we commit ourselves to the cause of Christian unity, for division among the disciples of Christ has certainly impaired our mission. Your meeting therefore draws together members of different Churches and Ecclesial Communities, united in the love of the Bible and in the desire that 'listening to the word of God should become a life-giving encounter...which draws from the biblical text the living word which questions, directs and shapes our lives' (*Novo Millennio Ineunte*, 39).

"Whatever differences remain between us, the promotion of the Bible is one point where Christians can work closely together for the glory of God and the good of the human family. The Great Jubilee of the Year 2000 was a splendid occasion for all Christians to rejoice in celebrating the Incarnation of Jesus Christ not just as a past event but as an enduring mystery. It is my fervent hope that this momentum will continue to inspire Christians to a still deeper love and knowledge of the Holy Bible, thus encouraging the work of the Bible Societies. Praying that Christ himself will 'touch your ears to receive his word and your mouth to proclaim his faith, to the praise and glory of God the Father' (*Rite of Baptism*), I gladly invoke upon you the abundant blessings of Almighty God, whose word endures for ever."

Ashley Scott represents BFBS that happy Easter in Rome and treasures a photograph taken of himself with the Pope. I asked Ashley to tell me his most vivid recollection of the day.

"Despite the inevitable boundaries of protocol," he replied, "and in the fleeting moment of personal introduction, one was aware – at one and the same time – of a frail humanity and an indomitable, inner strength that was simply inspiring."

This journey of reconciliation between Catholic and Protestant lovers of Scriptures is surely one of the happiest stories in the history of the Bible Society movement – and full of even more promise for the future.

A passion to make the Bible heard

Albuquerque, New Mexico, September 1993

Enter Neil Crosbie, Philip Poole and Gary Hodgson

Three members of Bible Society's staff arrive in Albuquerque, on the Rio Grande, the largest city of New Mexico, encircled by Indian pueblos, opposite a pass between mountains to the east. Neil Crosbie, Philip Poole and Gary Hodgson visit the team from the organisation Hosanna, which manages the Faith Comes by Hearing (FCBH) programme. Neil will come to look back on the visit as the first visible signpost to a new approach which will characterise the Society's work in England and Wales as it approaches its bicentenary.

The visit is intended as a "get to know each other" session. Both the BFBS trio and the Hosanna leaders expect discussions about the Society's involvement with FCBH to come later in the week. However, as Neil says later, "God has his own agenda for such meetings." During the conversation with the Hosanna team, Neil finds himself reflecting on the significance of the meeting in the light of the whole history of Bible Society. As the conversation unfolds, he stops talking at one point and looks at Philip Poole, only to find that Philip is looking at him. They both interpret each other's expression in the same way: they are sure they will be recommending the introduction of FCBH into Bible Society. "Exactly when that decision was made," says Neil, "we didn't really know, but it was clear that the Lord himself had made it, and that our response was to get in line with His will."

FCBH is finally launched in 1995 after the economics have been worked out and the Board's approval sought and given. An important challenge is to find the right people to staff the programme. Recruiting a team to work on the telephone in such a spiritually open way is not something the Society has ever attempted before, and raises huge challenges for the Society's management. One person, Peter Duke, is an obvious choice, not least because of his enthusiasm for the whole venture. The other person, Lesley Whelan, is transferred from a lower profile job in the Society to what becomes a critical position in the years that follow and a role which she performs admirably.

When the launch day for the FCBH programme finally arrives, Neil Crosbie decides to come into Bible House early in the morning to pray, and particularly to pray against any final resistance that may be experienced. "As I sat in the FCBH area on the ground floor," he remembers, "it was as if all the lights in the building came on (but they were still switched off – I opened my eyes to check!). God was present in all His power and majesty, and there was nothing for me to do except to bathe in the experience."

During his time as the Society's Chief Executive, Neil Crosbie attaches importance to developing an organisation which is not just an effective business unit but also has the spiritual and communal life that will combine with the programme activities to form an effective *mission agency*. His thinking is influenced by the advice and friendships made in Hosanna and the Northumbria Community.

Neil's time with the Society also coincides with a period of intense debate about the role of BFBS in England and Wales. Staff and Board members agree that the Society's traditional but vital support of translation and distribution of the Scriptures abroad should continue. This means that approximately two-thirds of annual expenditure is channelled via the United Bible Societies to worthwhile programmes across the world – translation, literacy projects inside and outside schools, in prisons, amongst AIDS patients, with visually handicapped people, and in countries ravaged by war and famine.

But what is to be the role of the Society in England and Wales? Is it going to be publishing, offering a wide range of products now that the "no note and comment" rule has been relaxed? Is it going to be church growth and training? Is it going to be a concentration on new electronic methods of spreading the Good News of the Bible? Is the focus going to be on providing new and better products and programmes, or is the emphasis and approach going to be on mission? What is the relationship of the Society to the church – servant, partner, cajoler, provider of expertise or what?

Enter Lesslie Newbigin

A number of people make their input into the thinking. There is Lesslie Newbigin, missionary, bishop, and author of many books on the Gospel in contemporary culture. Lesslie, who worked for many years in India (and died in 1998), used to recall a brilliant Hindu scholar friend of his who, from his wide knowledge of the sacred books of the world's religions, said to him, "I find your Bible something quite unique. It is a unique interpretation of universal history, and therefore an interpretation of the human person as a responsible actor within history." Newbigin warmly welcomes the Open Book project which the Society manages for Churches Together in England as a way of providing the churches with an opportunity to recall society to the true "metanarrative" – the biblical story which can make sense of both our public and private lives.

Enter Dan Beeby

Dan Beeby is close to Newbigin and works as a consultant to the Society on the Recovery of Scripture programme. He is committed to the view that Bible Society has a role to play in enabling the church to become oriented for mission and to recover the Scriptures as truth for the public life of society. "This must be," says Beeby, "a mission to culture as we strive to recover the biblical narrative as the foundation for society's renewal."

Enter Martin Robinson and Colin Greene

Martin Robinson (working closely with Colin Greene), author and the Society's Director of Mission and Theology, is adamant that the biblical narrative is as much public story as private conviction. Reflecting on BFBS history, he notes that the Society owed its birth to men who energetically and successfully campaigned to change society. "William Wilberforce and the Claphan Sect," says Robinson, "saw the need to generate a new vision for the society of their time. Theirs was a campaigning agenda, arguing for what Wilberforce called 'the Reform of Manners' by which he meant attempting to make goodness fashionable."

And so a new campaigning strategy for the Society emerges. In May 2000 UBS General Secretary Fergus Macdonald presents a thoughtful paper to the UBS Executive Committee on the subject of Bible Societies and Scripture engagement. In October of the same year, at the World Assembly in Midrand, South Africa, Bible Societies formally recognise that their mission reaches beyond Bible distribution to seeking to promote the Bible's impact understanding and use.

At the start of 2001 the Society embarks on the process of talking to and listening to the church in England and Wales about its intended campaigning strategy. Conversations with senior church leaders reveal a high level of agreement on the need to change public thinking about the Bible and the church and to engage society in a conversation – as well as challenging it with the Christian world view.

In June 2001 a new visual identity with the strap line *Making the Bible heard* is introduced to the public and the Society's supporters. The idea is not simply to provide a dynamic new look for the 21st century but to emphasise that the Society is now in the business of Bible advocacy as much as Scripture distribution.

England and Wales, September 2001 to May 2002

The Society stages 37 roadshows throughout England, Wales and the Channel Islands for its supporters and church leaders to talk about the new approach and enlist local involvement.

"Our aim," says the Society's President, John Taylor, introducing the new approach, "is to endeavour to increase the Bible' presence, reputation and profile everywhere. From the translation and distribution of Bibles where there are none, to encouraging fresh encounters with the Bible, to helping people think differently about the Bible – we believe that, together with the church and our supporters, we can achieve the vision of bringing the Bible to the heart of our culture."

Clive Dilloway, who has been Chairman of the Board of Trustees since June 2000, points out that the work is not just for England and Wales. "It is a work that involves a Global Alliance of people with a passion for making the Bible heard. In a world of contrasts, where some still do not have access to a Bible in their own language, and others, in our own society, are still not touched by the relevance and power of the Scriptures in their own lives, the task is enormous."

Neil Crosbie will leave the Society at the end of 2001, after 21 years of contributing to its work. He goes on to become Chief Executive at the United Bible Societies in succession to Fergus Macdonald. Neil summarises the vision of the Society as being for a world

- where the narratives of the Bible are known and loved in a vibrant Christian church
- where people who are searching for direction and fulfilment find a connection between their yearnings and the timeless truths of the Bible
- where the Biblical vision of forgiveness, justice, freedom and hope are lived out in nations, among communities and in the hearts of individual people
- where everyone has the opportunity to encounter the drama of the Bible for themselves, bringing purpose, vitality and dignity into their lives

The Society's new campaigning vision is widely welcomed. Dr Rowan Williams, then Archbishop of Wales, says: "For almost 200 years Bible Society has demonstrated its dedicated commitment to communicating the message of the Bible to a vast range of cultures and individuals. I am delighted to see that, in response to the changing needs of society, the Society is expanding its vision, thereby ensuring a continued relevance for the 21st century and beyond."

Vincent Nichols, the Roman Catholic Archbishop of Birmingham, notes that Bible Society is not afraid of the intellectual challenge that expanding its vision involves. Commissioner Alex Hughes of the Salvation Army says that "the footprints of Bible Society can be seen everywhere from the playgroup to Parliament and from finance to fashion".

Stonehill Green, Swindon, 7 January 2002

Enter James Catford

The new arrival at Swindon Bible House grew up in a town which is famous in Bible Society history – Haywards Heath, Sussex, where UBS was born. He was much involved in the life of All Saints' Church in Lindfield. After university, he went back there for a year and ran the youth work before doing postgraduate studies in Bristol.

James Catford has been responsible for publishing for three major British publishing houses, IVP, Hodder Headline and HarperCollins – where his authors included Margaret Thatcher, the Pope and, just before he left, Archbishop Carey whom he signed up to write his autobiography. When invited by Bible Society to apply for the post of Chief Executive, after Neil Crosbie took over the running of UBS, James took time to reflect. "I knew that it was a mission agency," he says, "respected across the main denominations and with around 100 staff, and I quickly felt that this job was what I'd been waiting and praying for."

Staff at Swindon Bible House soon discover that he has charm to match his good looks – and also a well-articulated vision for the Bible. "I would like to see the Bible entering the market place of our everyday lives," James says. "Up on a shelf somewhere it might be beyond contradiction, but it is also gathering dust. I'd like to see it consulted when people are looking for advice and guidance, listened to as much as people listen to the radio, and taken as seriously as people take sport or exercise. Then we will know that we are making an impact on society as a whole."

The Bible is a collection of 66 books written over many hundreds of years, but James is impressed by its consistency. "Everything in the Bible tells the same story: everyone can find an abundant life with God. The Bible invites us to enter a life full of righteousness, peace and joy. In fact, it is the very life of Christ that is being offered to us in the Bible. It is intended to be experienced right here, right now, and not just when we die. I'm passionate about discovering this life that the Bible describes, in all its implications for individual people, societies and nations."

As he takes over the helm at Stonehill Green, a biblical phrase keeps coming to James's mind. "It is the one that Matthew records at the very start of Jesus' ministry: 'Repent for the Kingdom of Heaven is near' (Matthew 4:17). John the Baptist and Jesus are both saying, 'Think about your thinking; think about it in the light of the reality that the Kingdom of God is now open and available to you.' It is a simple invitation, running throughout the New Testament, to rearrange our lives in the light of this."

Just as the Bible challenges us to personal repentance, so it matters to public and political life today. "Deep down it is very simple," says James Catford. "We believe that it is the best source of information or wisdom available to humankind concerning the most important issues of life. Actually it is unique; whatever part of the church we come from, this is what we should grasp. Public and private matters are always tightly intertwined with these 'matters of life'. And that's why the witness of Scripture concerning them needs to be clearly heard in our day."

James recognises that in many countries having access to or owning a Bible is the most pressing need. "That is why," he says, "we continue to translate and distribute Bibles worldwide as a priority." One of his first foreign visits is to Ethiopia.

THE SOCIETY AND ETHIOPIA

Christianity was introduced to Ethiopia in the fourth century, and the Ethiopian Orthodox Church is one of the oldest churches in the world. As early as 1811, the Society's annual report tells us that, stimulated by pressure from the Edinburgh Bible Society, the General Committee decides to produce an Ethiopic version of the Psalms. A few years later, the Society manages to secure a complete version of the Bible in Amharic which has been translated by an elderly monk called Abu Rumi. Amharic has for centuries been the colloquial speech of much of Ethiopia (in the 19th and early 20th century always referred to as Abyssinia).

In 1856, at the request of Bishop Samuel Gobat of Jerusalem, the Society sends 300 Bibles and Testaments in Amharic and a supply of Ethiopic Scriptures to Ethiopia. Two missionaries from the London Jews Society take them into the country in large boxes. One rumour is that the boxes are full of gold and silver from Jerusalem for the "King of Kings" (the ancient title of Ethiopian Emperors).

"Have you brought me a gunsmith?" the Emperor asks, when the boxes arrive at his home.

Although the missionaries' answer is a disappointment, he treats them kindly. But he takes a dim view of the Ethiopic Scriptures.

"Why do you bring such books which nobody understands? What is the use of them? The Amharic are far better. They are understood by everyone."

Abuna, however, the head of the Ethiopian Church, is glad to buy a whole case of Psalters and Testaments in Ethiopic. He will not touch the Amharic Scriptures.

"A profane tongue, unfit for prayer, a desecration of the Word of God."

He sees Ethiopic as the "holy language", even though 95% of the clergy cannot understand it.

The Society sends another two consignments in April 1859. The batch includes 100 Bibles in red leather, a special gift for the King to help him furnish the churches and to enforce his reform that every Sunday and feast-day the clergy should read to their congregations some chapters of the Old and New Testaments in their everyday speech.

When Menelik II becomes Emperor in 1889, the Society

presents him with some handsome gifts. Menelik is delighted with these and, as we saw in Act 29, in May 1892 he presents to the Society two large elephant tusks which are proudly displayed in London Bible House.

Early in the 20th century, the Society's agent in Egypt, C T Hooper, manages to secure an interview with the Metropolitan of the Ethiopian Church and gets his agreement to open a Bible House in Addis Ababa to be managed by the Society. Eventually, after the Society has secured a plot of land, the Addis Ababa Bible House is begun in 1924. In the same year, His Imperial Highness Ras Tafar Makonnen (who in 1930 will become Emperor Haile Selassie I) makes a donation to the Society which allows it to commission a marvellous "translations globe". This stands about four foot six inches high and is held in a wooden frame. Written in red, in the appropriate locations on the globe, are the names of all the languages into which the Bible has been translated and for which the Society has been responsible to that date. It sits today in a prime position outside the suite of rooms occupied by the librarian and deputy librarian at Cambridge University Library.

On Ascension Day, 13 May 1926, Ras Tafar Makonnen opens the completed Bible House at a colourful ceremony. Following their invasion of Ethiopia in 1936, the Italians drive the Society's agent in Addis Ababa out of the country, although his wife, a Dane, stays in the country as long as she can to oversee Bible work.

In 1966 the Bible Society of Ethiopia is established as a fully-fledged Society in its own right and in 1972 becomes a full member of UBS.

Addis Ababa, January 2003

Enter James Catford

"I've never met a militant fundamentalist before," says James, "but I did in Ethiopia. The man was fighting against Communists in Afghanistan before he had a dramatic encounter with God. Now he is a mild-mannered and gracious disciple of Jesus who has a warm smile to match his tender heart. I met him in a church in Addis Ababa where he has become a wise and effective teacher of the Bible and a leader of his congregation."

With his Bible in his hand he tells James how God has met him and transformed his life. "The Bible tells me everything I need to know about the love of God for all people."

This man is not the only person James meets in Ethiopia who is hungry for the Bible. He finds that the Scripture version most people have access to in Ethiopia is written in Ge'ez – an ancient language that few people understand today and is more like reading Chaucer or Latin for people in Britain.

With Yilma Getahun, General Secretary of the Bible Society of Ethiopia, James visits a monastery on an island in Lake Tana where they have no modern Bibles. A young monk is so excited to receive a Bible in modern Amharic that he asks for it to be autographed.

"I should like to have copies for everyone in my community," the head monk says.

Using funds provided by Bible Society, James and Yilma distribute 100 copies of a contemporary Amharic Bible to a Mission of Mercy training centre in the middle of Addis Ababa. The centre is for children who have been abandoned by their parents, or who have not been able to afford education. They have almost nothing in the world. James is thrilled by the expression on the children's faces as they receive their Bibles.

James hears about the work of the Ethiopian Bible Society. In cooperation with churches and other organisations, it has recently completed three major Bible translation projects: the common language Amharic Bible revision, the Gurage: Chaha Bible translation and the Wolaytta Bible. The Society distributes Scriptures by vans, shops, from warehouse and by churches. Free Bibles are given to seminary graduates at graduation ceremonies and to prisoners through churches and other organisations.

Towards the end of 2001 the Society embarked on a Faith Comes by Hearing programme, making cassettes available in Amharic – Ethiopia's official language since the Second World War.

In addition to its regular devotional time, the Society has had a weekly prayer time on two prayer items. One was about regaining its Bible House which was nationalised during the Communist rule and the second one was about opening a shop in Awasa, a very strategic town of the southern regions of Ethiopia. "God, who is able to do the impossible," says the General Secretary, "answered our prayers. We received a donation of Birr 50,000.00 from a young lady (who is in [her] twenties) towards the purchase of a Bible House in Awassa. The staff was encouraged by this donation and agreed to give 20 per cent of their one-month salary and raised Birr 5,375.00. Consequently, a total of Birr 55,375.00 was raised and then the house was bought for Birr 55,000.00 at a good location. In the efforts made to recover our Bible House, the Government accepted our claim, and an agreement is reached to give back the building to the Bible Society of Ethiopia. We have received a letter to this effect and we hope we will move soon into our Bible House."

The Ethiopian Orthodox Church has long accepted the use by its members of Scriptures in their colloquial language. Now the Church has asked Bible Society to do more and the door is open as never before.

MAKING THE BIBLE HEARD EVERYWHERE

Working through a global alliance of supporters, churches, other organisations and a network of over 130 Bible Societies around the world, Bible Society's vision is to make the Bible heard everywhere. Over 2,300 languages now have some part of the Bible. During James Catford's first year at Swindon, thirteen languages received a complete Bible for the first time. However, many groups of people are still reading the Bible in a language which is foreign to them, but technological development is now playing an important part in what can be a lengthy translation process. In other languages, new translations are being prepared in a clear, modern idiom that is easily understandable to today's readers. You can read more about this on the Society's website at www.biblesociety.org.uk/translation.

Bible Society's Machine Assisted Translation (MAT) team

researches ways to apply mathematics, linguistics and computer technology for the benefit of Bible translators. As a result of this research, the team develops software that can be used to assist translation projects around the world.

In countries where literacy rates are low, national Bible Societies produce specially designed Scriptures to help new readers and develop other ways for people to encounter the Bible, including videos like the *Jesus* film, audiocassettes and CD-ROMs.

Bible Society helps to fund the distribution of Bibles and parts of the Bible across the world – for children, marginalised peoples, Christians, and people exploring Christianity for the first time, or in response to an emergency situation or natural disaster. Working through the global alliance, the Society not only funds the provision of Bibles, but also supports the distribution teams and the lorries, motorcycles and bikes that enable them to do their work.

Bible Societies in the Middle East sell Scripture products annually at book fairs – like the Bible Society of Egypt at the Cairo International Book Fair, the Bible Society of Jordan at the Book Fair in Syria, and the Bible Society of Lebanon in Iraq.

SELLING BIBLES IN BAGHDAD

The Society's popular report issued in July 1928 said, "For many years the Bible Society has been active in Baghdad and the neighbourhood. Its headquarters were in a little unpretentious Arab shop much too small to house the necessary stock. In 1914 a friend presented to the Society an excellent site on the main thoroughfare running through the city parallel with the Tigris. Upon this a Bible House, a one-storey building, has now been erected at a cost of £1,300. It was opened in May of this year. A deep, covered veranda provides shade for pedestrians who wish to shop and read the Scriptures displayed in the window. From Baghdad over 10,000 copies of Scripture were put in circulation last year. It is hoped that with the increased facilities provided by these new premises this number will be greatly increased in future."

Today, the Bible Society in Lebanon has responsibility for

the troubled land of Iraq. When I asked Tom Hoglind whether the Bible House in Baghdad still exists it was clear that he knew it well. But since the advent of Saddam Hussein's regime it has not been possible to use it for Bible work. In 1978 "Bible Society lost a great shop on Rashid Street," he told me, "on the shore of the famous Tigris river right in the centre of Baghdad – the city of dreams". He remembers sitting in the home of the Director of the Bible Society of Iraq as he "kept the TV on during the whole time of fellowship in case there'd been some listening device in the home".

However, "we overcame the fear of those days and were able to see God move in an amazing way during the rest of Saddam's reign of terror and make it possible to supply large quantities of Scriptures to the Iraqi Church".

In 2001 the Bible Society of Lebanon ran three exhibitions at the Baghdad International Book Fair. "Bishop Jean Suleiman gave us the largest hall in the Cathedral of St Joseph to fill with Scriptures and Christian books," says Lucien Accad. "And the chairman of the National Protestant Church in Iraq generously opened his church's doors to us. Suddenly we were faced with the challenge of running three exhibitions simultaneously! During our ten days in Baghdad thousands of books were sold to the visitors who crowded to these three sites."

In 2002 the Bible Society in Lebanon's Just for Kids drama troupe toured three Iraqi cities, performing to thousands of Iraqi children.

ART, EXHIBITIONS AND POSTERS

The Bible Society of Belarus is working with an art college to incorporate an Opening the Bible module into their course. The students' work is then displayed in Minsk Central Children's Library for everyone to see. We saw earlier how BFBS's Assistant Chief Executive Philip Poole has taken a special interest in Belarus and made at least one visit there every year since 1992, most recently in May 2003.

Bible Societies are using interactive and multimedia exhibitions to communicate the stories of the Bible and how the Bible came to us. The Bible Society in Lebanon's Bible World exhibition in Beirut comprises a traditional museum as well as a time travel experience and computer game.

The Bible Society of Egypt runs an outdoor advertising campaign to encourage people to study the Scriptures. The huge hoardings at the side of the Cairo–Alexandria highway and other billboard displays raise awareness and promote Scripture products.

PUBLISHING AND RESOURCES

In collaboration with HarperCollins the Society is a co-publisher for the still top-selling Good News (GNB) and the latest Contemporary English Version (CEV) Bible ranges. The Society is the sole publisher of the New Welsh Bible.

As well as Bibles, the Society supplies quality creative resources such as *The Miracle Maker* film and *Tales from the Madhouse* video series to churches, schools and individuals.

Each year, the Society produces resources for churches to celebrate Bible Sunday (now the last Sunday in October) and fundraises for Bible Society work around the world.

FAITH COMES BY HEARING

We have seen how Neil Crosbie's team first entered into partnership with the American ministry Hosanna. Today, the New Testament has been recorded on to CD and audiocassette in more than 90 languages, giving tens of thousands of people in Britain and around the world the chance to encounter the Bible in their own language in a way that fits their lifestyle.

Rev. David Pickett told the Society that his church, Thundersley Congregational in Essex, decided to devote its monthly prayer meeting to Faith Comes by Hearing. "The month before I preached, they prayed for people to catch the vision," he said, "for the outcomes and for opportunities to share the Word with non-believers. When I preached more than two thirds of the congregation committed to take part in the 40-day listening!

"Now some are listening again, but in more depth, as a sort of meditation. My PA, Pat, listened in the morning and read the same passage again in the evening. She said that this helped cement it in, though she found that listening brought out different things to those she noticed when reading. She said, 'The voice of Jesus really got to me, it was so soft.'"

MAKING THE BIBLE HEARD IN OUR CULTURE

The Society is working in four key areas: politics, arts, media and education.

In a Society in which several of its early Committee members, and four of its first five Presidents, were politicians, it is a natural development for it to seek to raise the profile of the Bible in political discussion. Working with the Parliamentary Christian Fellowship, a cross-Party, cross-House group, the Society is beginning to play a key role in providing Scriptural perspectives on contemporary issues for debate.

In partnership with the Northumbria Community, The Telling Place has been set up to develop a network of storytellers and story circles around the country in venues as diverse as churches, pubs and front rooms. A storytelling performance of Mark's Gospel successfully toured local theatres.

The Society commissioned two powerful dramas, written by Murray Watts, the screenwriter of *The Miracle Maker*. *The Walk* is a dramatic retelling of the story of William Wilberforce. *The Way* is an inspiring performance introducing the challenges facing mission and ministry today.

Tales from the Madhouse is a series of monologues retelling the Easter story. The Society worked with the award-winning film producer Norman Stone in providing a portion of the finance and theological advice. First shown on BBC Television, the series was later released on video along with church and schools resources developed by the Society.

Working in partnership with others, the Society ensured that *The Miracle Maker*, an animated film about Jesus based on the Gospel of Luke, was shown in cinemas up and down the country.

The award-winning series of BBC programmes *The Test of Time* explores four of Jesus' key teachings – about forgiveness, money, commitment and peace – and how they have stood the test of time.

To help teachers in the classroom, the Society has developed a partnership with Exeter University School of Education to conduct research into how the Bible is taught in schools, and the attitudes of young people towards the Bible. The Biblos project has produced resources for use in the classroom and activities to inform and influence policy-makers and syllabus writers.

Nottinghamshire, England, October 2003

"Should Lisa seek revenge on Phil in *Eastenders*?" Huge billboards and posters appear overnight, asking this question arising from a popular TV "soap", and inviting people to text vote or email their answer.

The posters appear on bus shelters and in university and pub washrooms asking the question. But no one knows who is asking or why.

In fact it is Bible Society asking the question, in partnership with the churches of Nottinghamshire, using the *Eastenders* storyline to stimulate debate about a biblical theme: is it right to take revenge?

Two weeks after the teaser posters and adverts appear, more posters, radio and supporting publicity reveal all: stories in soaps explore themes first dealt with in the Bible. If one grips the nation, why dismiss the other?

Steve Bassett, who developed the campaign for the Society, explains that the secrecy adds intrigue. "The Bible has become so misunderstood and ignored," he says, "that our vision to make it heard is a challenge of breathtaking proportions. The posters and ads initially did not mention the church, Christianity, the Bible or Bible Society because today most people do not want to be preached at, to be told what to do and how to do it – they want to explore things for themselves. So, we hoped that by using a national soap opera storyline we would be able to have a genuine conversation with the culture around us."

After the revelation that it is Bible Society behind it all, the campaign moves on with special resources including a booklet and special website (www.getthestory.co.uk), offering more on how the themes relate to everyday life and setting out a range of opportunities to follow up any questions. An information centre provides more help — telling people about local churches, accessing useful resources and information on where to get help on various social issues.

And so the aim of the campaign is to get people talking about things that matter to them and, with an open mind, start to see how the Bible might connect with these things — from how we live, to the world we'd like to live in. The impact of the campaign will be assessed. The Society's Board of Trustees (the more recent name for the old General Committee) will discuss with staff and the Society's supporters the opportunities presented by this sort of campaigning to make the Bible heard and how it fits with the traditional "no doctrinal note or comment" stance of Bible Societies.

ACTION GROUPS

In the 1970s the old Auxiliaries were renamed Action Groups. They are, as they always have been, at the heart of the work of Bible Society. Around 400 of them are working in their local churches and communities to support the Society's work through prayer and fundraising. They also organise activities to make the Bible heard in their local communities — from passion plays in the street and regular storytelling evenings to handwritten community Gospels and "readathons". As I write this in December 2003, I am looking forward to joining the Crediton Action Group in Devon for a favourite carols evening. The oldest surviving Action Group is also in Devon, at Hatherleigh: it has loyally supported the Society without a break since 1810. The Secretary of the Exmouth Action Group showed me an almost continuous set of minutes of meetings going back to 1820.

Morecambe Bay has been crossed on foot and by stagecoach at low tide for centuries, and members of local Action Groups from Lancashire and Cumbria recently repeated a similar crossing on foot. "An Exodus experience is how it was described," Brenda and Richard Gill, the Society's former local representatives in the north-west said recently. "Thunder and lightning crashed overhead as hundreds gathered on the Arnside sands. Before them lay three hours of tiring walking on wet, ridged sand, knowing they would be forced to cross deep water including a river reaching, for some almost to waist height. Hundreds were walking, but the group quickly became dwarfed in the vast expanse of the Bay, moving quickly and eagerly." The destination of this journey may not have been the "promised land", yet the £6,500 sponsorship that flowed through the accounts of many Action Groups introduced the promise of hope and love to many lives through the distribution of more Bible Society Scriptures – Good News for the world.

Llanfihangel, Wales, 29 June 2002

Enter Heswall and District Action Group

We come towards the end our story of Bible Society where it began – in a tiny Welsh hamlet. Sturdy Bible Society supporters from the Mersey area gather at the ruins of Mary Jones's childhood home at Tyn'y-ddôl to repeat her famous walk to Bala. One half of the group will do the 28 miles in one day while some, not quite as determined as Mary, plan to take two days. They all hope by their sponsorship money to swell the funds of Bible Society. What they have not envisaged is the other benefits they gain from their experience.

First, they spend two days amongst some of the loveliest scenery imaginable, with time to get to know each other. Then they have a strange feeling of identification with Mary herself. They come from such a different society and enjoy benefits beyond Mary's wildest dreams, but in these surroundings, cut off from the bustle of modern life and amid scenery which has not greatly changed since her day, they can just about make the leap of imagination across the intervening 200 years. They keep thinking how Mary would have been amazed at their equipment. What would she have made of their high-tech gadgets like digital cameras or global positioning systems – and would she have appreciated their Gortex walking gear?

They keep thinking of the faith which drove her to undertake such a demanding walk and how far their own commitment falls short of hers. Nevertheless, no one who takes part in the walk is untouched by the experience. "We shall long remember the fellowship enjoyed," says Mike Jackson, "the glorious scenery around us which was a continual reminder of the 'wonders of his work'."

WHAT OF THE FUTURE?

Clive Dilloway, an Anglican from All Saints', Lindfield, West Sussex, who spent his career in the oil industry, steered the Society's Board of Trustees through important changes in their governance structures. He became Chairman of the Board in June 2000 and will remain so into the bicentenary year. During Clive's time as Chairman, as with his predecessors Douglas Scott, Alan Dyer and Arthur Scotchmer, Board and staff members have appreciated spending time together at regular two-day residential meetings – enjoying Christian fellowship, getting to know each other and having more time to discuss strategic issues. Julian Smith agrees that it is a very different atmosphere from when he first joined the General Committee in 1968!

Looking to the future, Clive sees the core work of the Society continuing unabated to meet an increasing demand for Bibles that people can read in their own languages and buy at prices they can afford. Alongside this core work, Clive sees the Society's work in England and Wales helping it to identify possible future needs in other countries with three areas of activity likely to develop further.

The first concerns changes in the way that textual information is communicated and studied. When Bible Society was founded it would have been common for a copy of the Bible to be the only book in a house and for it to be read frequently and in great detail. In contrast, nowadays most reading is purely for entertainment whilst the use of textbooks is progressively being displaced by access to Internet study resources which present textual information in very different ways. The challenge for the Society will be how to meet the needs of the Internet age and to develop biblical material in a form that goes beyond the first generation of Bible CD-ROM without compromising the faithful reproduction of the Scriptures

The second area of activity concerns an even greater and more insidious change in our culture since the beginning of the 19th century. The popular status of the Bible has been progressively eroded until it is common now for it to be spoken of as just another book of religious wisdom, whilst those who conscientiously study the Bible are regularly derided, sometimes even within the church, as being ultra-conservative in their beliefs. That wall of prejudice has to be broken down and ways found to encourage people to look at the Bible with an open mind. Encouraging the wider circulation of the Scriptures in England and Wales today means attacking the problems of lack of demand rather than historical problems of lack of supply.

The final area of activity is a by-product of Bible Society's need to work with a scattered church. The mandate to work without note or comment in the Society's objective ensures that the Society does not become embroiled in doctrinal disputes and has thereby earned it widespread respect for the conscientious way in which it has published unbiased versions of the Scriptures. In consequence the Society is now well placed to serve as a unifying influence within the church by providing a neutral meeting point around a common belief in the importance of the Scriptures. Without compromising its doctrinal neutrality, the Society need to use that influence to encourage greater use of the Bible throughout the church and to support Bible-based debate on issues of the day by providing appropriate extracts from the Scriptures and reference aids.

Clive's successor during 2004 will be Alan Emery, a Methodist from Bristol, who recalls his introduction to the work of the Society as a young person through the local Bible Society summer garden party. This was an event of meticulous planning a which the local Christian leaders would want to be seen.

Alan believes the original work of Bible Society is only half complete. Over 2,300 translations, in full or in part, of the precious resource for life represents a story of success. But in a world where there are more than 4,000 different languages it is not enough. And burgeoning population growth creates a ready market for more copies of the Bible. The case for continuing to pursue that original objective of encouraging the wider circulation of the Bible is strong. The monthly information sheet from UBS bears testimony to the numbers of people who, having encountered the Word in written or spoken form in their own language, have found their lives transformed for the better.

But the world context in which the Society's work must now be done is very different today than when it started. In every sense it was a missionary endeavour facilitated by the presence of Empire. That political context no longer exists. The work was also seated in and driven from a church that was fundamentally stronger than it is today. Indeed it may be argued that the Bible is now better known and understood with confidence in the places where the best of the Society's work has been done than it is in the home territories. It may be then that the decision in 1984 to expand the Society's purpose to include the use of the Bible alongside its publication and distribution was an inspired move.

The founding fathers knew their Bibles and applied that knowledge to their lives. In so doing they caused the world in which they lived to change for the better. In England and Wales today where more than 70% of the people have an idea of God, the Bible is not generally taken seriously. It is widely available at affordable prices and in many different forms but remains for many the owned but unopened, given but unread book.

Alan Emery believes that three things would be achieved by placing the Bible once again at the centre of religious, cultural, social and political thinking. First, a revitalised and strengthened church that will be confident in its support of the work of publication, distribution and use. Second, a work that will remain not just interdenominational but be respected across even the internal divisions within each denomination. And third, a society that is a better place for all of God's people. What better vision for the future can there be?

Act
50

Good News for the world

A fifteen-year-old girl walks 28 miles across the side of a mountain to buy a Welsh Bible from a Methodist minister. He is so impressed by the enthusiasm that she and others show to read the Scriptures in their own language that he makes the case in London for a special Society to provide affordable Welsh Bibles. His colleagues on a small committee quickly see that such a Society is indeed needed – but that Bibles in the language of the people must be made available not just in Wales but throughout the world.

You have almost finished reading the drama of what happened next. The story of Bible Society is a remarkable strand in the last two centuries of British history. Indeed, when we think of the Bible Houses the Society built, bought or renovated, whether in Port Said, Addis Abba, Warsaw, London, Shanghai, Vienna or Kobe it is a strand of British history which has physically left its mark around the globe.

The human story you have read has an intriguing blend of charm and irony. Mary Jones's 80-year-long life was poor and hard – but not without its joys, interests and sense of purpose. At the age of 71 she gave a half-sovereign to the Society's appeal to print and circulate a million Chinese New Testaments and lived through almost the whole of the Society's 52 years at its first Bible House. The Society whose formation she unwittingly triggered quickly attracted within its orbit Kings, Queens, Princesses, a Russian Tsar, an Ethiopian Emperor, Prime Ministers, Governor Generals, Chancellors of the Exchequer, reforming Earls, political campaigners, Archbishops, Bishops, Patriarchs and the initial hostility of Popes! Mary Jones might well have said, "Hold on a moment, I only wanted a Bible!" Well, she got three and started an international movement with profound repercussions.

But if the impact on history has been extraordinary, and the marks left on the planet visible, the spiritual results have been incalculable. In 1800 it is believed that, counting every version in every land, in manuscript or in print, there were no more than 4 million Bibles in the world in approximately 50 languages (including some which are no longer spoken). During its first 154 years, Bible Society issued 600 million copies of the Scriptures in 852 languages. Figures since that date (1958) cannot usefully be given separately for BFBS since it has worked as a member of a growing family of national Bible Societies throughout the world. The latest (March 2004) figure for the number of languages into which some part of the Bible has been translated is 2,355. Total sales of Bibles since 1816 − by far the world's best-selling book − is estimated by *Guinness World Records* to be 2.5 billion copies.

When you consider the amount of work involved in translating even just one Gospel into a foreign language − particularly if it has never been written down − this is a mind–boggling success story. And behind the statistics, you have read the stories of individual lives which all over the world have been transformed by an encounter with the Bible and the God of whom it speaks.

Is there a simple explanation for the remarkable success of Bible Society in its first 200 years?

One reason certainly has been the unprecedented broadmindedness of its principles. No one had any doubt from the start that the Society was not to be confined to any one section of the Christian church, nor to any party within the church. The first prospectus laid it down that "the principles upon which this undertaking will be conducted are as comprehensive as the nature of the object suggests they should be. In the execution of the plan it is proposed to embrace the common support of Christians at large, and to invite the concurrence of persons of every description who profess to regard the Scriptures as the proper standard of faith".

On the whole, the Society has kept well to this principle − but like every organisation in the world it has had to make do with flawed individuals to run it, work for it and support it, and some have had a better appreciation of what the Society was about than others. Generally though, the openhearted principle has been well understood. "If we cannot reconcile all opinions, let us at least unite all hearts," the Society's second President said.

The Society expressed its sole objective from the start with admirable clarity and simplicity: to encourage the wider circulation of Holy Scripture, without note or comment. It has been wary of interpreting Scripture, and has declined to propagate any doctrine about the Bible or teach any particular theory of inspiration.

With these noble objectives, the Society quickly captured the imagination and gained the support of all levels of Society. Having followed the story, we can point to a whole series of other partial explanations of the Society's success: the ability and quality of its leadership through the years; the loyalty, enthusiasm, dedication and self-sacrificial giving of its supporters; the courage, hard work, spirit of adventure, linguistic abilities and sheer faith of its agents, correspondents and colporteurs at home and abroad; its partnership with missionaries and translators throughout the world; the sheer prestige, as time went by of being associated with such a successful and internationally respected organisation; and the useful coincidence that the Society was able to follow the flag into an ever-expanding British Empire. The sun that never set on Queen Victoria's Empire never set on Bible Society's army of agents and colporteurs.

I think there is truth in all these explanations. But I believe there is another more important reason for the success of the Society. I think it has been doing God's work as a custodian of his Book supported by the prayers of God's people.

Bible Society marked its centenary and will celebrate its bicentenary with a special service at St Paul's Cathedral. In the south aisle you can see Holman Hunt's magnificent painting *The Light of the World*. The Bible is a book of light. It begins with God's majestic command "Let there be light" and ends with the Holy City ablaze with light. In its pages we meet the subject of Hunt's painting, whose voice echoes through the centuries, "I am the light of the world."

No book can stand comparison with the Bible. It seeks admission to every language, claims to belong to every nation, knocks at the door of every home, and would find its way into every heart. Every home that possesses a Bible is enriched. The Bible "fits into every fold of the human heart".

The Bible has always been mobile. The circulation of the books of the New Testament goes back nearly as far as the origin of the books themselves. The Apostle Paul writes a letter: a messenger sets out to carry it to its intended destination. The colporteur — the first of God's packmen — is early on the stage of the drama and busy at a task which will become worldwide.

The New Testament comes from the burning hearts of men who tell a story they cannot keep to themselves. Great as is the genius of the Apostle Paul, and wonderful his work, the explanation of the expansion of Christianity does not lie solely with him. Everyone in the first century who receives Christ as Lord and Saviour becomes a missionary of faith. The Good News for the world spreads from lip to lip. One loving heart sets another on fire and so Christianity spreads across the civilised world of the day — a tide that no one can resist.

If the colporteur goes back to the dawn of Christianity so does translation. The church in the hour of its birth at Pentecost experiences the miracle of the translated word, and translation is from the beginning a characteristic and indispensable method of expansion. In the seventh century the tide of Scriptural translation first washes the shores of Britain. It happens at Whitby on the Yorkshire coast where Caedmon sings in Anglo-Saxon some of the Bible stories — the first attempt to give the English the Bible in their own language. The task is taken up by Wycliffe, Tyndale, Coverdale, the men of Hampton Court and then, through the work of Bible Societies, the Good News travels to every corner of the world.

Because this Book contains a message that all humanity needs, it could never be imprisoned in one or two languages. The translation into over 2,000 languages and dialects was inevitable as soon as men and women realised that it enshrined a secret that must become an open secret — open to the whole world.

Ever since the disciples first proclaimed it, the Gospel has been proving that it is able to break through the barriers of language. The experience of the Day of Pentecost was a symbol and a prophecy of the victories which God's Good News could win, despite the world's confusion of languages. To 999 out of every 1,000 people, the Bible has to be translated if it is to speak at all. The people and scholars who regularly read the Bible in ancient Hebrew and Greek are few and far between. For most of us such reading is impossible and always will be.

God's Book was meant to be translated, and God's purpose is realised as the Bible speaks to every man, woman, boy and girl in their own language.

The Bible is astonishingly translatable because it deals with things which are common to all humanity: the sky, the wind and the sea, bread and wine, the kisses of children and tears shed beside a grave – these things never grow stale or obsolete or out of date. The Bible goes down to the root of our deepest needs, our darkest sorrows. It speaks with accents that are not of this world about the only things that really matter in the end to every human being.

The Bishop of Durham and Vice-President of the Bible Society, Tom Wright, makes an important point when he tells us: "Whatever view of the Bible you take, if you are to be in any way obedient to the Bible you cannot make the Bible itself the centre or focus of your attention. It points away from itself. From the Christian point of view, the centre of attention can never be merely the Bible; it must always be Jesus of Nazareth, Jesus the Messiah, Jesus the Lord of the World."

"In fact," as Bible Society Chief Executive James Catford puts it, "it is the very life of Christ that is being offered to us in the Bible."

The Bible is not first of all a theological treatise, although it is full of theology. It is not history pure and simple, although much of it is historical. It is not a poem, although it is steeped in poetry. It is not drama, although there is a great deal of drama in it. It is not biography, although it vividly tells the stories of many lives: Abraham, Isaac, Jacob, Samuel, Saul, Ruth, David, Elijah – how truly human these Old Testament characters are! Peter, James, John, Andrew, Mary, Martha, Paul, Barnabas, Timothy – how equally human, flawed and interesting! And it tells of one life in particular – the Son of God himself who never sinned and whose character, words and actions have held the world spellbound for 2,000 years. The Bible is a book about God the heavenly Father, the Author of everything that is good and beautiful and true, and the mysterious relationship he has with his children. As such it never wanders far from life's greatest interests and problems. That is what the Society's recent campaign in Nottinghamshire has tried to demonstrate.

Confronted with Christ in the pages of the Gospels, we forget we are reading a book. We lose sense of time and place. The centuries disappear. We are neither in England, nor on the shore of Galilee, nor in Russia, Spain, Korea, Japan, China or Africa. We are in the presence of the eternal Christ.

Jesus has special reverence for bread. He uses it to feed 5,000 people. He breaks it with his disciples. But he reminds a materialistic world in every century since, that "Man cannot live on bread alone, but needs every word that God speaks" (Matthew 4:4, Today's English Version). He tells the world, "I am the bread of life."

Soon after Jesus announces that he is the bread of life, we read in John 6:66–68 that many of his disciples turn back and stop following him. Then Jesus asks his twelve disciples if they are going to leave him too.

Simon Peter answers, "Lord, there is no one else we can turn to! Your words give eternal life."

Some of the people you met with their dates

Tsar Alexander I, 1777–1825
George Bell, Bishop of Chichester, 1881–1958
George Borrow, 1803–1881
Mildred Cable, 1877–1952
William Carey, 1761–1834
Thomas Charles, 1755–1814
Elizabeth Fry, 1780–1845
Ebenezer Henderson, 1784–1858
Selina, Countess of Huntingdon, 1707–1791
Mary Jones, 1784–1864
Henry Martyn, 1781–1812
Robert Moffat, 1795–1883
John Paterson, 1776–1855
Spencer Perceval, Prime Minister, 1762–1812
William Platt, 1893–1993
Ellen Ranyard, 1810–1879
John Ritson, 1868–1953
Earl of Shaftesbury, 1801–1885 (known as Lord Ashley until the
    death of his father)
Granville Sharp, 1735–1813
Sydney Smith, 1764–1840
Karl Steinkopf, 1773–1859
Lord Teignmouth, 1751–1834
John Temple, 1885–1948
Henry Thornton, 1760–1815
Nicholas Vansittart, 1766–1851 (becomes 1st Baron Bexley in
    1823)
William Wilberforce, 1759–1833

Further reading

In order to keep the length of this book manageable and to have it published in time for the Society's bicentenary celebrations, I have had to omit a great deal of material I should like to have included, and to refrain from going down a whole series of inter- esting and intriguing avenues. Some of these topics are explored in the book *Sowing the Word: Essays on the History of the British and Foreign Bible Society, 1804–2004*. To be published by Sheffield Phoenix Press towards the end of 2004 or early in 2005, this col- lection of essays (to which I have contributed a chapter on "no note and comment") has been prepared by Stephen Batalden, Kathleen Cann and John Dean and is highly recommended.

CONTACTING BIBLE SOCIETY

If you would like to contact Bible Society you should visit www.biblesociety.org.uk or ring 01793 418100 or write to Bible Society, Stonehill Green, Westlea, Swindon SN5 7DG, UK.

Index

Uyeno Park, Tokyo 254-6

Vansittart, Right Hon Nicholas –
    see Bexley
Vatican 155-6, 419-24
Venn, John, rector of Clapham 70-1
Victoria, Queen of the United
    Kingdom and Empress of India
    218-19, 272
Vienna 119, 354-63, 446
Villa Seca, south of Madrid 206-7
Villiers, George (Earl of Clarendon),
    British Ambassador in Madrid
    185-6, 195-6, 204-5

War, First World 316-20
War, Second World 349-64
Warsaw 352-3, 407-10, 446
Watson, John 397, 401
Weller, John 402, 404

Westminster Abbey 384-5, 390-1
Wilberforce, William 39-40, 56, 69,
    77-8, 95, 162, 173-4
Wilkinson, Arthur 344-5, 382-3
Williams, Crwys, District Secretary
    328
Williams, Lewis 45
Williams, Rowan, Archbishop of
    Canterbury 429-30
Wilson, Daniel 169
Worthing-Davies, Richard 402, 411,
    416
Woudschoten, Zeist, Holland 346-8

Young Bin, Secretary of Korean
    Bible Society 389
Young-Jin Min 297-8

Zwemer, Samuel 323-4